CAPITALS OF CAPITAL

International financial centres have come to represent a major economic stake. Yet no historical study has been devoted to them. Professor Cassis, a leading financial historian, attempts to fill this gap by providing a comparative history of the most important centres that constitute the capitals of capital – New York, London, Frankfurt, Paris, Zurich, Amsterdam, Tokyo, Hong Kong, Singapore – from the beginning of the industrial age up to the present. The book has been conceived as a reflection on the dynamics of the rise and decline of international financial centres, setting them in their economic, political, social, and cultural context. While rooted in a strong and lively historical narrative, it draws on the concepts of financial economics in its analysis of events. It should widely appeal to business and financial professionals as well as to scholars and students in financial and economic history.

YOUSSEF CASSIS is Professor of Economic and Social History at the University of Geneva. His previous publications include *City Bankers, 1890–1914* (1994) and *Big Business: The European Experience in the Twentieth Century* (1997).

Capitals of Capital

A History of International Financial Centres, 1780–2005

Youssef Cassis

Translated by Jacqueline Collier

CAMBRIDGE
UNIVERSITY PRESS

CAMBRIDGE UNIVERSITY PRESS
Cambridge, New York, Melbourne, Madrid, Cape Town, Singapore, São Paulo

Cambridge University Press
The Edinburgh Building, Cambridge CB2 2RU, UK

Published in the United States of America by Cambridge University Press,
New York

www.cambridge.org
Information on this title: www.cambridge.org/9780521845359

First published 2006

Printed in the United Kingdom at the University Press, Cambridge

A catalogue record for this publication is available from the British Library.

ISBN-13 978-0-521-84535-9 hardback
ISBN-10 0-521-84535-1 hardback

Contents

Tables

Foreword

Past performance is no guarantee of future returns ... this well-known warning – printed regularly on all investment prospectuses, and rightly so – demonstrates quite simply how much financiers tend to focus on the future and on what tomorrow might bring rather than dwelling on the past. But looking ahead does not mean ignoring yesterday's lessons. Although no two financial shocks are ever the same, they often display strikingly similar patterns: when speculative bubbles – whether in tulips in 1637, railways in 1845 or the Internet in 2000 – burst, it is always sudden, investors change their minds without warning and, with the crisis at its height, markets simply grind to a standstill. The risks facing investors are legion, but no matter how much they remember these past mishaps, there is no way of predicting the exact timing or repercussions of tomorrow's shocks. In this respect, knowledge of the past is useful, but by no means vital.

There is, however, another part of the financial universe that evolves less erratically, tracking a more predictable course: the business of settling transactions, transferring deposits and assets, trading securities, organising the structure and legal status of the main intermediaries – a complex set of functions encompassing most back-office banking operations and the hidden cogs of the financial sector's machinery. Highly intensive in physical and human capital, structures of this sort are always slow to change. Moreover, in the financial arena, the infrastructure is so vast and so expensive to construct that individual players have naturally sought to keep costs down by grouping many related activities in one location, more often than not close to a stock exchange's trading floor. This drive towards greater concentration was so strong all around the developed world that it finally gave birth to the so-called 'financial centres'. Whilst most such places confined their business to their immediate horizons, either local or national, a select few extended their activities way beyond their original and natural territory to turn themselves into international financial centres – the true world's *capitals of capital*. These capitals soon laid down the operating standards for finance, imposing their skill and technical innovations – some would even go so far as to say their fashions and whims – on the rest of the sector operating in more remote and less prestigious areas. Every decision-maker in finance should thus have some notion of how these centres have evolved, as details of their history are necessary background knowledge for anyone trying to reshape, either partially or totally, any kind of financial activity. Will these capitals of capital continue to dominate world finance, pushing for even more concentration centred around them and marginalising weaker or smaller centres even further? Or will they fade in importance or even very slowly vanish into oblivion, dissolving into a plethora of dislocated and increasingly fuzzy trading networks, as physical trading floors disappear one by one, cheap information is disseminated instantaneously worldwide and business procedures everywhere are standardised? Two questions, countless opinions, but the various answers could have a major bearing on many strategic investments and (re) location decisions, some of them vital for the future of specific cities, regions or even entire countries.

As a 200-year-old private bank that has weathered many a crisis, recession and war, Pictet & Cie of Geneva has garnered a wealth of experience and tradition. Interestingly, a number of key elements in the Bank's history have closely mirrored developments in the world's leading international financial centres even though Geneva, our birthplace and home still today, has always tended to rank among the second tier of financial market-places worldwide. At its inception in 1805, our establishment was a merchant bank, ready to undertake all sorts of banking business and trading operations. Often working closely with other private bankers in Geneva, it gradually evolved over time into an investment bank, placing its capital in various ventures, such as shipping, before setting up an investment trust in US and Mexican shares in the early years of the twentieth century. Finally, from 1910 on, Pictet & Cie turned to specialise in private banking and, later in the century, branched into institutional asset management to become eventually what it is today: a small international banking group dedicated to wealth management. Although, through the decades, Pictet & Cie has retained its structure as a private bank and not been transmuted into a limited liability company or a universal bank, many of Pictet's partners in the nineteenth century served as directors on the boards of the deposit banks set up at the time to smooth settlement procedures and interbank clearing. Understandably, much of Pictet & Cie's knowledge concerns Geneva and private banking. Nevertheless, this accumulated wisdom inherited from our local past and particular specialisation is no longer sufficient for a bank like ours which is seeking to develop and excel in today's financial universe, even if only within the confines of a rather narrow, but well-known niche. For us, strategic planning and long-term decisions need to be based upon a thorough examination of our environment and its mechanisms, which calls, among other things, for a sound grasp of how the great financial centres have functioned in the past and how they do so now.

Unfortunately, no single book until now traces the history of the 'capitals of capital' in a clear and comprehensive manner, although there is no shortage of articles on specific areas or particular cities. To mark its bicentennial, Pictet & Cie thus decided to fill this gap, calling on an expert in this field, the historian Youssef Cassis – recently appointed Professor of Economic History at Geneva University after having lectured in London and Grenoble – to summarise in a single volume 200 years of history of the world's most significant international financial centres. He has masterfully risen to this challenging task, portraying the main trends, human networks and technical changes that, little by little, have shaped and transformed these international centres into what they are today. The text will, of course, be of interest to students or anyone curious to learn more about this topic, but, thanks to its extensive array of notes and the extent of the literature consulted, professional economic historians themselves should also find it a rich source of useful and informative material. We, therefore, firmly believe that this book will become a reference in the field.

Claude Demole
Partner
Pictet & Cie

Preface

This book was written to mark the bicentenary of Pictet & Cie, Geneva's large private bank. Among other events, the partners wanted to commemorate this anniversary by publishing an academic work that would contribute to banking and financial history. This desire to support a scholarly project reflects a broadness of outlook, characteristic of the Genevan humanist tradition, which is probably not unconnected with their bank's extraordinary longevity. I suggested to them that I write a history of the main international financial centres over the last two centuries, an important topic that had interested me for a long time and that I had broached in some of my publications, but that, oddly enough, had not yet been the subject of a comprehensive historical study. I would like to thank the Banque Pictet's partners, especially Ivan Pictet and Claude Demole, for giving me the opportunity to write such a book and, hopefully, to help fill this gap.

I wrote this book with several audiences in mind. Without sacrificing scholarly rigour, the style adopted is not intended primarily for specialists, even though they should find plenty to appreciate here too. This work by a historian, rooted in a narrative account, nevertheless draws on some of the concepts of financial economics as it endeavours to analyse and interpret events. I hope that both academics, particularly historians, economists and political scientists, and practitioners of banking and finance who have a sense of history's importance, as well as others curious about the international financial issues that carry a great deal of weight in today's world, will find reading this work worthwhile and pleasurable. History does not offer any lessons for decision-makers and even less any ready-made solutions, but it does allow us better to understand the present –and being unaware of it can only lead to serious errors.

This book has been designed as a creative synthesis, largely based on existing literature, but new by virtue of its purpose, its long-term perspective and its comparative approach. It would have been impossible for me to write it without the help and advice of numerous colleagues and friends whom I would like to thank here: Balaji Ambigapathi, Stefano Battilossi, Philip Cottrell, Michel Dacorogna, Howard Davies, Lucie Drevon, Olivier Feiertag, Jakob Graf, Joost Jonker, Ginette Kurgan van Hentenryk, David Kynaston, Margaret Levenstein, Alain Plessis, Laure Quennouëlle-Corre, Richard Roberts, Catherine Schenk, André Straus, Richard Sylla, Samuel Tilman, Patrick Verley, Eugene White, Mira Wilkins and Fiona Wood. I would also like to thank Jacqueline Collier Jespersen for her meticulous translation of a book that I opted to write in French, as well as the various employees, permanent or temporary, of the Banque Pictet, who allowed me to produce this work. I am, of course, responsible for any errors that may remain and for the views that are expressed in it.

YOUSSEF CASSIS

Introduction

International financial centres have come to represent a major economic stake. Indeed, the advantages that they bring, especially in terms of jobs, incomes and wealth concentration, to the countries and cities that host them seem highly desirable – even though they come at a price, the most visible to date being the strengthening of inequalities.[1] Such benefits apply above all to the most important centres: New York and London, or even Frankfurt, Paris, Zurich, Tokyo, Hong Kong and Singapore, to name but the leading ones. However, there are far from insignificant benefits for the numerous secondary centres in developed countries confronted with the competition and challenges of the post-industrial era, or for those in emerging economies to which they offer further prospects of enrichment and development.

The extent to which defending and promoting these centres has reached today reflects the importance of these stakes, which are far from solely the concern of pressure groups from the financial sector. Politicians also enter the fray whenever national interests are concerned. Has the British chancellor of the Exchequer, Gordon Brown, not provided the best example of this by making the preservation of the City's international competitiveness one of the five conditions for the pound sterling's entry into the European Monetary Union?

These stakes are also mirrored in the increasing number of publications devoted to this subject over the last twenty years or so. Their authors, usually economists or financial analysts, have endeavoured to define and classify international financial centres and organise them into a hierarchy. In so doing, they have sought to establish, both analytically and prescriptively, the conditions underlying the centres' successes and failures. Until now historians have not really followed this trend – yet it is hardly a new phenomenon. Without going back over ancient history, the mere mention of today's main international financial centres evokes an often brilliant and at times turbulent past that for some of them goes back to the eighteenth century, or even earlier, and above all that provides an abundance of lessons to help understand their recent development.

1

Historians have obviously not lost sight of this past's significance; but until now they have only analysed it within a specific framework. Their interest has focused on isolated financial centres, first and foremost the City of London, and on specific institutions, like banks, the capital market or even, to a lesser extent, stock exchanges and insurance companies. No historical study has been undertaken to date on the main international financial centres as a whole from the beginning of the industrial age up to now, with Charles Kindleberger's pioneering study in 1974[2] being particularly concerned with the emergence of these centres on a national level and mainly focusing on banks. This book attempts to fill the gap.

What is an international financial centre? David Scholey, chairman of S. G. Warburg & Co., a renowned City merchant bank nowadays incorporated into UBS, acknowledged in 1987 before an audience of young Swiss bankers that, 'Although we would like to pretend otherwise ... the financial markets are, basically, pretty simple things. All they require is a surplus of capital ... a roughly offsetting deficit of capital ... and an intermediator or intermediation process ...'[3] The definition is clear, even if its last point is worth explaining. A financial centre can thus be considered the grouping together, in a given urban space, of a certain number of financial services. Or in a more functional way, it can be defined as the place where intermediaries coordinate financial transactions and arrange for payments to be settled.

In both cases, this concentration can chiefly be explained by what are usually called external economies – in other words, cost reductions that firms can make not through their internal organisation (for example, economies of scale linked to growing mass production), but thanks to the effects of the competition, proximity and size of the sector or the place in which they are developing. For a financial centre, what really matters is the liquidity and efficiency of markets; the diversity and complementarity of financial activities; professional services (primarily legal and accounting); technological expertise; workforce skills; and, arguably above all, access to high-quality information.

This concentration can be found at national, regional (in the sense of a grouping of several nations in one part of the world) and world levels, depending on the extent of the geographical area served by one financial centre or another. All the international centres do not, therefore, have the same functions or the same importance. Consequently, their more or less explicit hierarchical order has become one of the main themes of the literature devoted to this subject. Back in 1981 for example, the American economist Howard C. Reed proposed an initial ranking of international financial centres, at intervals of ten or fifteen years from 1900 onwards,[4] based on a set of quantitative criteria, such as the number of foreign and multinational banks or the relative amount of non-residents' banking deposits existing in a centre. For 1980 he divided the eighty centres under consideration into five ascending categories: forty were classified as host international financial centres, twenty-nine as international financial centres, eight (including Frankfurt, Hong Kong, Paris and Zurich) as supranational financial centres of the second order, New York and Tokyo as supranational centres of the first order, and just one, London, as the supranational centre par excellence. Such an approach has its limits. Admittedly, it allows a large number of centres to be compared, but, in the end, the indicators used give only very limited information on the centres' true nature.

Subsequent analyses have put forward a number of variations on this theme. Geoffrey Jones, for example, has slightly adjusted Reed's model by using a more qualitative selection method and by reducing the categories from five to three: the national financial centres, which he calls subregional and whose relations with the other centres are essentially of a bilateral nature; regional financial centres that cater to the needs of one region of the world; and global financial centres, whose vocation is truly worldwide.[5] Richard Roberts suggests a fairly similar subdivision, adding offshore centres to the three preceding categories.[6] Other classifications are more functional: Gunter Dufey and Ian Giddy, for instance, distinguish between traditional financial centres, based in large capital-exporting countries; financial entrepôts serving as hubs for international capital flows; and offshore centres that work on behalf of non-residents.[7] The list is not exhaustive.[8]

A different approach has been adopted in this book, above all because its purpose is different. It does not aim to draw up a ranking, taxonomy and history of all the international financial centres over the last two centuries. Such a task would in any case be impossible, if only because of the lack of documentation available prior to the mid-twentieth century. Instead, this book concentrates on the most important centres – those that truly make up *capitals of capital*. Given the transformations in the world economy, their number has remained remarkably stable, yet without being rigid. In Europe, barely half a dozen centres have really made a difference in the financial field since the end of the eighteenth century: London and Paris; Berlin, followed by Frankfurt after the Second World War; then, to a lesser extent, Zurich (which can be combined with Geneva), Brussels (especially before 1914), Amsterdam (before 1800 and during the 1920s) and perhaps Luxembourg (as an offshore centre). At world level, New York should of course be added from the end of the nineteenth century and, much more recently, Tokyo, Hong Kong and Singapore.

The aim of this book is to undertake a historical and comparative analysis of the role of the international financial centres over the last two hundred years or so, with particular emphasis on the dynamics of their rise and decline. It is not merely a matter of ranking them according to predefined selection criteria, since the reasons for a centre winning or losing influence – a world leader or a less important centre – are complex. They can only be understood within the economic, political, social and cultural context of a particular age. And to grasp how these general factors have influenced a centre's development, it is necessary to investigate its inner workings and operations.

An international financial centre's importance depends primarily on its financial capacity and on the way in which this is implemented by its institutions and markets. It can be gauged from the amount of capital exported by the country that hosts it; from the development of its capital market; from the size of its main financial institutions, even if it is not always easy to separate their international activities from their national ones; from the presence of foreign banks in this centre, as well as from the spreading of domestic banks outside their borders; and finally, from the network of both formal and informal relationships developed by its main players. On top of this come all the services provided by a centre, varying in range according to how important the centre is. So, in addition to banks and capital markets, there are insurance companies, finance companies, commodity markets and professional services.

These institutions and markets' operations, organisation and inter-action – nowadays called the financial architecture – fall within a framework that is predominantly national. The banking system prevailing in each country, especially its degree of specialisation, plays a key role in this respect. Here the classic contrast lies between the German model, dominated by universal banks, and the British system, in which deposit banks are complemented by a more active capital market.

An equally crucial and variable role is played by central banks. Before the First World War, those in existence – after all, this was not the case in Switzerland before 1907 or in the United States before 1913 – were not all prepared to act as lenders of last resort, thus they were unable to fully assume their role of central banks; after the Second World War, many having lost their independence, the question of their relationship with the state became the dominant issue. The financial architecture is also influenced by regulations and the control exerted by governmental authorities over banking and finance, which vary considerably in scope according to the time and the country, from near total *laissez-faire* at one extreme to almost complete state control over financial institutions and circuits at the other. Finally, it is necessary to take into account the monetary conditions under which the various centres operate. The role and status of the national currency – a strong or weak currency, a reserve currency or even the leading currency at world level – have a positive or negative impact on the influence exerted internationally by each financial centre, the effects varying according to the exchange rate regime – fixed exchange rates or floating exchange rates – and its relative stability.

The rise or decline of an international financial centre cannot be understood independently from the economic and social environment of the country in which it operates; from the weight carried by the financial sector in this economy; from the preference given to it compared with other activities, especially industrial, by the political authorities; and from the political influence that the financial elites are able to exert. There are so many elements, whose balance can never be taken for granted, which serve to remind us that in the end it is men – far less women, even if they have increased in number over the last twenty years – from grandees of finance to office clerks via salaried managers, who are the driving force behind the international financial centres. All these factors, both institutional and human, create an atmosphere that is unique to each centre and that is vital to its success, even if it is neither quantifiable nor always easy to detect. This expresses itself in the way that a centre's premises are laid out, its traditions, its unwritten rules, its interpersonal relationships, its attitude towards the outside world and its unique culture.

The development and interaction of these various factors, themselves influenced by changes occurring in the world political and economic order, explain the ups and downs in fortune of the main financial centres. Periods of war or peace, of revolution or counter-revolution, of prosperity or slump, of the speeding-up or slowing-down in trade, of technical innovations – none of these affect different countries, and thus different financial centres, in the same way. These parameters form the analytical grid used here to approach the history of these centres.

The book is divided into six chapters that follow a chronological order whose various – and inevitably debatable – stages cover the major phases of the world's economic and political history. For each of these periods, there is a corresponding hierarchy of international financial centres. This work endeavours, among other things, to identify changes in this hierarchy and to explain the reasons for them.

Writing a history of international financial centres represents a challenge for the historian. How can international operations, which make up the subject of this book, be separated from national activities? What is the exact purpose of the study? It is not a history of the banks, and yet it is not possible to exclude those that have been the key players in all the centres. The same could be said of the capital markets that have formed the very essence of these centres, of the stock exchanges that have set their pulses and of a good many other agents, institutions or markets. The history of the financial centres encompasses the history of all financial activities without being that of any of its constituents in particular. Hence its relevance, as well as its difficulty. When all is said and done, it is perhaps another way of writing the history of banking and finance – a way that helps us grasp both its global nature and its intimate association with its environment.

1   The age of private bankers, 1780–1840

For Walter Boyd, an ambitious young Scottish businessman determined in the early 1780s to cut a figure on a larger stage, London, Paris and Amsterdam were at that time the three great international financial centres upon which Europe's trade depended. Where to seek one's fortune? Boyd opted for Paris. He settled there in 1785 and in the space of a few years became one of the capital's most influential bankers, but had to flee to London in 1792. After brilliant initial successes in issuing loans for the British government, he went through some difficult years, eventually recovering his fortune only after Waterloo.[1]

Walter Boyd's route illustrates fairly well the changes that occurred within the leading international financial centres during the French wars, as well as the new international hierarchy which formed at the beginning of the nineteenth century: the pre-eminence of London; the resurgence of Paris, which emerged as the second major market; and the eclipse of Amsterdam, relegated to the rank of a lesser centre, along with cities like Brussels, Frankfurt, Hamburg and Geneva, in a hierarchical order that was not easy to determine. This hierarchy was obviously not of a permanent nature. It nevertheless left its mark on the whole of the nineteenth century, despite the coming of Berlin, which to some extent replaced Frankfurt after 1870, and then the emergence of New York at the turn of the twentieth century.

Our Scottish banker's reversal of fortune also shows the extremely turbulent nature of the 'age of revolutions'[2] – the Industrial Revolution, which started in England around 1780 and subsequently spread to the United States and north-western Europe, and the political revolution, triggered by the fall of the Bastille in 1789, which spread to most of Europe thanks to the strength of its ideas and that of the French revolutionary armies. Nowadays the notion of 'revolution' tends to be put into perspective: economic growth never exceeded 2% in England during the Industrial Revolution,[3] and in many respects the Ancien Régime persisted in Europe until the First World War, particularly owing to the influence of the landed elites.[4] Whether emphasis is placed on breaks or on continuity, it is undeniable that the changes that took place between the 1780s and 1830s profoundly transformed the western world.

Similarly, the revolutions, wars and reconstruction that followed clearly constituted a watershed in the history of the financial centres, not only as far as their international ranking was concerned but also their internal organisation, on account of new institutional arrangements being introduced and some players being replaced. We will examine these developments, which took a different course in each of the main centres. But whatever these differences, business was conducted everywhere through the same type of financial institution: the private banks, joined by – and the distinction was not always very clear during this period – merchant firms, stockbrokers and other financiers. Unless working on an individual basis, all of those involved formed associations in the shape of partnerships.

It was the private banks that above all characterised financial centres during the early decades of the nineteenth century, which for them constituted a real golden age. With the exception of central banks, joint-stock banks only started to matter from the 1840s. Significantly, a private bank in the nineteenth century and during most of the twentieth century was a bank whose owners were also managers; and, more often than not, these were family firms, though people from outside the firm could also become partners. Their legal form was generally that of partnerships and general partnerships, with partners having unlimited responsibility; but there were also limited partnerships and even joint-stock companies, whose directors retained the major part of the capital. The private banks were, therefore, defined by their type of ownership rather than by their activities. It is only since the last quarter of the twentieth century that the notion of private banking has designated a specific profession – portfolio management on behalf of wealthy individuals. This term formerly designated commercial banks, as well as merchant banks, wealth managers and even universal banks. Specialisation in one activity or another resulted either from a strategic choice made by the partners or from the way, whether official or unofficial, that a given banking system functioned. In the main financial centres, these activities were in any case very closely linked to commercial activities. At the turn of the nineteenth century, the main function of an international financial centre was that of financing international trade, along with the complementary activities of currency exchange, insurance and shipping. The issuing of loans on behalf of foreign governments, which would grow increasingly important during the nineteenth century, was still subordinate to trade finance.

The grandeur and decline of Amsterdam

Amsterdam's decline was apparently rapid, brutal and without any real parallel in the history of financial centres. Contemporaries attributed it to the Napoleonic Wars and the French occupation. They believed that the old order would be restored upon the return to independence in 1813. But Amsterdam never recovered its position as the world's preeminent trading and financial centre that it had occupied in the seventeenth century and during most of the eighteenth century.

Trade and finance

In fact, Amsterdam's decline was a longer-lasting phenomenon. Its position as the world's trading and financial centre originally derived from the Netherlands' economic prominence, just like the position of the centres that would succeed it in the nineteenth and twentieth centuries – London and New York – derived from their own country's economic prominence. The Dutch took the lead from the end of the sixteenth century, as world trade shifted from the Mediterranean to the Atlantic, and this became particularly apparent through the Netherlands' higher level of urbanisation than that of other European countries, its more productive agriculture, more advanced industry and more developed international trade.[5] In 1700 the per capita income of the Dutch exceeded by 50% that of the English, the next in line.[6] The Netherlands' commercial supremacy was built above all on the role of entrepôt played by Amsterdam, with goods and foodstuffs flooding in from all over the world to its port, at that time the world's foremost. There the goods were sorted, treated, sometimes processed, distributed and then for the most part re-exported. These trading activities lay at the root of the development not only of an important service sector, dominated by shipping, insurance and financial transactions, but also of a significant manufacturing sector comprising, besides shipbuilding, the processing of raw materials into export products, such as sugar, soap, tobacco and printed calicos.

The foundations of this system were undermined during the eighteenth century as the centre of gravity of world trade gradually shifted towards London. Opinions differ as to when the Netherlands' commercial decline began. Some trace it back very far, to the 1670s, whereas others place it in the 1730s, which is more likely, with ups and downs during the subsequent half-century until the war with Great Britain between 1780 and 1784, which dealt a fatal blow to the country's trade. This decline was due mainly to international competition, particularly between the Netherlands and Britain, as well as to the fact that the direct trading links being established between countries meant that Amsterdam's role as an entrepôt was becoming redundant. Various remedies were considered to enable it fully to regain this role, including abolishing customs tariffs and making Amsterdam a free port in 1751, but all in vain.[7] In around 1780 London certainly overtook Amsterdam as a trading centre, judged by the number of ships entering its port, not only in relation to goods traffic but also to auxiliary services, such as insurance or even the acceptance of bills.[8]

Amsterdam asserted itself as the world's financial centre even though its commercial supremacy was crumbling. Its capital financed international trade or was invested in loans on behalf of foreign governments. This was partly the result of strategic choices on the part of the city's merchants, on the lookout for new business opportunities. From the seventeenth century, the leading merchants accepted bills of exchange; in other words, they undertook to pay the respective amount upon the bills' maturity date on behalf of other merchants and businessmen. In the eighteenth century, trade financing gradually became dissociated from trade itself. First, an increasing number of merchants worked on commission rather than on their own account; or to put it another way, they did not take the risk of purchasing and then reselling the goods but acted as brokers, putting purchasers and sellers in touch with each other and earning a commission on the price of their service. This solution enabled them to commit less capital, clear more stock and use their surplus in credit transactions. Second, numerous merchant houses gave up physical trade in order to specialise in financing it by accepting bills of exchange. According to contemporaries, the volume of acceptances reached 200 million florins towards 1750. In both cases, these financial activities were linked less and less to the port of Amsterdam and more and more to international trade.

Amsterdam's rich merchants also turned to what would become the most prestigious activity of international financial centres: issuing foreign loans. From the middle of the seventeenth century, the Dutch had lent considerable sums to foreign states, including Austria, Sweden and Britain, before investing heavily in the British public debt from 1688. But the development of a genuine capital market dates from 1713, when the Netherlands embarked on a policy of neutrality. From then until the end of the Seven Years War in 1763, foreign loans amounted to an average of 4 million florins per year (i.e., a total of 200 million) and flowed almost exclusively to Britain and Austria. They then increased markedly (to an annual average of 8.3 million between 1763 and 1780) and flowed to the whole of Europe, notably with issues on behalf of

Denmark, Sweden, Russia and various German states. They reached a peak during the fifteen subsequent years, between 1780 and 1794, when issues on the Amsterdam market reached an annual average of 20 million florins.[9] This was the apogee of the Hope & Co. bank, the market leader. Originating from a Scottish family that had emigrated to Holland, it was founded in 1734 and in the course of some twenty-five years transformed itself from a company involved in all manner of trading and financial business to a banking house specialising in acceptances of bills of exchange and above all of foreign loans. In particular, it handled the issuing of ten Swedish loans between 1767 and 1787 and eighteen Russian loans between 1788 and 1793. Hope was probably the largest bank in Europe at the time, with a capital of 10 million florins in 1780.[10] In 1800, seventy loans were listed on the Amsterdam Stock Exchange on behalf of fourteen different states, and the total Dutch foreign investment amounted, according to the most conservative estimates, to 500 to 600 million florins, representing twice the country's GDP. By way of comparison, the ratio would be one and a half times' GDP in the case of Great Britain on the eve of the First World War.[11] The Dutch would continue to invest heavily abroad, but the Amsterdam capital market would no longer play the unique role that it had played in the late eighteenth century.

Decline of a financial centre

There are several ways of assessing the decline of a financial centre. The first field of enquiry concerns the range of services offered and the destination of these services. In the case of Amsterdam, the world's leading financial centre, this boils down to wondering what remained of the influence that it had formerly exerted internationally. A second approach involves assessing the extent and consequences of this decline. Was it an absolute or relative decline? Losing first place does not necessarily mean any reduction in the volume of business, and not all banking houses and merchant firms are affected in the same way; while some collapse, others manage to extricate themselves. It is also necessary to examine the impact of this decline on the city itself and more generally on the domestic economy, in so far as the services provided by a leading financial centre are, in general, considered an important source of wealth. Lastly, there is a third criterion. Which strategies were adopted, first to curb this decline and then to adapt to the new world economic order?

Throughout the nineteenth century and even beyond, the services provided by an international financial centre continued to follow on first and foremost from financing international trade and issuing foreign loans. In these two areas, Amsterdam was relegated to the background by London, as well as by Paris.[12] The annual average of loans issued on the Amsterdam market fell to 5–10 million florins during the Napoleonic Wars, in spite of legal restrictions intended to limit the export of capital.[13] London took over. In 1794 the Austrian government did indeed apply to the Amsterdam bankers for a typical loan of 2.5 million florins; but at the same time it obtained, not without some initial difficulty, some 55 million in London and asked for more three years later. Such sums greatly exceeded Dutch resources. The markets lost during the war were never to be recovered. Between 1814 and 1860, loans were floated on the Amsterdam market to the tune of 345 million florins; in other words, an average of 7.5 million florins per year – a modest amount compared with London or Paris, and far lower than that of the issues at the end of the eighteenth century. More seriously, the main part of this amount (312 million) consisted of issues on behalf of the Russian government, which Hope & Co. had partly succeeded in retaining, the rest comprising some minor American issues rejected by London. From being an issue market, Amsterdam became, as Joost Jonker has noted, a market where securities issued abroad were traded.[14] This decline was, of course, due to competition from London and Paris; but it was also caused by the weakening of Amsterdam's banking houses and merchant firms, which could no longer call on the financial resources that their leading role in financing international trade had provided. Subsequently, acceptances dwindled as trading activities declined.

Although Amsterdam was marginalised in both of these major activities, it was still relatively important in some markets and therefore remained a magnet for foreign bankers. First, there was the stock exchange. The Dutch continued to be big exporters of capital, and a large number of foreign companies were listed on the Amsterdam Stock Exchange – a lightly regulated market, especially as regards access to the floor. For this period there is only a record of listed securities, without any indication of the companies' capital or market capitalisation. In number, foreign stock greatly exceeded domestic stock: 108 to 28 in 1820, 110 to 27 in 1830 and 126 to 34 in 1840; that is to say, by nearly four times as much. Nevertheless, in value, the difference was probably not so big, owing to the weight of the Dutch public debt. The Amsterdam market thus remained a favoured location for securities arbitrage and continued to attract foreign bankers throughout the first half of the nineteenth century. The majority of them belonged to the main German Jewish banking houses in Frankfurt, Cologne and Berlin

and were more often than not part of a network of relationships linking
Antwerp, Brussels, Vienna, London and New York.[15] They were able to
exploit the interest rate differentials between Amsterdam, where short-
term interest rates had traditionally been low, and the other European
markets, to set up flourishing arbitrage deals. Moreover, they used their
presence in Amsterdam and their access to its money market to support
the financial transactions of their entire network.[16]

Stock-market speculation was unquestionably fuelled by a major
element of the money market, the *prolongatie* – a variant of advances on
securities, or Lombard loans, specific to the Amsterdam market.[17] The
prolongatie were advances granted for one month, renewed by tacit
agreement, unless cancelled by one of the two parties, and backed by
shares or bonds whose nominal value exceeded by 10% the advance
granted. To avoid having to pay stamp duty and comply with other
formalities connected with Lombard loans, they were considered continuation contracts in the nineteenth century. The *prolongatie* system as
it operated at that time fulfilled the functions both of a futures market
and of banks, by attracting deposits and using them for loans. Flexible
and spread among a multitude of operators, both large and small, this
market offered direct intermediation between savers and investors,
without interest rate differentials, the only price difference being the
commission payable to the broker by the borrower. In spite of its
speculative nature, the *prolongatie* system was not only widespread
during the first half of the nineteenth century but was considered sufficiently stable and respectable to attract such conservative investors as
the savings banks, or to be manipulated by the financial adviser to King
William I in order to float an unpopular loan on the market. More
importantly for Amsterdam's role as an international market, the *prolongatie* market was widely used by foreign investors. From the 1820s
French and German bankers took advantage of the low short-term
interest rates available in the Netherlands to make substantial carry-over
transactions on the Amsterdam market. In the 1830s English bankers
took out large loans on the basis of American securities that they had not
managed to place.

Amsterdam therefore retained one or two truly international markets,
remnants of the world prominence that it had enjoyed a few decades
earlier. On the whole, however, as was the case for foreign loan issues,
the loss of this prominence was accompanied by a contraction in the
total volume of international business, as clearly shown by the position
occupied by the big banking houses and merchant firms. Overall, the
capital of the three most important among them[18] was estimated, and
probably overestimated, at some 30 million florins in 1773. Nearly 50

years later in 1820, the figure, probably underestimated, barely exceeded 13 million florins and fell below 10 million in 1835.[19] While, taken individually, some banking houses did better than others, they all moved down in the world hierarchy: in 1790 the big Amsterdam houses held more capital than their rivals in London; yet in 1840, perhaps with the exception of Hope, they would be ranked just above the average English provincial banks.[20] It is also significant that the number of big international banking houses and merchant firms barely increased during the first half of the nineteenth century, from 140 in 1826 to 145 in 1850, whereas that of companies involved in domestic trade went from 1,759 to 2,452.[21] This indicates that they adapted to a new situation, which was reflected in greater interest being shown in the domestic economy – a characteristic of international financial centres in decline. Moreover, new institutions that were more focused on the domestic economy were created, such as in 1806 the Associatie Cassa, the country's first joint-stock bank, and in 1814 the Bank of the Netherlands (Nederlandsche Bank) on the model of the Bank of England.

Defensive strategies

The foundation in 1824 of the Dutch Trading Company (Nederlandsche Handel-Maatschappij), with a capital of 37 million florins, to develop trading links with the colonial possessions in the Dutch Indies, came closest to a restructuring strategy. All the same, this strategy did not challenge the structures underpinning the Amsterdam market's role as an entrepôt, which had been the source of its fortune in the seventeenth and eighteenth centuries. The great merchants and bankers, who continued to form the economic and political elite of the city, were no more able or inclined to make a clean break with the old order than their predecessors in the middle of the previous century. They were criticised for rejecting change and blindly clinging to their glorious past – an understandable attitude when the past is still very recent. However, one cannot really speak of collective bankruptcy. A large number of firms were certainly conservative, but there were just as many that showed dynamism and a capacity for innovation. The problem was that there was no real alternative to the strategy followed – the factors that undermined Amsterdam's competitiveness were more than ever present.

Modelled on the former Dutch East India Company, the Dutch Trading Company came within the framework of the neo-mercantilist policy of King William I, who held a major stake in it. The goal was to substitute colonial trade for world trade by replicating, on a reduced scale and in a somewhat artificial fashion on account of the numerous privileges enjoyed by the company, the entrepôt system that had made Amsterdam what it was. Between 1830 and 1850, trade with the Dutch Indies, more than half of which passed through Amsterdam, increased at an annual rate of 5.4%, higher than any other economic activity. This helped revive the manufacturing sector, as well as the service sector, both of which depended on the city's rapid expansion in trade.[22] The Dutch Trading Company's successes do, however, need to be put into perspective, in spite of their by and large positive effects on the country's economy. Born of King William I's voluntarist reaction to foreign competition, the company in fact established a monopoly in a sector in which Amsterdam's merchants were still competitive and would probably have done better, both in terms of transaction volume and profitability.[23]

Amsterdam nevertheless succeeded in temporarily curbing its decline through a policy of colonial retreat. The urban population, approximately 221,000 in 1795, fell to around 180,000 in 1815 before recovering. By 1849 at 224,000, it had exceeded its level prior to the French occupation, even though immigration remained low compared with at its peak. The country's economic growth was admittedly slower, but its accumulated wealth did not disappear overnight; in 1820 the Netherlands' per capita income was second in the world after Britain's. And the upturn that took place in the second half of the nineteenth century assured it of a lasting place among the richest nations in the world. The decline of Amsterdam as an international financial centre should be seen in this context.

The rise of the City of London

The coming of the nineteenth century coincided with London's emergence as the top international financial centre. This phenomenon should come as no surprise. Expansion resulted primarily from the dominant position in the world economy that Britain had built up during the eighteenth century and that asserted itself in a striking manner just after the Napoleonic Wars. Already a great trading and colonial power, England was the cradle of the Industrial Revolution in the last third of the eighteenth century. It was in England that a series of technological innovations occurred (the mechanisation of the textile industry, the use of coal in the metallurgical industry and the use of steam as a source of energy) that was to transform production methods, allow huge productivity gains to be made, give the country a decisive competitive advantage, especially in the cotton industry, and bring about a considerable transfer of resources from agriculture to industry. England's lead would be maintained and even strengthened during the first half of

the nineteenth century, whether measured in terms of industrial production, of capacity for technological innovation, of trade, or simply of
income per inhabitant, which towards 1860 would reach twice that of
continental Europe as a whole. The City's pre-eminence was therefore
built up during this entire period on Britain's economic power, or rather
superpower.

During the first two-thirds of the nineteenth century, England may
well have served both as a workshop and as the world's banker, but the
link between the two was not necessarily self-evident. First, because of
the geographical divide between the industrial north of the country and
the south-east centred on finance and, more generally, on services. And
second, because of the time-lag between the financial revolution and the
Industrial Revolution, since all the elements that had led to the City's
emergence in the last quarter of the eighteenth century had been put in
place before industry took off in England.

Birth of a financial system

The financial revolution of the eighteenth century affected the public
sphere far more than the private sphere, and its causes lay in the need to
finance the war effort rather than in the development of trade and
industry.[24] It referred to the setting up of a modern system of government finance,[25] following William of Orange's accession to the throne in
1688, and to the founding of the Bank of England in 1694. As the
government's banker, the latter was given responsibility for managing
the public debt, even though it was a private institution whose profits
also derived from commercial banking activities and from the privilege
of issuing banknotes. The state's opportunities for borrowing were thus
greatly increased, with the public debt, which had been £14.5 million
sterling in 1697, growing steadily after each war (the Spanish War of
Succession, the Austrian War of Succession and the Seven Years War)
to reach £132 million in 1763 and £188 million in 1781 (the American
War of Independence).

The financial revolution also gave rise to a genuine capital market,
capable of attracting available savings, and where not only government
securities but also those of large joint-stock companies, first and foremost the Bank of England and the East India Company, were traded. At
that time, the agents who traded these stocks occupied part of the Royal
Exchange, the commodity market, established in 1571 at the suggestion
of Thomas Gresham and rebuilt after the Great Fire of 1666; but they
were soon dislodged by merchants, who were disturbed by their noisy
presence and considered these goings-on mere speculation. In 1698 they

moved to Change Alley, between Lombard Street and Cornhill, where there were plenty of taverns, places conducive to dealing with their clients. The busiest coffee house was Jonathan's Coffee House, which the stockbrokers and other regulars decided in 1773 to call The Stock Exchange.

The eighteenth century was also a period of spectacular growth in British overseas trade, whose volume doubled between 1700 and 1780. This dynamism can be explained chiefly by three phenomena: the increase in domestic demand for American and Asian consumer goods (sugar, tobacco, tea and coffee) and for raw materials from northern Europe (particularly timber); the re-export of American and Asian consumer goods to Europe; and third, the growth of markets in the American and African colonies, reserved for British goods.[26] But this commercial expansion also ensued from the British navy's ever-strengthening position and from the acquisition of colonies in Canada, the West Indies and India, which would more than compensate for the loss of the American colonies, a loss that moreover barely affected trading relations between the two countries. London, far more than the other British ports (Bristol, Liverpool and Glasgow), whose growth was however by no means insignificant, was at the heart of this 'commercial revolution', which brought about a remarkable development in auxiliary services.

First of all, there were the commodity markets. Although the Royal Exchange remained the main rallying point for the City's traders, more specialised markets began to form alongside it, most often in the neighbouring coffee houses, where transactions were carried out and the latest information shared: the Jamaica for trade with the West Indies, the Jerusalem for the Orient, the Virginia for the American colonies and the Baltic for north-eastern Europe.[27]

Next came insurance, starting with the marine insurance market. Lloyd's origins are partly legendary. Everything began in Edward Lloyd's tavern in Tower Street, in that part of the City near the Port of London. Nobody really knows how far the establishment dates back, but it existed in 1688–89. Its clientele of seafarers frequented it to do business rather than to relax. In particular, it was a place where ships were bought and sold and where auctions were held, especially for wines and spirits. It is not really known when insurance started to be taken out there, but these activities developed during the period of commercial prosperity under Robert Walpole's government between 1721 and 1742, on the occasion of the Austrian War of Succession, and then throughout the second half of the eighteenth century. At the same time, the tavern underwent the transition from a meeting place to a subscribers' association. In 1769 several of the subscribers left Lloyd's tavern, where more and more bets were being made on eminent people dying, founded the new Lloyd's tavern, elected a committee and in 1773 moved into the Royal Exchange.[28] Despite Lloyd's near-monopoly on marine insurance, the first big insurance companies came into being at the beginning of the eighteenth century. The Royal Exchange Assurance Company and the London Assurance Company were both granted a Royal Charter in 1720 and developed their business in marine, life and fire insurance.[29]

Finally, there were banking activities, which, as we know, were still very closely linked to those of trade through the use of the bill of exchange as the main credit instrument. At the same time, a more autonomous banking profession developed – the private bankers of London. Many of them were former goldsmiths who since the seventeenth century had also acted as bankers, collecting deposits, granting loans, discounting bills of exchange and issuing receipts that were also substitutes for the first banknotes, before devoting themselves wholeheartedly to banking. The number of private banks increased considerably in the second half of the eighteenth century – from fewer than thirty in 1750, to fifty in 1770 and to seventy in 1800.

Very early on, there was a degree of specialisation within the profession between the bankers of the City and the bankers of the West End.[30] The former were more numerous.[31] They collected deposits, discounted bills of exchange on behalf of merchants and granted short-term loans to stockbrokers and all kinds of other brokers working in the City. From the end of the eighteenth century, these banking houses also acted as the London agents for provincial private banks, which mushroomed – from being a dozen in 1750, their number is believed to have reached 650 and possibly 780 in 1810 – and took charge on their own behalf of various investment and transfer operations. The West End group, which included Coutts & Co., bankers to the Crown, were above all connected with the landed aristocracy, whose funds they managed and to whom they granted loans, often of a considerable size. Finally, at the end of the eighteenth century, a third type of financial middleman developed who would form an essential cog in the banking system that was in the process of being set up in England – the bill broker. Bill brokers were brokers of bills of exchange, who, in return for commissions, obtained bills of exchange for banks that wished to discount them. In this way, they enabled funds to be transferred, usually via London, from agricultural regions where money was in plentiful supply but where there were few opportunities to spend it, to the industrial regions where demand for credit was high but where there were insufficient funds available locally. They were behind the huge discount market that developed in London in the following century.

The City's financial architecture – in other words, the combination of services that it was able to provide – was essentially in place by the second third of the eighteenth century. However, it was still Amsterdam that held sway over the international market. This was particularly evident in the two main functions fulfilled by a financial centre at that time: financing international trade and lending to foreign states. In these two fields, both the British government and British traders continued to be dependent upon Amsterdam. Things changed from the 1780s onwards, when Anglo-Dutch trade rivalry finally turned to Britain's advantage, as trade was strengthened between itself and its colonies, and British traders and industrialists became increasingly independent when it came to financing their exports to the United States.[32] The naval war that the two countries fought between 1780 and 1784, completely ousting Dutch ships from the Baltic, dealt a serious blow to Dutch pre-eminence. But it was above all the French wars that brought about a complete reversal of roles.

The French wars

As far as the financing of international trade was concerned, the use of bills of exchange drawn on merchants from the City and, to a lesser extent, from Liverpool, spread from the turn of the century, and in 1802 the private banker Henry Thornton considered that London had become 'the trading metropolis of Europe and, indeed, of the whole world'.[33] The figures are unreliable for this period, but the total value of acceptances in 1836 has been estimated at £30 to £40 million sterling, half of them given over to Anglo-American trade.[34] Accepting a bill of exchange means undertaking to pay the amount for which it was drawn when it falls due, generally within a period of three months, if its drawer defaults. This activity was not new but, particularly from the 1820s, it was undertaken by banking houses that tended to specialise in this type of credit. At the outset, these were all merchant houses – in other words, they were still directly involved in buying and selling merchandise – and almost all of them remained so in part until around 1850 or even later – whence the term of 'merchants' that they preferred to keep throughout the nineteenth century. Thanks to their knowledge of business matters and to the financial soundness of the nearby or remote merchants with whom they had dealings, they were able to distinguish the 'good' bills of exchange from the rest. They therefore began to accept more and more of these bills to the point where this became their main activity. They then became accepting houses, more commonly known as merchant banks. At Baring Brothers, for example, the commission received to finance these acceptances represented 50% to 65% of the bank's profits in 1830 and 75% twenty years later.[35]

At the same time, European states whose financial situation obliged them to take out a loan had no choice but to turn to London. The experience of the City's bankers and financiers in foreign issues was still recent and barely dated back to before the wars of the Revolution. In 1794 Walter Boyd had taken charge of the issue of the first Austrian loan for £3 million, and the practice had been so unusual and past experiences so discouraging that he had encountered some difficulty in finding subscribers. Yet it was already apparent that no other financial centre could offer better conditions. As Boyd wrote to William Pitt: 'Why should we forgo the advantages of being as it were the Banker of Europe?'[36] The apprenticeship continued during the war and enabled Baring Brothers to establish itself as the most powerful firm of the day. But it was an apprenticeship served under the tutelage of a foreign firm that had far more experience in this type of transaction – Hope & Co. from Amsterdam, with which Barings was closely connected. In 1802, for example, the two firms issued a Portuguese loan for 13 million florins, with Barings floating, not without difficulty, 5 million on the London market. The following year they took joint charge of a more important and more prestigious transaction – financing the purchase of Louisiana by the United States from France,[37] effected by means of American Treasury bonds for the amount of $11.25 million at 6% per annum, which Barings and Hope accepted in return for paying an equivalent sum in gold to France.[38]

Numerous foreign merchants and bankers came to swell the City's ranks during these years, attracted by the business opportunities offered by the country's economic dynamism. Above all, there was a huge expansion in British overseas trade, particularly in the export of cotton goods. There were also, to a lesser extent, loan issues and fund transfers to pay troops. Several of these arrivals left their mark on the history of the City. The Schröders, merchants in Hamburg, sent some young members of their family to London. Johann Friedrich arrived there in 1797 and founded the firm J. F. Schröder & Co. as early as 1800. Two years later his younger brother, Johann Heinrich, just turned 18, joined him. The firm specialised in exporting sugar – one of the main colonial foodstuffs re-exported to the Hanseatic city – became involved in the acceptance of bills of exchange and then, as Hamburg declined following its occupation by French troops in 1803, endeavoured to develop business with Russia. When this partnership disbanded in 1817, the younger brother set up his own firm, J. Henry Schröder & Co., which would become one of the leading merchant banks in the City, followed by another in Hamburg in 1819 and a third in Liverpool in 1839.[39] Other renowned merchant banks were founded by merchants and bankers from Germany.[40] The most important of these was obviously N. M. Rothschild & Sons.

Nathan Mayer Rothschild arrived in Manchester from Frankfurt in 1798, aged 21, sent by his father, the banker Mayer Amschel Rothschild, to export cotton goods to Germany and continental Europe. So the Rothschilds started out in England in trade. From 1806, however, following his marriage to Hannah Barent Cohen, the daughter of a prominent London merchant, Nathan turned increasingly to the banking activities that he was determined to specialise in. Involved in the City from 1808, he settled there permanently in 1811. The Rothschilds built their reputation and fortune over the course of the next few years by taking charge of transferring British government funds, needed partly to pay the duke of Wellington's troops and partly to meet the subsidies granted to Britain's allies. Nathan benefited from backing in high places and so was entrusted by the British government, even though he was still relatively unknown, with a responsibility for the war effort that was both crucial and highly profitable, thanks to the commissions received on transfers and arbitrage transactions on foreign exchanges. Along with his brothers, he carried this out extremely effectively, thanks to their presence in the main financial centres – London and Frankfurt, then Paris, where James, the youngest of the five brothers, had settled in 1812 – and by travelling the length and breadth of Europe.[41]

The role played by the London market in ensuring the Rothschilds' success, as well as their emergence as the main force in European finance – they were already on a more or less equal footing with Baring Brothers, the largest bank in Europe in 1815 – should not be underestimated. The City was important because of its geographical proximity to political power and, above all, because its capital market allowed Europe's resources to be mobilised, in spite of the war and the blockages, to finance the war by exchanging bills of exchange payable to London against cash.[42]

The loans earmarked for paying the French war indemnity marked the real beginning of London's ascendancy with regard to international loans. No indemnity had been demanded of France at the time of the Bourbon restoration, but the climate changed just after Waterloo. France had a war indemnity of Fr.700 million inflicted upon it, as well as the presence of an occupying army in the country until this indemnity was fully paid. Moreover, the maintenance costs of this army of 150,000 men also had to be borne by France. The Duke of Richelieu, Louis XVIII's prime minister, admitted that he would have to resort to a foreign issue. Baring Brothers and Hope, which seemed to be the leaders in international finance, agreed to take charge of the matter. The two banking houses continued to work in concert, even though the balance of power was henceforth largely tilted in the English firm's favour; Hope's partners had fled to London in 1795 and, although the bank reopened its doors in 1802, its activities were suspended in 1813 and it was purchased for some £250,000 by Alexander Baring, who decided to keep it afloat. A first loan of Fr.200 million was taken out in February 1817, a second of Fr.115 million in July and then a third of Fr.265 million in May 1818. The indisputable success of the operation reputedly led the duke of Richelieu to declare: 'There are six great powers in Europe: England, France, Prussia, Austria, Russia, and Baring Brothers.'

The pre-eminence of London

Although an English bank in partnership with a Dutch firm had directly underwritten the French loans, these loans were by no means fully subscribed on the London market. Barings and Hope ceded most of them back to other banking houses, which then took charge of placing them in the European financial centres, including and above all in France. The financial capacity displayed by the City was less of a quantitative nature – in other words, linked to the amount of capital available – than qualitative, through the trust that it generated on account of the prestige of its largest banking houses and the network of relationships that it could bring into play. Furthermore, French loans were denominated in francs and the interest was payable in Paris.

The Prussian loan of 1818 marked a new, even greater turning point in London's role as world capital of foreign loan issues. Like the other countries in the Holy Alliance – Austria and Russia – Prussia had to call on foreign capital markets to find the necessary money, given the state of its public funds (higher debt and currency devaluation), seriously undermined by the war. The first new element was the issuing of this loan by the Rothschilds, under the management of Nathan Mayer, head of the London house. It was the first step in the almost complete takeover of the loan issues for European states, which lasted an entire generation. Austria, Russia, Naples, Spain and Belgium followed in the first half of the twenties, until the stock-market crash of 1825. N. M. Rothschild soon completely overshadowed Baring Brothers, which entered a phase of relative decline as its head, Alexander Baring, gradually lost interest in the banking business and turned to the lifestyle of a country gentleman. But the Rothschilds' success was mainly due to their talent for business, the quality of their services, their network of relationships and their innovations in financial matters. Crucially, the Prussian loan was issued in pounds sterling, not in thalers, and the interest was payable in London instead of in Berlin. When a sinking fund was set up, modelled on the British public debt, there was, as Niall Ferguson puts it, an 'anglicisation' of foreign loans. Moreover, loans were issued simultaneously in Frankfurt, Berlin, Hamburg, Amsterdam and Vienna, representing a key step towards creating a genuine international market in government bonds.[43]

These innovations introduced by the Rothschilds would serve as the model for future issues that would soon become widespread. Between 1822 and 1825, at least twenty foreign loans were issued in London's financial centre, for a total nominal value of £40 million.[44] The City was taken over by a mania for lending to the new states of Latin America. These states gained their independence from Iberian colonisation with help from Britain, which was seeking outlets there both for its industrial products and for its capital. This mania led, alongside perfectly respectable issues such as those made on behalf of Brazil by Rothschilds or on behalf of Buenos Aires by Barings, to more adventurous transactions, including an issue for the imaginary kingdom of Poyais. In the highly specialised English banking system, foreign issues, like acceptances, were the preserve of the merchant banks; in particular, they were the prerogative of a very select group dominated by Barings and above all Rothschilds.[45] Other merchant banks came from abroad to set up in London and deal in acceptances and, to a lesser extent, issues, the most notable being George Peabody & Co. and C. J. Hambro, Sons & Co. The first of these was founded in 1838 by George Peabody, from Massachusetts, and it would have its hours of glory under the name of J. S. Morgan & Co., then Morgan Grenfell & Co. The second was founded in 1839 by Carl Joachim Hambro, son of a merchant and banker from Copenhagen and former American consul in Denmark.

The merchant banks were therefore the main players in the two activities upon which the City's position as the foremost international financial centre depended. Nevertheless, with the exception of Rothschilds and Barings, they were not the overall market leaders, since they were relatively new. It was the traditional private bankers, long established and more focused on the domestic economy, who still dominated the scene, certainly in terms both of social prestige and of personal and collective influence in the City.[46] What is more, they alone corresponded to the English definition of a bank, clearly formulated in the

1870s by Walter Bagehot: 'Messrs Rothschild are immense capitalists, having, doubtless, much borrowed money in their hands. But they do not take £100 in deposits payable on demand, and pay it back in cheques of £5 each, and that is our English banking.'[47] For London was also Britain's financial centre. At the beginning of the nineteenth century, domestic affairs clearly had the edge over international affairs and, in the workings of the City, the integration of the two was still a long way off. The traditional private banks were more a part of domestic money circuits and they constituted the cornerstone of a money market that was in the process of being set up. After the crash of 1825, which in the wake of a speculative fever led to the disappearance of some sixty private banks in London and in the provinces, the private banks placed most of their reserves in the form of money at call and short notice with bill brokers. From being brokers, the latter increasingly turned into real traders in bills of exchange, their profit no longer coming from commissions but from the difference between the bills' purchase price and selling price. This transformation was reflected in the name of 'discount house' that started to be given to them.

Other mechanisms were then set up to adapt to the needs of a market that was increasingly open to the outside world. Foreign loans were allowed to be listed on the London Stock Exchange in 1823, not without encountering a degree of opposition; in the committee, the serious risk of a large number of members seceding finally won the day. The Bank of England began to take on the role of lender of last resort, notably by undertaking to discount bills of exchange held by the discount houses; and in times of crisis, it was driven to rescue or to let founder both British and foreign firms involved in domestic and international activities.

The revival of Paris

The path followed by Paris's financial centre from the end of the *Ancien Régime* to the mid-nineteenth century showed greater continuity than London's, distinctly upward, or Amsterdam's, clearly downward.

The Ancien Régime *and the Revolution*

In the eighteenth century, Paris's role certainly relied on developing international trade, but it also relied on the state's financial needs and on the possibility of subscribing to its numerous loans. Paris already stood out on account of its cosmopolitanism. Many foreign bankers, above all from Geneva, had settled there. According to the royal almanacs, there were fifty-one banking houses in 1721 and more than seventy in 1780. In 1770 the capital's three main houses[48] were perhaps also the largest in continental Europe.[49] According to a contemporary: 'Paris has an incredibly wide-ranging sphere of banking activities; it could be said that there is no city in the universe that is superior to it in this respect.'[50] There were also notaries who played a key role in distributing private medium- and long-term credit, as well as in placing public issues, thanks to the information that they held on their clients and to the establishment of a system for sharing information.[51]

The importance of the financial institutions and markets should not be overlooked either. The Caisse d'escompte, founded in 1776 by Turgot, the general financial controller, at the initiative of the financier and speculator Isaac Panchaud, had the main goal of supporting trading activities by discounting bills of exchange and other negotiable bills, as well as by collecting deposits, making payments on behalf of its clientele, trading in gold and silver, and issuing notes, which were not, however, legal tender. Although modelled on the Bank of England, and in many respects the forerunner of the Banque de France, the Caisse d'escompte did not enjoy any kind of exclusive privilege. As a joint-stock limited partnership founded to serve the merchant community, it would, however, quickly be used by the state, notably by Necker, to provide for the Treasury.

The Bourse had been founded by an order of the Council in 1724. The shares of several large companies, such as the Compagnie des Indes and the Caisse d'escompte, were listed there. But it was mainly government annuities that were traded. During the decade preceding the revolution, their issue exceeded £1 billion – £600 million in perpetual annuities and £500 million in life annuities. The latter, particularly prized by investors in Geneva and Amsterdam, were based either on a person's life (or head), the payment ceasing upon his or her death, or on the lives of several people (in some cases more than a hundred), the payment decreasing as the heads disappeared. Nevertheless, listing foreign stock was prohibited by an order of the Council in 1785. The Bourse continued to be dominated by speculative transactions, the vast majority on the futures market, in spite of various attempts to restrict them and the tight regulation of stockbrokers' activities both by their own corporation and by the public authorities. Their number was limited to forty, then to sixty from 1785 onwards, and they were the only ones permitted to act as middlemen for the purchase and sale of securities. Another important market, which was both the driving force and a reflection of the influence exerted internationally by Paris, was the foreign exchange market. It too was located at the Bourse and was in principle reserved for banks authorised by the general financial controller – fifty-three names featured on the list in 1785. The exchange rate was set by the centre's largest banking houses on the basis of the rates applicable abroad, the supply and demand for drafts in the various currencies and, of course, the latest political news.

The Revolution, in particular the abolition of the monarchy in September 1792, inevitably put a brake on these activities. The economic and political conditions, in particular the measures decreed by the Jacobins in 1793 – closing the Bourse, liquidating the Caisse d'escompte, dissolving joint-stock companies, seizing currencies and stocks of colonial foodstuffs, and arresting monopolisers – were hardly conducive to making an international financial centre bloom. The bankers, inevitably suspected on account of their wealth and their foreign connections, were hit hard. Most of those who remained in the capital were arrested (this was the case for the Mallets and the Lecouteulx, two of the oldest Parisian banking houses belonging to the *haute banque*) and some, such as the Vandenyvers, of Dutch origin, did not escape the guillotine. Nevertheless, business picked up again after the fall of Robespierre in July 1794 and the 'opening of places known under the name of stock exchanges' in April 1795, in spite of measures taken against speculation, which hampered the market's normal functioning.[52] Tentative at first, the recovery gradually intensified, especially from the summer of 1807, when the Continental System was made more efficient, stimulating industry and encouraging initiatives. While some banking houses combined banking activities and industrial investment, the vast majority remained connected with trade.[53]

From the Revolution onwards, the monetary situation was unstable for a long time. Inflation turned into hyperinflation as the issuing of paper currency by the state raced out of control; the *assignats* (banknotes used during the Revolution), issued from 1790, lost their entire value and were abolished in 1796. Coins also tended to disappear from circulation, taken by *émigrés* or hoarded by the population. A brief period of free banking then began in France, as the Parisian merchants and bankers set up various banks, like the Caisse des comptes courants in 1796 or the Caisse d'escompte du commerce in 1797, which put banknotes into circulation. The creation of the Banque de France put an end to this situation. Bonaparte, having come to power after the *coup d'état* of 18 *Brumaire* (9 November 1799), was determined to set up such an institution and had already discussed this possibility with several Parisian bankers. On 18 January 1800 he signed a decree authorising a group of bankers, including Lecouteulx, Perrégaux, Mallet and Périer, to create the Banque de France in the form of a private company, with a capital of 30 million francs, managed by fifteen *régents* and overseen by three censors. It absorbed the Caisse de comptes courants, then the Caisse d'escompte du commerce and in 1803 obtained the privilege of issuing banknotes for fifteen years. This privilege would later be extended, but the state's grip did not take long to tighten. In 1806 a law put a governor and two deputy governors, appointed by the state and dismissible by it, at its head, resulting in an institution that was far less independent of political power than its British counterpart.[54]

The founding of the Parisian haute banque

The new development in the early nineteenth century was the ever-stronger appeal exerted by Paris, to the detriment of provincial towns, particularly Lyons. Indeed, French commercial and financial capitalism became increasingly concentrated in Paris, a city which, as Louis Bergeron wrote, 'since the Revolution, appeared to be both the home of business freedom and the nerve centre of contacts, information and speculation'.[55] Consequently, two dozen provincial houses established themselves in Paris to seek new business opportunities there; and these were only families and individuals belonging to a narrow 'politico-financial' elite owing to its shared interests with the state.[56] Among the most outstanding personalities, Claude Périer, a notable and business-man from Grenoble in the Dauphiné, should be mentioned. Having settled in Paris under the Directory, he was one of the bankers who financed the *coup d'état* of 18 *Brumaire*, before founding the Banque de France, whose statutes he drafted. Besides his business in Grenoble, Claude Perier took control of the Mines d'Anzin in the north during the Revolution, and his family retained a stake in heavy industry throughout the nineteenth century. Nicolas Seillière set up as a banker in Paris in 1796. His family was involved in business in Nancy, especially in financing the provision of sheets to the army; it was also involved in financing industry through its links with the Wendel family. Two other distinguished families from Lorraine, both Jewish, settled in Paris during this period: the Foulds and the Worms.

As an evident sign of its resurgence, Paris's financial centre also attracted numerous foreign bankers and merchants. For a start, the recovery meant the return to business of the Swiss, notably Genevan, bankers who had settled in Paris at the end of the *Ancien Régime*. Four banking houses came to dominate the scene: Mallet, Perrégaux, Delessert and Hottinguer.[57] The Mallets were already the second, and soon to be the third, generation of their family in Paris. The first bank had been founded in 1713 by Isaac Mallet, back from Geneva, where his ancestors had taken refuge one and a half centuries earlier. In 1794 the bank took the name of Mallet Frères, after a partnership agreement had been renewed between the brothers Guillaume and Isaac-Jean-Jacques, the founder's grandsons, and their cousin Jacques Torras. Mallet Frères was not one of the largest banks in the capital, but the length of time that it had been in existence and its soundness made it a prestigious house, and it was as such that it became co-founder of the Banque de France. Jean-Frédéric Perrégaux, who had arrived in Paris in 1765 from Neuchâtel, opened his own banking house in 1781. In 1788 he hired Jacques Lafitte, who became his partner in 1795. The bank barely interrupted its activities during the Revolution and emerged as the most important of the Parisian banking houses under the Empire; it took the name of Perrégaux, Laffitte & Cie following the death of Jean-Frédéric Perrégaux in 1808. The Delesserts were originally from the canton of Vaud. Etienne Delessert settled in Paris in 1777, after a detour via Lyons. He survived the Revolution and kept his fortune, despite being imprisoned in the second year, very probably because of transferring funds abroad. In 1795 his son, later joined by his brothers, succeeded him at the head of the bank, of which he remained a limited partner. The House of Delessert's power came chiefly from its subsidiary in Le Havre, more directly involved in trading activities. Jean-Conrad Hottinguer, born into Zurich's circle of big traders, set up in Paris in 1784. He left France for the United States in 1794, but returned to Paris in 1796 and re-established his bank in 1798. He was also the largest importer of cotton in continental Europe.

The other great wave of foreign immigration, from Germany, only really started under the Restoration. James de Rothschild arrived fairly unnoticed in Paris in 1812, within the framework of fund-transfer transactions organised by his brother Nathan, founded his own bank, de Rothschild Frères, in 1817 and quickly emerged as the dominant force within the Parisian *haute banque*. Other bankers from Frankfurt came to settle in Paris too. The Protestant Bethmanns, who played a leading role in placing foreign securities, especially Austrian, in Frankfurt's financial centre during the second half of the eighteenth century, sent a representative, whereas the Gontards made longer-term commitments there from 1827, while maintaining the hub of their activities in Frankfurt. Moreover, others, often of Jewish origin, arrived from Germany – the Oppenheims from Cologne, through their alliance with the Foulds,[58] the de Habers from Karlsruhe and the Seligman-d'Eichtals from Munich.[59]

The comparative advantages of Paris

The appeal of Paris's financial centre can be explained first by its role in financing domestic and international trade. Not only was almost all domestic trade handled in the capital, but numerous foreign merchants, especially Swiss, regularly drew bills of exchange on Paris. The Parisian financial centre's role as a centre of international settlements is partly explained by the banking houses of the *haute banque* and by the trust that they inspired in their clientele. Yet this explanation is inadequate. As Maurice Lévy-Leboyer has clearly demonstrated, Paris's role was above all due to France's position in the multilateral system of payments. In spite of its relatively modest foreign trade, France played an important monetary role, since it was the only country in continental Europe that had balanced trade with Latin America and a positive trade balance with the Anglo-Saxon countries. The franc was an international currency because, on the one hand, the British and Americans were trying to obtain bills of exchange on Paris to pay for some of their purchases and, on the other hand, the merchants of continental Europe were using the Paris centre to clear their debts with the Anglo-Saxon countries.[60]

This was indeed a new role for Paris, with its constraints but also its advantages, in particular the opportunity of creating a very active capital market. Capital accumulated in the French capital. Deposits, which represented up to 80% of the liabilities of certain banks, included, besides the accounts of members of the aristocracy and the bourgeoisie, as well as the funds of numerous French industrial and commercial firms, the proceeds from sales made in France by foreign merchants, who used them on the spot to make payments and to obtain new credits. This capital replenished itself. In particular, it lay at the root of the role that Paris would henceforth play in placing and then issuing foreign loans.[61] Issue activities had remained limited until the Restoration: Napoleon was not very keen on loans and the French wars had mainly been financed with the resources of occupied countries. As for the loans earmarked to pay the war indemnity, they had been managed by foreign banking houses – Barings from London and Hope from Amsterdam, which had ceded a part back to several French houses,[62] the Rothschilds only being involved in the last instalment. The French bankers therefore lacked experience in these matters and, even though France, along with Britain, was the main capital-exporting country, the number of loans floated on the Paris market only progressed slowly during the first half of the nineteenth century: three loans to the Kingdom of Naples between 1821 and 1824, managed by the Rothschilds, were mostly issued in Paris; the Spanish loan of 1823 was concluded under difficult conditions by the Paris banker

Guebhart; furthermore, four Belgian loans and two others on behalf of the city of Brussels were issued between 1831 and 1844; while papal loans were very easy to place in France between 1831 and 1839.[63]

The Paris Bourse also provided a secondary market both for loans that had been issued there and for those issued in other markets. French and foreign state loans largely dominated, until the 1840s anyway, when railway company stock began to compete with them. The listing of foreign securities had, nevertheless, been prohibited by Council decree in 1785, but this ban was lifted by royal edict on 18 November 1823, the same year that they were admitted for listing on the London Stock Exchange. Yet in Paris, this admission was not entirely subject to government authorisation; the government, approached over this matter, had preferred to delegate responsibility for it to the stock-brokers' own body, the Compagnie des Agents de Change. Regulations also extended to other areas, such as the stockbrokers' monopoly on trading public securities or the legal ban on the futures market, even though this was generally tolerated, with periods of greater or lesser leniency. These regulations were, however, circumvented by the existence of a parallel market, the *coulisse*, where, as far as possible, stocks not admitted to the official list were quoted and where forward transactions were carried out. Prior to the Revolution, the *coulisse* had been tolerated by the authorities, who knew perfectly well that they could not do without it. In any case, these transactions, whether of an official nature or not, required considerable funds, and these were mainly provided by banks, as well as by other institutions, especially insurance companies.[64]

Paris's international role thus depended first and foremost on the members of the *haute banque*, a group of some twenty banking houses (the exact number varying according to the observer), whose structure was built up by the waves of both native and foreign immigration to the French capital. The concept of *haute banque* is difficult to define. Length of time in existence, which would play a decisive role from the end of the nineteenth century, was not yet applicable to this recently established group. Size, network of relationships, activities and tacit peer recognition were the most reliable identification criteria. Denomination, on the other hand, was not. Although the members of the *haute banque* were above all Protestant, they were also Jewish and Catholic. Their activities resembled those of the London merchant banks: financing international trade, mainly through the acceptance of bills of exchange, an activity that was still usually connected with trade, and issuing foreign loans. While the first was common to the whole group, the second was largely dominated by one house: de Rothschild Frères.

The lesser centres

After London and Paris, several markets that were significant but secondary, compared with the capitals of the two largest European economies, played a key role in providing financial services to the international community. Amsterdam belonged henceforth among these lesser centres, but its recent status as the leading world market and the circumstances of its decline meant that it was accorded special treatment. Besides Amsterdam, three other centres deserve special attention: Frankfurt, Brussels and Geneva.

Frankfurt, Hamburg and Germany

In Germany there was no financial centre comparable to London or Paris before the unification of the country in 1871. Berlin, the capital of Prussia, hosted several leading banking houses, including Mendelssohn & Co., with links to Russia, but its international influence was still very limited. Cologne was integrated into the large European networks, but it did not play the same international role as the two main Germanic markets – Hamburg and Frankfurt. As continental Europe's first, and the world's fourth, port (after London, Liverpool and New York), Hamburg's importance as a financial centre was closely linked to its trading activities and to its connections with Britain. Frankfurt, on the other hand, was far more of a banking centre, and it was as such that it holds our attention here.

Frankfurt's fate has been astonishing to say the least. From being the leading German financial centre from the mid-eighteenth century to the mid-nineteenth century, it experienced an apparently irreversible decline after the unification of Germany in 1871, before recovering its pre-eminence in the wake of the 'economic miracle' that followed the Second World War. Frankfurt's international role can be traced back to its fairs, the first of which dates from the thirteenth century, as well as to its geographical location at the crossroads of the trading routes connecting Italy with north-western Europe, where its merchants were especially active. Nevertheless, Frankfurt experienced its hour of glory in the eighteenth century, just when its fairs were starting to be supplanted, in relative importance, by those in Leipzig. Trade, on the other hand, which continued without interruption between fairs, intensified. This mainly involved activities connected with shipping and transporting goods, as well as with the role of trade dealer. Moreover, it was in this line of business that the city's main banking houses started out.[65]

Frankfurt's speciality during the first half of the nineteenth century was above all its position as continental Europe's main centre for trading government bonds. A turning point was reached in 1776, when Bethmann placed a first Austrian loan for 200,000 guilders at 4% on the market; and then, the following year, two issues for 500,000 gulden at $4\frac{1}{2}$%, in bonds of 1,000 florins. From then on he made a name for himself as the banker to the Austrian imperial family, placing a total of fifty-four issues amounting to 30 million guilders on their behalf between 1778 and 1796. Other banks soon followed: Metzler with a Bavarian loan in 1779 and, above all, Mayer Amschel Rothschild with five issues between 1801 and 1806. It is hard to make international comparisons for this period. Between 1778 and 1796, government bonds for a total of just over 100 million guilders had been placed on the Frankfurt market, primarily for Austria, but also for Denmark, Prussia, Bavaria and other smaller principalities and territories. It was a high figure, but it probably represented less than a third of the issues on the Amsterdam market during this period, without counting the foreign securities, especially French annuities, held by the public.

The period of the French wars was far from being as destructive for Frankfurt as it was for Amsterdam. On the contrary, the placing of foreign loans on the Frankfurt market experienced strong growth after the occupation of Amsterdam in 1795. Upon the dissolution of the Holy Roman Empire in 1806, Frankfurt was integrated for seven years into the new Confederation of the Rhine, which united the large states in southern Germany (Bavaria, Wurttemberg and Baden), as well as various other territories, including Hesse-Darmstadt and Frankfurt. But the French occupation was to have a limited impact on economic life and, in particular, on the city's banking activities. From the 1820s onwards, the main development was the supremacy of the House of Rothschild in issuing and placing government bonds. The five brothers' home town remained a cornerstone in the strategy of the multinational bank run by Nathan Mayer in London.

Frankfurt's financial capacity clearly stemmed from the city's wealth and from the existence of a public attracted by foreign investment, not so much bankers and merchants, who did not generally keep these securities in their portfolio, as foundations and other investment companies, as well as of course individual investors. But it also derived from the existence of a strong potential pool of investors outside the city. In this respect, it is significant that only 53% of account holders at the Bethmanns Bank at the beginning of the nineteenth century were residents of Germany. Frankfurt's international calling was also due to the fact that the city was a real breeding-ground for bankers. In 1837, 118 banking houses were registered there, forming an extremely wide social and professional network, which not only survived but spread to the main European financial centres and somewhat later to the American ones. This was first and foremost the case with Jewish bankers, whose political emancipation won during the French occupation was challenged at the time of the Restoration; they had to wait until 1824 for civic equality and until 1854 for full political equality. The Rothschilds were, of course, the best-known example and the most spectacular success, but several other families installed a member of the family in Amsterdam, London, Paris, Brussels, New York or San Francisco.[66]

Brussels, Antwerp and Belgium

The Brussels financial centre was more recent. Various foreign loans were admittedly issued in Belgium in the course of the eighteenth century – first and especially for the Austrian government, which placed issues at $4\frac{1}{2}$%, 4% and 3%, adding up to a total of 30 million florins, mostly in Brussels through the Nettine bank, later Vve Nettine et fils. Some other foreign loans, including Swedish and Russian, were also issued in Belgium, usually for amounts not exceeding 2 or 3 million florins. In addition to these, there was considerable Belgian investment in the French public debt.[67] But, at the beginning of the nineteenth century, Brussels was still a European centre of secondary importance that had not yet established itself against the old centre of Antwerp. At that time, the main Belgian stock exchange was unquestionably Antwerp, where mostly foreign securities were traded (Austrian government funds, Russian and, to a lesser extent, Danish, Swedish and British government bonds), with Brussels focusing on the funds of various Belgian public entities.[68] Besides, Brussels only had a handful of provincial private banks like those found in large numbers in Antwerp or in the province of Hainaut.

Brussels began its rise in the 1820s, when a series of favourable events enabled it to eclipse its rival. This started with the founding of the Société Générale in 1822. The bank was established on the initiative of William I of the Netherlands, with the involvement of bankers from Brussels, with a view to developing credit and to exercising the functions of central bank and state cashier in the south of the country. With a capital of 30 million florins, it was a bank of European dimensions, whose headquarters were located in Brussels. Next came the independence of Belgium in 1830, which benefited Brussels by centralising government and politics in the capital but proved catastrophic for Antwerp.[69]

Furthermore, the Brussels financial centre ended up considerably strengthened during this period by the arrival of powerful private bankers originating from abroad, amongst whom German Jews formed the largest group. The most famous was undoubtedly Jonathan-Raphaël Bischoffsheim, who arrived from Frankfurt. When he settled in Brussels at the end of the 1830s, he already had strong connections with Amsterdam, where his brother had settled in 1820, and with Antwerp, where he had been living since 1827. His brother Louis opened a branch in London in 1840, finally opting for Paris in 1848. The name of Bischoffsheim is tied to the fate of the Banque de Belgique, rival to the Société Générale, founded in 1835, as well as to that of the Banque de Paris et des Pays-Bas in the second half of the century. The brothers Louis and Jonathan-Raphaël showed the way for a galaxy of bankers originating from Frankfurt and Mainz (their father's home town), who gradually settled in Brussels,[70] but contacts with Germany were maintained throughout the century. They also had ties with the Rothschilds. In 1843 Samuel Lambert, born into a family of merchants originally from Alsace, established in Lyons, opened a branch of the House of Rothschild in Antwerp. His father-in-law, Lazare Richtenberger, had himself represented the Rothschilds in Brussels since 1830. Upon his father-in-law's death in 1853, Lambert reorganised the Brussels and Antwerp branches under the name of Banque Lambert. Among the Protestant bankers originating from Germany, mention should be made of Frédéric Brugmann from Dortmund, who went into partnership with J. Engler, to set up first a wool company in Verviers around 1795 and then a banking house in Brussels, the house Engler, Brugmann et Cie. Between 1831 and 1839, J. Engler would be the manager of the Société Générale, before retiring from business.[71]

The establishment of the Société Générale contributed to developing the *haute banque* in Brussels. Between 1825 and 1830, approximately 51% to 54% of the Société Générale's largest shareholders had their residence in Brussels. By 1837 the proportion had reached 92% to 98%, as the Société Générale became a purely Brussels bank. The founding of the Banque de Belgique and the joint role of the two big banks in setting up the first large industrial enterprises further strengthened this trend. Shares in the companies that they had financed were traded almost exclusively on the Brussels Stock Exchange, which pushed aside Antwerp's for good.[72] However, the influence exerted by the Brussels centre remained above all domestic. Between 1830 and 1850, Belgian capital was chiefly invested in the first large-scale industrial limited companies, and investing in foreign stocks became increasingly rare. On the other hand, foreign capital came to be invested in Belgium. Indeed, during the first decade of its independence, Belgium got into debt with foreign countries. The state's creditworthiness was not sufficiently sound, whereas its needs were considerable, particularly as a result of building the railways, of which it had to bear the costs. At that time, most of the loans contracted by the new Belgian state were issued in Paris and London.[73]

Geneva in the French sphere of influence

Geneva was probably the smallest of the so-called secondary financial centres. Yet, from the beginning of the eighteenth century, its international role was out of all proportion to its size as a small republic. Geneva was able to take advantage of its neutrality and its position at the heart of the 'Huguenot International' to form a key link in the chain financing Louis XIV's wars, which required massive amounts of foreign funds. At that time, Geneva was a cosmopolitan city, what Herbert Lüthy has called 'a society without a definite nationality'.[74] This was not only because of its traders and bankers but also because of the composition, possibly unique in Europe, of its portfolio of securities, which included a mixture of French and English, and soon Dutch, Italian, Scandinavian and imperial, annuities. From the middle of the century onwards, Geneva also became an important centre for issuing foreign loans, with eight Sardinian loans between 1742 and 1752, a Danish loan in 1760 and an Austrian loan in 1765.

All the same, Geneva did not become a truly international financial centre. Its bankers' attention was almost exclusively focused from 1770 on financing the French debt. Throughout the eighteenth century, Geneva had kept close links with Paris, where its bankers had a strong foothold, but things only got moving when Necker was appointed general financial controller in 1776. Born in Geneva, he made his career in Paris, and his bank became one of the most important in the capital. During his five years in office, Necker borrowed £530 million, £386 million of which were in the form of life annuities, the famous *tontines*. The Genevan bankers were to transform this rather old-fashioned type of loan into a negotiable and highly speculative financial instrument. Their innovation consisted in 'scientifically' selecting lives – those of young women from families belonging to the Genevan bourgeoisie whose particularly long life expectancy had been noted; they perfected reinsurance plans guaranteeing payment of the annuity in the event of death and offered the possibility of purchasing annuities by paying in several instalments. The demand for annuities developed into a mania at the end of the eighteenth century, the investments of the Genevans exceeding £100 million. It spread to other cities through the Huguenot International networks and raced out of control in a speculative bubble that burst with the financial chaos brought about by the Revolution.

The Genevan centre thus felt the full force of the French Revolution. After the suspension of some smaller houses in November and December 1789, three banks collapsed in 1792.[75] As in France, the recovery began towards the end of the Terror, slowly at first, then more steadily, and continued after the annexation of Geneva by France on 26 April 1798. Until 31 December 1813 Geneva was the capital of the French department of Léman. As business recovered, Genevan banking reformed under new corporate names. Ferrier, Darier & Cie was founded in 1795, Henri Hentsch & Cie in 1796, J. G. Lombard & J.-J. Lullin in 1798 and de Candolle, Mallet & Cie – now the house of Pictet & Cie – in 1805.[76] At the same time, these bankers, like their European colleagues, were involved in various trading activities. Ferrier, Darier also dealt with transport; Henry Hentsch, which had represented the calico trader Picot, Fazy & Cie in Lyons, first founded a drapery business, which later became a 'silk goods and commissions' company.[77]

As we have seen, the recovery also meant the return of Genevan bankers to Paris. As a financial centre, Geneva remained well within the French sphere of influence even after joining Switzerland in 1814, a situation that afforded both advantages and disadvantages. But one thing was clear, and that was that the Revolution marked the beginning of Geneva's slow decline as a financial centre. Just like Lyons, it suffered from the new appeal exerted by Paris, where foreigners and people from the provinces felt the urge to be represented. It was, moreover, significant that the new banks founded in the French capital in the early years of the century, such as Schlumberger jeune, R. Vassal & Cie or André & Cottier, almost immediately exceeded in size the firms from Lyons and Geneva that had sponsored them.[78] And, above all, Geneva was no longer in a position to play the role in financing the French public debt that it had enjoyed under the *Ancien Régime*. When the French war indemnity was to be paid, the Genevan financiers, 'who had formerly held the top rank',[79] were no longer capable of responding to such calls for capital.

Geneva then witnessed a revival as a financial centre. New banking houses made their appearance,[80] and the private banks reoriented their activities in two directions. First, they gradually freed themselves from commercial dealings. De Candolle, Mallet & Cie, for example, rapidly made the transition from trade to banking and focused on foreign exchange transactions, discounting bills of exchange, and purchasing and selling securities, both on its own account and on behalf of its clientele; in 1821 (under the corporate name de Candolle, Turrettini & Cie), it was one of the first to go into insurance by becoming the Swiss agent for the Compagnie Générale d'Assurances sur la Vie, in Paris.[81] Second, in the same way as their Parisian counterparts, they began to attract a well-heeled clientele and to direct their activities towards portfolio management.

Interactions and networks of relationships

The existence of a hierarchy of international financial centres was clearly in contemporaries' minds. In Britain, in particular, there was a keen awareness from the turn of the century of the City's newly acquired role as the centre of European and even world trade – less thought was given to finance as such. The advantages of this position were not lost on politicians, even if they do not appear to have taken measures intentionally aimed at promoting the City against its main competitors. The pound sterling's return to gold convertibility in 1821, as well as the first steps towards free trade in the 1820s, two of the linchpins of Great Britain's economic policy in the nineteenth century that were generally considered beneficial to the City's interests, took place in conditions that clearly illustrated the reality and limits to the rivalry among financial centres at that time. It was, for example, symptomatic that, in both cases, the government showed far more enthusiasm than the City's businessmen.[82]

The return to gold was particularly revealing. The purpose was eminently political: it was a matter of shielding the government from domination by the money market and of putting an end to the profits, considered excessive by public opinion, of the period of non-convertibility introduced in 1797. If anything, the City, which feared a period of monetary constraints, tended to be against it. But William Huskisson, Tory minister and the real instigator of this action, was more farsighted and thought that resuming payments in gold could only strengthen the City's position. He explained this to the prime minister, Lord Liverpool:

I have no doubt that with the extent of our commercial dealings and operations of Exchange, which make this Country the Emporium not only of Europe but of America North and South, the Bank of England would make London the chief Bullion Market of the World ... The facility it would give to Trade in affording them the means of promptly rectifying the Exchange with any particular Country, and probably in the particular Coin of that very Country to which it might be desirable to remit Bullion, could not fail to form one of these inducements which would make London the *settling House* of the Money transactions of the World.[83]

There was already a clear view of the effects that such a political choice could have on the City's role as an international financial centre. But one could not speak of protecting or of promoting the centre, whose status was seen as the consequence of Britain's dominant position in world trade. Nor could one speak of real competition among centres; Amsterdam handled its decline as best it could, and Paris was not yet in a position to vie with London.

Instead, the characteristic feature of this period, as regards both competition and cooperation among financial centres, was the existence of networks of relationships and of subgroups within these networks. We have already come across some of them. At a time when merchant and banking houses were almost exclusively family firms, it was through these highly personalised channels that most international banking activities, particularly financing international trade and issuing foreign loans, were carried out. There were, of course, large networks formed by the Protestant and Jewish religious minorities. The Protestant banking network was dominant in the eighteenth century, but it grew weaker during the following century, even though it still had a strong foothold in the Parisian *haute banque* and in the family and business links that it maintained with Genevan private banking. The Jewish banking network left more of a mark on the first part of the nineteenth century.

These networks, especially those belonging to the Jewish banks, varied in density. The closest relations, between father and son and/or between brothers, struggled to last beyond the second generation. The borderline case was, of course, that of the Rothschilds. Not so much in the first generation; the simultaneous presence of five brothers in five international financial centres (Amschel in Frankfurt, Salomon in Vienna, Nathan in London, Carl in Naples and James in Paris) was not in itself exceptional. Other dynasties, like the Bischoffsheims, the Oppenheims or the Sterns, settled in London, Paris, Frankfurt or Brussels. Instead, it was in the ensuing generations that the Rothschilds distinguished themselves by managing to maintain a surprisingly high level of cohesion; in the second generation, fourteen out of eighteen marriages took place among members of the Rothschild family, and there were another thirteen out of thirty in the following generation!

As a rule, the more extensive the network, the more distant the degree of kinship, to the point of becoming non-existent. It is, therefore, wrong to speak of a single network of Protestant banking, as had been the case in the eighteenth century, or even of Jewish banking. On the contrary, there were several often interconnected networks, whose heart was formed by one or, more frequently, several families. This

was, for example, the case with the Oppenheims and the Foulds[84] or
the Bischoffsheims and the Goldschmidts,[85] around whom revolved a
whole succession of banks and families related by marriage and
friendship.

In the absence of a member of the family, or of a family related by
marriage, in a financial centre, it was necessary to turn to correspondent
banks or agents. The example of the Rothschilds is revealing here too.
Unwilling or unable to be directly represented in centres such as New
York, Berlin or Brussels, not to mention in countless other lesser centres, they dispatched or recruited an agent there or worked with a
partner bank. Auguste Belmont, for example, an employee of the house
of Frankfurt, was sent to the United States in 1837. The partners did
not originally intend to make him their agent in New York, but Belmont
decided to settle there and made a success of it, especially on a social
level. The Rothschilds, who did not succeed in convincing a member of
the family to settle on the other side of the Atlantic, gave their approval
in spite of a certain degree of distrust.[86] In Berlin, they had a special
relationship with Mendelssohn, whom Samuel Bleichröder endeavoured
to supplant.[87] Some agents entered the fold, such as Léon Lambert,
the Rothschilds' agent in Belgium, who married Baroness Lucie de
Rothschild, James' granddaughter, in 1882.[88] There was thus not
always a very clear dividing line between family representative and
agent, particularly in the context of networks where family ties were
fairly weak.

The existence of networks of special relationships, in which professional and family ties intermingled to varying degrees, was far from
limited to the religious minorities. The alliance between Barings of
London and Hope of Amsterdam, for example, in which business
relations took precedence over marriage bonds, extended to Hottinguer
in Paris and to Pictet in Geneva. The scattering of the Schröders in
Europe and in America was just as remarkable as that of the great Jewish
banking dynasties. When the company's founder died in Hamburg in
1821, his sons and nephews had set up firms in Bremen, Amsterdam,
London, Riga and St Petersburg. Over the following years they expanded to Liverpool, Trieste, Rio de Janeiro, Lima, New York, New
Orleans, Jakarta and Singapore.[89]

There is no need to draw up the complete inventory of these very
numerous networks, which in the first half of the nineteenth century
concerned above all the world of trade. These independent businessmen, with a foothold in the main trading cities where they settled on a
temporary or permanent basis, formed a real cosmopolitan bourgeoisie
whose liberal, progressive and individualistic ideology transcended

nationalist standpoints. This internationalism found expression particularly in integrating individuals and families of different nationalities,
both centrally, first in London, and on the periphery, like in Argentina.[90]
This world was to fall slowly apart as capital became concentrated,
starting in the mid-nineteenth century and intensifying during the two or
three decades preceding the First World War.

2 The concentration of capital, 1840–1875

Towards 1840 the City of London was the leading financial centre in the world, ahead of Paris, itself followed by a group of important but secondary centres, including Amsterdam, Brussels, Frankfurt and Geneva. In all of these centres the most prominent merchants and bankers ran their international businesses like private firms and within the framework of highly personal and family contacts. And the House of Rothschild held sway over the world of international finance thanks to its immense resources and to its key position in issuing loans on behalf of foreign governments. Things were not fundamentally different around 1875; the City of London still ranked top in the world, followed by Paris, private bankers retained control over large international financial transactions, and the House of Rothschild was still the largest bank in Europe. This did not mean that inaction was the dominant feature of these thirty-five years, far from it. Two major changes occurred during the second third of the nineteenth century. The first was the increased concentration of capital; the second was the strong growth in capital exports.

The concentration of capital was a fundamental shift, whose effects profoundly transformed the life of the financial centres. They were already noticeable in the 1830s even though, on the face of it, the old order barely seemed to have changed. The first big businesses of the industrial era were the railway companies and the joint-stock banks. The former required substantial investments, whereas the latter had huge resources available, comprising principally their clients' deposits. And yet the pioneer joint-stock banks did not come into being to finance the railways. The evolution took place more or less in parallel – a little earlier for the railways – in order to take advantage of a technological innovation in one case and a financial innovation in the other. And in both cases, private interests – bankers, financiers, merchants and industrialists – were the main promoters. This partly explains why the major private banks retained control of the large international financial centres until the 1870s. In the meantime, company laws in the mid-nineteenth century[1] eased restrictions on limited companies by no longer requiring government to give prior authorisation for them to be founded and by clearing the path for large firms to emerge and go on to dominate the industrial and service sectors in the twentieth century. For the financial centres, building the railways led to a considerable development in the capital markets, both the primary market, through issuing securities, and the secondary market, through listing them on the main stock exchanges. On the other hand, the emergence of large banks started the process of systematically draining savings and centralising available financial resources.

The effects of exporting capital were more immediately apparent and confirmed the existing hierarchy among the international financial centres. Foreign investment began to grow more substantially from the mid-1850s, the capital stock invested outside its country of origin going from just under $1 billion in 1855 to $7.7 billion in 1870.[2] This capital was chiefly exported from the London and Paris markets. The City certainly remained the foremost international financial centre, but its predominance was strongly challenged by Paris. The rivalry between these two centres was very real during the Second Empire, Paris endeavouring to supplant London in the 1850s and 1860s, through initiatives emanating from both financial and political circles. These attempts failed and, in any case, the chances of them succeeding were rather slim given the two countries' respective positions in the world economy. But it was the military defeat against Prussia in 1871 that really put an end to Parisian ambitions. The ensuing unification of Germany had the additional consequence of allowing Berlin, now the political and financial capital of the new empire, to work its way up in the international hierarchy, at the same time overshadowing Frankfurt's historic financial centre. On the other side of the Atlantic, New York established itself once and for all as the United States' financial centre and played a growing role on the international capital market – however, as a debtor market rather than as a creditor market.

The banking revolution

The term revolution is overused and that of 'banking revolution' is no exception to the rule. Changes, particularly in the economic field, in which archaism and modernity continue to coexist, are more often than not slow and gradual processes. It is, nevertheless, a fact that a 'new bank' appeared, then established itself in Europe during the second third of the nineteenth century; the situation was somewhat different in the United States, where it was both earlier and later in coming. What were this new phenomenon's original features? And how did it impact on international financial centres?

This bank was new in three respects: first, it was a joint-stock bank; second, it was a deposit bank – more precisely a bank that collected its deposits through a network of branches; third, it was an investment bank. These three characteristics did not always coincide in the institutions that stemmed from this banking revolution. The first was common to all of them, whatever their nationality or special field of activity; so was the second, but to a greater or lesser extent according to the banking system. It was particularly representative of the British banking system, as well as the French one, insofar as deposits in current accounts made up the bulk of their liabilities and, as a rule, long-term commitments were excluded from their assets. The third characteristic, which is usually combined with the second in what is known as a 'universal bank' or 'mixed bank', was more typical of the banking systems in central Europe (Germany, Switzerland and Austria), as well as in Belgium and Italy until the 1930s.

The specialisation of the English banking system

The model of the joint-stock deposit bank with its network of regional or national branches is usually deemed to have originated in Scotland in the last third of the eighteenth century, before spreading to England half a century later. It is perhaps a question of nuance, as the Scottish banks actually had only a small number of shareholders. In England, with the exception of the Bank of England, joint-stock banks were prohibited until 1826, when a law authorised their founding, but outside a radius of 65 miles around the capital. In 1833 a new law lifted this ban, on condition that the banks that decided to set up in London either did not issue banknotes or relinquished this right. The founding of London's great joint-stock banks[3] dates back to this period. But numerous similar establishments were also created in the provinces; there were 100 of them in 1844 and some would be called upon to play a major role in the City from the beginning of the twentieth century onwards.[4]

These banks were founded by City business people, with a view to taking advantage of the possibilities offered by banking activities, especially discounting, in the City. Moreover, they were made to feel very unwelcome both by the Bank of England, which at first refused to open accounts for them or to discount their paper, and by private bankers, who refused them access to the London Clearing House. And yet they would not drastically change the City's business life overnight. Their novelty lay in their legal status far more than in their conduct of banking business. As joint-stock companies, they had at their disposal a far larger capital than that of the private banks. The London Joint Stock Bank, for example, had a nominal capital of £3 million, of which £300,000 was initially paid at its foundation, whereas that of the main private banks rarely exceeded £500,000. But they needed time to reach the top ranking. In 1844 the deposits of the five London joint-stock banks reached nearly £8 million and those of the capital's sixty-three private banks exceeded £27 million.[5] From the outset, they also drew a very clear dividing line between ownership and management, the latter being entrusted to salaried general managers.

On the other hand, their activities remained those of deposit banks, as already practised by the private banks. For the most part, their resources consisted of their clients' deposits and they were mainly used for short-term loans and discounting. The difference in this field – and it was less a matter of innovating than of resuming a tradition that was already well established in Scotland – lay in the network of branches that the joint-stock banks would put in place, not only in the capital but also in the provinces, which would enable them to attract considerable resources to the City. This process only began to develop in the second third of the nineteenth century, but from the 1860s the future of the private banks gave cause for concern. This was especially the case after the buyout of the famous bank Jones, Lloyd & Co. by the London & Westminster Bank in 1864. Its head, the future Lord Overstone, one of the richest and most influential bankers of his time, was however one of the fiercest opponents of the first joint-stock banks; to him, the principal–agent relationship, to use a contemporary term, seemed particularly inappropriate for conducting banking business.[6]

Another type of joint-stock bank appeared in Britain during the same period – the overseas banks. These were British banks, insofar as their capital and management were British and their registered office was usually in London, but their sphere of activity was in the British Empire or abroad – whence the name of 'Colonial and Foreign Banks' that was also given to them. The first overseas banks were founded in the 1830s to operate in the British Empire, amongst which was the Hongkong and Shanghai Banking Corporation in 1865,[7] and in the 1860s they continued to expand into Latin America and the Near East.[8] From the 15 overseas banks that existed in 1860, with a total of 132 branches operating abroad, their number grew to 33 in 1890 and that of their branches to 739.[9]

The overseas banks were set up by business people from the City, generally merchants dealing with the country or the region where the bank was operating, often in association with private bankers.[10] These were independent companies and not subsidiaries of big commercial banks. Their goal was to finance trade with the regions in which they were established and to obtain exchange facilities so that they could conduct these activities. They also offered financial services in regions often lacking in banking infrastructure, thus winning a clientele from among well-off members of the local community. In this respect, they were deposit banks, and applied the same principles to conducting their business as their counterparts did back home.

The emergence of this new type of banking in England did not, therefore, challenge the specialisation of the English banking system that had been taking shape at the turn of the nineteenth century. Banks in the strict sense of the word were deposit banks, otherwise known as clearing banks or joint-stock banks, once the banks organised as joint-stock companies had totally supplanted the partnerships, but this would not happen before the 1870s. For the time being, the London private banks that had made a name for themselves in the second half of the eighteenth century – Glyns, Barclays, Smiths and several others – retained their prestige and their pre-eminence. International credit was provided by the merchant banks, through their two main activities – accepting bills of exchange and issuing foreign loans – Rothschilds and Barings continuing largely to dominate the scene until the end of the American Civil War in 1865. The overseas banks were deposit banks specialising in a particular geographical area and thus did not pose much of a threat to the merchant banks in their issuing activities. The bill brokers, for their part, continued to act as middlemen on the discount market; but from brokers of bills of exchange, working on commission, they increasingly turned into dealers, operating on the basis of the day-to-day loans that the commercial banks granted them.

At the top of the edifice, the Bank of England more closely resembled the model of a modern central bank; in other words, of a lender of last resort. The Bank Act of 1844 attempted to control the fiduciary issue following the crises of 1825 and 1836, due to excessive lending on the part of small provincial banks that usually took the form of over-issuing banknotes. It made a clear distinction between its two departments, 'banking' and 'issuing'. The first functioned like a commercial bank, while being given responsibility for managing the country's currency reserves. The second issued banknotes, which had to be fully backed by gold as soon as they exceeded the amount of £14 million. These restrictive measures would often be untenable, on account of the bank money created by the commercial banks. At each serious crisis, the Bank Act would have to be suspended and Parliament would have to authorise the Bank of England to issue as many banknotes as the situation demanded.

A banking innovation in Belgium

The new banks appeared somewhat later in continental Europe, where very often they took on the features of investment banks or universal banks, even though the model of the English deposit bank met with a degree of success, particularly in France. The precursor of this type of institution was the Société Générale de Belgique, established, as we have seen, in 1822, which after 1830 clearly established itself as a mixed bank – in other words, as both a deposit bank and an investment bank, inspiring numerous imitators in France, as well as in the rest of continental Europe. From 1832 it embarked on a policy of acquiring stakes in manufacturing companies, in particular in the mines and the metallurgical industry in the region of Hainaut, boosted by the building of the railways, from Fr.3.8 million in 1835 to Fr.54.8 million in 1850.[11] Moreover, it systematically increased its collection of deposits, which reached Fr.44.4 million in 1838.[12] After losing its issue privilege following the founding of the Banque Nationale de Belgique in 1850, the Société Générale became more resolutely involved in investment banking activities, but it reverted to universal banking, or mixed banking as the Belgians prefer to call it, from the end of the 1860s, notably by setting up a network of sponsored banks modelled on the British deposit banks.[13]

The Société Générale's decision to opt for mixed banking at the beginning of the 1830s had not really been planned but it had been forced on it by the freeze on its short-term claims on companies in the Hainaut region. As Ginette Kurgan has written: 'By deciding, under the weight of circumstance, not to insist that debts be repaid, but to acquire holdings in companies by requiring that they transform themselves into limited companies, the bank embarked on a new course, largely anticipating the creation of the French and German universal banks in the second half of the nineteenth century.'[14] All the same, the first imitation occurred within Belgium itself, with the founding in 1835 of the Banque de Belgique on the model of the Société Générale, with which it immediately tried to compete.

Deposit banks and banques d'affaires in France

The father of new banking in France was most probably Jacques Laffitte,[15] undoubtedly the most eminent Parisian banker of his time, although known more on account of his plans for financing industry and large-scale infrastructure projects than for his concrete achievements, which came up against quite a few difficulties. From 1821 Laffitte proposed setting up a financial company to purchase the network of canals that the government submitted for the House's approval. The company's capital would have reached the huge sum of Fr.240 million, which would have been put at the state's disposal in return for certain advantages. This initiative met with strong opposition and came to nothing. The banker returned to the attack in 1825 with a plan for a Société Commanditaire de l'Industrie, with a capital of Fr.100 million, destined to act as an intermediary between capitalists hesitating whether to invest their money and industrialists searching for funding. Industrial financing was to be carried out by taking stakes in companies that were not only new but also innovative. In spite of the enthusiasm aroused by the plan, especially among the Saint-Simonians, he did not manage to convince the government, which considered its capital too high[16] and imposed restrictions, including the exclusion of foreigners, thus preventing him from fulfilling it.[17] The plan that finally took shape in 1837 was a rather toned-down version of previous endeavours. The Caisse Générale du Commerce et de l'Industrie – Laffitte relinquished the title of bank to avoid any idea of rivalry with the Banque de France – in fact differed little from an ordinary bank apart from its capital, whose total amount, Fr.55 million, remained substantial. Above all, it practised discounting and tried to increase its resources by attracting available savings through the issue of credit notes, whose maturity date could vary from three days to three months, yielding interest or not. But the Banque de France retained the monopoly on issuing bank notes. The originally declared intention of converting the Caisse into a genuine investment bank once again had to be abandoned.

The Caisse Laffitte nevertheless filled a gap in the French banking system and was a sign of the big banks to come, even though, to avoid governmental authorisation, it was organised in the form of a joint-stock limited partnership. In its form as a discount bank, it had numerous imitators during the July Monarchy; so much so, as Bertrand Gille has written, that Paris at the end of the reign of Louis-Philippe had several important banks, which provided indisputable services by facilitating discounting and lowering the interest rate, even if their paid up capital was still far below the amounts initially expected.[18] But unlike their English counterparts, whose position strengthened during the nineteenth century, they all disappeared during the economic crisis of 1847–48.

The big banks really made their appearance in France in the years 1848–52. The founding of two institutions symbolises this 'banking revolution': the Comptoir d'escompte de Paris and the Crédit Mobilier. While the former more closely resembled the model of a deposit bank, and the latter that of an investment bank, they shared several directors and numerous characteristics. Both had a decisive impact not only on the French banking system but also on Paris's role as an international financial centre. The first, the Comptoir d'Escompte de Paris, was created on 7 March 1848 – at the same time as sixty-eight other discount banks in the rest of the country – by the new minister of finance, Louis-Antoine Garnier-Pagès, to give a boost to the credit mechanisms that had been completely ruined by the economic crisis and, finally, by the February Revolution. Its capital was set at Fr.20 million, of which two-thirds comprised bonds of the city of Paris and Treasury bills, and one-third shareholders' subscriptions. It was, therefore, a kind of semi-public company, including in terms of its management, since the Ministry of Finance appointed the managers, even though it left the running of business to private circles. The bank passed entirely into private hands in 1854 and rapidly established itself as the foremost French bank.[19] There was another new aspect of the Comptoir d'escompte, which also distinguished it from the English joint-stock banks; it quickly set up branches abroad,[20] with the primary goal, as for the English banks, of financing international trade, except of course for the London branch, which tried to wrestle control over a small part of international big business.[21] This development certainly added a new dimension to the influence exerted internationally by the Parisian financial centre.

The second bank was the Crédit Mobilier, founded by the brothers Emile and Isaac Pereire in 1852,[22] with a capital of Fr.60 million, making it the country's second bank after the Banque de France. Far more than the Comptoir d'escompte, and probably more than any other large bank in France or elsewhere, the Crédit Mobilier acquired almost mythical status. Its very name evokes, not only in France but undoubtedly in Europe, the somewhat romantic notion of an 'entrepreneurial' bank at the service of economic development, ready to do battle against the banking establishment – symbolised by the Rothschilds – to impose new banking practices. Moreover, one still speaks of Crédit Mobilier-type banks to designate a hotchpotch of investment banks, merchant banks and mixed banks, even though historical research has seriously challenged the novelty of the initiatives taken by the Pereire brothers and traced their ancestry back to Jacques Laffitte or to the Société Générale de Belgique.[23]

The goal set by the Pereires at the Crédit Mobilier was an ambitious one, it involved allocating the available resources to firms in industry, transport and public utility. To this end, they planned to issue bank bonds, whose subscribed amounts would then be invested in these firms. Ultimately, their aim was to create an industrial monopoly; the Pereires longed to purchase the securities of the main manufacturing and railway companies, making the shares and bonds of the Crédit Mobilier a kind of universal security representing the capital of all the large firms grouped together under its control. Their achievements would not be so far-reaching, but they were remarkable all the same. In addition to creating numerous companies in France,[24] they were also involved abroad, particularly in railways (obtaining concessions in Austria and Spain) and in finance (contributing towards the founding of banks along the lines of the Crédit Mobilier). Their most noteworthy success was the creation of the Bank für Handel und Industrie in Darmstadt, also known under the name of Darmstädter Bank, the first bank of this type to be set up in Germany.

The heroic image that has been preserved of the Crédit Mobilier is largely due to the conflict pitting Emile and Isaac Pereire against James de Rothschild from the mid-1850s to the beginning of the 1860s. Its significance may have been exaggerated. James de Rothschild was opposed on principle to joint-stock banks and he considered the Pereires' plans, particularly the almost unlimited issuing of bonds, dangerous for economic stability. And even if some of the Crédit Mobilier's initiatives, among others in the railway and banking fields, were damaging to the Rothschilds' interests, it was an unequal combat, the capital of the five branches of the House of Rothschild[25] amounting to more than Fr.550 million in 1862, the French branch alone having more than Fr.200 million. By and large, James de Rothschild adopted a wait-and-see policy, but he succeeded in preventing banks modelled on the Crédit Mobilier from being founded in Naples and in Brussels. Moreover, when the Pereires showed signs of achieving their ends, he himself did not hesitate to encourage the creation of banks of this type, such as the Caisse du Commerce et de l'Industrie in Turin and, above all, the Credit-Anstalt in Vienna. Faced with the Pereires' plan to control the entire Austro-Hungarian railway network, he obtained concessions in Lombardy, Venetia, Hungary and Serbia. In France, the Rothschilds and their allies succeeded in preventing the Pereires from being involved in establishing the large railway companies, as well as in cutting their railway in the south of France off from the Paris–Mediterranean route.

The Pereires' final defeat was not, however, due to hostility on the part of the Rothschilds, but above all to the illiquidity problems brought about by the runaway expansion of their business. From the outset, the Crédit Mobilier had difficulty in placing the securities of all the companies that it had created and it often had to take them back itself or get other companies in the group to buy them. No longer authorised to issue bonds after 1854, it found itself forced to make increasingly risky financial arrangements, while being confronted with hostility from the Banque de France.[26] The Pereires' fall took place in 1867, following the bankruptcy of one of their city companies, L'Immobilière, from Marseilles, where huge sums were tied up. The Crédit Mobilier's shares were affected and fell below par from the month of April, forcing Emile and Isaac Pereire to leave their bank's board of directors. The Crédit Mobilier collapsed in 1870. The company of the same name that succeeded it survived until 1902 but played only a secondary role in the financial life of the country.

The other large banks that appeared during this period proved more stable and drew their inspiration more from the model of the English deposit banks. This was especially true of the CIC, founded in 1859 under the name of Société Générale de Crédit Industriel et Commercial, with a capital of Fr.60 million, at the initiative of the French banker Armand Donon, who was joined by a group of English financiers.[27] The Crédit Lyonnais was founded in July 1863 – also on the model of the English joint-stock banks – by Henri Germain with support from the main representatives of the Lyons business world, predominantly leading merchants in the silk trade, and with considerable Genevan involvement. At the time, its capital amounted to Fr.20 million, the maximum authorised by the very latest law on limited companies, adopted two months earlier. The founders' goal was to free themselves from Parisian control, but the Paris branch, opened in 1865, quickly established itself as the real centre of the firm, which in the 1880s had become the largest bank in the country.[28]

The Société Générale was also intended to be a deposit bank. It was set up in 1864 by a broad coalition of Parisian interests, coming from the Réunion Financière, formerly created by the Rothschilds in their struggle against the Pereires, which comprised various bankers and financiers,[29] including Alphonse Pinard, general manager of the Comptoir d'escompte and the majority shareholder in the new bank, with his partners Louis Bischoffsheim and Edouard Hentsch. Moreover, it was these three men who were behind the founding in 1863 of the Banque de Crédit et de Dépôts des Pays-Bas, whose merger with the Banque de Paris in 1872 gave rise to the Banque de Paris et des Pays-Bas, with a capital of Fr.125 million, of which half was paid up. From the outset, this bank established itself as one of the leading banks in the capital and, above all, as a *banque d'affaires*, working first and foremost with its own resources and whose assets consisted mostly of controlling stakes in various companies.[30]

As in London, the emergence of the new banks did not disrupt the Parisian world of finance. The *haute banque* remained in control until the beginning of the 1870s and, in particular, retained control over government loans. A turning point was reached in 1872 with the loans intended to pay the 1871 war indemnity to Germany. This persistence on the part of the *haute banque* was mainly due to the fact that the new banks had been formed recently and had not yet had time to make a name for themselves in big international business, in particular in the issue syndicates. It can also be explained by the role that the *haute banque* played in creating the new joint-stock banks, whether by being behind their creation, as in the case of the Société Générale or the Banque de Paris et des Pays-Bas, or by taking an active part in their formation;[31] even the Crédit Mobilier counted a majority of the long-established members of the *haute banque* among its first shareholders, with the exception, naturally, of the Rothschilds.

The German universal banks

In the end, the Crédit Mobilier played only a marginal role in developing the large joint-stock banks in France – but a far greater one in livening up the Parisian financial centre under the Second Empire. On the other hand, its posterity was more long lasting in Germany, where the big banks that appeared in the 1850s were all inspired, to a greater or lesser degree, by its model – starting with the Darmstädter Bank, the first German universal bank founded in 1853 by the Pereires and a group of private bankers from Cologne.[32] While the Schaaffhausenscher Bankverein, a private bank from Cologne before being transformed into a joint-stock company after the crisis of 1848, already had wide-ranging powers, the statutes of the Darmstädter Bank went further and authorised it to hold shares in other companies, to participate in issue syndicates and to organise mergers and acquisitions; in other words, to combine investment banking with deposit banking. Moreover, it mainly dealt in railway financing, industrial investment and government loans.

Another major universal bank, the Disconto-Gesellschaft, was established in 1851 by the former manager of the Bank of Prussia, David Hansemann. This was first of all in the form of a credit association in the small principality of Dessau and then, in 1856, to evade Prussian legislation that outlawed the creation of new limited companies, in the form of a joint-stock limited partnership, with a capital of 10 million thalers and its headquarters in Berlin. In the same year, a group of private bankers[33] set up the Berliner Handels-Gesellschaft under the same legal status. Then, other banks of the same type appeared in several other German cities,[34] but the financial crisis of 1857 put a brake on this trend that would only resume between 1870 and 1873, during the *Gründerjahre* that followed the foundation of the Reich. It was in 1870 that the Deutsche Bank was created in Berlin by a group of private bankers under the leadership of Adelbert Delbrück and Ludwig Bamberger,[35] and the Commerz- und Disconto Bank was founded in Hamburg by the city's main bankers and ship owners, including M. M. Warburg & Co.[36] The Dresdner Bank was established two years later by Eugen Guttmann, son of a minor private banker from Dresden, who persuaded the barons Karl and Felix von Kaskel to turn their respectable banking house into a joint-stock bank.[37]

The emergence of the big German universal banks therefore took place, at least at the beginning, away from the country's main financial centres. Darmstadt, a smallish city, was chosen by default, mainly because of its proximity to Frankfurt. Following the public rescue of A. Schaafhausen, Cologne found itself refused any new authorisation to create a joint-stock bank. In 1854 the Frankfurter Bank was founded in Frankfurt due to the concern provoked by the foundation of the Darmstädter Bank, but it was merely a bank of deposit and issue, and in 1856, pressurised by the powerful lobby of the city's private bankers, the Senate refused to authorise the creation of a Crédit Mobilier-type bank. As for the Hamburg banks, they continued to focus mainly on financing trading activities. In the end, it was Berlin that played the best game. Not only were two extremely important banks[38] created there during the first wave of the mid-1850s, but it was there that the Deutsche Bank was founded, destined to become the country's largest bank. Berlin, the political capital of the new German empire, would quickly develop into its financial capital.

The emergence of the big Swiss banks

The situation was similar, although slightly less pronounced, in Switzerland. New banks, modelled on the Crédit Mobilier far more than on the English deposit banks, were created in the country's main financial centres and large industrial towns. The first, the Banque Générale Suisse de Crédit International Mobilier et Foncier, was founded in 1853 in Geneva – the country's leading financial centre – with a capital of Fr.25 million, 5 million of which were paid up immediately. It planned to engage in all kinds of banking transactions: discounting, lending, underwriting government loans, acquiring industrial holdings and issuing banknotes. In line with its international calling, its board of directors included financiers from London, Paris and Turin. It led an eventful existence and was liquidated in 1869.[39] The second had a much longer-lasting and far more glorious destiny. It was the Crédit Suisse, founded in Zurich in 1856 by Alfred Escher, one of the most influential Swiss businessmen and politicians of his time, with the main goal of financing the building of the Swiss railways and shielding them from the threat of foreign, particularly French, domination. The Crédit Suisse quickly established itself as the country's largest bank and remained so until the end of the century. In 1862 in Basle, a group of private bankers created the Basler Handelsbank, and in Winterthur business circles from the canton of Zurich's second industrial city founded the Bank in Winterthur, forerunner of the Union Bank of Switzerland. The Eidgenössische Bank came into being in Bern one year later, thanks to backing from the CIC and to a large contribution of French capital. A trend was set, but the big banks still only represented a small part of the Swiss banking system – in 1870 barely 14% of the total assets of all Swiss banks (not including private banks), compared with 26% for the local banks, 19% for the cantonal banks, 22% for the mortgage banks and 19% for the savings banks.[40]

The American banking system

The American banking system did not evolve along exactly the same lines as in Europe. In certain respects, it modernised earlier. The 'Federalist financial revolution', to use Richard Sylla's expression,[41] which occurred in the 1790s, was comparable partly to the English financial revolution of the eighteenth century and partly to the banking revolution of the nineteenth century in Europe. On the one hand, Alexander Hamilton, the first American Treasury secretary, stabilised and modernised the public funds;[42] he created a central bank, the Bank of the United States, which in 1791 obtained, not without a degree of controversy, a federal charter, and opened branches throughout the country; he opened a Mint, having the dollar adopted in 1792 as the monetary unit of the new state. On the other hand, these measures led to the setting up of a financial market, where government securities and central bank securities were traded, and to the extremely rapid development of the banking system. Whereas the United States had only three banks in 1790, none of these going back more than three years, their number increased to 35 in 1800, approximately 100 in 1810, some 300 in 1820 and about 700 in the mid-1830s. Furthermore, the vast majority of these banks comprised limited liability joint-stock companies, well before this way of organising became widespread in Europe.

There were, however, limits to the financial revolution and to its effects. First, experimentation with a central bank lasted barely beyond the 1830s. From the outset, the Bank of the United States, whose charter expired in 1812, had to face opposition from agrarian circles and opponents of any federal prerogative. In 1816 it was replaced by the Second Bank of the United States, but in 1835 President Andrew Jackson vetoed the renewal of its charter. The country would remain without a central bank until the eve of the First World War. Universal banks did not really catch on across the Atlantic either, at least not until the end of the century, partly owing to the unfortunate experiences of the Bank of the United States, which, registered as a bank in the state of Pennsylvania after losing its federal charter, went bankrupt in 1841. Since opening branches in another state was prohibited by law, banking expansion occurred within states. The banks that developed, the state banks, were commercial banks that issued notes, had no branches and benefited from a charter from the state in which they operated. The system produced a large number of banks. There were 1,500 of them in 1860 and they issued 9,000 different types of banknote. The system worked in a more or less satisfactory manner, counterfeiting remained limited, and money circulation was controlled fairly well. But in the absence of banknotes at national level, transaction costs were high.

The Bank Acts of 1863 and 1864, decreed right in the middle of the Civil War, attempted to standardise the issuing of banknotes by introducing a new category of bank, the national banks, and these were granted a charter from the federal government. They were obliged to invest a third of their capital in federal government bonds – what the federal government needed at that time to finance its war effort – and could deposit these securities with the Treasury to underwrite their issuing of banknotes,[43] the total amount of which could not exceed 90% of the market value of these securities. The law was equally restrictive in relation to reserves. The national banks could either keep them in the form of cash in their vaults, or place half in the national banks situated in one of the seventeen so-called reserve cities. The latter, in turn, had the opportunity to place half of their reserves in one of the national banks in New York, thus strengthening the central role of the country's financial capital. These new laws did not do away with the old state banks, which could retain their status if they did not wish to comply with the federal regulations. But their banknotes were hit with a 10% tax, which resulted in quite a number of them disappearing; others, in greatly increasing numbers from the 1890s, continued their banking activities without issuing notes.

The railway adventure

The railway adventure did not start in 1840. The first rail link, between Stockton and Darlington in the north of England, was completed in 1825, and several others followed in the 1830s.[44] But the real railway boom dates from the 1840s. In Britain, the end of the 1830s was marked by an initial wave of investments, the average annual amount being approximately £6 million but growing to more than £25 million during the fever of the mid-1840s and remaining at this level throughout the boom of the 1860s. In 1875 the British rail network was more than 70% complete, having over fifty years required capital to the tune of £630 million, more than 60% of which was required after 1850.[45] In France, where the first speculative fever gripped the public in the mid-1840s, the railways' accrued expenditure went from a little over Fr.1 billion in 1852 to more than Fr.7 billion in 1869. In Germany, the overall cost of building rail links was less per kilometre than in Britain. Net investment in the German railways increased steadily during the third quarter of the nineteenth century and went from an annual average of 88 million marks at the beginning of the 1850s to a little over 500 million at the end of the 1870s.[46] In the United States, the railroad network grew from 3,300 miles in 1840 to 30,600 in 1860; by this date, more than $1.2 billion had been invested in the railways.[47]

Never before had private companies requested such sums from the public. Part of their success in doing so was certainly due to state intervention, except in Britain where the financing was entirely private. In France, for example, the state bought the land and undertook the excavation work, while private companies supplied the rails, buildings and rolling stock, and obtained the right to operate the network for a period of 99 years. Moreover, the state guaranteed a minimum return on the capital invested – a guarantee found in most countries. In the United States, companies also received considerable donations of land in the regions opened up by building the railways. Nevertheless, the capital markets still had to meet the demand and organise or reorganise themselves accordingly, which naturally led to the strengthening of the most important financial centres. Indeed, mobilising capital and trading issued securities could only be undertaken in centres that were large enough in terms of both networks of relationships and access to information. Here both national and international aspects should be taken into account. The bulk of this capital was invested in building a national network, especially during the first phase that lasted from the 1830s to the 1870s. But even though most European countries called, to some extent, on foreign capital to build their own network, in return they – primarily Britain and France – made considerable contributions towards financing the railways in other European countries and overseas. In this respect, as with the emergence of the big banks, the financial centres' national and international roles in the large industrialised countries became increasingly closely linked.

The City's reserve

Yet things had not always started out this way, particularly in the country that was the home of the railway. In Britain, the first wave of building was financed mainly by local capital, independent of the London market.[48] Similarly, the securities of these first companies were traded chiefly in the provincial stock markets that appeared during these years – in Liverpool and Manchester in 1836, then throughout the entire country. On the whole, the City's bankers and financiers resisted this trend. The two main merchant banks, Rothschilds and Barings, despite being accustomed to large issues, were not involved in promoting companies, whether new lines or the big mergers that took place during the boom of the 1840s. One exception proves the rule – the involvement of George Carr Glyn, partner in the private bank Glyn, Hallifax, Mills & Co., soon to be known as the railway bank and, if the Rothschilds are excluded, destined to become the largest private bank in the City.[49] Some other private banks also embarked on the adventure, but they remained isolated cases.[50]

The City's role in financing the British railways intensified, however, during the boom of the forties. First, London capital was increasingly channelled towards these regional firms, sometimes for purely speculative purposes. The brokers' house Foster & Braithwaite, for example, specialising in railway securities, saw its annual income grow from £4,200 to £50,650 between 1839 and 1845. At the same time, the London Stock Exchange gradually established itself as the leading market for the securities of the main companies, especially after the speculative fever. In 1853 stock representing a nominal capital of £194 million – in other words, 70% of the entire capital issued by the railway companies – was listed on the London Stock Exchange, and the prices set by transactions in London were imposed on the provincial markets.[51] The City thus played a more important role as a secondary market than as a primary, capital-raising market. In 1853 the railways represented 16% of the nominal value of all securities listed on the London Stock Exchange – in second position, though far behind British government securities, which exceeded 70% of the total capitalisation. But the public already considered the bonds of the main companies to be as safe an investment as Consols, the British national debt. In twenty years, from 1853 to 1873, the nominal value of the securities of the British railway companies listed on the London Stock Exchange went from £194 million to £374 million; and that of foreign railway securities, including the British Empire, from £31 million to £354 million – that is to say, nearly as much.

The City was more active during this second phase of building the railways, dominated by foreign railways – in the first place American. Here too, the most reputable merchant banks, in particular Rothschilds and Barings, generally stayed away from the first issues in the early 1850s; although Barings, together with Glyn Mills, did take on an unfortunate issue in 1853 on behalf of the Grand Trunk Railway Company of Canada. Instead, the initiative was taken by George Peabody, an American banker based in London, who in 1852 introduced the securities of Illinois Central, the first American railroad company to be advertised in the British press.[52] In the 1850s, numerous securities of American railway companies were, moreover, allotted in England to pay for the huge deliveries of English rails to the United States, before being traded on the stock exchanges of Britain or of continental Europe, where they were often resold. With the fever that gripped the American railways after the end of the American Civil War, all the main banking houses in the City joined the trend, led by Baring Brothers and J. S. Morgan, who succeeded George Peabody.[53] In the early 1870s, issues on behalf of the American railways represented approximately 70% of all the railway issues placed in London and roughly 45% of all the issues on behalf of private companies.[54]

The commitment of the Parisian haute banque

The Parisian market, on the other hand, was deeply involved in the railway adventure at all stages of setting up the national network, just like the state for that matter, whose presence was much more keenly felt in France than in Britain. On the level of the primary market, the Parisian banks played an active role in the process of launching companies as soon as they had reached a certain size – in other words, from the end of the 1830s,[55] then during the first real boom of the French railways between 1844 and 1846. They played a key role in making the financial arrangements for investments – either as bidders or as guarantors that the capital required for building the line could be raised – an indispensable condition for accepting a bid.

The main Parisian members of the *haute banque* were all part of this trend and both competed and cooperated with each other. Before the Crédit Mobilier was founded, they were central to three of the four large groups that took shape during this period.[56] James de Rothschild's group[57] controlled the Nord railway company. Charles Laffitte's and Edward Blount's,[58] backed by British capital, obtained several concessions, including Paris–Rouen and Rouen–Le Havre, but was also party to several agreements with the other groups. Finally, the group led by François Bartholony[59] controlled the Paris–Orléans and the Centre. The fourth group, run by the engineer Paulin Talabot, did not include any member of the Parisian *haute banque* and remained relatively weak financially speaking, a weakness that was compensated for by support from the Rothschilds; its position was strong in the Sud-Est and it endeavoured to control the route linking Paris to the Mediterranean.

Parisian bankers' financial commitments were far from insignificant.[60] At the height of the boom, in 1845 and 1846, the capital issued by the railway companies[61] totalled Fr.919 million, approximately three-quarters of the entire railway capital issued since the first concession of 1833. At that time, the amount subscribed by nine of the main banking houses[62] reached Fr.225 million; in other words, nearly 25% of the grand total. Some subscriptions constituted long-term investments, starting with the Rothschilds' Fr.51 million – out of Fr.200 – in the Nord. For the most part, however, the bankers played the role of middlemen, whether simply by acting as brokers, or by reallocating, usually with a premium, all or part of these issues to their clientele. Yet these subscriptions also represented opportunities to influence companies and to be on their first board of directors.[63]

The Parisian bankers remained deeply involved in developing the railways under the Second Empire, even though the composition of the groups changed as a result of the initiatives taken by the Pereire brothers and by the Crédit Mobilier, which threatened established positions. Two camps clashed during the 1850s: the Pereires and their allies (including certain members of the *haute banque*) on the one hand, and the Réunion Financière on the other. The fight ended in the Pereires defeat;[64] and the French rail network scene was set for good from 1857, following the merger trend encouraged by the state, which gave rise to six large companies: the Nord, the Est, the PLM, the Ouest, the Paris–Orléans and the Midi. Although the *haute banque* continued to be widely represented on the boards of directors of these companies, it quickly ceased to play a significant role within the companies, since the bulk of power was entrusted to salaried managers.

Paris was the financial centre most directly involved in the railway adventure, not only in France but also abroad, especially in Mediterranean Europe (Spain, Portugal and Italy), Russia and the Austro-Hungarian Empire; in other words, in the main areas of confrontation between the Rothschilds and the Pereires.[65] The role of the Paris centre was due not only to the commitment of the *haute banque* but also to the concentration of numerous auxiliary services in the French capital – especially the engineering offices, which played a decisive role in designing projects – to say nothing, of course, of the presence of political power. On the Paris Bourse, railway securities, more than 80% in bonds, exceeded Fr.10 billion in nominal value in 1869; that is to say, about a third of all securities listed, after government securities that still represented more than 50% of the total. As in England, it was not long before they became, in the eyes of investors, as safe as government stock.

Decentralisation in Germany and the United States

In Germany and in the United States, private bankers went into the railway business from the outset without, at least to start with, any financial centre really occupying a key position. Berlin and New York only gradually established their predominance.

In Germany, the earliest initiatives were taken by Cologne's private bankers.[66] Abraham Oppenheim himself played a major role in founding in 1835 the company in charge of building the line linking Cologne to Aachen and Antwerp,[67] as well as in the negotiations underway since 1833 to build the line from Cologne to Minden – this line was essential to developing industry in Westphalia, and his bank, along with other banking houses from Cologne, contributed a major part of its financing.[68] Frankfurt also followed the trend thanks to the omnipresence of the House of Rothschild, to the wealth of its private bankers and to the importance of its stock exchange. The banks in Berlin were also involved – in the first place Mendelssohn & Co. Apart from participating in the first issues, including the Berlin–Stettin in 1836, it created in 1870, in partnership with an engineer by the name of Plessner, a railway construction company that obtained the concession for several lines, mostly in the middle of Germany. The firm went bankrupt in 1875, causing Mendelssohn to withdraw from industrial finance.[69] The other banks in Berlin[70] also joined issue syndicates and, if the need arose, were more directly involved in the financial management of the companies – Bleichröder, for example, as the banker and director of the Cologne–Minden.[71] What was also distinctive about the way in which the German railways were financed, setting it apart from the British, French or American cases, was the role played by the state. Some stretches were certainly built and operated without its assistance, but for others, like the Cologne–Minden, state involvement took the form of purchasing shares and guaranteeing interest, while the state itself built and operated the main lines. Besides, most of the network would be nationalised by Bismarck in the 1880s.

In the United States, the commitment of bankers to promoting the railway companies coincided with the emergence of the investment banks – banks specialising in granting long-term capital, through issuing and trading in securities. These activities had been undertaken since the very beginning of the century by merchants, stockbrokers or even commercial banks, before being taken charge of by specialised banking houses from 1850. This transition was no doubt speeded up during the American Civil War by the government's financial needs and by the need to call on domestic savings. But it was the financing of the railways, then that of the large industrial companies, that would lend credibility to the investment banks during the last quarter of the nineteenth century – in particular to J. P. Morgan & Co. and Kuhn, Loeb & Co.

The earliest initiatives were taken in the 1840s. The bank Winslow, Lanier & Co., founded in 1849 with the main goal of trading in railway securities, established itself within the space of a few years as the most important firm in this field of activity, helping to make New York the main centre for American railroad finance. In the years following the American Civil War, the leading light was Jay Cooke, who founded his own banking house, Cooke & Co., in Philadelphia in 1861. After playing a very active role in placing government loans, he turned to railway securities in 1870, financing the Northern Pacific, over which he wielded considerable power.[72] But in mid-August 1873, this company owed him more than $5 million, and anxious depositors began to withdraw their money. On 18 September 1873, the 'first bank of the United States' was obliged to close its doors, unleashing acute panic on Wall Street and a change in leadership in the world of the investment banks.[73] The most distinctive feature of American railway financing was, however, the recourse to foreign capital on a massive scale. In evidence since the earliest initiatives, this would reach huge proportions during the last quarter of the nineteenth century.

In its early stages, the building of the railways in the large European countries had required the services of the main financial centres, primarily in a national context. Very quickly, however, these activities acquired an international dimension, especially in London and in Paris. Along with government loans, the railway company securities at that time constituted the main demand for funds addressed to these centres. These responded according to the funds that they had available, sometimes competitively, but more often through one form of co-operation or another, and on yet other occasions independently from one another, each enjoying its own special spheres of influence.

Rivalry between London and Paris

The international financial centres were constantly on both competitive and cooperative terms, with the latter generally tending to prevail. The periods during which two or several centres fought for world or European supremacy were rare – in the 1850s and 1860s between London and Paris, in the 1920s between London and New York, and in the 1990s, to a lesser extent, between London and Frankfurt at the European level – and the true nature of these conflicts was in many respects deceptive. The rivalry between Paris and London in the mid-nineteenth century was both the most illusory, Paris barely standing a chance of gaining the upper hand, and the most real, because it was sustained by dynamic entrepreneurs and ambitious politicians and affected all the fields of activity that an international financial centre was involved in.

International trade and its financing

In the mid-nineteenth century, a centre's financial capacity still depended largely on the scale of its trading activities. Banking and finance were offshoots of trade, and it was on this front that London had a decisive advantage over Paris. It is true that the United Kingdom clearly occupied a dominant position in international trade, providing more than 20% of world trade in 1850 and about 25% in the 1860s – approximately twice France's share (11% in 1850 and 13% in 1860).[74] But, above all, the bulk of this trade was handled directly by the City. Throughout the nineteenth century, the City of London remained much more of a trading centre than a financial centre. The presence of the Port of London, the largest in the world, which stretched away immediately to the east of the Square Mile, goes a long way towards explaining London's enduring role as an entrepôt and the considerable weight, both in numbers and in prestige, carried by the great merchants: 'A merchant's office ... is more representative of the City than any other', declared the *Financial News* in 1934. 'Banks exist in Lombard Street because the merchants of old created a demand for them. Shipping companies flourished ... because of the freights with which the merchants provide them. Lloyd's is but the necessity of these mercantile freights and bottoms. And the stock exchange lives light-heartedly on the patronage of the banker whom the merchant brought into being. So it is not too much to say that it is the merchant who has made the City of London.'[75]

Until the 1870s, what one might call the physical trade in merchandise ranked top among the City's commercial activities. This involved handling products intended for import, export or re-export that passed through London and transited the warehouses sometimes located within the City itself. A second type of activity began to develop from the 1850s and involved organising and coordinating the movement of merchandise that never physically passed through London – whether British exports and imports brought from other towns in the kingdom or commercial trade between third countries. Finally, there was a third field of activity – the commodity markets, where auctions took place and forward contracts were negotiated – colonial products[76] in Mincing Lane, and cereals and the chartering of ships at the Baltic Exchange. The Royal Exchange, in decline, increasingly ceded its place to more specialised markets, which over the rest of the century assumed a more formal structure.[77]

The importance of this entrepôt role for the City's prosperity was not lost on the promoters of the Paris financial centre, including the Pereires. Paris's geographical location is obviously not comparable to London's, but the advent of the railways brought about some changes, cutting the time needed to reach the capital from the main ports, especially Marseilles and Le Havre.[78] This meant that it was worth considering equipping Paris with warehouses to rival the London docks. Such possibilities fitted in with the public works policy that was in full swing under the Second Empire, encompassing major urban development programmes, the setting up of the railway network and the modernisation of the ports, above all Marseilles, whose future looked very promising following the opening of the Suez Canal in 1869.[79] From the beginning of the 1850s, various companies were formed with a view to opening warehouses near Paris stations, including that of the Docks Napoléon at the Place de l'Europe that had a direct rail link to Le Havre, but these initiatives were on a relatively modest scale. It was the Pereires who strove to bring a new European dimension to the plan for Paris warehouses, but they would fail.[80] Despite the railway network converging on the French capital, despite Universal Exhibitions being organised in 1855 and 1867, and despite Haussmann undertaking the spectacular modernisation of the city, Paris was unable to threaten London's prominent role in international trade.[81]

Foreign loans

On the other hand, Paris rivalled London in the financial sphere, though not in the financing of international trade, which became the exclusive preserve of the City. It was in loans to governments and the financing of companies abroad that competition from Paris began to make itself felt. Comparing the financial capacity of the two centres in such a far-off period is no easy matter. The main banks were still private banks that did not publish their balance sheets, so it is impossible to compare their size. Under the Second Empire, the House of Rothschild in Paris was larger than that in London, yet they were known to be part of the same group, whereas Baring Brothers was far more important than the other members of the Parisian *haute banque*.[82] In contrast, the joint-stock banks were much more developed in London and, even if they did not yet play leading roles, they tipped the balance in the City's favour. The London Stock Exchange was also larger than the Paris Bourse, the nominal value of securities listed in London adding up to £1.7 billion sterling in 1863 and £2.3 billion in 1873, compared with 1 billion – £1.3 if the *coulisse* is included – in Paris in 1869.[83] The amount of capital exported by Britain and France does, however, give some idea of the financial clout exerted internationally by their capitals.

On a purely quantitative level, the differences were minimal. From 1840 to 1870, Britain and France exported very similar amounts each year. This was in the order of about £2 million to £6 million per year, on average, in the 1840s, £15 million to £20 million in the 1850s and £30 million to £35 million in the 1860s.[84] All the same, if one of the two nations had to be given the advantage, it would be France. Britain was certainly in the lead in the 1830s and 1840s – especially until 1848 – with an annual average of £6 million, compared with a very slightly negative balance of payments in France. Yet France very definitely had the upper hand in the early 1850s, as well as during the 1860s, exporting more than twice the amount that Britain did.

However, the rivalry between the two centres is not evident from these figures. For this capital did not have the same destination – French capital flowed mainly towards Europe,[85] whereas British capital flowed towards the high seas.[86] Europe absorbed more than two-thirds (67.4%) of French investment between 1852 and 1881, but less than a third (29%) of British investment between 1865[87] and 1881.[88]

An international division of labour was thus established between the zones of influence of the two great European centres. This by no means implies that there were no points of friction,[89] but this competition did not necessarily pit the two centres against each other. There could have been a degree of rivalry between groups of bankers and financiers operating in several centres at the same time, or the stakes could have been of a more political nature. To take just one example: the loan of £4 million issued in London in 1851 by C. J. Hambro & Sons on behalf of Piedmont, when the House of Rothschild, particularly the Paris branch, traditionally managed this country's finances, had nothing to do with any rivalry between London and Paris. Baring Brothers had, moreover, turned down the loan request. The change – in any case on an entirely temporary basis – was due to the desire of Cavour, Piedmont's minister of finance, to escape from the stranglehold that the Rothschilds had over Sardinia's external finances at that time.[90]

Far more than rivalry over one field of operations or another, it was the City's financial hegemony that French officials wanted to challenge. 'For a long time, London's financial centre has had a monopoly over foreign loans', reported a Ministry of Finance memorandum in 1865.

> But when England lent, it was driven to do so by far more significant advantages than the interest paid on its capital. On the one hand, it assured itself of a huge annual tribute ... at the same time as imposing its commercial dominion over the whole world. The nations that it had financed became its industry's clients and some, like Portugal, fell entirely under its commercial sovereignty.[91]

These were the benefits that Paris was seeking to appropriate. Even though France exported as much, if not more, capital than Britain and even though foreign government bonds had been accepted for listing on the Paris Bourse since 1823, more loans – to which foreign banks and investors also subscribed – were issued in the City of London. As far as the securities of private companies were concerned, the French political authorities adopted a liberal attitude in 1859, merely requiring notice from the government for them to be listed, after having tried to restrict their admission during the three preceding years.[92] In today's terms, it was a deregulatory measure intended to retain or bring back to Paris businesses that had a tendency to move to London.

By the 1860s, these efforts seemed to bear fruit: 'Today France shares with England the honour of providing capital to the industry of the world', the Ministry of Finance's 1865 report declared. Between 1861 and 1865, forty-two loans were issued in London, for a total of Fr.2,127 million. This compared with fourteen in Paris, for a total of Fr.2,106 million – of which Fr.447 million, admittedly, were on behalf of the French government.[93] It is interesting to note that both in number (fifty-six loans out of seventy-three) and in value (Fr.4.2 out of Fr.5.6 billion), three-quarters of the public loans taken out in Europe during this period were issued in one of these two centres.

Paris also became the main hub for foreign exchange in continental Europe, as foreign governments that borrowed on the Parisian market tended to index their currency to the franc, in order to make their securities more attractive to French investors. This was notably the case with Austria-Hungary, which immediately following the defeat at Sadowa in 1866 and its exclusion from the *Zollverein*, undertook to purchase French products and adopted a monetary unit linked to the franc. Spain did the same in 1868. From then on, Paris served as a clearing house between France and its various debtors,[94] as well as between these countries and Britain.[95] Another of Paris's competitive advantages was the solidity of the Banque de France, whose metallic reserves continually increased in the second half of the 1860s, while being easily accessible thanks to the policy of buying and selling gold at a set price practised by the central bank.[96] Significantly, Walter Bagehot acknowledged that until 1870 there were two great reserves of specie in Europe – the Bank of England and the Banque de France.[97]

Towards a universal currency?

One of the most striking signs of Paris's new ambitions was the proposal made by France in December 1866 to introduce a universal currency based on the franc. This proposal was addressed to all European countries, as well as to the United States, and it was based on the signing of a monetary convention between France, Italy, Belgium and Switzerland the previous year, which would quickly become known as the Latin Monetary Union. The purpose of this convention was in fact rather limited – to reach agreement on the proportion of silver contained in the low-denomination coins of the four countries.[98] Inevitably, those coins with the highest proportion of silver had been disappearing from currency circulation. In practice, this decision meant that coining continued and that all the signatories to the convention accepted the Fr.5 coin, the ecu.[99] The delegates also agreed that gold coins could be freely struck and accepted at par by all the member states. On the other hand, at France's request, they did not discuss the more fundamental issue of the transition from bimetallism to gold monometallism.

These technical details, which concerned metallic currency and not banknotes, should not mask the importance of this agreement. As clearly shown by Marc Flandreau, the Latin Monetary Union was more a reflection and the consequence of France's commercial and financial influence in continental Europe than any diplomatic initiative of the emperor aimed at capturing a leading position.[100] The proposal for a universal currency that suddenly became all the rage at the end of the 1860s went along the same lines.[101] France invited the other states either to join the Latin Monetary Union[102] or to attend an international conference to discuss the possibility of introducing a fixed gold exchange rate between the franc and the other currencies. The plan was based on the idea of a new Fr.25 gold coin – corresponding to the British sovereign,[103] the American $5 coin and the Austrian 10 florin coin – that could be shared by the four large states. However, adopting this coin required a certain number of parity adjustments to be made – the pound sterling was in fact worth Fr.25.2218, the dollar Fr.5.1824 and the Austrian florin Fr.2.4693. Overall, the French proposals were favourably received, especially by lesser powers, and the United States also showed an interest in the project. On the other hand, agreement with the German states remained dependent upon discussions relating to their own monetary union. For its part, Britain was far more reticent; it did not envisage any changes to the existing monetary system and would only participate in the planned discussions as an observer. An international conference was held at the Quai d'Orsay in Paris from 17 June to 6 July 1867, attended by twenty countries. The principle of monetary union was accepted there, on the basis of coordinating the existing systems and adopting gold monometallism.[104] It was also planned to strike a gold Fr.25 coin, which would be considered international currency and would create a visible link between France, Britain and the United States.

In the context of the rivalry between London and Paris, the significance of the French initiative and the advantages that the Parisian financial centre expected from it appeared far more symbolic than truly tangible. The proposal for a universal currency was above all supported by a visionary, Félix Esquirou de Parieu,[105] motivated by his liberal convictions, by his enthusiasm for the gold standard and by a clear idea of France's role in the world. While he had the backing of the Ministry of Foreign Affairs, he came up against resistance from the Ministry of Finance and especially from the Banque de France, both of which were satisfied with the monetary system as it was and were believers in the benefits of bimetallism. Similarly, whereas merchant circles supported the initiative, the world of finance was opposed to it, if only because it would mean an end to lucrative arbitrage opportunities on currencies.

In the fervour surrounding the establishing of Paris as an international financial centre, the plan for monetary union seemed like a way of possibly extending French prestige and influence in the world. This goes a long way towards explaining British lack of enthusiasm. Given that the City was the world's foremost financial centre, British public opinion found it inconceivable that the pound should adapt to an international system devised around the franc – even if the merchants reckoned that they were likely to gain by a more competitive market, or even if Britain's membership of a union of this type would represent a *de facto* obstacle to French hegemony. Besides, the report of the parliamentary commission of inquiry appointed in 1868 by Disraeli recognised the benefits of an international currency but thought that the pound sterling would constitute a more appropriate basis for this. Popular opinion expressed a patriotic commitment to the pound, its long history, its stability[106] and its role in international payments. In the end, only the fear of being isolated on the international stage led certain officials to consider the possibility of rallying to an international agreement. But the City was sceptical and emphasised, through Goschen's voice[107] among others, that the single currency would have only a minor impact on international trade, since the main transactions were settled in gold bars and not in cash, and that it would not prevent fluctuations in the exchange rate caused by likely gaps in trade balances. Refusals on the part of the British and the Germans would eventually scuttle the plan.

Paris thus showed a great deal of vitality under the Second Empire – the dynamism of the challenger, one might say. While, at that time, the City was packed with entrepreneurs, Paris had more striking or more colourful personalities – James de Rothschild, who established himself as the true head of the multinational bank after Nathan's death in 1836; the brothers Emile and Isaac Pereire with their Saint-Simonian ideal; or even talented 'imitators' of the English banking model, like Armand Donon or Henri Germain. This dynamism, fed by the ambitions of Napoleon III, was reflected in the modernisation of the capital undertaken by Hausmann. The defeat by Prussia in 1871 put an end to Parisian ambitions. First, there was the non-convertibility of the franc, officially maintained until 1878, which left the pound sterling unrivalled as an international payment instrument; second, the suspension of cash payments by the Banque de France, making London the only world market for precious metals; and finally, the settlement of the war indemnity, with Bismarck demanding the colossal sum of Fr.5 billion. Although France was able to pay this off without too much difficulty by mobilising national savings, owing to its huge success in raising loans in 1871 and 1872, there were hardly any other opportunities for exporting capital. Without accounting for the German indemnity, the French balance of payments still showed a deficit of Fr.468 million in 1871 and Fr.741 million in 1873, displaying only a slight surplus of Fr.129 million in 1872.[108] The export of French capital continued to decline throughout the 1870s and was henceforth markedly lower than that of British capital.[109]

Even so, Paris was gripped by great feverishness during these years. Issues involved enormous sums, rarely reached within the framework of operations of this type, and attracted French and foreign bankers. As the manager of the Parisian headquarters of the Crédit Lyonnais wrote in February 1871: 'All interested parties are on the alert; each one is trying to keep abreast of developments; but initiative lies in the hands of Bleichröder, Rothschild and highly influential English people…'[110] In Paris, the Rothschilds and the *haute banque*[111] retained supreme control over the two large government loans, even though they had to cede back one-third of the various transactions linked to the loan of 1872 to a syndicate led by the Banque de Paris et des Pays-Bas. In London, Rothschilds and Barings took charge of issuing an instalment of some Fr. 500 million, but the German banks were excluded from this business.

The rise and fall of the lesser centres

Behind London and Paris, the lesser centres enjoyed varying fortunes. Few changes occurred in Amsterdam, whereas Geneva and especially Brussels increased their activities and their international influence. Frankfurt, on the other hand, overshadowed by Berlin, began a protracted decline that lasted nearly a century. It would not be long before unified Germany's new capital found its place among the major international financial centres, as did New York, which consolidated its financial pre-eminence in the United States during these years.

Amsterdam, Brussels and Geneva

Having joined the ranks, Amsterdam continued to play an international role that resembled that of a secondary far more than a primary market.[112] Backed by the system of *prolongatie*, discussed in the previous chapter, the Amsterdam Stock Exchange was probably the largest in Europe after London and Paris and was largely open to foreign stocks. American stocks, especially in the railways, grew considerably during these years, going from 8% to 33% of the total number of securities, both national and foreign, that were listed there between 1855 and 1875.[113]

The internationalisation of the Brussels centre became much more pronounced from 1850, under the twin effect of the resumption of capital exports and the arrival of new private bankers related to families already based in Brussels. Foreign investments were partly attributable to investors seeking higher returns, especially after the conversions made by the Belgian government in 1852 and 1856, lowering the government bond coupon from $5\frac{1}{2}$% to 4%. Above all, they could be explained by the method of financing the exports of Belgian metallurgical and building firms. Just as in the British case, orders that were placed with them by foreign railway companies were actually settled by means of shares and especially bonds in these companies. These securities were then resold through public issues handled by a bank or group of banks or were introduced directly on the stock exchange.[114] The banks were also involved in setting up firms abroad. The Société Générale, in particular, was induced to back the formation of railway companies, since orders from these companies benefited the metallurgical and mining firms that it sponsored.[115] The private bankers' network of international contacts grew during the third quarter of the nineteenth century with the arrival of new bankers and financiers, including Maurice de Hirsch, Jacques Errera and Franz Philippson,[116] all integrated into very dense networks of alliances forged by families such as the Bischoffsheims, the Oppenheims or the Lamberts. After 1850 their sphere of influence spread to the most important European centres, particularly London, Paris and Frankfurt.[117]

The international significance of Brussels took on a new dimension following the Franco-Prussian War of 1870–71. Belgian neutrality not being in jeopardy, Brussels became a safe haven for foreign capital and saw intense activity during these few years. New banks were created, amongst which were the Banque de Bruxelles in 1871, at the initiative of the Oppenheim group, with the backing of banker relations and friends in Germany and the cooperation of several important banking houses in Belgium. A large number of banking and foreign exchange houses also made their bow. Representatives of German banks formerly established in Paris came to set up in Brussels, at the same time as the French banks strengthened their presence there. With the prosperity that Belgian industry experienced immediately after the war of 1870, this expansion of international business laid the foundations for the remarkable development of Brussels during the forty years before the First World War.

Despite being a small international financial centre, Geneva was nonetheless one of the cities in Europe that had the highest number of banks per inhabitant, chiefly private banking houses. It also had some joint-stock banks, including the Banque Générale, the first of the large Swiss banks, and some banks with a mainly local purpose, like the Banque du Commerce, the Banque de Genève and the Comptoir d'escompte, founded between 1846 and 1855. Yet it was the private banks that gave Geneva the characteristics of an international financial centre. These banks cooperated more closely from 1840 onwards, essentially in order to undertake transactions that were beyond the means of each one alone. It was about this time that the Quatuor was formed, an informal grouping comprising the centre's four main banking houses[118] and particularly interested in the Ouest-Suisse railway, the mines of the Loire and loans to Piedmont and other places. In 1849 the Omnium was created, a more organised grouping endowed with a capital of Fr. 2 million,[119] whose goal was to buy and sell government securities, as well as stocks and shares, in any country and finance new businesses, amongst which featured the Rio Tinto mines, the Corinth

Canal and various gas companies, including those in Marseilles, Naples and Vienna.[120] Gas businesses also constituted one of Genevan banking's fields of expertise during this period. The Quatuor and the Omnium were, of course, led to cooperate, their cooperation being formalised in 1872 with the forming of the Association financière de Genève, an investment bank that – like many others set up in Europe at that time – enabled private bankers to join forces in order to obtain stakes in big business while preserving their autonomy.

Still closely connected to France, Genevan bankers were actively involved in the founding of the Crédit Lyonnais in 1863. There were more than 70 Swiss shareholders, chiefly Genevan bankers and stockbrokers, among the 353 original shareholders, and 3 Genevans sat on the board of directors.[121] However, relations deteriorated, the directors resigned in November 1868, in circumstances that have not been clarified, and the number of Swiss holders of shares in the Crédit Lyonnais steadily declined.[122] A representative office was opened in Geneva in the autumn of 1870 during the Franco-Prussian War. At that time, Geneva was able to provide a fallback position should Lyons be occupied by German troops, but it was closed as soon as the hostilities had ended. Nevertheless, it supplied significant services, primarily as an intermediary, for many foreigners' transactions in French francs, as a haven for families and stocks belonging to the bourgeoisie of Lyons, and for subscriptions to the war loan issued by the London banking house J. S. Morgan & Co. in October 1870. A branch was finally opened in 1876. In the event, the Genevan financial centre now began to attract foreign banks. The first was the Banque de Paris et des Pays-Bas, present from its foundation in 1872 and managed in Geneva by representatives of private banks, amongst others Chenevière & Cie and Lombard, Odier & Cie.[123] With the exception of the Eidegenössische Bank,[124] established in Geneva since 1866, the large Swiss banks would not follow until much later.

The other major development affecting the Genevan centre was the creation of the Geneva Stock Exchange in 1850 – the first in Switzerland and the only one in existence until the mid-1870s. From the eighteenth century, foreign exchange brokers acted independently, buying and selling bills of exchange and trading the first stocks and shares appearing on the market. The creation of an organised market dates to the initiative taken in 1849 by the stockbroker Jacques Reverdin to publish thrice weekly a list of exchange rates and some government securities. The Société des Agents de Change was founded in the following year with a twin goal – the joint publication of a list and the stockbrokers' meeting organised daily in a set place and at a set time, from 12 p.m. to

12.30 p.m. Strictly private at first, these meetings were made open to the public under pressure from the private bankers in 1852 and then from the cantonal authorities in 1857. The Geneva Stock Exchange quickly agreed to list various foreign securities, particularly Italian, Austrian, German and French, then American and Mexican. Although smaller than Amsterdam's, it was one of the main European stock exchanges at that time.[125]

From Frankfurt to Berlin

While the German unification process, which culminated in the war of 1870, led to Paris's relative but not steep decline, its consequences were far more serious for Frankfurt. The fate of Germany's foremost financial centre had in fact been sealed somewhat earlier following Austria's defeat in 1866 and Frankfurt's annexation to Prussia the following year. Frankfurt was undoubtedly an important centre but of lower rank on the international level, alongside Amsterdam, Brussels and several others, including Berlin. It would gradually regress to the rank of regional centre, admittedly with a glorious past, hosting prestigious names and benefiting from a dense network of international affiliations, but incapable of competing with the new political, economic and financial capital of the Reich, and even less so with London or even Paris.

Frankfurt's decline meant, first and foremost, the loss of its political autonomy.[126] The city was henceforth integrated into the Prussian province of Hesse-Nassau, of which it was not even the capital, this role having been allotted to Wiesbaden.[127] On the municipal level, the new institutions that were set up – a representative council and an executive council – were subordinate to the Prussian institutions. Germany's monetary union, with the introduction of the mark in 1871 and the foundation of the Reichsbank on 1 January 1876, also deprived Frankfurt of its monetary autonomy, even if the Frankfurter Bank retained an issue quota until it was integrated into the national central bank in 1901. Frankfurt's political leanings, particularly its friendly relations with Austria, did not work in its favour either. In the monetary sphere, the private bankers showed, through the Chamber of Commerce, a clear preference for the French bimetallist monetary system, especially because of the city's links with Austria and southern Europe; and in their cosmopolitan tradition, they welcomed with great enthusiasm the proposal for a universal currency put forward at the monetary conference in Paris in 1867. Prussia, on the other hand, was more reticent and, once unification had been completed, it decided to align itself with Britain and opted for the gold standard.

Frankfurt's decline was thus apparently attributable to political causes – the metropolis on the Rhine would not be in a position to face, on equal terms, competition from Berlin, which would benefit from a whole string of advantages associated with its status as the capital of Prussia and of the new Reich. This explanation, however, is only partly accurate. There is little doubt that Berlin's political role had strengthened its position as a financial centre. The new German Empire was certainly a federal state, but it was dominated by Prussia, whose imposing bureaucracy was controlled by the emperor, who was at the same time the king of Prussia. The significance of political power is vividly illustrated by the example of the Reichsbank, whose supervisory board was chaired by the chancellor of the Reich, with the chairman of its executive board duty bound to act in accordance with the directives laid down by the chancellor.[128] The fact remains that Berlin was not a financial centre created from scratch at the end of the 1860s, whereas Frankfurt showed signs of entrepreneurial failure long before being annexed to Prussia. From the mid-nineteenth century, Frankfurt seemed to be a backward-looking centre, but Berlin a forward-looking one. Frankfurt persisted in its attachment to government loans, but Berlin opted for industrial shares. Frankfurt remained the capital of private bankers, but Berlin became the capital of the big banks. These factors significantly influenced the contrasting destiny of the two centres from the middle of the nineteenth century.

In a gesture of defiance, Frankfurt's private bankers established the Frankfurter Bankverein in January 1871, with a capital of 36 million marks (that of the young Deutsche Bank amounted to 15 million at that time), to demonstrate that Frankfurt's appeal as a financial centre was still intact. It would be taken over by Deutsche Bank in 1886. When the French war indemnity was paid, Frankfurt did indeed enjoy a mini-boom in placing governmental loans, its special field of expertise since the end of the eighteenth century. But this was a mere flash in the pan. After 1870 large foreign loans placed in Germany were issued in Berlin, usually under the management of the big banks. The disparity between the two cities is clearly reflected in the employment figures in the financial sector (banks, the stock exchange and insurance companies), which recorded 7,000 people in Berlin in 1882, compared with only 2,100 on the banks of the Main. The most striking symbol of Frankfurt's decline was unquestionably the disappearance of M. A. Rothschild & Söhne, bought up by the Disconto-Gesellschaft in 1901.[129] Like the Rothschilds, the most dynamic members of Frankfurt's numerous other banking dynasties left to enrich the other leading international financial centres.

New York, financial capital of the United States

One of these was New York. By 1840 it had asserted itself as the financial capital of the United States at the expense of its main rivals – Boston, Baltimore and Philadelphia. However, commercially speaking, the die was cast as early as the 1820s. New York had indisputable natural advantages – a large natural port near to the high seas and a river, the Hudson, which gave it access to a vast hinterland – that its business people well knew how to turn to good account by obliging all American exports and imports to pass through it. They achieved this by developing the port and by improving links to the rest of the country.[130] New York also established itself as the main port of import for European products, particularly following the organisation of auctions of British products from 1815 onwards and the launching of a regular steamship service to Liverpool in 1818. Its position further strengthened with the building of the first railway lines and quickly became impregnable. By the end of the 1850s, two-thirds of American imports and one-third of its exports passed through the port of New York. Boston, Philadelphia and Baltimore, its main harbour rivals, were left far behind; together, they barely represented a quarter of the value of the merchandise that transited New York.[131]

The development of finance, just like that of industry, went hand in hand with this commercial expansion. In the 1820s and 1830s, New York became an important centre for banking and insurance. The New York Stock Exchange was founded in 1817 and, ten years later, the shares of nineteen insurance companies and twelve banks were traded there. Even so, New York was not yet the United States' financial capital, and its stock exchange remained a local market alongside the stock exchanges of the main cities on the east coast. Its predominance dates from the revolution in telecommunications that started in the 1840s. In the banking sphere, the way was decisively clear from 1836, when the charter of the Second Bank of the United States, its headquarters located in Philadelphia, was not renewed by President Andrew Jackson.[132] The country no longer had a central bank, but due to New York's growing economic importance the banks of other states took to depositing their reserves there – a situation ratified by the banking laws of 1863 and 1864. The emergence of the investment banks further strengthened its position as the country's financial centre. At the beginning of the 1860s, New York was already one of the richest cities in the world, surpassed only by London and Paris.[133] In spite of its strong American leanings, it would be one of the cornerstones in the globalisation of the world economy – about to get under way.

3   A globalised world, 1875–1914

Globalised economy or age of empires? To ask the question is to highlight, from the very outset, the ambiguous nature of the globalisation of the world economy during the three or four decades before the First World War. Opening up the world – with the revolution in transport and communications, population shifts and the free circulation of capital – went hand in hand with establishing colonial empires and with the imperialist powers extending direct or indirect domination over most of the world on an unprecedented scale. In 1914 the British Empire stretched over 30 million square km and included 450 million inhabitants, while the French colonial empire stretched over ten million square km with 50 million inhabitants. On top of this, they informally held sway over regions as vast as China, the Ottoman Empire and Latin America. These two phenomena are only partly linked, yet they are not completely unconnected either – as revealed by arguments among contemporaries, as well as among generations of historians, about the primacy of politics or of economics in spreading imperialism at the end of the nineteenth century. But in either case, the international financial centres were more involved in opening up the world than in colonial imperialism.

Whatever one's viewpoint, the political and economic environment prior to 1914 was particularly conducive to the rapid development of international financial centres. In many respects, it was truly a golden age for them and one that they would not encounter again before the late twentieth century. With the financing of international trade, their main activities continued to revolve around foreign investment; in other words, essentially issuing securities on behalf of governments and companies abroad, and trading these securities on the secondary markets.

The changes that characterise this period and explain why the concept of globalisation is so applicable to it fall into three categories. The first is quantitative – exported capital reached hitherto unheard of, and even undreamt of, sums. Moreover, it was invested in the four corners of the world and was used to finance a multitude of public and private activities. The second important change was the closer integration of the international financial centres, made possible by the much faster transmission of information and by the free circulation of capital. Evident signs of this were the harmonisation of the prices of stock traded simultaneously in several centres and the strong international convergence of interest rates.[1] The third change was the increase in the number of international financial centres. Whereas London and Paris had been the only financial centres of any note until 1870, Berlin, then New York, now joined them, though not posing any real threat to them; smaller centres, like Amsterdam, Brussels, Zurich and Geneva, found a role that suited them, usually in certain niches where they enjoyed a competitive advantage. Nevertheless, at the same time, there was a very clear hierarchy among these centres and a truly global or supranational centre, London, emerged at their head. In this respect, the forty years preceding the First World War constituted the 'classic' period of the City of London as the world's financial centre.

The globalisation of the world economy

Globalisation has been defined in a thousand different ways, not only in economic terms, but also in social, political and cultural terms. From the angle that most interests us here, five phenomena are worthy of note: movements of people, transport facilities, communication speed, expanding trade and transfers of capital.

Trade, transport and communications

The free movement of people, without the need for a passport, was perhaps the most obvious sign that the world was opening up. From 1850 international migration increased on an unprecedented scale; 36 million Europeans left the Old World between 1870 and 1915, most of them, some 70%, heading for the United States and almost all the others for Argentina, Australia, Canada and Brazil; in other words, to temperate regions where European immigration was still recent. To this should be added intra-European migration, which was on a lesser but far from insignificant scale; the proportion of foreigners residing in the whole of Europe went from less than 0.7% of the population in 1860 (or approximately 1.5 million inhabitants) to 1.8% in 1910 (or approximately 5.6 million inhabitants).[2] By and large, the rest of the world – namely Africa, Asia and a part of Latin America – remained unaffected by these trends.

Such migration would hardly have been possible without advances in transport, which made the world smaller and brought countries and continents closer together. The building of railway lines, started in the 1830s, continued on a much larger scale, world mileage increasing from 205,000 km in 1870 to 925,000 km in 1906. Railways spread to every continent, admittedly to varying degrees, linking the coasts to the interior and facilitating the movement of both people and goods, whatever interests their developers may have had in the formal and informal empires. Maritime transport also made considerable progress with the development of steamships, which really got underway in the 1890s, when steam tonnage finally overtook that of sailing ships. The duration of a voyage between New York and Liverpool fell from three weeks on the outward leg and five on the return leg (due to the head winds) at the beginning of the nineteenth century to less than a week from the 1880s.[3]

Telecommunications sped up to the point of becoming instantaneous, first with the telegraph, then the telephone and finally wireless telegraphy. The earliest telegraph links date back to the 1840s, following the invention of Morse code in 1832, and they developed rapidly in Britain and the United States, spurred on by the railway companies. Under the English Channel, a cable linked Britain to the European continent as early as 1851, and the first transatlantic cable between London and New York was laid in 1866, after ten years of effort. Land lines were quickly established between Europe and Asia, and telegraph links were set up in the colonial empires.[4] In this way, the whole world became linked up.[5] The telephone made long-distance communications more personal and quickly spread to a wider geographical area.[6] It acquired an interurban dimension in the United States from the 1880s, then an international one a decade later, notably with the Paris–London line in 1891, transatlantic links having to wait until the 1920s. Wireless telegraphy[7] enabled messages to be transmitted across the Atlantic from 1901, and when the Titanic sank in 1912 it already played an important part in ocean navigation.

The globalisation of the world economy did not necessarily go hand in hand with the abolition of trade barriers. Between 1880 and 1914, the golden age of the first phase of globalisation was marked by a return to protectionism, following a phase of free trade that had been opened up in 1860 by the treaty between Britain and France. Among the large countries, Germany was the first to take the plunge: in 1879 Bismarck introduced protective tariffs on both agricultural and industrial products. France followed in 1892 with the Méline tariff, which substantially increased customs duty on manufactured goods and, to an even greater extent, on agricultural goods. As for the United States, it remained highly protectionist throughout the nineteenth century, with the average customs duty on manufactured items being in the region of 40% to 50%, whereas at the end of the century it was no higher than 20% in any European country, except for Russia. Only Britain remained loyal to free trade until 1932. Yet this return to protectionism did not lead to any slowdown in trade. On the contrary, foreign trade grew dramatically in the nineteenth century. In the case of Europe, the proportion of exports, measured as a percentage of GDP, went from 9% in 1860 to 14% in 1913. Paul Bairoch has observed that foreign trade increased more rapidly during the protectionist phase than during the free trade phase, a paradox that he explains by the fact that economic growth was stronger during the protectionist period.[8]

These characteristics of a globalised economy had repercussions on business in the international financial centres. Apart from its economic and sociocultural impact, migration brought in talent to enrich the main centres; the growth in trade brought about an increase in business to finance international trade, which tended to concentrate in the large centres – first and foremost the City of London; the transport revolution not only underpinned the increase in this trade but required huge investments that only the large financial centres were able to provide.

Capital flows

However, in the last analysis, it was the transfer of capital that lay at the heart of the globalisation process and of the international functions fulfilled by the financial centres. Foreign investment saw very strong growth during the 1880s and, above all, from the final years of the nineteenth century. In 1913 the stock of capital invested abroad reached a total of $44 billion, Great Britain being far and away the largest exporter of capital, followed by France, Germany and the United States (see Table 3.1). Together, the Netherlands, Belgium and Switzerland, traditionally large providers of capital and, in any case, among the most important per head of population, invested almost as much abroad as Germany did. It is revealing that this ranking is the same as that of the main international financial centres. London was firmly established at the top of the hierarchy; then came Paris, no longer able to challenge the City's financial hegemony but remaining securely in second place; Berlin, whose third rank was higher than that previously attained by Frankfurt or Hamburg; New York, Brussels and Amsterdam; and for Switzerland, Zurich and Geneva, completing the group of financial centres of truly international calibre.

Table 3.1. *Stock of foreign investment in 1913 (in billions of dollars)*

Assets in foreign countries		*(%)*
Great Britain	18.3	*(42)*
France	8.7	*(20)*
Germany	5.6	*(13)*
United States	3.5	*(8)*
Belgium, Netherlands, Switzerland	5.5	*(12)*
Miscellaneous	2.4	*(5)*
Total	44.0	*(100)*
Liabilities towards foreign countries		
Europe	12.0	*(27)*
North America	10.5	*(24)*
Latin America	8.5	*(19)*
Asia	6.0	*(14)*
Africa	4.7	*(11)*
Oceania	2.3	*(5)*
Total	44.0	*(100)*

Source: United Nations, *International Capital Movements during the Interwar Period*, New York, 1949.

Europe, in which Russia has to be included, was the main recipient of this investment, closely followed by North America, Central and South America, Asia and Africa, with Australasia trailing far behind. The supply of capital was, therefore, a far more decisive factor than demand in developing the financial centres, even though New York's position was more attributable to the latter than to the former. Even if the role played by centres such as Vienna, St Petersburg or Constantinople should not be underestimated, their influence remained above all regional – just like that of Sydney or Buenos Aires.

This overall distribution of the capital-exporting countries' assets masked very different destinations, which were both the cause and the consequence of the main financial centres' specialisation and way of operating (see Table 3.2). British foreign investment was spread worldwide, with a distinct preference for the two Americas, the rest being shared out more or less equally among Europe, Asia, Africa and Australasia. The British Empire's share represented 40% of the total, the largest part being allocated to India and to the settlement colonies with white populations (Canada, South Africa, Australia and New Zealand).[9] French investors, on the other hand, expressed a more marked preference for Europe, including Russia, as well as for the Middle East, the Ottoman Empire and Egypt – which absorbed more than 60% of their assets abroad, Russia taking the lion's share, with 25% of the total. Although British and French investments in Latin America

Table 3.2. *Distribution of the major powers' foreign assets, 1913*

	UK (%)	France (%)	Germany (%)	United States (%)
Europe	13	55	53	20
North America	34	4	16	25
Latin America	17	12	16	46
Asia	14	}	–	–
Africa	11	}9^a	9	–
Oceania	11	}	–	–
Middle East	–	12	–	–
Rest of the world	–	8	6	9
Total	100	100	100	100

Note: [a] French colonial empire.

Sources: M. Simon, 'The pattern of new British portfolio investment, 1865–1914', pp. 15–44; R. Cameron, *France and the Economic Development of Europe 1800–1914*, Princeton, 1961, p. 486; H. Feis, *Europe the World's Banker, 1870–1914*, New York, 1961; L. E. Davis and R. J. Cull, *International Capital Markets and American Economic Growth 1820–1914*, Cambridge, 1994, p. 82.

were roughly the same size in percentage terms, this was far from being the case in North America, where British investment was much higher. Similarly, France invested less than Britain in its colonial empire – of less economic significance than the British Empire. But investment from the metropolis was by no means insignificant; according to Jacques Marseille's estimates, it represented more than 13% of French foreign investment in 1913, which ranked it in third position behind Russia and Latin America.[10] For their part, German assets abroad were more or less equally shared between Europe and the rest of the world; however, the importance of Turkey and the Balkan countries, with 15% of the total, and that of Austria-Hungary, with 13%, should be noted. As for the stock of capital exported by the United States, it essentially remained on the American continent, with its two immediate neighbours – Canada (24.7%) and Mexico (24.3%) – in the lead, followed by South America (10.4%), Cuba and the Caribbean (9.6%); yet, for all that, Europe was not overlooked.

Which economic realities were concealed behind this exported capital? First, the amount of capital was rising sharply compared with the mid-1870s. The stock of British capital invested abroad approximately quadrupled between 1875 and 1913, and that of French capital nearly tripled,[11] with prices remaining practically constant. On the other hand, its flow represented a major proportion of the available savings: around 40% for Britain between 1880 and 1914, and between 20% and 25% for France. In 1913, the year that it reached its highest level ($1.1 billion, compared with an average of $700 million between 1906 and 1910 and $225 million between 1901 and 1905), capital exports amounted to 67% of the available savings in Britain. At that time, the British invested more abroad than they did in their own country.

These overseas assets were for the most part (about two-thirds) portfolio investments – mainly foreign government stocks and railway company, chiefly American, bonds (more rarely shares), as well as the securities of other large companies in the public utilities (electricity, water and gas), mines or, to a lesser extent, manufacturing industry. For its part, direct investment represented approximately one-third of the supply of capital exported in 1914.[12] The distribution between these two types of investment was not, however, the same in all countries. The United States was a special case; direct investment represented three-quarters of its overseas investment, and even more than 80% in the case of investment destined for Europe and Latin America.[13] Whereas American capital exports remained fairly modest on the whole prior to 1914, several large industrial corporations – in sectors such as oil, car manufacturing and machinery – were already well established abroad. The share of direct investment was also higher than average in Germany's case (45%), for broadly similar reasons, but in different sectors – first and foremost the chemical industry. The distribution was closer to the average in the case of British overseas investment; but on a global scale, Great Britain owned 45% of the supply of direct investment abroad in 1914, compared with 14% each for the United States and Germany, and only 11% for France.[14]

Unlike portfolio investments, which were made by subscribing to issues floated in the main international financial centres or by purchasing securities on the secondary market, direct investments often took the form of transactions within large companies. The bulk of British direct investment before 1914 was, however, the preserve of a particular type of company that Mira Wilkins has called the 'free-standing company'.[15] These were not large companies that were firmly rooted in their national markets, but were founded with the specific goal of conducting business abroad. The nature of this business was extremely varied, but investment in the primary sector (plantations and mines) and in services, including financial services, largely predominated. The number of such companies has been estimated at several thousand during the thirty or forty years preceding the First World War. Some were only short-lived, but others survived and became major corporations. These included the overseas banks,[16] the big mining companies – such as South Africa's diamond trust De Beers Consolidated or the Rio Tinto zinc mines in Spain – and oil companies, such as Burmah Oil. These firms maintained only a minimal presence in London (hence the designation 'free-standing'), where their registered office was generally located, but a presence that was sufficient to keep control (hence their characterisation as multinational corporations). One of the main duties of the London headquarters was to provide the company with various financial facilities by having recourse to the City's capital market.

A dominant economy: Great Britain

Even if globalisation is, by definition, a global phenomenon, it takes place within the framework of an economic order that hinges on a dominant economy. Today this is the United States, but before 1914 it was Great Britain.[17] Yet after an interval of a century, the relative positions of the two Anglo-Saxon powers have different underlying foundations. From the beginning of this period, Britain was no longer the world's leading economy. It had been overtaken by the United States in terms of total national income by 1870, and in terms of per capita income shortly before 1914.[18] Nor was Britain the world's foremost industrial power any longer, it had been overtaken by the United States towards 1880 and by Germany towards 1905, even though its level of industrialisation, measured in terms of per capita industrial production, was probably still the highest in the world.

The fact that Britain remained the dominant economy until 1914 was partly thanks to the leadership that it retained in numerous fields of activity, such as foreign trade, services and finance on the one hand, and to its key position in the system of multilateral trade on the other hand. Its considerable share of capital exports has already been noted; unlike at the end of the twentieth century, the dominant economy of the day was a creditor and not a debtor power. In 1913, despite pressure from its competitors, British foreign trade still represented some 14% of world trade, and the British merchant navy was the world's foremost navy, with one-third of world tonnage, operating most of the traffic between non-British ports.

Above all, Britain was located at the centre of the system of international payments and trade. This was on account of its trade deficit with the major industrial countries, from which it purchased mainly manufactured goods, and its surplus with its colonial empire that absorbed more than a third of its exports, especially with India – the main outlet for the English cotton industry and paying an annual tribute to the British Crown. At the end of the nineteenth century, the industrialised countries significantly increased their imports of primary products from India and other countries of the future third world, without increasing by the same proportion their exports to these countries, where Britain was in a position of strength. This resulted in a system of multilateral settlements, in which Britain's surplus with India was partly used to offset its deficit with its other partners.[19]

Britain's weight in the world economy was, in short, due to the role of the pound sterling. The main international trading and reserve currency, it formed the cornerstone of the international monetary system in force at that time – the gold standard. This standard was widely adopted during the last quarter of the nineteenth century; and the first globalisation of the world economy coincided with a period of great monetary stability, as exchange rates between the major currencies only fluctuated within the gold points, the level at which it became more advantageous physically to import or export gold. By 1868 the gold standard had been adopted, apart from in Britain, by only a handful of countries in the British sphere of influence (Portugal in Europe, Australia and Canada, Brazil and Chile in Latin America, Egypt and the Ottoman Empire). The rest of the world was divided between a silver monometallic system (with notably the German states, Austria, the Scandinavian countries, India, China and Japan) and a bimetallic system (including the United States, France and the other countries of the Latin Monetary Union). Forty years later, all these countries, except for Guatemala, Honduras, El Salvador, China and Persia, had changed over to the gold standard.[20]

The reasons for the spread of gold monometallism were numerous and complex. First and foremost, there was the collapse in the price of silver from the 1870s,[21] combined with the ease with which gold, as a precious metal, could be used for international transactions and with the generally held conviction that gold monometallism was superior to bimetallism with regard to monetary stability. But it was clear that the determination to fall in step with the foremost economic power of the time – Britain – played a not insignificant role in the main Western European countries' decision to adopt the gold standard from the 1870s, starting with Germany right after unification. The German decision, discussed below, certainly helped tip the scales, more on account of the new Reich's economic weight in Europe than on the further depreciation of silver that it brought about in a marginal way. The Scandinavian countries and the Netherlands were the first to follow their big neighbour, and those of the Latin Union soon joined them.

One of the reasons why the international monetary system was so stable during the quarter of a century preceding the First World War was, apart from Britain's regulatory role in the world economy, the growing cooperation among the various central banks.[22] To use Keynes's expression, the Bank of England was the 'conductor', whose leadership the other central banks were willing to follow in order to coordinate the setting of their discount rates and to which they provided assistance in times of crisis, particularly when the gold reserves were threatened.

World financial capital: the City of London

'We are, it is admitted, the financial centre of the world; this is more than a phrase, it is a fact. Our position has indeed been assailed, but so far without effect.'[23] This was the view expressed in December 1903 by Felix Schuster, chairman of the Union Bank of London, one of the capital's largest banks, to his colleagues, gathered at one of their monthly meetings at the Institute of Bankers. There was nothing new about this standpoint. London had held the top rank among the international financial centres since the beginning of the nineteenth century. Its position was strengthened from 1870 onwards, and for about forty years the City was the hub of international financial relations. The strengthening was of a quantitative nature – the City's working population more than doubled, growing from 170,000 people in 1871 to 364,000 in 1911.[24] It was also of a qualitative nature – the City was the first modern financial centre where an unrivalled range of hitherto unavailable, or at least hard-to-find, services were provided.

Operating mechanisms

The City's financial predominance was assured by a combination of financial institutions whose operating mechanisms were carefully designed. The linchpins of the mechanism were the banks, diversified due to the specialisation of the English banking system. Other significant financial intermediaries were the insurance companies, which played a growing role on the capital market from the 1880s, and the finance companies, especially the investment trusts, which channelled a major part of savings overseas. The City's pulse beat to the rhythm of its markets, headed by the London Stock Exchange, the Gold Market (London's prerogative in the era of the gold standard), the Baltic Exchange (specialising in chartering ships) and the London Metal Exchange (a commodity market for copper, tin, lead, zinc and silver). The City also hosted the headquarters of a multitude of large enterprises: shipping companies, particularly because of the trading role and proximity of the Port of London; railway companies; large breweries, like Guinness and Whitbread, which at that time were among the largest companies in Europe; oil firms, like the Shell Transport and Trading Company; not to mention the London branches of companies established abroad but whose financing was largely provided by the City, such as the South American railways or the South African gold and diamond mines.

In addition to these companies, but closely connected with them, the City teemed with private firms, both large and small: bankers, merchants, financiers, stockbrokers, insurers, arbitragers and brokers in the various commodity markets, chartered accountants and lawyers, all gathered within one square mile. This geographical concentration constituted one of the main characteristics of this financial centre. It was a world unto itself, where people met continuously and where contacts were made orally among businessmen whose offices were a couple of minutes away from each other. The City had its dress code and its unwritten rules – but, above all, it jealously guarded its independence from government. This independence, which extended to all the institutions, including those carrying out duties of a public nature like the stock exchange or the Bank of England, was symbolised by its own municipal administration, led by the lord mayor of London and separate from the rest of the capital.

The City's operational mechanisms, in place, as we have seen, since the beginning of the nineteenth century, were far more oriented towards international rather than national financial needs during the thirty or forty years that preceded the First World War. As pointed out by *The Economist* in 1911, 'London is often more concerned with the course of events in Mexico than with what happens in the Midlands, and more upset by a strike on the Canadian Pacific than by one in the Cambrian collieries.'[25] The large deposit banks – the clearing banks, whose activities continued to be limited in principle to short-term lending and discounting – were firmly anchored in the national economy, whereas international credit was provided by specialised banking houses – the merchant banks. It was these banks that accepted, or upon which were directly drawn, the bills of exchange, generally for three months, that constituted the main instrument for financing international trade. The good reputation of these banks turned these bills of exchange into negotiable instruments. Well before they reached their maturity dates, they were discounted, also by specialised banking houses – the discount houses – which then resold them to various British or foreign banks present in the City; and thus these bills lay at the heart of the huge discount market that existed in London and in which the banks of the entire world took part, whether directly or indirectly.

So it was the specialisation of the system, as well as its complementarity and profound unity, that broadly speaking sustained its own growth. By making available deposits collected all over the country, the clearing banks provided cash, in the form of day-to-day loans, to discount houses that discounted the bills of exchange accepted by the merchant banks. But in order to be able to meet their various payments, the beneficiaries of these bills of exchange – wholesale dealers, merchants and industrialists – replaced the liquid assets that they had obtained through discounting them in the deposit banks. It was the deposit banks that made the whole wheel of international trade financing turn. The Bank of England had pride of place at the top of the edifice, guaranteeing the country's gold reserves, essential to the smooth running of the system.

The merchant banks also specialised in issuing loans on behalf of foreign companies and governments. These securities were offered to the general public, mainly made up of individual savers, as well as to institutional investors, especially insurance companies and investment trusts. The British and foreign banks, whatever their specialisation, as well as stockbrokers, finance companies or even finance tycoons, took part, in both stable and variable combinations, in syndicates set up for issuing these loans. These securities were then traded on the London Stock Exchange, where they represented more than half the nominal value of all the securities quoted. This huge market too was sustained by money at call supplied to stockbrokers by the deposit banks and, like the discount market, it offered unrivalled opportunities for the use of short-term funds.

The merchant banks

The City's main financial institutions thus each represented an essential cog in the mechanism, but it was the merchant banks that really formed the cornerstone of the system that enabled the City to play its role as the world's financial centre. Indeed, more than any other activity, the financing of international trade lay at the heart of the City's international calling. The volume of acceptances on the London market grew from approximately £50 million or £60 million in 1875 to some £140 million in 1913; in other words, by more than 120%. This activity remained the prerogative of the merchant banks, which held 70% of the market on the eve of the First World War.[26] Baring Brothers was definitely in the lead until 1890, when its liabilities on acceptances reached £15 million, but in that year the bank went through a serious crisis that threatened to bring it down and that temporarily depressed the entire market.[27] From then on, the hierarchy among the major banking houses changed, with the more dynamic and aggressive merchant banks making a name for themselves – first and foremost Kleinwort, Sons & Co. and J. Henry

Schröder & Co., whose liabilities on acceptances totalled £13.6 and £11.7 million respectively in 1913, compared with only £6.6 million for Baring Brothers. The competition exerted by the large banks was also much stronger, especially on the part of the foreign banks established in the City, as well as the English clearing banks. Nevertheless, a large number of their acceptances were finance bills – purely financial drafts, intended for making advances or funding transfers and not for financing commercial transactions – and were thus riskier, since those issued by foreign banks were not re-discountable at the Bank of England.[28]

The merchant banks also succeeded in keeping supreme control over the City's other major activity, which was also experiencing a boom during this period – the issuing of foreign loans. Between 1870 and 1914, they were in charge of an average of 37% of the issues placed on the London market, far ahead of the overseas banks with 15% and the English commercial banks with 10%. Furthermore, some issues were directly floated on the market through the official or semi-official agents of foreign governments and, for large companies, through their banker.[29] This growth in demand naturally brought about a quite substantial increase in the number of merchant banks. Estimates vary on account of the diversity of tasks undertaken by these houses and the vagueness of their designations. The number of private banking houses involved in the City's international operations, including those that were still involved in some commercial activities, is said to have increased from 45 in 1885 to 105 in 1914 or, according to a more conservative assessment, from 39 in 1890 to 63 in 1910.[30] As for the select circle of top-ranking accepting houses – those invited to the first meeting of the Accepting Houses Committee in August 1914 – it comprised a mere 21 names.[31]

As in previous eras, this increase was largely due to the arrival of new talent attracted by the business opportunities offered by the London market. Some even managed, in less than one generation, to reach the heights of fame within the City.[32] Although the market was larger and more competitive than during the first two-thirds of the nineteenth century, positions did not change radically between 1875 and 1914. Most of the well-established banking houses managed to retain their competitive advantage. This was the case for the 'Big Five': Rothschilds and Barings, as well as Morgans, Schröders and Kleinworts (set up rather more recently in London, in the 1850s).

At the beginning of the 1870s, N.M. Rothschild & Sons was unquestionably the foremost merchant bank in the City, with a capital of £6.5 million in 1873 – three times higher than that of Baring Brothers. It probably still ranked top on the eve of the First World War, but only just. Its capital had barely increased (£7.8 million), but this was still far higher than Kleinworts' (£4.4 million), the new number two. A lot has been said about the decline of the House of Rothschild from the end of the nineteenth century onwards. In actual fact, its decline was a relative one. N. M. Rothschild & Sons grew at a slower rate than its competitors and displayed a degree of conservatism – understandable in view of the bank's incomparable prestige and the family's huge fortune. Yet the partners were willing to acquire substantial holdings: it was in the 1880s and 1890s that the Rothschilds of London, in cooperation with their cousins in Paris, built their mining empire (gold, diamonds, non-ferrous metals and oil) with, among other spectacular achievements, De Beers Consolidated and Rio Tinto. But, above all, the Rothschilds continued to control the issuing of government loans; between 1865 and 1914, they took charge, alone or with others, of issuing nearly three-quarters of the government loans floated on the London market.[33]

Baring Brothers was the Rothschilds' great rival throughout the nineteenth century. Firmly ensconced in second place at the beginning of the 1870s, it had slipped back a little by 1914. Between these two dates, the bank grew very rapidly at first, was almost bankrupt in November 1890 and then made a quite remarkable recovery. Until 1890 Baring Brothers was the largest acceptance house in the City. While it was no match for Rothschilds on the government loan market, it dominated, on the other hand, that of the American railways that were booming in the 1870s and 1880s.[34] It was in Argentina, however, that the bank was most active. It earned plenty of money there, but its illiquid assets brought about its collapse in 1890. Since the bankruptcy of such an important and prestigious bank would have had devastating consequences not only in London but all over the world, a rescue operation was immediately organised by the banking community, under the leadership of the Bank of England.[35] Baring Brothers, reorganised in the form of a limited liability company, was helped back on to its feet. The fact that the bank was not fundamentally insolvent at the time of this crisis – its assets could be liquidated easily – certainly played a role in this rebirth, as did the determination of the younger generation which took control – first and foremost John Baring, the second Lord Revelstoke. From the beginning of the twentieth century, it was once more a force to be reckoned with in the world of international finance, especially in Argentine matters,[36] and in Russia, where it regained the government's confidence – an ace that would prove invaluable during the First World War.[37]

The growth of J. S. Morgan & Co. – a bank originally known under the name of its founder, George Peabody, and then that of his successor, Junius Spenser Morgan[38] – was steadier, more as an issuing house than an accepting house. During the 1870s and 1880s, it was particularly involved in issuing American railway securities – far less so in government loans. It was, however, active in placing in London part of the $1.4 billion worth of bonds issued by the federal state between 1871 and 1879 to consolidate its debts incurred during the American Civil War. From the 1880s onwards, it extended its influence to other parts of the world, especially Argentina, where it managed its first issue syndicate in 1884. Competition with Barings would be tough during subsequent decades, even though the two banking houses remained allies. One of Morgans' main competitive advantages was its ability to give Argentina access to both the London and New York capital markets. Of all the City's merchant banks, J. S. Morgan was the one that had the closest links with the United States, where John Pierpont Morgan, the son of Junius Spencer, became the greatest American investment banker. In 1900, during the Boer War, it was through him that the chancellor of the exchequer, Michael Hicks-Beach, decided, to the Rothschilds' dismay, to place a loan of £10 million in New York – a hotly debated decision in the City. At that time, J. S. Morgan was one of the best-known firms in the City, probably just behind N. M. Rothschild and Baring Brothers. But control over it was in the process of being transferred to the other side of the Atlantic. In 1910 J. P. Morgan & Co. of New York became a partner, with a 50% stake in the London branch, from then on renamed Morgan, Grenfell & Co.[39]

The rise of J. Henry Schröder & Co. and Kleinwort, Sons & Co. was based above all on acceptance credit, in which they held the two top places in 1914. Schröders, however, achieved a breakthrough in foreign issues at the beginning of the twentieth century, particularly in Latin America, and won acclaim in 1908 with the issue – which had been turned down by the Rothschilds – of a Brazilian loan of £15 million (the San Paolo Coffee Valorization Loan), intended to stabilise the price of coffee. The success of these two firms can be explained, for the most part, by their dynamism and especially by the fact that they were willing to take more risks than the longer-standing banking houses.[40]

Trade and finance

Close to the merchant bankers, the large merchant houses operated on the boundary between commercial and financial activities. In numerical terms, these merchants were still the largest group of businessmen in the City; in 1911 commercial activities represented 49% of the jobs there, compared with 17% for finance (including the banks) and 17% for various professional services (insurance, accounting, legal services and others).[41] Their prestige and weight in the City were measured by their strong presence in the Bank of England's Court of Directors.[42] Over time, however, their activities grew to resemble those of the financial sector proper. Indeed, developments in telecommunications dealt a severe blow to their role as intermediaries between foreign exporters and the brokers in charge of selling to the public. The link between producers and wholesalers could henceforth be made directly or nearly so, eliminating or considerably reducing the number of intermediaries and resulting, for those who managed to continue their activities, in a substantial reduction in their margins. To survive, the merchant houses had to face up to these changes. Various strategies were often simultaneously adopted within the same firm. Some merchants, amongst whom were the new arrivals often of foreign origin, chose to specialise either in one part of the world where their services were still needed or in products, generally new or with high added value, in which they had a very clear competitive advantage – for example, Marcus Samuel & Co. in oil (with Shell), Harrison & Crosfield in rubber, Chalmers, Guthrie & Co. in coffee, Czarnikow in sugar and Vestey in meat.[43]

Others moved from commercial activities to service activities – in other words, from physically trading goods to organising this trade on behalf of third parties – especially by taking charge of chartering ships from London, loading and unloading them, and handling customs formalities and insurance, among other things.[44] Yet others turned to increasingly financial activities and came to resemble merchant banks, without however losing their identity. This most recent change led most of these houses to take on organising and financing the commercial, financial and manufacturing operations carried out abroad and in the empire by their branches and correspondents. These were what Stanley Chapman has called investment groups – a useful concept to designate the variety of firms that lay somewhere between the traditional merchant houses and the merchant banks.[45] While, for the foremost among them, their capital was comparable to that of the merchant banks, namely around a million pounds, that of the entire group that they controlled reached far greater magnitudes at the beginning of the twentieth century – often exceeding £4 million,[46] which easily put them among the fifty largest European companies of the day.[47] Moreover, it became clear that, like the merchant banks, these investment groups simultaneously fulfilled the two main international functions of the City: a larger or smaller part of their business was acceptance credits, and they played a far from insignificant role in exporting capital, mainly in the form of direct investment.

The opening up of international markets also offered opportunities to financiers who specialised in handling large-scale financial affairs: promoting, buying and selling companies, organising international issue syndicates, direct investment and stock-market transactions. These were generally new men, ready to risk considerable sums to attain glory in the City. Some were reliable businessmen, others unscrupulous adventurers, but it was to this group that the real financial entrepreneurs belonged – the handful of individuals who, in each generation, left their mark on their surroundings. One of them would be especially remembered – Ernest Cassel, probably the outstanding personality in the City from the 1890s and one of the great international financiers during this period. The son of a small banker from Cologne, Cassel arrived in London in 1870, at the age of 18, and, when he died, he left a colossal fortune of just over £7 million sterling – a fortune that he had built by financing often risky projects abroad and always independently, without being a partner in any firm. He started out in the City in 1874 as a manager at Bischoffsheim and Goldschmidt's,[48] then during the 1880s and 1890s took charge of organising the American and Mexican railways,[49] working with his friend Jacob Schiff, partner of the investment bank Kuhn, Loeb & Co. in New York. In Egypt, he agreed in 1897 to finance the first Aswan Dam – a project that Rothschilds had rejected – founded the National Bank of Egypt the following year, to attract British capital to the Nile and to finance new projects, and established the Agricultural Bank of Egypt in 1902, to lend money to the fellahs. It is impossible to draw up a complete list of all his activities. In 1909, on the initiative of the Foreign Office and in cooperation with Lord Revelstoke, the head of Baring Brothers, he founded the National Bank of Turkey to strengthen British influence in the Ottoman Empire.[50] Cassel was also involved in financing British industry through his long association with Vickers, Sons & Co., the armaments and shipbuilding giant. His success culminated in the social and political sphere; he was not only one of the most prominent socialites in the entourage of the prince of Wales, the future Edward VII, but also one of the most sought-after advisers to the Treasury and, in certain circumstances, an emissary of the Foreign Office. A keen advocate of lasting friendship between Britain and Germany, he was, for example, dispatched to Berlin in January 1912 to present a note to Chancellor Bethmann-Hollweg intended to sound out German intentions on the issue of easing the arms race.[51]

The big banks

Private family businesses and independent businessmen thus retained supreme control over the main activities that underpinned London's position as the world's financial centre. This phenomenon is remarkable during a period in which the big joint-stock banks experienced unprecedented growth. This was, above all, the result of the amalgamation movement that intensified between 1890 and 1914 and ended not only in the almost complete disappearance of the private deposit banks but also in the emergence of a dozen banks based in London with a regional or national network of branches, which controlled nearly two-thirds of the country's deposits.

Until 1890 the main private deposit banks, which since the end of the eighteenth century had formed the City's aristocracy, resisted the growth of the joint-stock banks as best they could, but they disappeared one after another during the recession that followed the Baring crisis. Their handicap against the joint-stock banks grew, particularly since they had no branches in the provinces to collect funds that could be transferred to London, where they could be put to more lucrative use. One of their main activities, acting as correspondents in the capital on behalf of provincial private banks, also tended to disappear as the latter were absorbed by the large deposit banks. They also received enticing takeover bids.[52] While ten of them were still members of the London Clearing House in 1890, there were only five left in the following year, two in 1900 and only one on the eve of the First World War – Glyn, Mills, Currie & Co.

The large joint-stock banks set up their own network of branches in the provinces. The National Provincial Bank and the London and County Bank were the first to do this and, with the London and Westminster Bank that was present solely in London, they remained the country's three largest banks until the end of the 1880s. During the 1880s and 1890s, provincial joint-stock banks arrived in the City and followed an extremely dynamic policy of mergers and acquisitions. Lloyds Bank, originally a private bank founded in 1750 in Birmingham, made its entrance there in 1884, and the Birmingham and Midland Bank adopted the name of London and Midland Bank after having transferred its headquarters to the capital in 1891.[53] At the beginning of the twentieth century, Lloyds and Midland became the two largest banks in the country; between 1890 and 1914, they took over thirty-three and twenty-three banks respectively. Another spectacular rise was that of Barclays Bank, founded in 1896 through the simultaneous merger of twenty London and provincial private banks, all interlinked through family ties and shared membership of the Quaker movement, which established itself as the sixth bank in the country. The *Bankers' Magazine* talked of a *coup d'état* and the Barclays people of an act of legitimate self-defence. Caught up with and then overtaken, London's old commercial banks in turn embarked on mergers. In 1909 two of the

Table 3.3. *The 20 largest commercial banks, 1913*

		Total assets (in millions of pounds sterling)
1.	Crédit Lyonnais (France)	113
2.	Deutsche Bank (Germany)	112
3.	Midland Bank (United Kingdom)	109
4.	Lloyds Bank (United Kingdom)	107
5.	Westminster Bank (United Kingdom)	104
6.	Société Générale (France)	95
7.	Comptoir National d'Escompte de Paris (France)	75
8.	National Provincial Bank (United Kingdom)	74
9.	Dresdner Bank (Germany)	72
10.	Société Générale de Belgique (Belgium)	72
11.	Barclays Bank (United Kingdom)	66
12.	Disconto-Gesellschaft (Germany)	58
13.	National City Bank (The United States)	57
14.	Parr's Bank (United Kingdom)	52
15.	Credit-Anstalt (Austria)	50
16.	Union of London and Smiths Bank (United Kingdom)	49
17.	Guaranty Trust Co. of New York (The United States)	47
18.	Bank für Handel und Industrie (Germany)	44
19.	Capital and Counties Bank (United Kingdom)	43
20.	London Joint Stock Bank (United Kingdom)	41

Source: P.L. Cottrell, 'Aspects of commercial banking in northern and central Europe, 1880–1931', in S. Kinsey and L. Newton (eds.), *International Banking in an Age of Transition*, Aldershot, 1998, p. 109; *Banking Almanac*, 1914.

City's most venerable institutions, the London and County Banking Company and the London and Westminster Bank, merged – the future Westminster Bank – to recover their place as frontrunners.

The size of the largest banks also took on new dimensions. In 1891 the deposits of the National Provincial Bank – the largest bank at the time – came to £41 million, and in 1914 those of the Midland Bank – it had, in the meantime, taken first place – to £126 million. The number of branches followed a similar trend: from 248 in 1897 to 639 in 1913 for Lloyds Bank, overtaken in that year by the Midland Bank with 725 branches. On the eve of war, these two banks were, in terms of total assets, among the world's five largest banks (see Table 3.3). And yet, when it came to banking activity, these new giants did not play such a different role from that of the former private deposit banks. They were the main purveyors of short-term credit in the City, and it was their vast resources that sustained the entire financial activities of the London market. These banks loaned, on a very short-term basis, to other banks,[54] to bill brokers and to stockbrokers and jobbers at the London Stock Exchange. They also granted huge advances, especially to colonial administrations and public authorities in Britain. But their two main operations remained discounting and loans to private and corporate clients – acceptances and investments featuring far less on the assets side of their balance sheets.[55]

The largest among these giants began, nevertheless, to come out of their torpor from the early twentieth century onwards. Within the limits of the specialisation of the English banking system, the large commercial banks played a more active role in the City's international affairs. They opened foreign exchange departments, an activity that until then had been the prerogative of the specialised private banking houses, usually of foreign origin. Under the leadership of Edward Holden, its fiercely ambitious leader and the architect of its spectacular growth, the Midland Bank was the first to take the plunge in 1905. These banks significantly increased the volume of their acceptances and participated on an increasingly regular basis in the issuing syndicates of large international loans. Some of them even undertook to issue such loans: Parr's Bank for Japan in 1899, the Midland Bank for a Russian railway in 1909 and Lloyds Bank for the city of Budapest the following year.[56] But the international activity that saw the most spectacular growth during this period was that of London agent for a foreign bank – a growth that went hand in hand with the City's assertion of its international pre-eminence.[57] These big English banks held the London deposits of foreign banks and undertook various transactions on their behalf, especially on the money market.[58]

The growth of the overseas banks was not as spectacular, but it was steady nonetheless. Taken as a group, their number stayed approximately stable from 1890 to 1913 – around thirty – with mergers and acquisitions remaining rare in this geographically specialised sector. On the other hand, the number of their branches abroad went from 739 to 1,387,[59] while the deposits of the ten largest among them increased nearly tenfold between 1873 and 1913.[60] Taken individually, they were noticeably smaller in size than the large English commercial banks, with deposits nearing £30 million for the Hongkong and Shanghai Banking Corporation and fluctuating between £17 and £22 million for the five other major banks in 1913.[61] Although chiefly operating abroad, the overseas banks had a strong foothold in London and were active on its money and financial markets. And yet, just like the English deposit banks, their influence over international business, particularly foreign issues, remained limited despite their special links with countries that regularly called on the London capital market.[62] In particular, they suffered from competition from the merchant banks, with houses like Barings for Argentina or Rothschilds for Brazil being far better placed, on account of their expertise and their networks of contacts, to see such transactions through to a successful conclusion. The exception here was the Hongkong and Shanghai Banking Corporation, which played a pioneering role in Chinese government loans (amounting to at least £60 million between 1895 and 1914), as well as in Japanese loans issued in London. The bank had a unique competitive advantage thanks to its knowledge of Far Eastern business, its relationships in the City, especially with the Rothschilds, and finally support from the Foreign Office, owing to the political nature of a number of these loans.[63]

One consequence of the City's financial predominance was that it attracted large foreign banks that came there to seek profitable business opportunities. In 1870 the Crédit Lyonnais opened a branch upon which it pinned great hopes: 'It should bring us the business that we want, such as advances to governments, the purchase and sale of Turkish and Egyptian bonds, etc. ... We have to be aware of everything that is happening by way of loans, whether consolidated or temporary.'[64] Deutsche Bank followed in 1873, and during the ensuing decades most of the large foreign banks opened a branch in the City. They numbered thirty in 1913, belonging to twelve different countries, and included the four main French deposit banks and three of the four German 'Ds'.[65] The competition to which the English banks were subjected was fierce, especially in the field of discounting and acceptances, but this was interpreted more as a sign of the City's health than as a real danger. The *Bankers' Magazine* noted in 1905 that, 'In all probability, no other city in the world has such a cosmopolitan collection of banking institutions, and this fact in itself is a tribute to the standing of London in international business.'[66]

However open the City was prior to the First World War, British banks definitely held a leading position in all the markets. It is revealing in this respect that the status of a foreign bank in the City only partly depended on the position that it held in its national market. It took the Crédit Lyonnais more than twenty years to become the leading foreign bank in London, and to do so it had to submit to the City's liquidity requirements.[67] Moreover, even though foreign banks had a strong foothold in the acceptance market, they had far less of one in the market for foreign loans, which remained the City's most prestigious pursuit. The big French and German banks certainly took part in the issues floated jointly on several markets, but they did not compete with the English banks on their home ground and in London participated in issue syndicates merely as members.

Insurance companies and investment trusts

Insurance was the City's other great speciality. Besides its not insignificant contribution to the British balance of payments,[68] it collected vast
funds and played a growing role in the financial markets. Insurance
activities experienced a considerable boom from the 1870s on. If marine
insurance, to a great extent dominated by Lloyd's, is excluded, the total
amount of fire insurance premiums went from £4 million to £29 million
between 1870 and 1914, a growth that can be explained mainly by the
expansion of British companies abroad, particularly in the United
States, which alone paid 40% of the total premiums collected. The
overall amount of life insurance premiums went from £10 million to
£29 million over the same period, chiefly thanks to the enlargement of
the domestic market and to the penetration of life insurance into the
less-well-off levels of society.[69] This growth was accompanied, as for the
deposit banks, by a trend towards increasing concentration. From
the beginning of the twentieth century, the ten largest companies,
including the Royal and the Commercial Union, took more than 70% of
the premiums collected in the field of fire insurance and 43% of those in
life insurance, with a giant, Prudential, controlling more than 50% of
the life market.[70]

This development was also accompanied by an increase in and the
diversification of their reserves. Between 1870 and 1914, their assets
increased nearly fivefold, going from £110 million to £500 million,
whereas British domestic and foreign assets both did little more than
double. The diversification of their portfolios was accomplished in three
main ways. First, there was a very significant reduction in the relative
proportion of mortgages, which went from approximately half to less
than a quarter of the total between 1870 and 1914, even if they continued to grow in absolute value. Second, there was an equally spectacular increase in foreign investment, which, from 7% of the portfolio in
1870, went up to around 40%, perhaps more, in 1914. Third, and
supporting the preceding trend, there was strong growth in the proportion of stocks of private companies, which during the same period
went from some 13% to nearly 40% of the total amount invested, a
diversification that was accomplished to the detriment of insurance
companies' traditional types of investment – government securities,
loans to local authorities and British railway bonds – whose yields
dropped considerably at the end of the nineteenth century. Overseas
investment, at first limited to colonial administrations, ventured
into private companies at the beginning of the twentieth century;
railways, first and foremost, then public utilities, mines and others.[71]

Furthermore, the riskier nature of these new types of investment made it necessary to develop a policy of portfolio diversification that, to be implemented successfully, could no longer be assigned to actuaries but had to be entrusted to investment specialists.

The diversification of assets was, moreover, the *raison d'être* of a new kind of financial institution that appeared on the scene in the 1870s – the investment trusts.[72] In England, the Foreign and Colonial Government Trust, founded in 1868 and specialising in foreign and colonial government bonds, was the first to apply the principles of the investment trust – namely, not taking controlling stakes in other companies but spreading risk by purchasing large numbers of different stocks and by using a part of the surplus as a redemption fund to reimburse the initial capital.[73]

In spite of these promises, the investment trusts were only marginally successful in England during the subsequent twenty years. By 1886 only twelve of them were quoted on the London Stock Exchange. In Scotland, on the other hand, they enjoyed a remarkable boom, epitomised by the foundation in 1873 of the Scottish American Investment Trust, whose secretary Robert Fleming is considered the 'father of the investment trusts'. Following his Scottish successes, he moved to the City in 1888, and his arrival coincided with a wave of investment trusts being set up. The nominal capital of all investment trusts quoted on the stock exchange grew from nearly £5 million in 1887 to some £50 million in 1890. Yet they were viewed with a great deal of suspicion by the City establishment. Profoundly shaken in the early 1890s, following the Baring Crisis, the investment trusts were held responsible for all the fraudulent transactions associated with setting up limited liability companies. The main criticism directed at them was that they were a vehicle for enriching their founders, who benefited from half the profits once a previously fixed dividend had been distributed, thanks to the preferential shares allocated to them. Moreover, they did not hesitate to commit their shareholders' capital by subscribing to dubious stocks or by setting up new companies to buy up the even more doubtful shares of companies already in trouble.[74] But eventually the investment trusts won acceptance, as a new wave of them came to the fore with renewed vigour after 1905 – this time thanks to the involvement of the City's aristocracy. Their assets reached £90 million in 1913, mainly invested in foreign stock, primarily American. Like the insurance companies, they found themselves at the heart of the City's networks of relationships, through overlapping boards of directors – one banker in three was a director of at least one investment trust, and one in two of at least one insurance company – and they were often members of the issue syndicates for the main foreign loans.[75]

Professional services

It is difficult to measure quantitatively the growth in professional services provided in the City during the forty years before 1914, but there is some data available: in 1891 about 700 accountancy and 2,000 law firms were working there. These are considerable figures, but they include a vast majority of tiny firms that had no involvement at all in international activities on the London market. On this level, the importance of these services in the City's inner workings was qualitative rather than quantitative, and they tended to be concentrated in the hands of a few key companies.[76] Among these, the law firms were the oldest, for example Freshfield & Sons, lawyers to the Bank of England since the early eighteenth century.[77] Other important law firms developed in the late nineteenth century, such as Ashurst, Morris & Crisp, and Slaughter and May, both specialising in issue activities.

The chartered accountants probably formed the group that was most representative of this new era, marked particularly by the dramatic rise in limited liability companies and the demand for auditing accounts. The main firms, most of them destined for a bright international future, made their appearance in the 1840s and 1850s: Deloitte & Co. in 1845, Price Waterhouse in 1849 and Cooper Brothers in 1854. But the chartered accountants still did not count for much and they acted above all as liquidators. It was not until the end of the nineteenth century that auditing overtook liquidations in terms of its share of income. And in this auditing work the firms' main clients were the City's large companies. Price Waterhouse, for example, was the co-auditor of the National Provincial Bank and the London and Westminster Bank. It was also involved in the City's international activities in two ways. First, by auditing the accounts of companies based in London but operating abroad or in the empire; from 1871, for instance, Cooper Brothers audited the accounts of the National Bank of India and the British South Africa Company. And second, by setting up abroad themselves to follow their clientele or to build up a new one. Price Waterhouse played a pioneering role in this; in 1890 it opened a branch in New York and in 1892 another in Chicago – America's second financial centre – where its business took off very quickly. Another firm that was particularly active abroad, McAuliffe, Davis & Hope, founded in 1895, opened an office in Baku in 1903, to audit the accounts of oil companies, and established itself in Rio de Janeiro in 1908.[78] In spite of this progress, chartered accountants before 1914 did not achieve a socioprofessional status comparable to that of bankers and of the great merchants, nor to that of the more long standing professions, such as barristers and solicitors.

The London Stock Exchange

The City's other major activity as an international financial centre was the London Stock Exchange, where the nominal value of the securities listed there went from £2.3 billion in 1873 to £11.3 billion in 1913; in other words, more than the New York Stock Exchange and the Paris Bourse combined.[79] As evidence of its highly cosmopolitan character, foreign stocks, which represented between 35% and 40% of the total in 1873, exceeded 50% from 1893 onwards. By 1914 one-third of all negotiable instruments in the world were quoted on the London Stock Exchange.[80]

From the outset, both the management and operations of the London Stock Exchange were based on a dualistic principle. Management was divided into two committees. One – the Committee for General Purposes – represented the users, in other words the stockbrokers and jobbers who were members of the stock exchange. The other – the nine managers, also called trustees – represented the shareholders of the company The Stock Exchange, which actually owned the building. The first was elected by the members of the stock exchange and controlled the business conducted there. It decided whether to allow a security to be quoted on the stock exchange, dealt with any matters relating to its members, especially disputes, and elected new members by secret ballot. The second was appointed by the shareholders of the stock exchange and managed it like a business. At its disposal it had the money paid by its members as annual subscriptions, and it set the membership fees for new members. As for the way that the market functioned, it was based on the separation of roles between jobbers and brokers. The jobbers were securities traders and, like any other traders, they earned their profit from the difference between the purchase price and the selling price. But they could not buy or sell securities directly to the public, which did not have direct access to the stock exchange. For all its stock-market transactions, the public, whether as individuals or companies, was obliged to go through a broker who, in return for a commission, would negotiate with the jobber. A broker could, of course, speculate on his own account, but when he worked for a client, stock-exchange rules did not allow him to sell a security for more than he had purchased it.

This way of being organised and operating was the source both of the stock exchange's problems and of its competitiveness.[81] It is not hard to imagine the problems, particularly conflicts of interest between members and owners. The owners obviously benefited from admitting as many members as possible and making them pay a high annual subscription fee, whereas the members had a diametrically opposed interest. Nevertheless, conflicts remained minor. Even if the membership fee increased considerably between 1870 and 1914,[82] the number of members grew regularly, from 1,046 in 1870 to 4,855 in 1913, in a more or less equal proportion between brokers and jobbers. Some worked independently but, more often than not, they worked with one or more partners: the number of firms went from 529 in 1882 to 910 in 1914.

The separation between the two roles came under threat, however, from the 1890s. Certain brokers acted as direct middlemen between banking houses outside the stock exchange and their clients, effectively bypassing the jobbers and thus collecting two commissions. Moreover, these banking houses were usually foreign banks recently established in the City. As for certain jobbers, they dealt directly with the provincial stock exchanges, bypassing the brokers, thus depriving them of their commissions. Although this overlapping of roles was a natural development in the way that the stock exchange operated, the management of the London Stock Exchange decided in 1908 to impose a number of measures prohibiting brokers from fixing prices and from collecting two commissions, and prohibiting jobbers from dealing with non-members. These regulations were unquestionably a victory for the small brokers and jobbers in danger of becoming extinct if the separation of roles were not maintained; their position was further strengthened by the decision taken in 1912 to impose fixed commissions.[83]

These specific characteristics of the London Stock Exchange were also advantageous in terms of openness and costs. The members of the London Stock Exchange were far more numerous than those of the New York Stock Exchange and, above all, than those of the Paris Bourse, bringing about an increase in the volume and diversity of business and, at least until the regulations of the years 1908–12, a far more competitive climate. The separation between brokers and jobbers offered guarantees of security to the public, since the broker with whom it negotiated made no profit on the difference between the purchase price and the selling price, and competition among jobbers assured clients of a narrow margin between the purchase price and the selling price – at least for continuously traded stocks, which however was less the case for shares in British industry.[84]

Apart from functioning as a market organised for trading negotiable stocks, and even more so for speculating on these stocks, the London Stock Exchange represented an important outlet for short-term funds, which came to London from all over the world in search of a use. The City's various financial institutions had, and used, the possibility of investing short term on the stock exchange, by buying and reselling securities over short periods to obtain slightly higher yields than the money market's discount rate. These transactions were risky nevertheless, and the banks tended increasingly to lend these funds to brokers and jobbers, who placed them themselves – at their own risk.[85] In 1914 half the very-short-term credit granted by both the British and foreign banks in London were loans to members of the stock exchange, backed by securities pledged as collateral.[86]

The main outlet for short-term funds was, however, the London discount market, which took on a truly global dimension once the bill of exchange on London had been adopted as the preferred instrument for financing international trade. From then on, Lombard Street belonged to the whole world.[87] On the eve of the war, there were nearly £350 million worth of bills in circulation, the bulk of them in the form of bills of exchange, but a growing proportion of them in riskier finance bills. This growth and internationalisation of the discount market placed particular responsibilities on the Bank of England.

The Bank of England

The Bank of England, which retained its organisational structure dating from the Bank Act of 1844, found it increasingly difficult to control the money market. This was due partly to the very expansion of this market and partly to the growth of the big deposit banks that, through successive mergers, had become absolute giants from the end of nineteenth century. More and more, it was the market rate – in other words, the rate used by commercial banks – that served as a benchmark and, inasmuch as it determined the flow of gold entering or leaving the country, could directly threaten British currency reserves. As Hartley Withers, one of the most respected financial authors of the day, wrote:

The general adoption of the gold standard by the economically developed countries of the world, accompanied by the fact that London has remained the only market in which every draft and every credit are immediately convertible into gold as a matter of course, has greatly intensified the responsibility of the Bank of England as custodian of a gold reserve, which is liable to be drawn on at any time from all quarters of the habitable globe from which a draft on London may be presented.[88]

No longer able to control the market merely by adjusting its discount rate, the Bank of England had to resort to other means of making its interest rate effective, in particular, borrowing on the market in order to raise the price of money and thus attract gold to London.[89] In times of crisis, it could also rely on support from the central banks, especially the Banque de France, and could often obtain assistance from the big banks. The Bank of England asserted its authority over the City during this period. It took a decisive step in this respect by intervening when Baring Brothers was on the verge of bankruptcy, no longer being able to pay the £16 million for acceptances that fell due on 15 November 1890. The governor, William Lidderdale, organised the famous merchant bank's rescue through concerted action by the banking community. He strengthened the Bank of England's position by borrowing £1 million worth of gold from the Russian government and £3 million from the Banque de France, through the Rothschilds. He obtained the support of the British Cabinet, which refused to intervene directly but promised to support the Bank by leaving sufficient funds in its own account. Finally, he set up a guarantee fund to cover any losses that might result from the liquidation of Baring Brothers, to which all the main banks contributed.

Nevertheless, the problems continued. The matter of the country's gold reserves was the subject of ongoing debate in banking circles, as well as in some political circles, following the rescue of Baring Brothers and up until the First World War. There was the question of their adequacy. Were they really insufficient, or was it acceptable to count on London's ability to attract gold if need be, bearing in mind the drawbacks caused by interest rate fluctuations involved in doing so? And there was the matter of safeguarding these reserves. Should the gold reserves accumulated by the banks be deposited at the Bank of England, which would therefore remain the sole guardian of the country's gold reserves, as proposed by Felix Schuster, the chairman of the Union Bank of London and the City's main theoretical authority from the beginning of the twentieth century? Or should each bank keep its own gold bars and coins, and publish their total amount on its balance sheet, meaning that authority over managing the currency reserves would no longer be assured by the Bank of England but by a committee also made up of the big deposit banks, as suggested by Edward Holden, the fiery chairman of the Midland Bank? A source of ongoing tension, the contradiction between the Bank of England's duties as a central bank and its commercial banking activities would not be fully resolved before 1914.

A brilliant second: Paris

The notion of decline is relative, especially when applied to the Parisian centre's fate between 1870 and 1914. Paris had undoubtedly given up vying with the City for world supremacy, but it was indisputably continental Europe's foremost financial centre and continued to play a leading international role, surpassed only by that of London. This rank of brilliant second was perfectly honourable and corresponded better to Britain and France's respective positions in the world economy; at the end of the day, it was reflected quite clearly in the amount of capital exported by each of these two countries. Far from declining, Paris had its finest hours during the forty years preceding the First World War, particularly during the *Belle Epoque* from the beginning of the twentieth century. Paris's strength as an international financial centre was due above all to its long-term capital market. Unlike London, it played only a minor role in financing international trade and constantly lacked enough acceptances to support a vigorous discount market. Paris remained the favoured place, after the British metropolis, for issuing foreign loans, usually on behalf of governments rather than for private companies, as well as for trading these securities on its secondary market.

The big banks

One of Paris's main competitive advantages was the size, diversity and influence of its main financial institutions. The three big banks held the top place, with more than half the deposits collected in the country.[90] The Crédit Lyonnais and the Société Générale experienced rapid growth after they were founded in the 1860s, as did the Comptoir d'escompte that had appeared about fifteen years earlier. The Crédit Lyonnais established itself quite quickly as the leading French bank and then as the world's top bank at the turn of the century. By 1913 it was one of the five biggest banks in the world (certain rankings even put it first), and the two others were in the top ten (see Table 3.3), in spite of the bankruptcy, after speculating unsuccessfully on copper, of the Comptoir d'escompte in 1889 and its restoration under the name of the Comptoir national d'escompte de Paris. While these three big banks reached a size that was comparable to that of the English deposit banks, their growth was for the most part internal, without recourse to mergers and acquisitions, the Crédit Lyonnais only buying up a single bank and the Comptoir d'escompte eight before 1914.

Another difference from their City counterparts was that these French banks were very involved in international business. They took part in all the issue syndicates, even if, with the exception of the Crédit Lyonnais, they rarely headed them, and they played a major role in successfully issuing and above all reselling loans. Indeed, they had considerable placing capabilities, which made them indispensable, thanks to their network of branches spread throughout the country and to their ability to sell securities to their clientele, usually without having to resort to a public subscription and even before listing them on the Bourse. They were also very involved abroad and noticeably extended their network of foreign branches during this period; in 1913, and without counting those in France's colonial empire, the Crédit Lyonnais owned twenty, compared with eight in 1878, and the Comptoir d'escompte twenty-eight.[91]

The French banks were also very active abroad through the overseas banks, although their development was not comparable with that of the City's overseas banks, owing partly to competition from the deposit banks but mainly to France's weaker presence in the world. In 1914 the total number of overseas branches of all French banks reached a maximum of 500 – in other words, barely more than a third of those of the British banks. There were, however, some important overseas banks, including the Imperial Ottoman Bank and the Banque de l'IndoChine that both benefited from the privilege of issuing local paper money. The first, founded in 1863, was officially an Anglo-French bank, with one board of directors in London, another in Paris and its management in Constantinople.[92] In fact, it became more and more of a French bank, mainly on account of the far larger French economic interests in the Ottoman Empire, for which British investors showed little enthusiasm.[93] The Banque de l'IndoChine was the main means of French economic and financial intervention in the Far East — the counterpart of the Hongkong and Shanghai Bank, despite being half the size in terms of its total assets.[94]

Thus, the *banques d'affaires*, which perhaps best symbolised the Parisian centre's international character, did not have a monopoly on public issues, even though the foremost among them, the Banque de Paris et des Pays-Bas (Paribas), had a particularly strong foothold in this sector, especially at the head of issue syndicates.[95] The Banque de Paris et des Pays-Bas experienced impressive growth during the *Belle Epoque*, its total assets, lower than those of deposit banks as it worked mainly with shareholders' equity, going from Fr.277 to 716 million between 1902 and 1912. Foreign government loans formed its main field of activity, especially on behalf of Russia, where from 1901 it was the market leader with the Crédit Lyonnais, Morocco and Latin America. As a *banque d'affaires*, the Banque de Paris et des Pays-Bas was also responsible for issues on behalf of private companies, issues that were usually linked to its acquiring stakes in these companies with representation on their boards of directors.[96] Although it was a joint-stock company, it retained an aristocratic air on account of the numerous private bankers sitting on its board of directors, as well as the very nature of its activities: high finance. This was even more true of the second French merchant bank, the Banque de l'Union Parisienne, set up in 1904 by the main houses of the Parisian *haute banque* in association with the Société Générale de Belgique.[97] Smaller than Paribas – its portfolio of securities came to Fr. 80 million in 1913 – it enabled members of the *haute banque* to handle transactions that exceeded the capacities of their own banks, a strategy used by European private bankers since the mid-nineteenth century.

Paris also attracted big foreign banks, which were mainly involved in foreign exchange and in financing external trade. The British overseas banks[98] were the most visible in Paris, where they had become established long before the clearing banks, which made a tentative entrance only on the eve of the First World War.[99] In total, around fifteen foreign banks, belonging to seven different countries, had a branch or subsidiary in Paris in 1913, amongst which were three Russian banks and three Spanish banks. The big German banks were not themselves present in the French capital, but they were represented by French banks – nearly always, private banks – in which they usually held a significant stake, assuring them of greater facilities than they would have been able to obtain through a correspondent bank.[100]

The Haute Banque

The vigorous development of joint-stock banks did not mean the end of private banks. There is no official list of the members of the *haute banque* – membership of the group was a matter of status rather than of functions. At the end of the nineteenth century, it was generally considered to have comprised eight banking houses: Rothschild, Hottinguer, Mallet, Vernes, Mirabaud, de Neuflize, Heine and Demachy Seillière.[101] In this group, de Rothschild Frères was way ahead of all the others. Its capital was fixed, for fiscal reasons, at Fr.50 million when it was re-formed in 1905, after the death of Alphonse de Rothschild and the dissolution of the partnership between the banks in London, Paris and Vienna the previous year. But the Paris house had far greater means at its disposal, its internal accounts revealing assets fluctuating between Fr.500 and Fr.600 million from 1874 to 1904.[102] By way of comparison, the capital of Mallet Frères, the longest-established member of the *haute banque*, was Fr.7.1 million in 1913, including its partners' reserves and deposits.

In many ways, the French Rothschilds were in a similar situation to their British cousins. Their legendary fortune and their immense prestige inevitably led them to adopt a more cautious attitude by this time.

Simultaneously, they had to brave the competition from ever more powerful joint-stock banks, a threat that they could ill afford to ignore. In the government loan sector, where they reigned almost supreme until the 1870s, the French Rothschilds remained a major force until 1914, on account of their prestige and their network of relationships, even if they were led to cooperate with the big banks and to give them a share of the cake. This is how they ended up having to share Russian business with the Banque de Paris et des Pays-Bas from 1888, then to give it the upper hand from 1901. The Rothschilds' power also made itself felt through the companies that they controlled.[103] During the 1880s and 1890s, in conjunction with the London house, they acquired major stakes in non-ferrous ores – with Peñarroya, Le Nickel or Boléo – and in oil – with BNITO – which are said to have reached Fr.100 million in 1900.[104] The Rothschilds' position in Paris before 1914 should not, therefore, be underestimated, their position ultimately being based on their vast financial resources. De Rothschild Frères remained by far the largest holder of securities on the Parisian financial market, with a portfolio estimated at 500 million francs. On this market, even at the beginning of the twentieth century, any withdrawal of funds on its part could not fail to trigger off an upheaval.

The other banking houses belonging to the *haute banque* had been eclipsed from the outset by the Rothschilds, and they were even more overshadowed by the rise of the large banks, especially in the issue business and in other large financial operations. This did not, however, mean that they were in decline. Thanks to their prestige and their network of relationships, they still played a role in international financial business out of all proportion to their size. Some continued to act as bankers for foreign governments and to pay the coupons of loans that they had issued in the past, for example, like Hottinguer & Cie, which held the large deposits of the Russian and Ottoman governments. They were also entrusted with the funds of a rich clientele and, at the beginning of the twentieth century, wealth management started to become their main activity. They were, moreover, heavily represented on the boards of directors of the railways, insurance companies, *banques d'affaires* and, of course, the Banque de France. Most of them experienced sustained growth throughout this period. The balance sheet of Mallet Frères, for example, went from Fr.17 million in 1860 to Fr.45 million in 1913, owing to the expansion of its international activities, in particular its acceptances that increased more than tenfold, and its deposits, amongst which the proportion of non-resident accounts increased from one-third to two-thirds[105] – a development comparable to that of London's merchant banks.

Although the Parisian *haute banque* did not, as a group, carry the same weight on the capital market as its British counterpart did, the Paris of finance was, nonetheless, packed with private banking and finance houses, which were more or less large and more or less recent, contributing significantly to its cosmopolitanism and vitality.[106] Those that were closest to the *haute banque* took an interest mainly in wealth management, whereas others were involved in activities of a more financial nature (promoting limited companies, acquiring holdings, arbitrage and others), usually in relation to a particular part of the world. Traditional banking business, like collecting deposits (by offering attractive rates) and granting short-term credit, had not completely disappeared. Some banking houses specialised in discounting bills of exchange, and others in acceptances. These varied activities reflected the Paris financial centre's vitality before 1914, as well as the fact that a number of private banks were of foreign origin and formed part of international family networks present at the same time in several financial centres, especially London and New York.[107] Others worked in close cooperation with large French or foreign banks.[108] As for the long-established merchant houses, those that had leanings towards activities of a more financial nature were, of course, less numerous than in London. The most famous was Louis Dreyfus & Cie, one of the world's leading cereals trading companies – present on five continents and especially powerful in Russia – which set up its own commercial bank.

The Paris Bourse

The importance of the Paris Bourse matched the Paris centre's international influence. In terms of size, with listed securities having a nominal value of £6.2 billion in 1913, it was in second place, quite far behind London (£11.3 billion) but just ahead of New York (£5.3 billion) and Berlin (£5.3 billion). In terms of openness, it was just as international, or almost, as the London Stock Exchange – a little over half the stocks officially quoted were foreign. In terms of volume, on the other hand, the transactions there were markedly smaller than those in London or even New York, because the big banks were involved in directly placing new stocks and in carrying out internal arbitrage on securities. The very way that the market was organised, in particular the official character and monopoly of *agents de change*, also served as a brake and tended to reduce the volumes traded.

Indeed, throughout this period, the Paris Bourse preserved the duality that had characterised it since its very beginnings: an official market, the *parquet*, where the number of stockbrokers, appointed by the government, was limited by law (set at sixty in 1724, it was increased to eighty in 1898), and a free market, the *coulisse*, that was open to everyone. Due to the total amount of listed stocks, the *parquet* was far more important and it offered security guarantees because of its official nature and the collective responsibility of the stockbrokers for forward deals. The *coulisse* was more dynamic, its turnover sometimes exceeded that of the *parquet* and it was able to decide whether to introduce new securities, particularly the funds of foreign states, onto the Paris market; but in principle it lost the right to trade in them once they had been accepted onto the official list and become subject to the stockbrokers' monopoly.

The conflict between the two markets was rekindled during the 1870s, after the *coulisse* became increasingly important in placing national loans earmarked for paying the war indemnity to Germany. The *parquet* demanded that the *coulisse*, tolerated by the government, be disbanded, whereas the *coulisse* called for the stockbrokers' monopoly to be abolished. An understanding was reached in 1892, leaving Russian bonds to the *parquet* and Turkish, Egyptian, Spanish, Hungarian and Portuguese stocks to the *coulisse*, but it did not last long. The situation was finally regulated by the law of 1898, which obliged the *coulisse* to restrict its operations to stocks not admitted to the *parquet*, but a private agreement authorised it to carry out forward transactions in French fixed-term annuities. These were important restrictions; the *coulisse* could no longer encroach upon the *parquet*. But, for the first time, it obtained legal recognition that made it lose, to a certain extent, its free-market character. Its members were henceforth part of a corporation and the admission criteria became more rigorous, notably with limited companies being excluded and private banking houses having to prove that they had sufficient capital. The most striking feature of the early twentieth century was, nevertheless, the far closer cooperation between the two markets. The *coulisse* was given the right to take orders for stockbrokers and thus had an interest in increasing the *parquet*'s turnover. For its part, the *parquet* received orders from the *coulisse*, often issued by clients who considered it too risky to deal directly with it. The Paris financial market could thus benefit from the twin advantages of the *coulisse*'s dynamism and the *parquet*'s security. On the other hand, the fact that the stockbrokers, who enjoyed a monopoly on the official market, were not traders and thus could not make a market harmed the Paris Bourse.

The role of the Banque de France

When all is said and done, it was the Banque de France that best reflected Paris's status as an international financial centre and made a vital contribution towards it. Unlike the Bank of England, which relied on being able to import gold into London whenever necessary, the Banque de France had huge gold reserves at its disposal – the largest in Europe after Russia. The purpose of these reserves was both strategic (having a war chest available should a new conflict arise with Germany) and economic (maintaining as low and stable a discount rate as possible, while assuring the convertibility of its banknotes). But the size of its reserves also enabled the Banque de France to play a key role in running the international monetary system. Whereas the Bank of England was the 'conductor', in many respects the Banque de France maintained regulation and stability by allowing its gold to flow to Britain when the need arose or by voluntarily making it available to the Bank of England on a temporary basis. This cooperation between central banks, particularly across the English Channel, was crucial in ensuring the smooth running of the pre-1914 gold standard.

But why did the Banque de France and the other European central banks agree to cooperate? Before 1914, was there an ideal of a higher pursuit that would apparently evaporate during the interwar years? In fact, the notion of altruistic cooperation between central banks is unrealistic. Several recent studies have shown that the central banks were at best indifferent and at worst hostile towards each other – and that they were willing to help each other only when they benefited directly. As Marc Flandreau has explained, the Banque de France did indeed adopt a policy against financial crises, which entailed releasing its gold in times of monetary tension and recovering it later. But it did so in its own interests.[109] This enabled it to prevent or reduce increases in bank rate in Britain that it would, in any case, have been forced to follow had the situation deteriorated.[110] And by discounting heavily bills drawn on London at a lower rate than that offered by its English counterpart, as it did for example in 1907, the Banque de France made a profitable investment in pounds sterling, at the same time as calming down a situation that was likely to disrupt the French monetary system. Things began to change as war loomed, with the Banque de France, as well as the Reichsbank, becoming far more attached to their gold reserves.

The rise of Berlin

Berlin's rise to the top ranks in the hierarchy of international financial centres seemed a natural consequence of Germany's economic weight following unification and the country's extremely vigorous economic growth during the forty years preceding the First World War. The world's second industrial power after the United States – Germany overtook Britain at the turn of the twentieth century – naturally had to have a financial centre of comparable dimensions.

Origins and development

Yet Berlin did not start from nothing as a financial centre just after the German Empire was founded. For one thing, it was the capital of Prussia, in other words, of a state belonging to the coalition of powers whose financial needs, especially for conducting wars, led to a local capital market being established from the end of the eighteenth century. From the 1840s, this market expanded rapidly because of its role in financing railways. In purely quantitative terms, Berlin was already a financial centre on a par with Frankfurt and Hamburg; but its focus was national rather than international, and industrial – whether in the activity of its banks or its stock exchange – rather than financial (like Frankfurt) or commercial (like Hamburg). In qualitative terms, Berlin's private bankers had some of the most prominent names in German high finance in their ranks: in first place, Mendelssohn & Co., the capital's most prestigious banking house, and S. Bleichröder, whose main partner, Gerson von Bleichröder, was Bismarck's banker and advisor.[111] Active in foreign issues, they formed part, alongside the centre's two leading joint-stock banks, the Berliner Handels-Gesellschaft and the Disconto-Gesellschaft, of the 'Prussian Consortium' set up in 1859 to issue a loan of 30 million thalers intended to finance the mobilisation of the Prussian army following the French victory against Austria at Magenta. This consortium (under the name of the Imperial Loan Consortium) would continue to take charge of issuing Prussian, then German, government loans – whence its prestige and the coveted admission of new members.

Berlin was also the headquarters of the Prussian central bank, Germany's longest-established issuing bank, the Preussische Bank, founded by Frederick the Great in 1765.[112] It was transformed into a limited liability company in 1846, the Prussian state keeping only one-sixth of the capital. Its share continued to shrink following several increases in capital, but the bank continued to be managed by high-ranking civil servants. Of the five issuing banks in Germany before the unification of 1871, it had by far the highest number of banknotes in circulation – ahead of the Frankfurter Bank. The creation of the German central bank in 1876, by transforming the Preussische Bank into the Reichsbank, of course reflected Prussia's dominant position in the new Reich. But German monetary union had already been well under way since the 1860s, through the medium of the Prussian thaler, which spread throughout the German states and became the common currency for everyday needs.[113]

The foundation of the Reichsbank in 1876 went hand in hand with the creation of the German single currency, the mark – a gold-convertible currency. The decision made by the German political and monetary authorities was an important one: for the international monetary system, for Germany and for Berlin as an international financial centre. In spite of reservations on the part of some people, notably Gerson Bleichröder,[114] who feared its deflationary effects,[115] opting for gold appeared to many German leaders to be synonymous with opting for modernity and the monetary system of the world's leading industrial and trading nation, as well as the path to follow in order to catch up with it.[116] To German banking and financial circles, the gold standard also seemed the best way of freeing German foreign trade financing from the twin controls of the pound sterling and bills drawn on London. National pride was certainly involved, but the profits made by English bankers, estimated at around 6 million marks per year for German trade with Latin America alone, were also enticing.[117]

The adoption of the gold standard, as well as Germany's industrial and commercial development, quickly made the mark one of the main reserve currencies in the world, alongside the pound sterling and the franc. Berlin's position in Germany was also strengthened – to the detriment of Hamburg and Frankfurt – in the two basic activities of international financial centres, namely the financing of international trade and foreign issues. The large-scale involvement of the big banks, all based in Berlin, in these activities played a decisive role. As far as trade financing was concerned, these banks enabled Berlin to benefit far more than Hamburg from German monetary union, which had however been a long-standing demand of the merchants and bankers of the Hanseatic city, and from the mark's international status. As for international issues, even though the Frankfurt bankers' expertise remained indispensable for a long time, the big Berlin banks, which largely controlled national industrial issues, succeeded in appropriating them due to the trend towards integration in German banking.[118]

The big banks

Business in Berlin was dominated by the big banks, headed by the four 'Ds': Deutsche Bank, the Dresdner Bank, the Disconto-Gesellschaft and the Darmstädter Bank. On the eve of the First World War, all four were among the world's twenty largest banks, Deutsche Bank taking top place in some rankings (see Table 3.3). And yet, taken as a group, the capital's nine big banks collected a mere fraction of the country's banking resources: barely 12% in 1913. There were still several hundred local and regional joint-stock banks, whose joint resources were more or less equal to those of the big banks, as well as at least a thousand private banks not included in the Reichsbank's statistics. But the bulk of the deposits lay elsewhere – almost three-quarters were in the hands of savings banks, mortgage banks, banking cooperatives and other specialised banks.

The big banks' significance stemmed essentially from three factors. First, from their size and from the huge resources that each of them had at their disposal. What is more, these means were reinforced by the specific forms that banking concentration took in Germany, with far less reliance on mergers and acquisitions than on 'communities of interests' – acquisitions of cross-holdings and profit-sharing – between big banks and provincial banks. In 1904, for example, Deutsche Bank had links of this type with fourteen banks and found itself at the head of a group whose capital and reserves amounted to 700 million marks.[119] Second, the big German banks were universal banks, engaged in both deposit and investment banking. This involved them in national industrial financing on the one hand,[120] and in large international banking and financial transactions, especially in issuing foreign loans, on the other hand. Even more so, and it is this third factor that made them important for Berlin as a financial centre, it was the big banks that controlled most of these international transactions. The other categories of bank were nearly completely excluded from them, with the exception of Berlin's most prominent private bankers and, to a lesser extent, centres like Hamburg, Frankfurt or Cologne.

The private banks continued to dominate international finance until the 1880s. In Berlin, Gerson von Bleichröder, ennobled in 1872, became the city's most famous financier immediately after unification and, as Bismarck's personal banker and advisor, had privileged access to information, in spite of palace intrigues. He was involved in industrial financing, played a major role in nationalising the railway network during the 1880s and took charge of issuing several foreign loans, usually in connection with German foreign policy, especially in Russia. However, he opposed the famous *Lombardverbot*, the ban placed by Bismarck in 1887 on the Reichsbank accepting Russian securities as loan guarantees – a ban that lasted until 1894 and led to Germany being replaced by France as Russia's main creditor.[121] Little is known about the activities of Mendelssohn & Co., other than that its prestige and vast fortune stemmed from its position as banker to the Russian government; the huge sums deposited to pay the coupons and interventions on loans were a regular and appreciable source of profit.[122]

From the 1880s onwards, the big banks increasingly took over operations, sometimes opposed by the private bankers who had been responsible for setting them up. The issue syndicates were henceforth dominated by Deutsche Bank and the Disconto-Gesellschaft, rather than by Bleichröder and Mendelssohn, particularly for areas like South America, China and the Ottoman Empire; the more personal relations of the private banking networks continued to play an important role in financial transactions with the United States and Russia. The private banks certainly continued to have a strong foothold, sometimes running the show but more often than not as members of the various syndicates, consortia and other international concerns orchestrated by the big banks.

Berlin also had, although to a lesser extent than London and even Paris, some overseas banks specifically set up to finance German foreign trade and to encourage foreign investment. Having arrived on the scene later than their British and French counterparts, they had all been founded by one or more big banks, sometimes with the involvement of private banking houses.[123] In 1886, for example, Deutsche Bank set about creating the Deutsche Überseeische Bank, active in Latin America,[124] and the Deutsch-Asiatische Bank in 1889, this time in conjunction with the Disconto-Gesellschaft and Bleichröder.[125] However, the activities of the overseas banks remained limited in Berlin, because, apart from the Deutsch-Asiatische Bank, they undertook barely any issue activities in connection with parts of the world where they had commitments, leaving this initiative to their parent companies.

The big German banks were also actively involved in direct investment abroad and set up new companies for this purpose. This contrasted sharply with the London market, where such initiatives were taken either by the merchant banks or by individual financiers. In oil, for instance, Deutsche Petroleum was founded in 1904 under the auspices of Deutsche Bank, whereas the British Shell Transport and Trading Company continued to be managed by its founder Marcus Samuel and his partners; there was also the case of the financing of the Baghdad railway, managed by Deutsche Bank but whose British negotiators were Baring Brothers, J. S. Morgan and Ernest Cassel, until the prospects of cooperation failed in 1903.

The Berlin Börse

The Berlin Börse reflected the market's financial traditions, namely a more pronounced focus on the national economy and on railway and industrial stocks, as opposed to Frankfurt's specialisation in foreign government bonds. In this respect, it was indicative that the first share had been traded in Berlin in 1804 and in Frankfurt in 1816. Further-more, the Berlin Börse asserted its predominance over the other German stock markets following the boom of the *Gründerjahre*. Nearly one thousand limited companies, with a capital nearing 3 billion marks in total, were created during the two years of euphoria that followed the unification of Germany in 1871 and ended with the crisis of 1873 – a brutal phase of stabilisation after the speculative fever that had taken hold of the country. From then on, even though it was challenged by the provincial stock exchanges, particularly those in Frankfurt and Hamburg, the Berlin Börse continuously increased its lead. At the end of the nineteenth century, its transactions – gauged according to taxes paid between 1882 and 1893 – represented 66% of those carried out on the German secondary markets, compared with 12% on the Frankfurt Börse and 9% on that of Hamburg.[126] This was a substantial lead, comparable to that of New York in relation to the other American stock exchanges or to the Paris Bourse in relation to the French provincial stock exchanges.

Smaller than those of London and Paris in terms of the volume of securities that were listed there, the Berlin Stock Exchange was also less international, even if almost half (192 out of 413) of the government loans that were listed there were foreign government bonds. This is, of course, mainly explained by the fact that Germany exported less capital than Britain and France. Even so, the regulations to which it was sub-jected did not help matters much. The law of 1896 (*Börsengesetz*), intended to curb speculation and combat fraud, introduced tight control over stock-market activities. It put in place new supervisory bodies, including a government commissioner, a stock-exchange board and a tribunal. But above all, it considerably limited forward transactions, prohibiting them on securities in mining and manufacturing companies, and only authorising them in other sectors on shares in companies whose capital exceeded 20 million marks. Consequently, speculative transactions, which represented the bulk of stock-market business, tended to move out of Germany, attracted towards the Amsterdam and London stock exchanges in particular.[127]

Limits to Berlin's expansion

Berlin had never been in a position seriously to rival London or even Paris on the international financial scene. As far as foreign issues were concerned, its ultimately inferior position was due to the fact that Germany invested far less abroad than Britain and France did, even if a handful of big German banks and private bankers had managed to find themselves a place in the sun. The situation was more complex when it came to financing international trade, given the phenomenal growth that German foreign trade experienced during this period.[128] In spite of the German banks' avowed intention of shielding this trade from control by the British banks and the pound sterling, Berlin's role in this field of activity remained limited. While the mark was used in Germany's commercial transactions with a certain number of European countries[129] and even partly with the United States, and while in other parts of the world, like Asia and Latin America, it presented itself as a possible alternative to the pound sterling, use of the pound in financing German foreign trade increased even more rapidly than that of the mark. Admittedly, German banks succeeded in winning market share, but they did so by strengthening their presence in the City and by continuing to use bills drawn on it denominated in sterling. Indeed, London's money market enjoyed advantages in terms of efficiency and costs that Berlin, like New York and Paris, was unable to compete with. Paradoxically, the growth in big German banks' business in relation to trade financing strengthened the London market more than it did the Berlin market.

The German capital's weight as a financial centre owed more to its position as the united Reich's financial centre than to its international influence. Furthermore, Berlin was not only an administrative and financial capital but also a major industrial centre – the second in Germany after the Ruhr – particularly for electrical engineering, with the presence of giant enterprises like AEG and Siemens. The big banks had also won praise by contributing to industrial growth. Their expansion abroad, the robustness of which impressed a number of contemporaries,[130] quickly enabled them to venture beyond the relatively narrow confines of Berlin's financial market.

The rising star: New York

New York's accession to the rank of foremost international financial centre took a different route from that followed by London, Paris and Berlin, even if the four centres had one thing in common: each was the financial centre of one of the four greatest economic powers of the day. New York's two distinctive features lay elsewhere. First, the city became a major financial centre as an entry point into a capital-importing country and not as an exit point from a capital-exporting country. Second, it mostly kept this status until 1914, by which time the United States had become the world's leading economic power. In 1870 America's GDP only just exceeded Britain's, even though the latter maintained its supremacy in the manufacturing sector, providing nearly one-third of world production. In 1914, on the other hand, it was on a par with that of Britain, Germany and France combined. Thus it hardly comes as a surprise that the United States' financial centre should become one of the main international financial centres.

Until the end of the nineteenth century, New York's role as an international financial centre was inversely in line with the big European centres – first and foremost London – importing capital on the west coast of the Atlantic and exporting it on the east coast. As for the financing of American foreign trade, this remained largely dependent on the City of London. So New York did not yet fulfil all the functions of a global international financial centre, but its importance became increasingly decisive for three reasons: the total amount of foreign investment in the United States, the dynamism of the American economy, and the city's position as the country's financial centre. On the eve of war, the United States was the top destination for overseas investment, having accumulated some $7 billion worth of liabilities, of which nearly two-thirds were from British creditors. Yet this foreign investment only made a limited contribution (less than 5% between 1799 and 1900 in net value) to the huge domestic accumulation of capital (nearly $60 billion during the same period), although its importance varied considerably between periods and sectors.[131] On the microeconomic level, the United States rapidly became the country of very large businesses, starting with the railway companies and followed by the industrial giants that sprang from the wave of mergers that left its mark on the final years of the nineteenth century. Financing for these companies was mainly obtained through New York's capital market, which continued to grow in importance during this period, whether measured against the volume of operations handled or against the calibre of its main players. At the dawn of the twentieth century, John Pierpont Morgan was unquestionably the world's top banker.

The investment banks

The investment banks, of which Morgans was one of the most distinguished representatives, formed the cornerstone of New York's financial centre. Revealingly, the most important among them were those that had the closest links to foreign financial centres, above all the City of London, thereby illustrating Wall Street's national and international roles. Most of the banking houses had been founded in the first half of the nineteenth century, but it was only from the 1870s that they really took off. They comprised two groups that were quite distinct in terms of their social and denominational origins: one Anglo-American and Protestant, which included J. P. Morgan & Co., Kidder Peabody & Co.

and Lee Higginson & Co. in its ranks; the other German and Jewish, with, among others, Kuhn, Loeb & Co., Speyer & Co. and J. & W. Seligman & Co.

J. P. Morgan & Co.'s origins lay partly in one of the City's main merchant banks, J. S. Morgan & Co, which bore the name of John Pierpont Morgan's father. After a short apprenticeship in his father's bank and several lucrative years in the banking business, in 1871 he became a partner in the Drexel & Co. bank,[132] whose leadership he took over six years later and which he renamed J.P. Morgan & Co. in 1895. Kidder Peabody was originally from Boston, where during the 1820s it started various banking and brokerage activities under the name of John E. Thayer. In 1865, when the last member of the Thayer family retired, three employees decided to keep the business going and formed a new general partnership that took the name of Kidder Peabody & Co. Lee Higginson & Co., also founded in Boston in 1845, offered investment services to a rich New England clientele after the American Civil War. Moreover, these two banks continued to be based in Boston, but strengthened their foothold in New York from the end of the nineteenth century.

Unlike the 'Anglo-American' investment bankers, who hailed mainly from the world of trade and finance, those of German Jewish origin, who had arrived in the United States during the 1840s and 1850s, tended to be of more modest extraction.[133] Most of them had started out as pedlars, before venturing into the retail or wholesale trade and then moving to New York to go into banking or finance. This was the case with Joseph Seligman, who left his native Bavaria in 1837 with $100 on him. He worked for a year in a shop in Pennsylvania and then became engaged in various peddling activities. His capital reached $500 in 1839, when two of his brothers, William and James, joined him, soon followed by four others. By 1843 they owned four shops in Alabama where, however, they felt rather cramped, and in 1846 they set up a haberdashery import company in New York. In 1850, at the height of the gold rush, two brothers went to San Francisco with $20,000 worth of goods. They sent gold from San Francisco to New York, then from there to London to pay for their wool and silk imports. When they opened their banking house, J. & W. Seligman & Co., in New York in 1862, they already had $1 million in equity capital at their disposal. They started to sell government bonds, particularly in Germany, during the American Civil War, before opening a branch in London in 1864, followed by others in Paris, Amsterdam and Berlin.

Abraham Kuhn, also originating from Bavaria, and his brother-in-law Salomon Loeb opened up an outfitter's together in Indiana around 1850 and moved to Cincinnati several years later, before setting up their banking house, Kuhn, Loeb & Co., in New York in 1867 and turning to selling government and railway bonds. The firm's fortune took a new turn from 1875, when Jacob Schiff arrived as a partner and lost no time in taking control and in making it the country's top investment bank for railway financing.[134] In this group, Speyer & Co., founded in 1845, was in some way the exception that proved the rule. Philip Speyer, belonging to a prominent banking family from Frankfurt, went to the United States with the specific goal of opening a branch of the parent company there – just like Auguste Belmont, the Rothschilds' representative in New York since 1837.

The position of the investment banks strengthened, above all in the national context, due to them financing the railways during the 1870s and 1880s and the large limited liability manufacturing companies in the 1890s, as well as to their role in the sweeping trend towards mergers at the turn of the twentieth century. This trend culminated in the founding of the United States Steel Corporation in 1901 – the largest enterprise ever created in the world, with share capital exceeding $1 billion for the first time. The investment banks' main task was to supply these firms with capital, usually through public issues. They could do this by providing them with capital when the companies were set up; they could contribute towards financing their growth by granting increases in capital; they could intervene in times of crisis by undertaking to reorganise their capital; finally, they could direct mergers and acquisitions by providing them with the capital needed to bring such operations to a successful conclusion. More often than not, they were present at each of these stages in a company's development, especially since privileged and lasting links developed quickly between a company and its banker. The banker not only played the role of the firm's financial advisor but was usually represented on its board of directors and was involved in running the business. Such services, epitomised by those offered by J. P. Morgan, probably had a positive impact on these companies' performance.[135]

Yet the investment banks' activities also took place in an international context. A larger or smaller proportion of the capital that they raised, depending on the company and the period, actually came from Europe, primarily Britain; the most powerful New York banking houses thus had a strong foothold in the City of London and, frequently, in one or more of the other European financial centres too.[136] J. P. Morgan & Co. held a special position owing to its connections with J. S. Morgan & Co. in London and with Morgan, Harjes & Cie in Paris, since John Pierpont Morgan, who inherited from his father, was a partner in both banks.[137] Family ties bound Speyers and Seligmans to the houses of London, Paris and Frankfurt.[138] Kidder Peabody was closely linked to Baring Brothers, for which it became the exclusive agent in the United States from 1886.[139] Jacob Schiff, the head of Kuhn, Loeb & Co., maintained social and business relations with his former compatriot, Ernst Cassel, as well as strengthening his firm's links with Warburg & Co., the bank from Hamburg that was on a roll from the 1890s onwards, particularly in issue activities.[140]

Other financial players

The capital of domestic origin available on the New York market was still the most important type of capital. Like the City's merchant banks, Wall Street's investment banks could call on the increasingly plentiful resources of the large American financial institutions, first of all the banks and insurance companies, to which they were connected through various links, particularly multiple overlapping directorships.

New York's national banks benefited from the status of central reserve city enjoyed by the United States' financial capital. New York was the only city granted this status until 1887, when Chicago and St Louis also obtained it, but it continued to attract the bulk of these funds. The centre's banks had to pay for these deposits, but they were able to put these resources to highly profitable use in New York itself, chiefly in short-term loans to brokers at the stock exchange, as well as on the capital market, particularly in the various issue syndicates managed by the investment banks.[141] By 1910 the deposits of other banking institutions represented nearly half the total of $1.3 billion deposited in New York's national banks.[142] Moreover, the biggest national banks were themselves involved in investment banking. This was the case with the National City Bank. During the 1890s, under the leadership of its chairman, James Stillman, it took up issue activities and, thanks to its network of relationships, won the accounts of numerous large American companies.[143] The National City Bank established itself as the country's largest bank at the turn of the century and came closer in size to the large European banks (see Table 3.3).

The trust companies and insurance companies also had a strong foothold in the capital market. The former, whose function initially consisted in collecting deposits from a better-off clientele than that of the numerous 'savings and loans' – American savings banks – and investing them in stocks and shares, turned into real banks at the end of the nineteenth century, without however being subject to the regulations of the national banks as far as reserves were concerned. The largest of them – Bankers Trust, Guaranty Trust Company of New York and Manufacturers Trust – outmatched most of the national banks in size and played a major role in financing companies through their investment and holdings in the various issue syndicates.[144] As for the insurance companies, especially those in life insurance, whose resources went from $403 million to $1.7 billion between 1875 and 1900, they purchased more and more shares in railway and manufacturing companies. But following the Armstrong Commission's findings, a law passed in 1906 prohibited them from taking part in issue syndicates.[145]

The New York Stock Exchange

The predominance of the New York Stock Exchange over the other American stock exchanges dates back to the telecommunications revolution, with the introduction of the telegraph in the mid-1840s, the ticker tape (which recorded the prices of all transactions and transmitted them to everybody who had subscribed to this service) in 1867 and the telephone in 1878. The prices listed in New York were known immediately and inevitably influenced those on the other stock exchanges. The New York Stock Exchange thus emerged as the United States' real national financial market, with 45% of the nominal value of the securities listed on all the American stock exchanges in 1912, but 69% of the total number of shares sold in the country in 1910 – and even 91% (in value) for bonds.[146]

The New York Stock Exchange had its own way of organising itself that differed from that of the three large European stock exchanges, which had repercussions on both the nature and the volume of its operations. Like the London Stock Exchange, that of New York was autonomous and did not benefit from any monopoly conferred upon it by a political authority, whether the city or state of New York or the federal government. But in contrast to London, the users of the stock exchange, in other words the members of the New York Stock Exchange, were also its owners, and a single management board ran the entire business. This goes some way towards explaining why the membership criteria, without being as restrictive as those at the Paris Bourse, were far stricter than those in London. The number of members, set at 1,060 in 1869, did actually go up to 1,100 in 1879 to finance the costs of equipping the building in Broad Street; but there was no further increase after this date despite the large growth in the volume of business, the nominal value of listed securities rising almost fivefold (from $4.2 to $19 billion) between 1879 and 1909.[147] As a result of this blockage, numerous brokers found themselves denied membership, either because of its price or the absence of an available vacancy, whereas the lack of members meant that the volume of business had to be limited.

The New York Stock Exchange was, therefore, driven to specialise in a certain type of stock – that of large companies with solid reputations. The committee meticulously examined the securities eligible for listing on the stock exchange list, more concerned with finding a reason for rejecting them than for accepting them. That is how it came to neglect the insurance companies and mining firms for a long time, favouring securities in the larger railway companies and then, at the beginning of the twentieth century, those in the large manufacturing companies. Another restriction imposed upon the members was the obligation to charge a fixed commission of $\frac{1}{8}$% on all transactions, whatever their amount, thus preventing any competition among them. Whereas the New York Stock Exchange was trying to win the general public's trust by posing as the guarantor of the quality of the securities listed there, these restrictive practices primarily benefited its own members, who thus enjoyed an absolutely guaranteed income. Such practices led to the development of rival New York stock exchanges; yet for all that, little harm was inflicted on its main activity.

In New York, various small, specialised markets merged in 1885 to create the Consolidated and Petroleum Stock Exchange, which offered railway company securities at half the rate of commission charged by the New York Stock Exchange, which reacted by forbidding its members to belong to both institutions and by endeavouring to cut all telegraphic or telephone communication between the two stock exchanges. Although it could not stifle the initiative, it succeeded in slowing the momentum of Consolidated, whose business and membership continued to decline. It nevertheless represented 13.4% of the number of shares sold on the American stock exchanges in 1910, which put it in second place behind the New York Stock Exchange. Relations were different with the curb market, an informal market where securities with a weak nominal value, mostly in mining firms, were traded in the street. The New York Stock Exchange tolerated the curb market without officially recognising it. In fact, it used the curb market's members (between 150 and 300 in 1908) to extend its own field of activity and remained in constant contact with it, so that about 85% of the curb market's business was conducted on behalf of members of the New York Stock Exchange. As for the main stock exchanges in other cities, they were used mainly to trade the securities of companies, not always small ones, that were well integrated into local networks. However, any firm expanding on a national scale tried to get a listing in New York.[148]

One of the factors that enabled the New York Stock Exchange to retain its pre-eminence was the fact that the commissions charged on operations between members were well below that of the $\frac{1}{8}$% imposed on external transactions. There were plenty of these internal transactions, especially because the regulations in force in New York, unlike those in London, did not require all the partners of a broker house to be members of the stock exchange. In reality, some partners were little more than sleeping partners, with stakes in large companies, but benefiting from the status of member through the broker that they financed, when it came to commissions. The volume of internal transactions naturally increased, while external funding flowed into the stockbroker houses, enabling these firms to reach a far greater size than in Paris and London.

Even more than the London Stock Exchange, the New York Stock Exchange played a crucial role in using short-term funding, especially for insurance companies and banks. In the absence of a discount market modelled on London's, which New York's financial circles would not get round to putting in place until the eve of the First World War, these funds made their way to the stock exchange. What is more, given that settlements took place on a daily basis in New York – unlike in London and Paris, where they were made once a fortnight – postponing the sale of a security until a more propitious moment usually meant having to borrow day-to-day funds that the banks were all the more willing to provide if they were extremely short term, hence in principle low risk.

Limited internationalisation

This way of organising the capital market, in many respects comparable to that of the City, continued to focus on financing American companies with the help of foreign capital. However, New York's international role began to grow as the first foreign issues were introduced at the beginning of the twentieth century. One of the most important in quantitative terms – £10 million – and intensely significant symbolically was the part of the British loan of August 1900 aimed at financing the Boer War, placed in the United States through John Pierpont Morgan. The issue was a resounding success and the American public subscribed for part of the four subsequent British war loans.[149] On the whole, the City was not too happy about resorting to the American market, fearing, as noted by a well-connected stockbroker, that 'permanent injury had been done to the London market by last year's arrangements. What had to be faced sooner or later was that New York would "cut out" London; and nothing had "put on the hands of the clock" in that direction so decidedly as these arrangements under which the example was set by the British Finance Minister.'[150]

The fear of future competition from New York could not have been more clearly expressed. But, for the time being, the City's position was secure, even if other major issues took place in New York, starting with the placing of $75 million worth of Japanese government bonds in 1905 by a syndicate under the leadership of Jacob Schiff. Nearly 250 foreign loans in total were issued in the United States between 1900 and 1913 for a nominal value of over $1 billion – for the most part, on behalf of European municipalities, principally German, as well as for consolidating the Mexican railways, organised by Kuhn Loeb and Speyers, and financing the electrification of the London underground, managed by the houses of Speyer in London and New York.[151]

New York's international influence was still somewhat limited. On the one hand, a legal brake was applied to American banks' expansion abroad until 1913.[152] On the other hand, few foreign banks set up on the banks of the Hudson, since the state of New York prohibited them from carrying out banking activities, such as collecting deposits, discounting and issuing loans, on its territory. They could, however, take part in financing foreign trade and operate on the foreign exchange market. This was how twenty foreign banks gained a foothold in New York in 1914. Eleven of them were British overseas banks,[153] five were Canadian banks, of which the most important was the Bank of Montreal, and the rest was made up of a Cuban bank, an Italian one, a Japanese one and a Czech one. Of possibly even more significance was the fact that none of the big British, French or German banks were represented. They made do with using the services of correspondents.[154]

At the end of the day, New York was still dependent upon the City of London. Beyond the vast exports of British capital to the United States, there was the far more sensitive issue of American foreign trade financing, a good part of which continued to be obtained by means of bills drawn on London, a situation that aroused resentment and envy among the bankers of Wall Street, just as it did in Paris and Berlin. The explanation for this lies partly in American banking legislation – until 1914 the national banks were not authorised to accept bills of exchange – and partly in the higher discount rates in New York than on the other main money markets, primarily London's. New York, and through it the entire American banking system, also depended on the City for obtaining liquid assets and, ultimately therefore, gold. Even though the United States had become the world's leading economic power, it was still a country that basically exported agricultural produce, with a markedly seasonal demand for credit from rural regions. Yet the American banking system, the bulk of whose resources was concentrated in New York, had great difficulty in coping with these fluctuations. This was due to the fragmentation of a system that prohibited networks of branches from being set up across different states, to the rudimentary nature of banking habits in rural areas and, finally, to the lack of a central bank. This dependency on London was, moreover, an ongoing source of instability for the international monetary system and could undermine it in times of crisis.

The most serious test came in October 1907. The crisis was primarily an American affair and it resulted in one of the biggest recessions that the country had ever seen.[155] It was caused by the failure of an attempt at cornering the copper market, involving several banks, particularly trust companies. A run on the most important of these, the Knickerbocker Trust Company, forced it to close its doors on 23 October and risked provoking a chain reaction. Panic was avoided and the situation re-established thanks to the joint intervention of the secretary to the Treasury, George Cortelyou, and of the banking community, led by John Pierpont Morgan. The former deposited $25 million in the main reserve banks in New York to enable it to cover withdrawals. The latter organised a pool of $25 million, followed by a second of $10 million, to prevent the stock exchange from collapsing. Morgan, then aged 70, came out of semi-retirement to act, single-handedly, virtually as a central bank. But the crisis took on an international dimension not only because of the interaction among financial centres, but because the inevitable tightening of the New York money market occurred at the height of demands for credit from cereal exporters – demands that could only be met by purchasing huge quantities of gold in London. The Bank of England had to raise its discount rate, at first to 6%, then to 7% at the beginning of November, its highest level since 1873, and maintained it until January 1908. While the British central bank was unable to check the flow of gold to the United States, it attracted it from twenty-four other countries and in fact forced the Banque de France to temporarily lend it £3 million worth of gold.[156] But it was a severe blow, with the prospect of an increase in the discount rate to 8% or even 9% paralysing the City until the situation had calmed down in the United States.

The Federal Reserve system

The vote in 1913 on the law establishing a Federal Reserve System was certainly influenced by the crisis of 1907 and by the desire not to leave the country's fate in the hands of one man, whatever the admiration aroused by Morgan in certain circles. It was also influenced by the evidence (including John Pierpont Morgan's) provided to the Pujo Commission[157] – appointed in 1912 to investigate the existence of a 'money trust', of the heavy involvement of bankers in the boards of directors of manufacturing companies, and of the concentration of issues in the hands of a few investment banks, cumulatively giving the impression that Wall Street was controlling the country's business.[158] The inquiry's findings were inconclusive, and the commission's recommendations (tighter control of the stock exchange and higher standards for presenting information in relation to issues) had no effect. But the fears aroused by the money trust helped overcome the resistance that for generations had prevented the creation of a central bank.[159]

The system established was, above all, aimed at solving the problem of the inelasticity of the money supply in the face of seasonal fluctuations in demand and of the absence of a lender of last resort. It did so by setting up a decentralised structure, dividing the country into twelve districts, each of which was provided with a Federal Reserve Bank located in the main city in the district[160] and whose capital had to be underwritten by the national banks and, ultimately, by the other local banks and trust companies that wanted to avail themselves of these new refinance facilities. The Federal Reserve banks had the power of rediscounting bills, serving as a clearing house for member banks and monitoring them. The entire system was overseen by the Federal Reserve Board, a body with eight members based in Washington and responsible for defining overall policy in agreement with the twelve Federal Reserve banks.

But the new system was also important for New York's international role. Real power lay in the hands of the New York Federal Reserve Bank, which had a number of prerogatives, particularly for anything relating to contacts with European central banks and to the foreign exchange markets. Its first governor, Benjamin Strong, former chairman of the Bankers' Trust, was a fully paid-up member of the east coast banking establishment. Relieved of their responsibilities for maintaining reserves and with a lender of last resort at their disposal, New York's national banks could henceforth embark on riskier ventures. They were also authorised to open branches abroad and to accept bills of exchange, a practice made possible by the rediscount facilities offered by the Federal Reserve Banks. The conditions were now ripe for developing a discount market in New York, able to rival London's. The outbreak of the First World War would provide it with exceptionally favourable opportunities for growth.

Niches and specialisations

Behind the financial centres of the world's four largest economic powers, several markets of lesser rank played a key role in international financial relations. These were primarily the financial capitals of the three countries with the highest per capita income in Europe after Britain: Belgium, the Netherlands and Switzerland – all three large providers of capital. Unable to compete on all fronts with the great centres, these markets tended to specialise in certain niches where they had a competitive advantage, while being integrated into the large international networks through which movements of capital flowed on a worldwide scale.

Brussels

Brussels probably ranked top among these centres and fourth in Europe, after London, Paris and Berlin. Its importance was mainly due to the international activity of the big Belgian banks, above all the Société Générale de Belgique, the tenth European bank in terms of its total assets in 1913, just behind the Dresdner Bank, but ahead of Barclays and the Disconto-Gesellschaft (see Table 3.3.) and way ahead of the biggest Swiss and Dutch banks.[161] The Société Générale de Belgique was not only big in size; during this period, it developed an extremely dynamic international strategy and, between 1891 and 1913, acquired holdings, usually with controlling stakes, in at least nineteen foreign banks and financial institutions, including 40% of the capital of the Banque de l'Union Parisienne.[162]

The international influence of Brussels was also linked to Belgian manufacturing companies abroad. In the last quarter of the nineteenth century, the need for capital on the part of the tramways, and then the power industries, took over from that of the railways, and their financing was mostly obtained through finance companies, set up by the banks, which usually took the form of holding companies.[163] Brussels was ideally placed to host the headquarters of these firms, owing to the plentiful Belgian domestic savings that preferred this type of investment to foreign government funds, to the not very restrictive legislation on companies, especially in fiscal matters, and finally to the country's neutrality, enabling these companies to attract foreign – mainly German and French – capital. One of the most important of these companies was the Société Générale des Chemins de Fer Economiques, founded in 1880 by various Belgian and French banks. By 1914 it had become one of the most powerful holding companies, with tramway firms in several countries, including Italy, Egypt and Spain,[164] while the Compagnie Générale des Chemins de Fer Secondaires, launched in 1880 by Belgian and German banks, owned tramway firms in Italy, Germany, Austria and Brazil.[165]

In the power industry, holding companies dated from the last years of the nineteenth century. In 1895 the Société Générale Belge d'Entreprises Electriques was created under the auspices of the Banque de Bruxelles, the Banque de Paris et des Pays-Bas and a German finance company, Gesfürel, which was a subsidiary of the electrical equipment manufacturer UEG.[166] The latter also acquired a large stake in a holding company destined for a great future, Sofina (Société Financière de Transports et d'Entreprises Industrielles), founded in 1898 by a group of private bankers that would later be joined by the Banque Liégeoise. On the eve of the war, the Société Générale Belge d'Entreprises Electriques, Sofina and the Société Générale des Chemins de Fer Economiques held more than Fr.700 million worth of holdings in tramways and power companies.

The private bankers thus continued to play a not insignificant role in the international activities of the Brussels centre, even if their importance inevitably declined from the end of the nineteenth century. Families like the Lamberts, Bischoffsheims, Goldschmidts and Oppenheims and their networks of cosmopolitan contacts unquestionably reinforced its international character. One of the most noteworthy success stories was that of the Banque Lambert,[167] to which Léon Lambert gave a new impetus, particularly through his support for King Leopold II's infamous exploits in the Congo.[168] Although fresh arrivals from abroad were less numerous than they had been, new native private banks came into being and contributed to the centre's dynamism, the most prominent of which was Josse Allard, particularly active in founding Belgian and foreign companies. And, of course, there was also Edouard Empain, a self-made man who made his fortune setting up transport companies and power firms and who founded his own bank, the Banque Empain, in 1881.

The private bankers who had been arriving in Brussels since the beginning of the nineteenth century were henceforth joined by the subsidiaries of the large European banks. There is no complete list available, but all the big French banks had branches there.[169] There were fewer German banks, only Deutsche Bank opening a branch in 1910, its third one abroad after those in London and Constantinople, the others working with correspondents or friendly banks in which, if need be, they had purchased a stake.[170] This was notably the case with the Banque Internationale de Bruxelles, created in 1898 and whose main shareholders were the Banque Centrale Anversoise (itself founded with German capital) and a group of German banks. The weight of the foreign banks was reflected in their holdings in new issues of Belgian companies, up from 6% in 1888 to 37% in 1911[171] – a degree of openness to international business that would be seen again in the late twentieth century.

Zurich, Geneva and Switzerland

In Switzerland, international financial activities remained less geographically concentrated than elsewhere, including in federal states like Germany or the United States. At the beginning of the 1870s, they were shared among Basel, Geneva and Zurich. On the eve of the First World War, none of these markets had attained a dominant position comparable to Brussels in Belgium or even to Berlin in Germany; but from then on, Zurich definitely outperformed the two border towns, at the same time as a certain division of labour became established among the three centres. Zurich's growth went hand in hand with the development of the Swiss economy, whose centre of gravity shifted with the arrival of electricity in the north-east of the Confederation. As the country's real industrial heartland, Zurich also benefited from the banking concentration that intensified towards the end of the nineteenth century: the share of bank deposits controlled by the big banks went from a mere 12% in 1880 to 27% in 1913.[172] It was these large institutions that, along with the private banks and finance companies, were the most active on the international scene, and most of them were based in Zurich. By 1908 the total assets of the four big Zurich banks represented 51% of those of the seven biggest Swiss banks, compared with 29% for Basel and 20% for Bern.[173] At that time, Geneva did not host the headquarters of even a single big bank, the Banque Générale Suisse having been wound up in 1869 and the Comptoir d'escompte de Genève only being considered a big bank after 1914. Two other categories of bank were also involved in international financial operations: finance companies and private banks. The first also had a strong foothold in Zurich, whereas the second, whose weight and influence should not be underestimated despite the lack of statistics, were more important in Basel and above all in Geneva.

A third factor confirmed Zurich's pre-eminence: the presence of the Swiss National Bank, founded in 1905 and operational in 1907. Switzerland was the last European country to be endowed with a central bank, some years before the United States. Arguments about creating a bank of issue had raged throughout the second half of the nineteenth century – interventionists versus non-interventionists and centralists versus federalists – leading to the scuppering of a number of bills and initiatives. Predictably, the central institution was a compromise between these diverse tendencies: it was a limited liability company with public shareholders (most of the shares being held by the cantonal governments) and private ones, enjoying considerable independence from the government, but with only limited means of intervention.[174]

The issue of its headquarters had always been a sensitive point in dis-cussions preceding the bank's foundation. It had even been the reason why an initial project had foundered in 1899. The choice was between Bern, the political capital, and Zurich, the country's economic centre. The compromise eventually reached accorded Bern the legal head-quarters and Zurich the administrative and banking headquarters of the new Swiss central bank.[175]

The big Swiss banks' influence on the international scene was limited until 1914. A not insignificant proportion of their assets was made up of overseas assets (55% in 1906 and 32% in 1913), but these banks had very little physical presence outside their country's borders.[176] In 1910 the Crédit Suisse founded the Schweizerische-Argentinische Hypothe-kenbank, with a capital of Fr.10 million, after a very promising report had been published on opportunities for developing this type of bank in Argentina; the country was in need of capital to exploit its natural resources and improve its agricultural production, and the normal Argentine interest rate of 8% yielded a sizeable profit margin on banking business.[177] The Hypothekenbank's success led the Crédit Suisse to set up the Schweizerisch-Südamerikanische Bank (Banco Suizo-Sudamer-icano) in 1912, with a view to developing banking operations between Europe and South America while fostering trade links between Switzerland and Argentina.[178] The only other example of a Swiss bank abroad was the London branch of the Swiss Bank Corporation, opened in 1898.[179] The Swiss Bank, as it was then called in London, quickly created a niche for itself in the City. It was particularly active in monetary transactions, arbitrage on currencies, executing stock-exchange orders, discounting and accepting bills of exchange, as well as in participating in issue syndicates. In 1912 the Swiss Bank Corporation also opened a branch in the west end of London to increase its share in foreign exchange operations and in the various transactions connected with tourism.[180]

Although smaller in size, Geneva was in many respects a more cos-mopolitan financial centre than Zurich, largely on account of its privi-leged links with France, as in previous decades. First of all, Geneva attracted more foreign banks than Zurich, where there were hardly any before the 1920s. Two big French banks opened branches in Geneva in the 1870s: the Banque de Paris et des Pays-Bas in 1872, the year of its foundation, and the Crédit Lyonnais in 1876. Geneva was part of the *système Paribas*, the Parisian *banque d'affaires*' international expansion strategy, which spread in concentric circles from the Parisian head-quarters to the three branches in Amsterdam, Brussels and Geneva, and then to the main foreign capital markets, through a complex network of subsidiaries and correspondents.[181] The reasons for opening up a branch of the Crédit Lyonnais in Geneva in 1876 are not very well documented, but they were mainly due to the financial and trading links between Geneva, Lyons and the Rhone valley. Switzerland's membership of the Latin Monetary Union – French, Swiss and Belgian francs and the Italian lira all had exactly the same value and circulated freely within the Union – could also offer an explanation, as could the existence of the free zones of Upper Savoy and the Gex region, which gave Geneva an economic hinterland in neighbouring France.[182] The Genevan market nevertheless had its own appeal for the French bank.[183] Among other things, the Geneva branch provided wealth management services to a rich French and Swiss clientele and used the funds collected by other branches and by the registered office in Lyons, overwhelmingly in short-term investments.[184] Alongside these two French banks, other foreign banks also opened branches, albeit short-lived ones, in Geneva during the decades preceding the First World War.[185]

But Geneva's international character came above all from its private banks, of which the ten most important at the time were: Bonna, Chenevière, Darier, Ferrier Lullin, Galopin Forget, Hentsch, Lenoir Poulin, Lombard Odier, Mirabaud and Ernest Pictet.[186] Although easily outmatched in size by the big banks, they did well in a Swiss banking system that was still highly fragmented. They were able to preserve a niche in which they had a unique competitive advantage, based on a well-established reputation for financial expertise, their network of international contacts and Switzerland's budding role as a haven for foreign capital. The activity of the Genevan private banks was not, however, limited to wealth management. They were actively involved in the various trades of the merchant banks, above all in issue activities. Following the tradition of cooperation instituted from the 1840s by the Quatuor, the Omnium and the Association financière de Genève, they founded the Union Financière de Genève in 1890, with a capital of Fr.12 million, created from the merger of the Association financière and the Banque nouvelle des chemins de fer.[187] The centre's ten leading private banking houses were involved in setting it up, and their heads formed its entire first board of directors. The Union Financière, whose purpose was to 'handle all financial operations in Switzerland or abroad or to participate in them', offered them the possibility of taking part in loan issues and in financing companies that were beyond the individual capacities of each of them. It acquired a holding in the issue syndicates and then shared it among the members of the group.[188]

The Union Financière was particularly active in setting up or leading a series of joint ventures, known in Switzerland under the name of 'holding companies', in various regions or economic sectors.[189] For Geneva, the preferred regions were France, Italy and the United States, while, like elsewhere in Switzerland, the dominant sector was electricity. One man played a pioneering role in this: Guillaume Pictet, senior partner of the House of Pictet & Cie, who after two trips to the United States was quick to realise that the securities of companies producing and distributing electricity represented an interesting and fairly low-risk alternative to the railway bonds to which most of his Swiss colleagues limited themselves when investing across the Atlantic.[190]

The holding companies were not the preserve of the Genevan market but were also much in evidence in Basle and above all in Zurich. More so than the big banks or even the private banks, it was in fact finance companies that constituted the backbone of Switzerland's role on the international capital market during the quarter of a century before the First World War. Their importance stemmed essentially from their contribution towards developing the power industry via their links with big German banks and electrical engineering companies. Indeed, Swiss finance companies played a key role in the so-called *Unternehmensgeschäft* strategy adopted by German manufacturers of electrical equipment, faced with still wavering investors, which consisted in financing their client companies (tramway and lighting companies, among others) via finance companies set up to offload the weight of these loans from the balance sheets of the electrical engineering firms. The most commonly used method was that of securities substitution, since securities in finance companies found buyers in the general public more readily – at least to begin with.[191]

The most important of these companies was the Bank für elektrische Unternehmungen, better known as Elektrobank. It was founded in Zurich in 1895 by the German electrical engineering giant AEG and a group of German and Swiss banks, led by the Berliner Handels-Gesellschaft, Deutsche Bank and the Crédit Suisse.[192] Under the *de facto* control of AEG, Elektrobank operated in Germany, Italy, Latin America, Spain and Russia. The Société Suisse pour l'Industrie Electrique (Indélec) was founded the following year in Basle at the instigation of AEG's great rival, Siemens, with a nominal capital of Fr.10 million. Operating in Russia, Italy, Germany and France, Indélec was, however, less sound than Elektrobank, due to the relative weakness of the group of banks associated with Siemens.[193] Lastly, in Geneva, the Union Financière, the Banque de Paris et des Pays-Bas and the French industrial concern Schneider & Cie took part in founding the Société Franco-Suisse pour l'Industrie Electrique in 1898, with contributions from the Crédit Suisse and the Swiss Bank Corporation. In spite of

Schneider's involvement, the Genevan holding company decided from the outset not to link up with a manufacturer of electrical equipment, though its activities remained chiefly focused on France.[194]

The competitive advantage enjoyed by Switzerland was mainly thanks to legislation on holding companies that was far more liberal than that in force in Germany at the time.[195] Added to this was the boon of Swiss neutrality, which could give German groups access to politically sensitive markets, as well as the Swiss banks' experience in dealing with finance companies, their recognised expertise in the power industry and their geographical and linguistic proximity to Germany and, to a lesser extent, France.

Competition and cooperation

Discussing the role of the main financial centres at the time of the world's first phase of globalisation has given us an insight into two apparently contradictory aspects of their relations – intense competition and cooperation that took a multitude of forms. This point is worth exploring further, by distinguishing among three different levels of interaction: that of the firm, that of the financial centre and that of the national economy.

Interaction among the players

Relations among the financial centres essentially took the form of business ties among firms operating in those centres. These ties strengthened from the last quarter of the nineteenth century, thanks to the absence of any constraints on the free movement of capital and to ever-faster telecommunications. This resulted in ever-closer integration among the main international financial centres, which were beginning to form, within certain limits, a genuine international capital market.

On the level of the primary market, one of the clearest indications of this integration was the simultaneous floating of an issue in several financial centres. There are no precise statistics available, but this practice became commonplace at the beginning of the twentieth century. It was the case, for example, for the Argentine loans issued in London by Baring Brothers in cooperation with the Banque de Paris et des Pays-Bas in Paris and with the Disconto-Gesellschaft in Berlin. Several issues of shares in railway companies, soon followed by those in other sectors of activity or in companies like AT&T, were floated simultaneously in New York and London.[196] On the level of the secondary market, the financial centres grew closer through international arbitrage operations.[197] The success of such operations, which involved buying stock in one centre and reselling it in another, taking advantage of the price differential between the two, meant that the same security had to be quoted in at least two centres, that there had to be a sufficiently developed secondary market to enable immediate buying and selling, and that information could circulate quickly enough between the two centres. These three conditions were indeed met with increasing frequency from the 1880s onwards.

More and more securities were quoted in at least two centres: American railway securities in London and Amsterdam by 1873, Brazilian government bonds in Paris and London by 1891, Argentine government bonds in London and Berlin by 1892, shares in electric traction companies from all over the world in London and Brussels by 1914, to cite just a few examples of relations between London and each of the main European financial centres. But it was the links between London and New York that were by far the closest. In 1884, £571 million worth of government bonds and railway company securities were listed in the two centres. The figure came to £2.09 billion in 1914, not counting municipal bonds and securities in commercial and manufacturing companies like US Steel. A number of securities were traded in several centres and they became genuine international stocks, starting with those in the large North American railway companies that were listed on the New York, London, Berlin, Frankfurt, Amsterdam and, to a lesser extent, Paris stock exchanges from the 1870s onwards. They were followed by those in South African gold mines, like Rand Mines or the Central Mining Corporation, traded on all the main European markets and, of course, in South Africa, where there was intense stock-market activity during the boom of the 1890s; then by those in manufacturing companies, like Nobel Dynamite Trust and US Steel, which continued to grow in importance in the early twentieth century.

At the same time, instantaneous information on the conditions prevailing in several markets became widely available. It was, however, only of interest to a limited number of brokerage houses with international contacts. Due to the complexity of arbitrage operations, some of these houses came to monopolise this type of operation and often specialised in a particular part of the world or in a specific sector. In 1909 only 262 firms, out of the approximately 1,500 on the London Stock Exchange at that time, formed a partnership with a firm in another centre with a view to conducting arbitrage operations. But they had an extremely wide network of relationships: 102 of them reported having a link with a European financial centre (including 27 with Paris, 16 with Amsterdam and Brussels, and 13 with Berlin) and 60 with North America (including

39 with New York). Less is known about relations between the main
financial centres over and above their links with London. There were
certainly fewer of them and they were probably less important, since it
was London that was located at the hub of this truly international
financial market. More than any other financial centre, the City was the
conduit for information coming from the four corners of the world and it
benefited from a volume effect on account of the size and liquidity of the
London Stock Exchange, as well as the large proportion of foreign
securities quoted there. Unlike those of Paris and Berlin, the London
Stock Exchange was not subject to any interference from the government apart from a stamp duty, which was generally lower than that
charged in New York and in the other main European centres. Its
internal regulations, especially the division of labour between jobbers
and brokers, could have hindered international arbitrage operations if
they had been properly enforced, but a pragmatic attitude prevailed, no
doubt facilitated by the fact that these operations involved only a small
number of firms, and the market was able to benefit from the flexibility
needed to undertake international transactions.

Cooperation among financial centres, or rather among the banking
houses operating in different centres, thus seemed to be the dominant
characteristic as far as both the issuing and trading of securities was
concerned. Competition among firms took place primarily within a
given financial centre; in other words, in the same place that they
conducted their business or negotiated contracts. In the case of big
international business, competition was not so much between the various centres as between rival groups and syndicates composed of companies operating in each of these different centres or on the international
capital market. It was, above all, typical of newcomers and, to a lesser
extent, of lower-ranking banking houses, whereas the leading lights in
the large centres were far more respectful of the territory that had traditionally been reserved for each of them.

Competition between financial centres

Even if the rivalry between the financial centres was not as intense as the
rivalry that had pitted London against Paris under the Second Empire,
there was nevertheless a degree of competition – though, in practice, it
was latent rather than real. It was mainly over capturing certain markets.
An illustration of this is Berlin's attempt to take over part of the
acceptance market from London immediately following German
reunification – more specifically, as we have seen, to take over acceptances aimed at financing German foreign trade. Similar intentions were

expressed in New York and began to take shape with the creation of the Federal Reserve System in 1913. From the early twentieth century, the City's bankers, anticipating the future, began to fear that the market for foreign issues would shift to New York. The possibility of trading securities in several financial centres also fostered competition among national financial markets: quite apart from arbitrage opportunities, a security listed on several markets was likely to be traded in the one offering the most favourable terms. Furthermore, this rivalry among financial centres was not free from a certain degree of nationalism. Even if the competition against London from Paris, New York and Berlin in all these fields should not be underestimated – as can be seen from the 'key currency' status enjoyed by the franc and the mark – the City's status as the only real global financial centre went unchallenged until 1914.

Finance and international politics

The large-scale international financial operations directed from the main financial centres were not, however, always purely commercial in nature. At a time of rivalry among the great powers, they were often subject to important political, strategic and diplomatic pressures. Such circumstances could make it difficult for bankers and financiers in different financial centres to cooperate with each other, or they could even foster competition among national groups and syndicates usually operating under the aegis of their government. Nevertheless, these circumstances were the exception rather than the rule for two main reasons. The first was that the big bankers and financiers preferred, less by inclination than by necessity, working within the framework of alliances or simply international coalitions, especially in a fraught diplomatic climate. The second was that areas of friction where political intervention relied on economic and financial weapons were relatively few and far between before 1914. The main examples were the Ottoman Empire and China, often described as semi-colonies – in other words, countries that were subjected to various forms of interventions and breaches of their national sovereignty, while remaining formally independent. Africa and the rest of Asia were under colonial rule. As for Latin America, the various forms of meddling and domination to which it was subjected remained, for the most part, of a purely economic nature.

Power struggles in the Ottoman Empire and China intensified from the 1890s and resulted in them being divided into spheres of influence, following complex negotiations on the eve of the war. In the meantime, these countries were mainly infiltrated by organising large loans on behalf of the local authorities and by obtaining railway concessions, the position of national financial groups being underwritten by their respective governments. In the Ottoman Empire, Paris used the Imperial Ottoman Bank, Berlin used Deutsche Bank and London used the National Bank of Turkey.

In China, the European powers' interests were represented by the Banque de l'Indochine, the Deutsche Asiatische Bank and the Hongkong and Shanghai Banking Corporation. Gravitating around these banks and a few others, like the Banque de Paris et des Pays-Bas in France, were groups of businesses comprising manufacturing, merchant and finance companies. These groups, whose top managements were located in the main international financial centres, maintained competitive and cooperative relations that varied according to the business opportunities available and the political initiatives undertaken by their governments.

These episodes made up the dramatic moments in the history of relations between high finance and imperialism. In reflecting upon relations between the financial centres, it is important to bear in mind that financial interests and political issues were closely intertwined. Businessmen can, of course, be seen as individuals who are, above all, pragmatic and preoccupied with developing their businesses while steering clear of political and ideological conflicts. This was, for example, the case when the Baghdad railway was built from 1889. Deutsche Bank's managers, who were in charge of the project, endeavoured to secure international financing for it and to attract British and French capital, despite opposition from the British and French governments. In any case, Franco-German cooperation, especially with the Banque de Paris et des Pays-Bas, continued on an unofficial basis right up until the eve of war.[198] But at the same time, the financial circles' pragmatism led them to use their government's support, as far as possible, to strengthen their position against foreign groups, as shown by the complex interplay of alliances and rivalries to obtain concessions in China following its defeat against Japan in 1895.

The *Belle Epoque* of the bankers

The height of the first phase of globalisation between 1900 and 1914 – the Edwardian age in England and the Belle Epoque in France – was truly a golden age for the world of banking and finance. It was partly the result of economic circumstances that were conducive to them and partly the successful outcome of the slower-paced development of social structures that lasted throughout the nineteenth century. While it was a flourishing era for everyone, there were differences, nonetheless, among the bankers and financiers in the main financial centres – differences in wealth, in socioprofessional status or in their degree of integration into the country's elites. These differences, one suspects, were not so much the consequence of one centre's international influence as the sociocultural context within which business life operated.

Wealth

The prime indicator of this golden age was the bankers, and financiers' material wealth. In Europe, they became, as a group, the wealthiest businessmen in their countries.[199] In Germany, 27% of business leaders worth $1.5 million (6 million marks) or more in 1911 were bankers, compared with 12% for ironmasters – the country's most powerful group of industrialists – and far lower percentages for other categories of businessmen.[200] Germany's richest bankers were not, however, all Berliners. In spite of its decline, Frankfurt continued to harbour great wealth, chiefly that of the Rothschild family.[201] But it was in Berlin that bankers were most numerous and, above all, it was there that the managers of the big banks were to be found – some of them drawing a salary and yet possessing vast fortunes. Arthur Gwinner at Deutsche Bank, Carl Fürstenberg at the Berliner Handels-Gesellschaft and Eugen Gutmann at the Dresdner Bank each owned just under $4 million (16 million marks) in 1913 – a fortune only exceeded in Berlin by that of private bankers.[202]

In Britain, bankers and financiers represented approximately 20% of the businessmen worth $2.5 millions (£500,000) or more who died between 1900 and 1939.[203] Even if it is not easy to make a comparison with Germany, it can be estimated that there were far more rich bankers and financiers in London than in Berlin.[204] The level of fortune was also higher in London, with a good half a dozen bankers and financiers worth $12 million (£2.5 million) or more, compared with not a single one in Berlin. This comes as little surprise; there were far more business opportunities in the City and, moreover, Berlin was handicapped by its relatively recent status as Germany's financial centre, as shown by the share of big banking fortunes retained by Frankfurt.

There are few comparable data available on France, as existing studies make few distinctions among categories of businessmen.[205] But if the concentration of millionaires in Paris and the vast fortunes of several *régents* of the Banque de France studied by Alain Plessis are taken into account, bankers and financiers must have made up a far from insignificant proportion of French millionaires.[206] The situation was somewhat different in the United States, mainly due to a level of wealth that was incomparably higher than in Europe. Whatever the differences among European countries, fortunes were roughly the same size. Across the Atlantic, the greatest fortunes reached $1 billion in the early twentieth century – an amount at least twelve times higher than the largest British fortune at the time.[207] Bankers were less wealthy, however. When Pierpont Morgan died in 1914, leaving an inheritance of $80 million, John D. Rockefeller is said to have announced: 'And to think – he wasn't even a wealthy man.'[208] Nevertheless, in spite of all the great fortunes made in industry in America, even more so than in Germany, the position of the banking and financial elites, forming 14% of the New York's largest fortunes in 1892, was still an enviable one.[209]

Social status

In all the financial centres, bankers and financiers led an aristocratic lifestyle. They lived in the most elegant neighbourhoods: Mayfair and Belgravia in London, the 8th or 16th *arrondissement* in Paris, the Tiergarten in Berlin or 5th Avenue in New York. Furthermore, most of them also had a residence or mansion in the countryside or abroad. Being a member of a prestigious club was also a sign of belonging to the upper echelons of society, especially in London, as well as in Paris and New York,[210] but less so in Berlin, where in any case social life was not as intense as in the other large financial cities.

Despite these similarities, the financial elites did not hold the same social position in their respective counties. In Britain, the City's bankers formed the country's dominant business group; on the whole, they were richer, more integrated into the old aristocracy and closer to political power than the industrialists from the north of the country – the division between the bourgeoisie of national standing and the bourgeoisie in the provinces broadly corresponding to the separation between the City and industry. Such a division between the capital city and the regions was even more pronounced in France but did not correspond to a division between finance and industry. The industrialists were better integrated into the upper classes than in Britain – if one thinks, for example, of steel magnates like Eugène Schneider or François de Wendel – and the French business upper-middle class was well established in Paris.

In this respect, New York had more in common with Paris than Berlin did. Indeed, the 1880s and 1890s saw an American business upper-middle class, mainly based in New York and within which bankers and industrialists held a privileged position, come into being to the detriment of the former commercial elite, typically New York based. The German upper-middle class, on the other hand, remained geographically divided. Berlin, the Reich's financial and political capital, as well as a major industrial centre, especially for electrical engineering, was not the capital for the country's leading group of businessmen, the industrialists of the Ruhr; while maintaining a political presence in Berlin, they continued to be based in Düsseldorf, Cologne and Essen. Moreover, the German business elite was far less integrated into the upper classes, which were dominated by a very inward-looking landed aristocracy, than its French and British counterparts were. Socially, it remained an isolated and introverted group, as shown among other things by its high level of intermarriage.

Another difference in the sociocultural structures of the main financial centres partly explains the privileged position held by the City's bankers: the religious factor. In Britain, the financial elites were not mainly composed of members of religious minorities. Most English bankers were Anglicans. There were, of course, some groups of non-conformists, primarily the Quakers, who had a strong foothold in the world of banking, but most of them had rejoined the Anglican Church by the turn of the twentieth century. It is generally believed that the merchant bankers were mostly foreign and Jewish. This was not the case at the highest level of the social and professional hierarchy, fairly well represented by the directors of the Bank of England. In fact, the only Jewish banker to accede to the court of directors of this institution before 1914 was Alfred de Rothschild. On a smaller scale, the position of the Genevan private bankers resembled that of their counterparts in the City – Protestant for the most part, they had no connections with any religious minority but, on the contrary, commanded a leading position among the city's elites.

In New York, the influential people within aristocratic banking – in other words, the investment bankers – were also Protestant, yet they included a significant number of Jews, who tended to be socially cut off from Yankee circles. The situation was somewhat different in Paris, where the *haute banque*, although quite varied from a denominational point of view, mainly comprised members of the Protestant and Jewish minorities. Finally, in Berlin, aristocratic banking was almost exclusively Jewish and, therefore, was less likely to become integrated into the dominant elite for which, as in Britain and to a lesser extent France, the old aristocracy continued to serve as a role model.

Benefits and costs

Did the international activities of the main financial centres benefit solely the bankers and financiers who stood at the helm? The question may seem trite, but it is worth asking by way of conclusion to this chapter, if only in the light of bankers' wealth during the *Belle Epoque*. It is a huge question that concerns the benefits and costs generated by the activities in these centres. It will be tackled briefly on two levels: the national economy, and the world economy.

Hosting a large international financial centre is nowadays seen as being particularly beneficial to the host country. The question was seen in a somewhat different light before 1914. At that time, it was much more closely linked to the country's trade and financial balance. In the case of the City, British political and economic leaders were very keenly aware how vitally important the income from its financial activities and that of some other centres – like Liverpool or Glasgow – was in maintaining the British balance of payments. In fact, since the income from commercial services, insurance and the merchant navy counterbalanced the traditional trade deficit, the balance of goods and services[211] was stable on the eve of war; so much so that the surplus on the British current account was entirely due to interest and dividends drawn from overseas investment, which exceeded £100 million net at the beginning of the century, and it was these that fed the flow of foreign investment. But dissenting voices were already making themselves heard, denouncing the negative effects of these capital exports on national growth.[212]

In France, the same concerns crystallised in the famous controversy that pitted Lysis against Testis in the 1900s. Lysis – the pseudonym of the journalist Eugène Letailleur – criticised the banks for their tendency to favour foreign investment that was not only risky but also diverted funds from national industry. Testis – probably the pseudonym of Alexis Rostand, general manager of the Comptoir national d'escompte de Paris – defended foreign investment, emphasising the higher interest rates offered abroad, the positive effects of capital exports on the export of goods,[213] and the diplomatic advantages that the country could derive from it.[214]

Recent research however, has, shown that capital exports barely affected the economies of centre countries. But was this also the case for those on the periphery? On the whole, there is little doubt that capital transfers, which constituted an international financial centre's *raison d'être*, played a positive role in their economic development. There were, of course, major differences among countries and regions depending on the period. Government loans were certainly not always put to productive use, whether in connection with military expenditure or, more often, with servicing an already contracted debt. The bankers and financiers in the main financial centres often 'forced' weak states to borrow beyond their means. It is, nevertheless, a fact that significant achievements were made, especially in infrastructure: railways, roads, docks, ports, power stations and urban development. These achievements enabled natural resources to be developed and exported, thus stimulating economic growth; and only foreign capital could ensure their success.

But at what price? From a strictly financial perspective, the cost of a loan was linked to the risks that the market associated with it – risks that the financial centres tried to assess as best they could. Banks undertook their own analyses: the Crédit Lyonnais, for example, was one of the first to have its own financial research service, set up in 1871.[215] The financial press and specialised publications, like *Fenn's Compendium*, appearing in London each year, published their own assessments. The criteria used at the time were not exactly the same as those in use today: the borrowing country's adherence to the gold standard was seen as a guarantee of good financial order;[216] membership of the British Empire provided additional assurance.[217] But, from the 1890s, a country's ability to shoulder its debt burden was mainly evaluated on the basis of its budget – more precisely through the ratio between the total annual cost of servicing its debt and its income from taxes. The higher this ratio, the bigger the risk was judged to be and the higher the rate of interest charged. For a long time, interest rates remained higher for countries that had defaulted, even after steps had been taken to realign the economy.[218] This apparently merciless analysis tends to underestimate the market's subjective judgements, but it is accurate on the whole. Borrowing on the international capital market was more expensive for Turkey than for Argentina or Russia, and even more expensive than for Australia or Japan.

Indebtedness could, however, have another price – one far more difficult to assess from a financial perspective. Was it by pure coincidence that the two main capital-exporting countries, Britain and France, were also the main colonial powers? The question not only preoccupied contemporaries but lay at the heart of debates on imperialism for several generations. In a famous book published in 1902, *Imperialism: A Study*, the English liberal economist John A. Hobson was the first to try and put forward a comprehensive explanation of imperialism, more specifically British imperialism, in terms of defending the financial interests at whose heart the City lay. Inspired by the writings on financial capital by the German economist Rudolf Hilferding, Lenin described imperialism as the ultimate stage of capitalism – that in which the division of the world among the colonial powers would follow on from its initial division among large capitalist groups. Over the last twenty years or so, these analyses have lost a great deal of their impact, and there is no longer any debate nowadays over whether the financial interests concentrated in London, Paris or Berlin were the driving force behind the spread of imperialism at that time. But the traditional argument espoused by those advocating the primacy of politics over economics, namely that the colonies acquired from the 1880s, when imperialist rivalry was at its height, received a mere fraction of the foreign investment, also seems somewhat trite. More attention is paid today to the complexities of the issue, especially to the at times artificial nature of the distinction between formal empire and informal domination, or to the interweaving of political and financial interests, which are not always easy to dissociate or put in order of priority. One only has to think, for example, of the Ottoman Public Debt Administration, established in 1880 and which directly managed part of Turkey's income; or of the occupation of Egypt in 1882 by British troops, whose primary motivation is open to debate *ad infinitum* – protecting bondholders or protecting the route to India? – or even of the controversy surrounding economic imperialism in Latin America. As far as the City of London was concerned, its role was not so much attributable to the financial circles manipulating political power as to the long-underestimated place held by London and, more generally, by the service sector in British economy, society, politics and diplomacy. P.J. Cain and A.G. Hopkins fully capture this context with the concept of 'gentlemanly capitalism' which they believed constituted the main dynamics in British overseas expansion.[219]

Imperialism was one of the major features characterising the first phase of globalisation, and the main international financial centres were fully engaged in it. First, because of the part played by the colonial economies in their business – a part that, as we have seen already, varied according to the location and the field of activity but was in no way insignificant. Next, because of their nationalism, their support for their governments' expansionist policies, even if it was sometimes critical, and their value systems that were deeply marked by the imperialist culture of the day. Ferdinand de Rothschild 'would cheer the Union Jack planted on every island of the Polynees, on every crag of the Himalayas, and on every minaret of the East ... '[220] and the members of the London Stock Exchange gave a rowdy demonstration of nationalism when the Boer War broke out in October 1899.[221]

This adherence to the prevailing nationalism of the day fluctuated and certainly did not imply that the businessmen who kept the wheels of the main international centres turning hankered after war between the great powers. On the contrary, trading, banking and financial activities flourish in times of peace, not in times of war. The financial circles did not really seek to reconcile nationalism and imperialism, or the risks of war and demands of peace, for the prosperity of their business. This is probably what explains the huge success of the book by the liberal journalist Norman Angell, *The Great Illusion*, published in 1910. For Angell, European countries had become so interdependent economically and financially that war risked ruining both the victor and the vanquished. A conqueror harming his adversary's trade or finance would suffer similar losses in return. While having some grounds for hope, bankers and financiers, at least the most clear-sighted among them, were well aware of the danger. 'War will still remain a possibility',[222] declared Frederic Huth Jackson, chairman of the Institute of Bankers in London, at a meeting devoted to discussing Angell's book in January 1912. When war broke out in August 1914, bankers and financiers were, on the whole, not in favour of it. But never mind! It was not their decision – and, even if they regretted it, they supported their government and were prepared to follow it.

4   Wars and depression, 1914–1945

On 4 August 1914, the day that Britain declared war on Germany, Gaspard Farrer, one of Baring Brothers' partners, noted in a letter: 'It is mortifying in the extreme to find how instantaneously the credit edifice which we have built for generations could tumble to pieces in a night.'[1] At the time, this view was widely shared in the major international financial centres. Nevertheless, few imagined that it would soon be known as the Great War. In this respect, Farrer's remark was fairly typical of bankers' short-sighted yet premonitory views. While being preoccupied above all by the serious crisis suddenly facing the City's accepting houses, at the same time he had a foreboding of a phenomenon on an altogether different scale – that of the end of an era, or of the transition from one economic order to another.

The period described by the historian Eric Hobsbawm as 'the age of catastrophe'[2] had profound repercussions on life in the international financial centres. Two world wars and the most severe economic crisis of the twentieth century indeed brought about major changes in the world economic and political order, the most important of which was the transfer of world leadership from Britain to the United States. This inevitably had an impact on the power struggle between Wall Street and the City. The financial centres were also affected by the vagaries of the international monetary system, with the suspension of the gold standard during the hostilities, its awkward restoration in the post-war period and its collapse in the early 1930s. The other significant change concerned continental Europe. Germany's rise was temporarily halted, whereas France was initially given a boost before having its momentum slowed by the Great Depression and then the rout of 1940 and the occupation. For the financial centres, this meant Berlin's decline during the 1920s and even more so during the 1930s, then its complete disappearance as such after Germany was defeated in 1945. For its part, Paris continued to play a leading role until the beginning of the 1930s, when it experienced a long eclipse. At the same time, the financial centres in small, neutral countries like the Netherlands and above all

Switzerland grew in importance during these times of monetary and political crises.

It is important to note that these changes were gradual and took nearly thirty years to be completed. New York did not replace London overnight in its role as the world's financial centre. In many respects, the City retained its top rank during the interwar years and the pound was only permanently replaced by the dollar as the main trading and reserve currency after 1945. The large economies continued to carry weight; until its autarchic retreat after the advent of National Socialism, Berlin remained a very active centre, even if Germany then became a capital-importing country. The significance of Amsterdam during the twenties and of Zurich during the Second World War was linked mainly to economic and financial trade with Germany. Changes were even slower, not to say non-existent, at world level. The challenge that certain countries, especially Japan, were able to pose to the old developed nations in staple industries did not give rise to new financial centres on a truly international scale.

Nevertheless, these permutations in the ranking of the financial centres, however important, were not the overriding concern of the time. On a political level, the period was overshadowed above all by the advent of totalitarian regimes – fascist Italy, Nazi Germany and the Stalinist Soviet Union – which pervaded every aspect of the history of the twentieth century and did not spare that of the financial centres. On an economic level, August 1914 put a brake on the first phase of globalisation at world level and ushered in an era of national or imperial retreat. While the illusion that the pre-war order could be re-established for good lingered throughout the 1920s, it was dispelled once and for all by the Great Depression, the symbolic turning point being the devaluation of the pound sterling and Britain's abandonment of the gold standard in September 1931. The activities of the international financial centres, already disrupted by the repercussions of the First World War, were henceforth curtailed or even brought to a standstill by the collapse in world trade, the introduction of exchange controls or other measures aimed at stemming capital flows, competitive devaluations, protectionist policies, the threat of war and, finally, the upheavals caused by the Second World War.

The Great War

International financial centres prosper in times of peace, not in times of war. Indeed for most bankers and financiers, the war meant a marked decrease in their activities, owing of course to disruptions in the trading of goods, services and capital among countries, as well as to growing state intervention in economic and financial affairs. A large number of services traditionally offered by the banks were henceforth superfluous, like commercial credit or issue syndicates, since governments at war tend to pay companies upfront or to borrow directly from savers.

Crisis management

During the final days of July and the early days of August 1914, growing rumours of war and then the outbreak of hostilities plunged all the financial centres into a deep crisis. The collapse of stock exchanges, interest rate rises, the withdrawal of funds from banks and, its corollary, the banks' demand that loans be repaid, on top of which came the risk of non-payment, cumulatively threatened to trigger off a series of bankruptcies and paralyse the entire credit mechanism. Only exceptional measures, calling for state intervention, enabled business to resume under conditions that few contemporaries imagined would persist longer than a couple of months.

As the world's financial centre, the City was the most exposed to these upheavals. The problem that it faced was simple in its enormity; bills amounting to £350 million were in circulation on the London discount market and would have to be paid when they fell due, in other words, within a period of three months. And yet, owing to the outbreak of war, a good third of these drafts, whose drawers were from then on in the enemy camp, were likely to remain unpaid, thus forcing the acceptors to honour the guarantee that they had provided to the holders of these bills. But the merchant banks were unable to do this, their own funds amounting to a mere £20 million, whereas their commitments to Austrian and German firms were estimated at between £60 and £70 million, in addition to a probably similar amount for Russia, with which all normal trading relations had been cut off. For their part, the members of the stock exchange collectively owed £100 million to financial institutions, 80% of which was to banks, on top of the £25 million's worth of unpaid and outstanding transactions amongst themselves. Moreover, bank loans amounting to a total of £250 million were secured by stocks and shares.[3] Given the drop in prices, the need to sell off these stocks to reimburse loans risked bankrupting several banking houses and triggering off a chain reaction. The London Stock Exchange, the last stock exchange still open in Europe, ceased trading on 31 July 1914, reopening only on 4 January 1915.

It was the City's complete credit mechanism that was in danger of collapsing. The commercial banks' huge assets, upon which the entire edifice was built, were at risk of being frozen; the rather panic-stricken reaction of their managers, that Keynes would denounce, did little to calm the panic that seized London's markets.[4] Disaster was avoided thanks to the combined intervention of the Bank of England, the commercial banks and the government; among other things, a moratorium on debt repayment was announced on 2 August 1914, while the central bank procured the liquid assets needed to keep the system functioning.

Similar measures were taken in Paris, where the amount of bank loans on the Bourse reached Fr.625 million, 400 of which were in the form of carry-over transactions. On 29 July the Compagnie des Agents de Change postponed, with the agreement of the minister of finance, the traditional monthly settlement. On 31 July the government decreed that commercial maturity dates and protest periods would be deferred, and on 1 August it authorised banks, faced with growing demands to withdraw funds at their counters, to limit withdrawals from deposit accounts and current credit accounts. This near suspension of payments, which had been avoided in London, was eased progressively from the end of the year.[5] Berlin was also panic-stricken; falling prices led the stock exchange to close its doors on 30 July, and a run on the banks reduced their deposits by some 20%. On the other hand, and unlike what happened in London and Paris, the Reichsbank did not introduce a moratorium on debt, of which Rudolf von Havenstein, its chairman, was moreover extremely proud. Instead, lending offices were set up to obtain liquid assets for banks in difficulty, a stopgap measure whose effects turned out to be highly inflationary.[6]

Neutral countries were not spared. The Swiss stock exchanges remained closed until mid-1916, except in Geneva where bond transactions were restored as early as 20 August 1914. On 30 July the Confederation suspended convertibility, and a banking moratorium was established *de facto* on 2 August, when the National Bank limited withdrawals to Fr.200 on deposit accounts and Fr.50 on savings accounts. Just as in France, commercial maturity dates and protest periods were deferred until the end of September. Wall Street did not avoid panic either. The New York Stock Exchange closed its doors on 31 July, a few hours after the London Stock Exchange did, following the huge sale of American securities and the growing difficulties confronting the banks and large numbers of brokers. The United States' liabilities also fuelled worries about the country's ability to pay its debts, leading to a drop – considered significant at the time – of some 1% in the dollar's value during the first months of the conflict.

In all the financial centres, the players involved in financial transactions had to confront new conditions. The merchant banks in the City, cornerstone of the international credit mechanism prior to 1914, were affected most directly by the crisis, with the acceptance of bills of exchange and the issuing of foreign loans in London coming to an almost complete standstill once hostilities had broken out. On 5 August 1914 the twenty-one most important banking houses[7] met to consider the situation and the delicate negotiations that they would have to carry out with the Bank of England; this resulted in the founding of the Accepting Houses Committee, which would become one of the City's most influential associations. The agreement concluded on 13 August when the Bank of England stipulated that the central bank, with the Treasury's backing, would discount all drafts accepted before 4 August. Furthermore, the Bank undertook to lend the necessary amounts, at 2% above the official discount rate, to acceptors who were unable to repay any bills presented that had fallen due.

Even though these measures undeniably revived the discount market, merchant banks made a very uneven profit from it. Everything depended on the relative value of their commitments to the central empires. There was a striking contrast between a firm like Baring Brothers, mainly involved in the Americas and the Far East, and a house like Schröders, with close ties to Germany and central Europe. The former's average supply of acceptances fell to just under £5 million between 1914 and 1918, compared with an average of nearly £7 million during the five years immediately preceding the war[8] – all in all, a limited drop. For Schröders, on the other hand, one of the two largest accepting houses with Kleinworts, the consequences of the conflict were catastrophic; the total amount of its acceptances dropped from £11.7 million in 1913 to just £1.3 million in 1918, having even reached its nadir, £634,000, in 1917 – average operating profit fell from £315,000 for the years 1905–13 to £9,000 per year during the war.[9]

Capital flows

Although the acceptance market subsequently recovered, especially with countries that had kept out of the conflict, foreign issues were still prohibited or subject to control by the British government, as they were by other belligerents. And yet, international capital flows did not cease during the war, far from it. Between 1914 and 1918, debts totalling nearly £4 billion or $19.4 billion – in other words an amount equivalent to the stock of British foreign assets on the eve of the war – were incurred among the Allies. The two main creditor countries were the

United States ($9.2 billion) and the United Kingdom ($8.5 billion), with France ($1.7 billion) trailing far behind. Only the United States never needed to take out loans abroad during the hostilities. The British had to borrow $4.2 billion and the French $2.7 billion from the United States, the French having to obtain loans for a more or less equivalent amount, namely $2.5 billion, from the British. The other Allies merely borrowed: Italy for $5.1 billion from the two Anglo-Saxon powers, Russia for $4 billion, mainly from Britain and, to a far lesser extent, from France, and the other small countries for $1.5 billion, also shared among American, British and French lenders. The contribution made by the small neutral countries was, however, much more modest. The credit granted by Switzerland, for example, barely amounted to $170 million.

Regardless of the problems that these inter-Allied debts would pose, such loans were essentially contracted between governments and did not activate the mechanisms usually associated with credit transfers between the international financial centres. France, for example, borrowed $2.9 billion from the American government compared with only $336 million from banks, and $2.1 billion from the British government, compared with $625 million from banks, including the Bank of England.[10] Only a few intermediaries and privileged partners were involved in these operations, most of which were managed from New York and London, from where they continued to offer their expertise and their network of relationships. In this respect, the First World War marked the end of the Rothschilds' supremacy in government loans, a supremacy that had begun to be contested from the turn of the century.[11] Their decline, above all, was due to their weak presence in the United States where the sinews of war would henceforth be located.[12] The United States quickly became the Allied coalition's sponsor, Germany being almost powerless to call on the American capital market in spite of the presence of a large contingent of investment bankers of German origin on the other side of the Atlantic. The vast majority of bankers and financiers on Wall Street were pro-Allies, and anti-German feeling grew among the American public after the submarine war began in 1915. Between 1914 and 1917, only $35 million worth of loans were issued in New York on behalf of the central powers.[13]

One banking house dominated these operations: J. P. Morgan & Co. Still in private hands, the big New York bank took over the syndicate responsible for issuing the first Anglo-French loan for $500 million in October 1915, the largest that it had ever issued. The conditions were difficult, due to the reluctance of one part of the public and the open hostility of another, which were in favour of Germany. Despite the efforts of the syndicate, composed of sixty-one banks and other finance companies, the bonds would never be fully subscribed. This did not stop Morgans from issuing four more loans amounting to a total of $950 million on behalf of Britain in 1916 and 1917. Morgans' other, perhaps more important, task was its role of agent for the British and French governments in the United States. Indeed, in January 1915 Britain broke with the practice of the War Office and the Admiralty themselves negotiating the purchase of munitions with British or foreign suppliers, since the scale of the demands made on American industry at that time meant that an agent with the necessary expertise and contacts needed to be present on the spot. J. P. Morgan & Co. was thus officially entrusted with making these purchases and with obtaining the best terms for the British government, in return for a 2% commission on the price of the goods worth up to £10 million and a 1% commission above that.[14] These transactions, estimated at some tens of millions of dollars when the agreement was signed, would reach $3 billion and earned Morgans some $30 million.[15] But things changed when the United States entered the war in April 1917 and started to lend directly to London. Besides, from August 1917 purchasing responsibility was taken over by the British war missions residing in the United States; Morgans continued, however, to act as a financial advisor.

In the City, Morgan Grenfell & Co., the group's London arm, acted as an intermediary between the British government and the New York bank, a supportive role that proved to be highly profitable.[16] For its part, Baring Brothers & Co. turned the war to even better account chiefly thanks to its role as Petrograd's official agent in London.[17] In this capacity, the bank was involved in negotiations for the increasingly huge loans granted by Britain to Russia to enable it to continue its war effort.[18] It made the tsarist government a certain number of advances (always guaranteed by the British government) and orchestrated several interventions to bolster the rouble on the foreign exchange market.[19] The most surprising thing was that Baring Brothers' huge profits stemmed principally from business deals with Russia, the weakest link in the chain of allied countries, though the Soviet default on Russian war debt would not affect the City's venerable house in any way.

The transformation of business life

Apart from the suspension, *de jure* or *de facto*, of the gold standard, the exceptional measures taken when hostilities broke out were gradually lifted in all the financial centres. And yet, as one can well imagine, business life did not return to normal. The war years were marked above all by massive departures to the front and high numbers of human loss that affected not only bank employees but also, especially in the City, the heirs to banking dynasties. At the Midland Bank, for example, 4,000 men, out of a total of more than 5,000 salaried employees in 1914, were mobilised during the hostilities and, of these, 717 were killed in action.[20] The departures to the front caused problems in recruiting and training staff that a bank like the Crédit Lyonnais struggled to resolve, being forced at the end of 1916 to close 76 branches – including 24 in Paris – out of just over 400.[21] In the financial sector, as in other economic activities, women quickly filled the posts left vacant due to the mobilisation of men. At the Midland Bank, for example, where no women had been employed before 1907, their number reached 350 at the beginning of 1915 and 3,600 three years later.[22]

In the field of financial activities, the most important transformation was the part played from then on in financing the growing needs of the state. The assets of the big German, French and British banks mainly comprised Treasury bonds and similar stocks at that time.[23] On the stock exchanges, government securities regained the part that they had played at the dawn of the first phase of globalisation, exceeding 30% of the securities quoted on the London Stock Exchange in 1920, compared with 11.5% in 1913.[24] Stock-market transactions were themselves disrupted, either by restrictions like the ban on arbitrage operations in London, or purely and simply by closure, as in Berlin, where the stock exchange only opened its doors in 1917. In the meantime, the buying and selling of securities was carried out solely through banks.[25]

Even if war was a terrible ordeal for all the financial centres, they were not all affected in the same way. Business as a whole certainly tended to slacken off, but new opportunities opened up in some fields such as foreign exchange transactions; one centre could win market share at the expense of another, for example in acceptance and issue activities. These changes and their medium- and long-term consequences were not all noticeable in the course of the hostilities, especially since the outcome of the conflict remained uncertain until the summer of 1918. Berlin's decline, for example, only really occurred after the German defeat. The big banks, which dominated the market before 1914, strengthened their position during the war through the Reich's loans and their international operations in Mitteleuropa and in the Ottoman Empire. Deutsche Bank and the Disconto-Gesellschaft indulged in fierce competition over Bulgarian loans, and the former continued its involvement in building the increasingly hazardous Baghdad railway. Paris, on the other hand, suffered more during the conflict but would rebound in the twenties. Not only was France partly invaded by Germany, but foreign issues, the Paris centre's speciality, came to a halt. To finance the war, it had to invest part of the gold held by the Banque de France and sell the bulk of its foreign assets, while the Russian Revolution of 1917 brought about the loss of a not insignificant share of the foreign stock held by French investors.[26]

Of all the large financial centres, it was the City that had the most to lose from any disruption to the world economic order. The war was 'the worst thing that ever happened to the City of London', as David Kynaston has written,[27] and the City did indeed weaken in favour of New York's financial centre. Britain sold $3 billion worth of American stocks to finance its war effort. The City also left New York a clear field in the area of international trade financing, use of the pound becoming more difficult following the introduction of exchange controls. Drafts in dollars tended to replace those in sterling, not only in financing American foreign trade but also that of other European countries, particularly with Latin America and the Far East. New York also learnt how to issue large foreign loans. From April 1917 the issue of more than $20 billion worth of American federal bonds through four Liberty Loans and one Victory Loan enabled Wall Street to improve its fund-raising mechanisms throughout the country, which would be the cause both of its successes and its failures in the twenties.

Other beneficiaries of the conflict were the financial centres of the small, neutral countries, above all Switzerland and the Netherlands. Switzerland did face some difficulties during the war because of its dependence on foreign countries, which led de facto to a loss of autonomy in the face of demands from the Allies and the central powers. But the Swiss banks were able to make use of the competitive advantage offered by the country's neutrality, with foreign exchange transactions in particular developing considerably in both Zurich and Geneva. And above all, these transactions laid the foundations for what would become the Swiss financial centre's forte throughout the twentieth century – the hosting of foreign capital – though in proportions that are still difficult to quantify. The assets of the big Swiss banks almost doubled between 1914 and 1919, going from Fr.2 million to Fr.3.8 billion, but this growth was almost entirely due to the inflation that hit the country at that time. Capital inflows did not really start to increase in scale before the political and monetary chaos that followed the end of hostilities and the crises at the end of the twenties.

The roaring twenties

Major conflicts greatly affect the destiny of international financial centres. Like the French wars or the Second World War, the Great War was no exception to the rule. Nevertheless, the changes that it brought about seemed less dramatic, at least in the medium term, than those caused by the other two cataclysms. The most radical transformations of the international order only occurred in the longer term, after 1945, at the end of a period that some have labelled the 'Thirty Years War of the 20th century'.[28] The fact remains that the world economic situation in 1919 was very different from what it had been four or five years earlier, even if contemporaries, in their eagerness to re-establish the pre-war order, were not always fully aware of this, especially since the changes brought about by the war were often sources of instability.

The legacy of the war

The first difference related to the powers' financial capacity, and thus that of the main financial centres that they hosted. The great victor was the United States, which in a few years changed from a debtor country to a creditor country; it went from having net private liabilities in excess of $3 billion in 1913 to having net assets of $4.5 billion in 1919. As for Europe, it was no longer the world's banker. Britain, France and Germany together lost more than a third of their foreign investment; in other words, some $12 billion. But the gaps between the three countries were far more significant than the Old Continent's collective destiny that too often tends to be emphasised. Germany lost nearly all its foreign assets, France most of them – probably three-quarters of its assets in Europe, mainly in Russia – and Britain only a part, chiefly the $3 billion worth of American stock that it was obliged to sell.[29] Moreover, opportunities for building up their portfolio of foreign stocks again were limited. Germany, burdened with reparations, became a huge importer of capital, France was crippled until 1926 by the weakness of the franc, capital flight and reconstruction requirements, and Britain found it increasingly difficult to regain its role of exporter of long-term capital because of the constraints weighing down its balance of payments, especially due to the loss of competitiveness of its staple industries.

The second major difference related to the international monetary system. The gold standard, which had underpinned it since the 1880s, indeed stopped functioning at the beginning of the conflict. France and Germany officially suspended the convertibility of their currencies at the outbreak of hostilities, and Britain did so unofficially, with some people, including Keynes, believing that abandoning gold at the first warning sign would be detrimental to London's status as the world's financial centre. After entering the war, the United States also maintained the convertibility of the dollar while making it difficult in practice. Between 1914 and 1918, the main currencies' rate was maintained thanks to intervention facilitated by American loans. Accordingly, the pound was index-linked to the dollar and the French franc to the pound from 1915. This stability ceased in March 1919, with the end of American support ushering in a phase of floating exchange rates.

However, restoring the gold standard system, as desired at that time by political and economic leaders, came up against numerous obstacles. The United States was the first to re-establish the convertibility of the dollar from 1919, but a widespread return to pre-war parities seemed difficult. Inflation was certainly rampant in all the belligerent countries, as well as in the neutral countries, but the scale of price increases varied considerably from one country to another.[30] And the differences became more pronounced in subsequent years among the countries that managed to bring inflation under control (the United States, Britain and the former neutrals), the more inflationist victorious countries (France and Belgium) and the defeated countries ravaged by hyperinflation (Germany and Austria).[31] The gold standard was essentially restored between 1924 and 1926, following efforts and crises that left deep marks on the workings of the major European financial centres in the first half of the twenties.

Monetary chaos was further complicated by the issue of reparations and, to a lesser extent, that of war debt. The Versailles Treaty attributed responsibility for the war to Germany and imposed reparation payments upon it. The amount was set by the Reparations Commission in April 1921 at 132 billion gold marks, or three times its GDP of the time; Germany would have to pay 2 billion per year from January 1922 plus 26% of its total exports over forty-two years. Germany initially accepted this programme, albeit unwillingly, but at the end of the year announced that it would not be able to pay the instalments scheduled for January 1922 and asked for a reduction in the amount set by the Commission. In response to the delayed payment of the instalments in kind, especially coal deliveries, Franco-Belgian troops invaded the Ruhr in January 1923, but in the face of passive resistance from the population obtained scarcely any results, apart from accelerating the hyperinflationary spiral on which the German government had embarked the previous year.

A solution seemed to have been found with the Dawes Plan,[32] which came into force in September 1924 and rescheduled reparations payments, with an annual amount of 1 billion gold marks until 1928, then

2.5 billion. The plan was backed by an international loan in dollars – the Dawes Loan – worth 800 million Reichsmarks, the largest of the time, issued simultaneously in several financial centres under the management of J. P. Morgan & Co. This enabled the German currency to be stabilised and confidence to be restored in the country's economy. The system seemed to function over the following years. Germany made its payments regularly and paid more than 10 billion marks up until 1930, though it did so by borrowing heavily abroad, chiefly in the United States, for a total sum estimated at between 25 and 30 billion marks. The mechanism risked jamming if the flow of foreign funds to Germany were to stop.

Were the reparations imposed on Germany excessive or realistic? The issue has been hotly debated among both contemporaries and historians. Keynes was the first to repudiate the policy, in a famous book published in 1919, *The Economic Consequences of the Peace*. He judged that an excessive amount would in fact not be in the victors' interest, since by crushing Germany it would compromise the prosperity of the rest of Europe. Others considered that, in view of its national income and its export capacity, Germany was perfectly able to pay the required reparations, especially as the inflow of capital into the country was far higher than the outflow comprising reparations. While the first underestimated the weight of public opinion in the countries most affected by the war and the desire to make Germany pay, the second underestimated the Germans' strong aversion to the reparations and their opposition to any increase in taxes to contribute towards their payment. Either way, the reparations had a crucial role in capital flows during the twenties and, therefore, had a direct impact on the organisation and functioning of the international financial centres, first and foremost New York.

The rise of New York

As the war drew to a close, New York seemed ready to take up the torch of the world's financial centre from London. Not only was American foreign trade finance freeing itself from London's control, but acceptances in dollars were posing a serious challenge to those in sterling. Furthermore, the huge expansion of the United States' merchant navy during the war – by 1920 as much as half of American freight was transported on ships sailing under the national flag – led to the parallel development of marine insurance. Finally, the national banks, permitted by the Edge Act of 1919 to set up joint-stock companies to develop their international business, started expanding abroad – the number of overseas branches of American banks increasing from 26 in 1913 to 181 in 1920.[33] And, of course, the United States lent heavily abroad. Some of these advances were limited, however. American banks were quick to retreat to their national territory after making some heavy losses, and by 1925 the number of their foreign branches had fallen back to 107; at the same time, the expansion of the merchant navy came to a halt, so that the country was once again dependent on foreign carriers.[34]

Acceptances and foreign issues. Acceptances enjoyed longer-lasting success partly thanks to the law of 1913 establishing the Federal Reserve System, which allowed the national banks to accept bills of exchange. Moreover, the rapid growth in acceptances was encouraged by a favourable international climate and by the setting up in 1919 of the American Acceptance Council aimed at promoting the merits of this type of financing, followed two years later by the International Acceptance Bank.[35] The volume of these acceptances, three-quarters of which were drawn on New York banks, went from $250 million in 1916 to $1 billion in 1920, reaching their highest level of $1.7 billion in 1929, more than 75% of them generally being connected with international transactions.[36] Despite this progress, New York did not replace the City as the preferred source of foreign trade finance. Indeed, from 1921 the bill on London regained a great deal of the ground lost during the war, British international acceptances reaching $1.8 billion in 1929.[37] While New York and London appeared to be neck and neck in this key sector, the figures are misleading. Quite a few of the New York acceptances were purely financial bills intended to compensate for the fall in American loans to the countries of central Europe, above all Germany, and so were not connected with any commercial transactions.[38] Nor did the development of acceptances lead to the creation of a true discount market in New York, demand for these among American banks remaining weak. In the United States, the money market continued to be dominated by brokers' loans that exploded in the second half of the twenties.

The change that hauled New York up to the top of the international hierarchy of financial centres was the export of capital – thanks to the American public's newly acquired enthusiasm for foreign stocks, combined with an abundance of savings in the United States and the east coast investment banks' expertise and networks of relationships. This investment capacity greatly exceeded Britain's potential, so that during the second half of the twenties foreign issues placed in New York generally exceeded those offered in London by 50%.[39] This foreign investment flowed mainly to Europe (41%), ahead of Canada (25%),

Latin America (22%) and Asia (12%), with a very marked preference for public bonds that made up more than 95% of issues between 1920 and 1929.

Financial architecture.   On Wall Street, large-scale international financial operations essentially continued to be the preserve of the investment banks and the national banks that had dominated the stage even before 1914. The main difference was, of course, that from then on they acted far more as intermediaries between American savers and foreign debtors than between European investors and American companies. The twenties were undoubtedly J. P. Morgan & Co.'s apogee. The bank was still the largest private banking house in the United States, and probably the world, with its total assets amounting to $680 million in 1929, in other words more than four times that of the City's largest merchant banks. It undeniably lagged far behind the large national banks in terms of size. But it was the country's top investment bank, capable between 1919 and 1933 of putting on the market, usually in cooperation with other banking houses, more than $6 billion worth of stock, including $2 billion in both public and private foreign securities. Furthermore, its close association with Morgan Grenfell in London and Morgan Harjes in Paris guaranteed it a strong international presence. J. P. Morgan & Co.'s prestige was derived, besides from the volume of its operations, from its position at the hub of the world of business and politics, particularly in the field of financial diplomacy during the twenties.

The other large pre-1914 private banking houses – Kuhn Loeb & Co., Kidder Peabody & Co., Lee Higginson & Co. and others – remained influential in international issues. In national matters, they felt more keenly the effects of competition from newcomers, able to mobilise investors who although of more modest means were distributed throughout the country, such as Halsey Stuart & Co. from Chicago or Blyth & Co. from San Francisco. Kuhn Loeb, with assets of over $120 million in 1929 – approximately the size of Baring Brothers or Schröders in London – remained firmly in second place thanks to its prominence in the railways. Dillon Read & Co., formed in 1921, was particularly active in issues on behalf of large German companies, including $100 million on behalf of the steel giant, Vereinigte Stahlwerke, between 1926 and 1928.[40] The national banks, for their part, continued as they had before the war and made more and more of a name for themselves on the international issue market. The leader was still the National City Bank of New York, which through its subsidiary, the National City Company, took part as a member or as the lead-bank of issue syndicates in more than a third of all the foreign loans subscribed in the United States between 1921 and 1929. Under the leadership of Charles Mitchell, who assumed control immediately after the war, it became among all the national banks the most perfect model of an almost universal bank, offering a complete range of services, including issuing and selling securities on a vast scale.[41] As the first American bank with assets exceeding $2 billion, it was nearly as big as the City's giants by 1929; however, the City banks remained the largest in the world.

The responsibilities taken on by the Federal Reserve of New York reflected the American financial capital's new status and at the same time helped its influence grow. Its chairman from 1914 to 1928, Benjamin Strong, certainly contributed to this both on the national level – his influence spread throughout the Federal Reserve System – and abroad. A convinced internationalist, aware of the importance of the United States and American capital in the post-war economic order, Strong shared the same orthodox monetary views as his friend Montagu Norman, governor of the Bank of England. The two men cooperated closely to re-establish and maintain the gold standard during the twenties. The Federal Reserve played its role to the full, as during the famous summit on Long Island in July 1927 that, besides Strong and Norman, brought together Hjalmar Schacht, chairman of the Reichsbank, and Charles Rist, deputy governor of the Banque de France; at the end of the summit, the Fed lowered its discount rate and conducted vast open-market operations to ease pressure on the Bank of England's gold reserves.[42]

Perhaps the most telling sign of the new role played by New York as an international financial centre was the fact that all the major foreign banks tried to establish a foothold there during the twenties. In accordance with New York's banking legislation, the branches of foreign banks had to be approved by the Empire State and were not authorised to collect deposits from the non-banking public. By 1929 they numbered twenty-six,[43] most of them being branches of British (all overseas banks), Canadian, Japanese and Italian banking houses, all mainly involved in financing international trade.[44] Other banks were represented by a subsidiary, usually set up jointly with another bank. The Comptoir national d'escompte de Paris, for example, set up a subsidiary there in 1919, the French American Banking Corporation, with two American partners.[45] The British clearing banks, on the other hand, continued to use the services of correspondents, as did most of the merchant banks unless they had a parent company in New York, as in the case of Morgan Grenfell, Lazards and some others. The partners of J. Henry Schröder & Co. went one step further by founding

J. Henry Schroder Banking Corporation in New York in 1923, with the initial intention of participating in the market for acceptances in dollars that at the time seemed to be developing on the banks of the Hudson. Very quickly, however, the bank went into the business of issuing and underwriting securities, taking advantage of the experience that it had acquired in the City of London, its international networks, especially in Europe and in Latin America, and the quality of its New York partners.[46]

The new finance companies. To make the most of the investment opportunities, new financial institutions made their appearance and fuelled the speculative fever that gripped the country. Not all of them were by any means real innovations in financial matters. The investment trusts, for example, had been known for a long time in Britain when they began to flourish in the United States in the twenties. From 40 before 1921, their number reached 770 by 1929, including 591 founded after 1927, in a frenzy reminiscent of the two or three years preceding the Baring Crisis in 1890 – as some American commentators could not help noticing. Between 1926 and 1929, their assets went from $1 billion to $7 billion and included a much higher proportion of American than foreign securities and of shares than bonds. Their sponsors were essentially finance or banking companies, which went from the most respectable, like the main investment banks and commercial banks on Wall Street, to the most dubious. Powerful groups bringing together several investment funds were also set up. The largest among them, the Founders Group, established in 1921, brought together ten investment trusts, whose total assets reached $626 million in 1929. The next largest was the Goldman Sachs group, which with three companies, including the largest in the country – the Goldman Sachs Trading Corporation – came close to $500 million.[47] Dillon Read, one of the most dynamic investment banks of the day, founded two investment trusts – the United States & Foreign Securities Corporation and the United States & International Securities Corporation – destined above all to place their own issues, especially foreign ones. On the whole, however, the investment trusts had a bad reputation, with incompetence, greed and dishonesty being the three main criticisms made of them. Their operating principle – in essence, collective investment and risk diversification – was fundamentally sound and basically the same as that of their British counterparts who served as a role model. But the practical application of these principles often left something to be desired, especially as far as the structure of their capital and the nature of their investment were concerned. For the investment banks and other financial institutions, the investment trusts were instruments that were well adapted for selling, directly to an uninformed public, stock that they had undertaken to issue and that had not found buyers. Of course, the problem lay in the quality of these securities and in their valuation; during these years it was widespread practice, as it had been in England during the 1880s, for a company to purchase the shares of another company in the same group in order to raise or artificially support prices. After the 1929 crash, the American investment trusts would fall even harder.

Another institution designed to encourage investment was a great success in the twenties – namely, holdings of public utilities. The first of these had made their appearance at the turn of the century, usually at the initiative of electrical engineering firms, to encourage the development of this sector, particularly in the production and distribution of electricity, which at that time were considered extremely risky. While these initiatives continued during the twenties, they quickly turned into a frenzy of new holding companies, similar to that affecting investment trusts at the time. Their establishment, with their group structures, cross-holdings and at times fraudulent schemes, served above all to enrich their founders. Even the prestigious Morgan Bank ended up bowing to the trend and in 1929 founded, jointly with Bonbright and Drexel, the United Corporation, whose assets exceeded $300 million at the time of the crash.

The lure of American stocks.   In spite of its new world role, New York remained just as much an American financial centre as a truly international one. Foreign issues played a secondary role – unlike in London before 1914 and even in the twenties[48] – despite the enthusiasm that they aroused among American investors; this enthusiasm was, moreover, encouraged by politicians and business leaders who saw them as a way of making the public more aware of the new role played by the United States in world affairs.[49] The main changes undergone by New York just after the war lay elsewhere. They were mainly connected with the incredible boom in issues of American stock. The twenties saw a period of strong industrial growth, of modernised production and management methods, and of mergers and acquisitions, with companies resorting far more to the capital market than to bank loans to finance themselves. To compensate for this drop in activity, the main commercial banks started issuing securities, usually through subsidiaries specially set up for this purpose. Between 1921 and 1929, nearly two-thirds of the issues that the National City Bank was involved in were on behalf of American companies.[50]

The democratisation of share ownership went hand in hand with this strengthening of the stock market. This can be explained partly by the experience that the American public had acquired through war loans and by the country's prosperity, as well as by a growing taste for risk-taking along with a desire to get rich quickly. There were far higher numbers of shareholders than previously and they did not belong solely to the wealthiest levels of society. That did not mean, however, that there was any less concentration of wealth; out of some 15 million holders of securities in 1925 (the highest estimate), 600,000, or barely 4%, were believed to own 75% in value. But the figure of the small investor held a central place in the collective imagination of the day, and his or her participation in subscriptions was sought after, as shown by the low nominal value of various shares. How willing were such people to support New York's new international role by subscribing heavily to large international issues? Probably not very, considering Americans' lack of familiarity with foreign stocks, which was one of New York's weak points compared with London during this period. Moreover, there were still far more numerous and tempting investment opportunities in domestic securities within the United States than in Europe.

At the same time, foreign capital continued to be invested in the American economy. Apart from long-term investments, which went from \$3 billion to \$5.8 billion between 1918 and 1929,[51] New York became the favoured market for the short-term deposit of foreign funds, which increased from \$1.7 in 1925 to \$3.6 billion in 1929.[52] The New York Stock Exchange mirrored this state of affairs. On the one hand, foreign investors, particularly European, were attracted by American stocks, especially with the bullish trend that marked the decade and saw shares almost triple, and those of public utilities, the most popular, more than quadruple between 1919 and 1929. On the other hand, the liquid assets of foreign banks supplied short-term loans to brokers, which constituted the bulk of the New York money market, where prices reached new heights with the speculative fever of the end of the decade. Furthermore, this interaction between national and international business was one of the main characteristics of the New York financial centre, which differentiated it from the City. While international issues handled in the two large financial centres attracted capital from all over the world, New York was far more successful than London in attracting funds looking to be invested in the domestic economy. The New York centre's tremendous vitality in the twenties came to an end with the Wall Street stock-market crash of October 1929.

Decline of the City?

In a book published in 1927, the American economist Leland Jenks, a specialist in international capital flows, considered it 'certain that New York in the next generation will be at least a close competitor to London for financial leadership'.[53] This authoritative opinion contrasts with the somewhat simplistic analyses claiming that the First World War signalled the City's irreversible decline and its replacement by New York as the world's financial centre. In reality, things were far more complex. That the City's influence had been on the wane since 1914 was indisputable. It was connected in the first place with the reduction in British assets abroad, above all in the United States, following the sale of American stocks to finance the war effort. It was also caused by the large increase in the public debt; in other words, by the huge needs of the British government, which absorbed the bulk of domestic savings that would normally have been invested elsewhere. Finally, there was the slump in the old British export industries – textiles, coal, steel and shipbuilding – that were being successfully challenged by newly developed countries. Crucially, this loss of influence occurred just as competition from New York was becoming keener following the new American financial legislation of 1913, which maximised the opportunities to capture market share offered by the war and by the United States' vast financial potential. The City's decline should be seen in this light – as a decline quite unlike the far more drastic decline of Amsterdam, the financial centre which had held sway over the world a little over a century earlier. At the end of the Great War, London still held some aces: unrivalled expertise, solid and well-established networks and client bases, considerable openness to the world and also, although to a lesser extent than New York, by no means insignificant financial capabilities, especially in relation to the size of its banks and its stock of capital invested abroad, which still ranked first in the world. These were aces that the British were determined to deploy to conserve for the City the top place that it had occupied before the war.

The pound's return to the gold standard. In order to achieve this, it was assumed to be necessary to first bring about the pound's recovery. For British leaders, restoring the pound's gold convertibility was a goal set even before the end of hostilities and made public in 1919 in the report made by the Commission chaired by Lord Cunliffe, wartime governor of the Bank of England. This return to the gold standard, one of the pillars of British economic policy in the nineteenth century, along with free trade, was intended to restore the mechanisms underpinning Britain's position in the world economy, above all to reactivate capital exports and thereby the export of goods, in order to restore to the City its undisputed leadership in international finance. The obvious question was the rate at which the pound should be stabilised. Should it go back to pre-war gold parity, which would mean a return to the traditional rate of $4.86 to the pound? Or should the pound be devalued both in relation to gold and to the dollar, which would take into account the higher inflation in Britain than in America during the hostilities and the real rate of the two currencies on the foreign exchange market? A large majority quickly emerged in favour of pre-war parity, apparently the only way to maintain the City's continuity, credibility and prestige. Keynes, one of the few dissenting voices along with Reginald McKenna, former chancellor of the exchequer and chairman of the Midland Bank, pleaded for a devaluation of 10% – a realistic measure, but deemed unacceptable, since it amounted to admitting in public that Britain had lost status in comparison with the United States, and the City in comparison with Wall Street.

Yet re-establishing the parity of 1914 was no easy matter; restoring British prices to the level of American prices required deflationary measures that penalised industrial activity. These measures would be taken, and in April 1925 Winston Churchill, then chancellor of the exchequer, announced the British currency's return to the gold standard with a parity of 7.32 grams of gold per pound, thus to its former exchange rate of $4.86 to the pound. This decision stirred up a great deal of controversy that we do not intend to discuss fully here.[54] According to the current consensus, after this decision the British currency found itself overvalued, in various proportions depending on the currency, probably more in relation to the French franc than to the dollar; and this overvaluation imposed a heavy burden on the British economy over a good number of years. To what extent did this put a curb on the City's decline? London, as we will see, remained the world's leading financial centre overall, even if it had to share this role with New York. Could an identical, or even better, result have been obtained by devaluing the pound? Some historians have maintained this, citing the example of Paris after the franc's stabilisation in 1926.[55] Nevertheless, at that time, such a solution seemed inconceivable to most of the London establishment.

The City's strengths and weaknesses.   In the twenties, London seemed to be a more international financial centre offering a far more comprehensive range of activities than New York, especially when it came to commercial financing and professional services. In this respect, the situation was not so different from what it had been before 1914, except for placing foreign issues, the capital henceforth coming from the other side of the Atlantic. Moreover, London suffered from restrictions placed on foreign loans, officially until 1919, then unofficially until 1925, due to subtle pressure from the Bank of England, on top of which came the handicap of a 2% stamp duty. The fact remains that, while Wall Street became the favoured place to which both public and private investors turned, the City was far from being abandoned, keeping well ahead of all the other European financial centres in this sector.[56] Besides, the issuing of foreign loans took off again in the second half of the twenties, on behalf of both traditional clients such as the governments of the Dominions, especially Australia, and newcomers such as big German companies.[57]

Elsewhere, the City retained all or part of the advantage that it had enjoyed before 1914, particularly in financing international trade. By 1920 the volume of acceptances in circulation on the London market had reached its 1913 level, namely £350 million in nominal value, but only about half in real value. After a net drop during the recession of 1920–21, it experienced robust growth, reaching a maximum of £415 million in 1926.[58] Thus, despite competition from New York, the draft on London remained the preferred instrument for financing international trade. Consequently, the London money market recovered a great deal of its dynamism and, above all, its attraction for investing funds on a short-term basis – not only in the form of bills of exchange, which traditionally constituted its backbone, but also in the form of short-term Treasury Bonds that were especially popular at the time.[59]

On the foreign exchange market, a field of activity that developed considerably in the climate of monetary instability following the war, the City established its predominance from the very outset, thanks to its high concentration of banks from all over the world. Currency transactions were, for the most part, interbank deals made by telephone, or by telegraph in the case of long distances, the market's very diversity calling neither for any formal organisation nor for a physical market. The foreign exchange brokers with some experience, like S. Japhet, Samuel Montagu or R. Raphael, made the most of the new opportunities; but it was Kleinworts, one of the main merchant banks, that established itself as the leader on the foreign exchange futures market through its partnership with Goldman Sachs in New York and a network of firms in Amsterdam, Berlin, Budapest and Paris. Its foreign exchange service employed from forty to fifty people at the time.[60]

While openness to the world remained one of London's characteristics during the twenties, a retreat to domestic financial business was nonetheless clearly perceptible. Foreign issues dropped to below half the total, whereas they had represented more than two-thirds before 1914. The stock exchange also mirrored this new state of affairs. With the dramatic rise in the public debt, which went from £700 million to £7,500 million between 1913 and 1919, British government securities once more held a prominent place on its list, with 34.6% of the nominal value of all securities, against only 11.5% in 1913. Conversely, the American stocks listed, above all railway stocks, declined noticeably following the sales made to finance the war effort. Even if it became less international, the London Stock Exchange nevertheless remained an attractive market for both British and foreign investors. In nominal value, the volume of negotiable papers increased markedly compared with 1913 to reach £18.5 billion in 1933. Government bonds, which represented an eminently sound and liquid investment, and the securities of large companies, like ICI, Unilever or Shell, found buyers abroad, especially in the United States; not to mention the ever-increasing share of foreign or colonial securities kept since 1914 or built up again after 1918. But the London Stock Exchange no longer played the international role that it had played before the war, as shown by Ranald Michie, of enabling short-term funds coming from all over the world to be invested in stocks distributed worldwide. In the first place, there was a decoupling of the money market and the financial market; the banks made far less use of their very short-term funds in loans to brokers, owing to their more cautious outlook and to the competition from Treasury Bonds and from the New York Stock Exchange. On the other hand, even if British investors partly built up their foreign assets again during the twenties, the loss of American stocks deprived the stock market of some of the most important securities listed and traded simultaneously in several financial centres, as well as of the facility that this allowed for international capital flows.[61]

Financial architecture.   London's financial architecture changed somewhat after the war. The first major change related to the Bank of England's role. Even if its primary mission, made more complex and more visible at a time of monetary unrest, remained to watch over the country's gold reserves, it henceforth provided the City's leadership. The Bank's increased authority coincided with the term of office of Montagu Norman, appointed governor in 1920 and who would remain so until 1944. This was an exceptionally long reign since, until then, almost all governors had remained in office for two years, the other major exceptions having been William Lidderdale, who stayed on for an extra year following the Baring Crisis, and Walter Cunliffe between

1914 and 1918. Montagu Norman, a strong character, was the typical central banker, steeped in his responsibilities and the high priest of monetary orthodoxy, perhaps ill-prepared for confronting a new monetary situation. A fully fledged member of the City establishment, Norman also usually had very good personal and professional relationships with the governors of the main foreign central banks, especially with the American Benjamin Strong and the German Hjalmar Schacht. However, contacts with the French Emile Moreau then Emile Moret were distinctly less cordial, no doubt because of the struggles for influence between Britain and France in central Europe and the rivalry between London and Paris as international financial centres.[62]

Norman made expert use of his network of relationships to fulfil his new role as leader of the City through what might be called his representative duties on the international level and his regulatory tasks on the national level. The former were not purely honorary, as the actions of the Bank of England, particularly in the international monetary diplomacy that was starting to develop, contributed to the prestige and influence of the City in the world, one of the avowed goals of its governor. The pound's return to the gold standard was an inherent part of this process, as were Norman's interventions in the Financial Committee of the League of Nations, the financial reconstruction plans for the countries of central Europe, and his initiatives to encourage cooperation among central banks, for which he was the true kingpin. The new regulatory tasks assigned to the Bank were not official. But the governor was able to impose his views informally, using moral persuasion deriving from the implicit gentlemen's agreement that at that time governed relations between the Bank and the City's other financial institutions. It was in this way that embargoes were put on some issues on behalf of foreign governments; restrictions were proposed on trading foreign stocks on the London Stock Exchange; and approval or disapproval were expressed with regard to such and such an initiative.

The second change was increased financial concentration, particularly in the banking sector, which led to the founding of giant enterprises without match in any other financial centre, including New York. In 1918, even before the end of hostilities, five mergers took place, bringing together, two by two, the ten largest banks in the country and giving rise to five giant clearing banks, immediately christened the 'Big Five': the Midland Bank, Lloyds Bank, Barclays Bank, the Westminster Bank and the National Provincial Bank. Based in London, they each had a national and, usually, international network of branches at their disposal, while collectively controlling more than 90% of the country's deposits. The three most important, Barclays, Midland and Lloyds, were at that time the largest banks in the world, with total assets exceeding £500 million in 1929 for the first two. It was not only their size but also their spheres of activity that added to their potency and, more generally, to the City's financial capacity since, even if the English banking system continued to be specialised and the clearing banks remained deposit banks, there started to be a degree of integration, especially in international financial activities.

First, the large banks presented a far more serious challenge to the merchant banks on the acceptance market, a good half of which was in their hands by the end of the twenties. Second, they became increasingly involved abroad, starting in continental Europe where most of them had already ventured on the eve of the war, then overseas.[63] Barclays took the initiative in this, under the leadership of its chairman Frederick Goodenough, who sought to establish a truly imperial bank; it took control of the Colonial Bank, the Anglo-Egyptian Bank and the National Bank of South Africa, to form in 1925 Barclays Bank DCO (Dominion, Colonial and Overseas), the largest multinational bank in existence at that time, with 506 branches abroad.[64] Lloyds Bank adopted a somewhat different strategy and acquired stakes, sometimes a majority, in a string of overseas banks without really trying to exert strategic control over them.[65]

On the whole, the City's influence exerted internationally through multinational banks based in London grew during the twenties and remained far more intense than that of any other financial centre. Between 1913 and 1928, the British banks' total number of foreign branches increased from 1,387 to 2,253, whereas the number of banks went from 31 to 27. The main overseas banks,[66] large firms with their total assets fluctuating between £50 million and £75 million sterling, consolidated their position in their respective spheres of activity but remained cautious when it came to geographical spread.[67] Similarly, the main foreign banking houses continued to maintain a presence in London, except for the large German banks which, having left at the start of hostilities in 1914, would not return to the City before the 1970s. On the other hand, the American banks – the National City Bank, Chase National Bank and the Bank of America – came to join the most important trust companies there, present since before the war. In total, fifty-five foreign banks had a branch or a representative office in the City in 1930, fourteen of which were American and seven French.

In spite of these changes, the merchant bankers continued to form the City's aristocracy, not only on a socioprofessional level but also, to a large extent, in the field of business.[68] The group of leading houses was the same as before 1914: Baring Brothers, probably the top house in the

twenties; Schröders and Kleinworts, still heavily involved in the acceptance business; Morgan Grenfell, closely linked with J. P. Morgan in
New York; Hambros, which worked its way up to the top ranks; and
Rothschilds, which was a waning yet ever-present force. These banks,
still all in family hands, were of course far smaller than the 'Big Five',
barely a twentieth of their size in terms of total assets. But they retained
more than just niches. In acceptance credit, their market shares remained
respectable – approximately 50%, compared with 70% before the war –
in spite of strong competition from the big banks. And even though they
suffered from the scarcity of foreign issues on the London market, they
kept supreme control over those that remained. Ultimately, it was at the
crossroads of finance and international politics that the City's merchant
bankers benefited from a decisive advantage – an advantage that they
owed to their social status, to their network of relationships and to their
presence in the Bank of England, particularly around the governor,
Montagu Norman, as well as to their expertise in the monetary questions
that dominated the problems inherited from the war.

Even if it did not hold the same position as before 1914, the City did
not seem like a financial centre in decline during the twenties. Admittedly, it had ceded the top place to New York in foreign issues, but it
retained its lead in almost all the other fields of activity. London was an
ambitious, forward-looking rather than backward-looking financial
centre. The grandeur of the buildings that the big banks were having built or rebuilt to house their headquarters, just like the Bank of
England's extension for that matter, showed self-confidence and a
feeling of superiority that had not been shaken by the First World War.
The permanence of these structures contrasted with the country's
general economic situation, particularly the shortfall in external sur-
pluses needed to fulfil the international role that the British financial
elites strove after for the City – a lack of which they were only too aware.
It contrasted too with the pound's fragility, apparent after 1927, which
France would know how to turn to its advantage.

Mixed fortunes for Paris

The Parisian financial centre seemed considerably weakened at the end
of the First World War. Two essential aspects of its pre-1914 international influence were suddenly lacking in whole or in part: a strong
creditor position *vis-à-vis* the rest of the world and a currency inspiring
full and wholehearted confidence among the public. As it happened,
France found itself cut off from 80% of its foreign assets, following sales
and above all the default by Russian and Ottoman creditors who,

together, had issued Fr.15 billion worth of loans on the eve of war. To this were added the war debts incurred with Britain and the United States, amounting to a little over Fr.5 billion. At the same time, the franc was swept along in the monetary upheaval at the beginning of the twenties, mainly because of the continuous increase in the French public debt, which went from Fr.33 billion in 1913 to Fr.297 billion in 1921. The deficit soared, with ever-growing expenditure on the one hand, caused among other things by the reconstruction of the *départements* occupied during the hostilities, and stagnating revenue on the other hand, resulting from politicians' refusal or inability to increase tax revenue, due to their conviction that, in any case, Germany would pay.

The crisis and stabilisation of the French franc. The problems posed by reparations and the worsening budgetary difficulties increased the pressure on the French currency, worth Fr.11 to the dollar – compared with 5 before the war – when currencies started to float in March 1919, subsequently fluctuating between 10 and 20 in the early twenties. In January 1924 an initial speculative attack made it drop to 29, but its fall was successfully halted by a counterattack from the Banque de France, with the support of Lazard Frères and a loan of $100 million from the Morgan Bank. But uncertainty surrounding budgetary policy lingered on and capital flight intensified after the left-wing Cartel des Gauches came to power in May 1924. The franc reached its lowest point of 49 to the dollar – just over a tenth of its pre-war value – on 21 July 1926. On that day, the prime minister, Edouard Herriot, resigned after the false balance sheet scandal at the Banque de France, which lent more to the government than permitted by law, was revealed to the Chamber. On the next day, his replacement by Raymond Poincaré, the former leader of the right-wing Bloc des droites, restored confidence; the franc picked up again, reaching Fr.25.5 to the dollar – 124 to the pound – by the end of the year. It was stabilised *de facto* at this rate, in other words at a fifth of its pre-war value, in December 1926 and *de jure* in June 1928. France finally returned to the gold standard, with a currency widely considered undervalued, unlike the pound.[69]

The crisis and the subsequent stabilisation of the franc had conflicting effects on the Parisian financial centre, and 1926 marked a very sharp turning point in its destiny. Until then, the weakness of the French currency had clearly been a handicap for Paris; the franc no longer inspired confidence among either French or foreign investors and, on the contrary, provoked capital flight, even if its depreciation encouraged French exports and helped to generate a surplus on the current balance. French citizens bought foreign stocks in Paris and in other financial centres, causing an often 'invisible' exodus of 'deserting capital'. This, nevertheless, helped French foreign assets, estimated at 25 billion Poincaré francs (or 5 billion gold francs) between 1921 and 1926.[70] But few issues took place in Paris except for some consolidation loans to European debtors and a relatively modest participation in the Dawes Loan.[71] The Paris centre's prestige thus decreased, and the Banque de France had to be on the defensive in the face of initiatives taken by the Bank of England to rebuild, under its leadership, the international monetary system through cooperation among central banks.[72] Following its stabilisation in 1926, the franc was once more a currency that inspired confidence. 'Deserting' capital returned to France, foreign issues picked up again and the Parisian market recovered a good part of its pre-war vitality, rekindling the ambitions of Paris economic and political leaders to compete with London and New York. According to Emile Moreau, the governor of the Banque de France: 'Reorganising the Paris market to make it one of the world's leading markets, coordinating and extending our banks' actions abroad will be the main tasks following stabilisation.'[73]

Acceptances and foreign issues. The most important plan was to create a vast market for international acceptances in Paris that would rival London's – similar to the situation from 1914 when the American authorities tried, successfully, to develop this activity in New York. Yet in 1913 French acceptances had barely represented one-tenth of British acceptances. From then on, they fell almost continuously, being worth only Fr.250 million in 1926, before going up again until 1929, when they reached Fr.1,300 million; in other words, just over £10 million, less than each of the main merchant banks in the City. Moreover, setting up such a market was intended to facilitate the emergence of a money market modelled on London's, where national and foreign funds on the lookout for short-term investments could always manage to find a use. In the absence of such facilities in their country, French companies and banks employed those available across the English Channel, thus depriving Paris of revenue from this activity and of another key aspect of a large international financial centre.

In addition to a propaganda campaign, various measures were taken to set up such a market, in particular simplifying the tax system and introducing rediscount facilities at the Banque de France. But the most important initiative was the founding on 20 December 1929 of the Banque Française d'Acceptations, with a capital of Fr.100 million, by the main French banks – *banques d'affaires* and deposit banks – in partnership with two Belgian banks and with backing from the central bank. Since all the French banks financed this type of credit, although each for a relatively modest sum, one of the goals of the new bank was to stimulate the development of acceptances for larger sums. The new bank made an encouraging start, with Fr.565 million worth of acceptances on its balance sheet at the end of 1930, but these quickly fell with the recession of the subsequent years. Although the slump certainly slowed business down, it is doubtful whether, even during a normal period, a discount market able to rival London's could have developed in Paris. Indeed, the French banks lacked experience and traditions in this field and, above all, they were reluctant to see the activities of bill brokers develop[74] – those traders of bills of exchange who in London and, to a lesser extent, in New York, made the acceptance market truly liquid. In any case, there was a long way to go: in 1930 the total amount of acceptances was estimated at Fr.4.8 billion francs in Paris, compared with Fr.40 billion in London and New York.[75]

On the Paris market, foreign issues, insignificant until 1928, then picked up, though only slightly, owing to the public's distrust due to losses suffered during the war.[76] They increased to 3.9 billion francs – $152 million – in 1930, that is to say 12% of all issues, for the most part on behalf of central and eastern European countries supported by French foreign policy in the region, namely Austria, Poland, Hungary and Romania.[77] This too fell far short of New York with its $1,100 million or even London with its $550 million.[78] On the Paris Bourse, the foreign securities still listed represented a quarter of French stock in the twenties; but their prices were inflated by the franc's depreciation, and this proportion somewhat exaggerated the internationalisation of the Paris market.

Financial architecture.   The big banks continued to dominate the Paris market during the twenties. However, war and inflation weakened their position, not so much within the country itself, even if they had to face growing competition from the main provincial banks (the Crédit du Nord, the Société Nancéenne de Crédit and others), as *vis-à-vis* the outside. Their assets decreased, not only in real terms compared with their 1913 levels but also against those of their foreign competitors, particularly the English 'Big Five', even though they had been almost the same size before the war.[79] With the stoppage, then the too slow resumption of international loans, the large banks withdrew to the national market and formed a cartel for the placing of domestic industrial issues.[80] Their network of branches abroad contracted somewhat following the disappearance of Russian branches, the closure of several offices in the Middle East and the gradual retreat from Latin America, but they remained present in the empire and in the world's main financial centres.[81]

The *banques d'affaires* too had to rethink their strategy and turn more towards financing the national economy. The share of French stock in the portfolio of the Banque de Paris et des Pays-Bas, for example, went from 23% in 1913 to 41% in 1928, that of industrial shares went from 11% to 33%. Similarly, purely banking activities, including the collection of deposits, became increasingly important in the bank's business, to the detriment of more financial specialities, like issues. Whereas the latter had generally produced approximately 70% of the bank's gross profits before the war, their contribution only exceeded half between 1928 and 1930.[82] The foreign banks present in Paris were more numerous – totalling thirty-five in 1923 – than before 1914, a little over half of them British and American banks. They had access to rediscounts at the Banque de France and their arrival did not fail to worry French bankers, who in 1920 expected to be able to limit competition from these banks in the national market, but without success.[83]

For their part, the members of the *haute banque*, particularly the Protestant banks (Hottinguer, Mallet, de Neuflize and Vernes) continued to prosper in the niches that they had carved out for themselves since the end of the nineteenth century, primarily in wealth management. They certainly remained prestigious and influential, if only because of their presence in the *Conseil des Régents* of the Banque de France and on the boards of banks, insurance companies, railway companies and others, but, from now on, it was up to others to take the initiative. As for the Rothschilds, who hovered above the rest before the Great War, they remained a financial power, but, with the coming of the third generation, they showed obvious signs of entrepreneurial decline, contenting themselves with managing more or less passively their industrial interests in the railways, mines, electricity or oil. As Jean Bouvier has written about Edouard de Rothschild, the head of the house: 'He is a man who is feared, who is consulted and needed. But it is true that the Rothschilds are no longer *rulers*.'[84] The most dynamic house was, without doubt, Lazard Frères, resembling an investment bank, which won acclaim by helping the Banque de France defend the franc in 1924 and became involved very early on in industrial financing, notably with Citroën, one of the largest European car manufacturers at the end of the twenties.[85]

At the top of the structure, the Banque de France looked like an institution undergoing massive changes; the ambitions that Emile Moreau, its governor from 1926 to 1930, set for the Parisian financial centre were all challenges that the central bank had to grapple with so that it could modernise itself. His initiatives to create a discount market in Paris aimed to strengthen both the Paris centre's international position and the capacity for intervening and the authority of the French central bank. In fact, the latter suffered from being unable legally to have recourse to open-market operations to try and offset the excess of liquid assets created by other instruments, such as direct advances to the Treasury before 1926 or sales of francs to maintain parity after the franc's return to the gold standard. Since the big deposit banks were, in these conditions, very liquid, the Banque de France found it difficult to control the market merely by using its discount rate. Moreover, the deposit banks were loath to apply to the central bank to discount their commercial paper, since they resented it as a competitor for continuing to practice direct discounting on behalf of the public and for having a bill portfolio that in any case amounted to 12% of that of the four big deposit banks in 1928. In these conditions, the French central bank's room for manoeuvre was small and limited in the domestic market.[86]

On the other hand, the Banque de France's international influence strengthened considerably in the three or four years that preceded the Great Depression and helped to enhance the Parisian centre's status at that time. From the stabilisation of the franc at the end of 1926, the French central bank built up huge quantities of gold and foreign claims, particularly in pounds, a build-up that can be explained by the surplus on the French balance of payments. The latter was due to the strength of exports, which benefited from the franc's undervaluation, the repatriation of French capital and the influx of foreign capital, all attracted by the strength of the currency, as well as to the weakness of capital exports. Furthermore, this accumulation of gold by the Banque de France gave rise to a great deal of criticism from Anglo-Saxon leaders, who saw this as a major cause of the instability of the international monetary system. But it put France in a position of strength in international monetary and financial relations – especially *vis-à-vis* Britain, for which it could cause serious difficulties owing to the overvaluation of the pound, forcing it to abandon the gold standard if the Banque de France were to convert its claims on London into gold.

The French authorities did not try to provoke a crisis in the international monetary system, but they were determined to take full advantage of the country's restored financial power to achieve a certain number of political and economic goals, including promoting the Parisian market. In this way, the Banque de France was henceforth able to extend its influence over the central banks of central Europe, an objective that corresponded to the broad lines of French diplomacy, whereas until then it had been obliged to leave the initiative to the Bank of England.[87] The pound's fragility and the franc's strength therefore altered temporarily the balance of power between Paris and London and put the Bank of England on the defensive. But it was, above all, a matter of international financial diplomacy, which certainly strengthened Paris as an international financial centre, but still left it far behind London when it came to the range of services offered, the networks of international relationships or even efficiency. Its money market and its capital market were also no match either for London or, indeed, New York. For a few years, the Parisian market recovered its glory of the Belle Epoque and the hope of supplanting the City; but its prosperity, essentially founded on the inflow of short-term capital, remained fragile and would not survive the shock of the thirties.

Berlin: the price of defeat

The crisis of the mark was far more serious than that of the French franc. German inflation, which saw the rate of the German currency go from 4.2 marks to the dollar in June 1914 to 4,200 billion in November 1923, has entered into the mythology of monetary history.[88] Until mid-1922 it was more or less under control, even if at that time the mark was worth only some 2% of its pre-war value, which at first encouraged the beginnings of an economic recovery. The situation deteriorated during the second half of the year – the assassination on 24 June of the minister for foreign affairs, Walther Rathenau, marking the transition from inflation to hyperinflation – and became uncontrollable with the Franco-Belgian occupation of the Ruhr at the beginning of 1923. On 15 November of that year, a brake was finally applied by the authorities, with the introduction of the transitional Rentenmark whose value was fixed at 1,000 billion inflation-adjusted marks. Stabilisation took effect on 1 September 1924, when the Reichsmark replaced the Rentenmark and was once again convertible to gold at the rate of 4.2 marks to the dollar.

The causes and consequences of this inflation have prompted plenty of ink to flow. The causes were both external, connected with the balance-of-payments deficit that grew under the effect of reparations and capital flight, and internal, with the increase in the budget deficit, the state's growing inability to stabilise its finances, and the unbridled recourse to printing money – in an attempt to meet the demands of various interest groups or, more generally, to resolve the contradictions and conflicts within German society, exacerbated by the defeat and establishment of the Weimar Republic. As for the consequences, although the fall of the currency was successful in the initial phase by stimulating exports, hyperinflation on the other hand ravaged the social fabric, notably by provoking the ruin of the German middle classes.

The effects of German inflation.   Like all large-scale economic or political upheavals, inflation in Germany made losers and winners – big business being indisputably in the second camp, though to varying degrees depending on the sector. Hyperinflation did little to strengthen Berlin's role as a financial centre, as it was of far more benefit to debtors than to creditors. Industrialists, who did not hesitate to encourage it, on the whole ended up strengthened, having taken advantage of the cir-cumstances to increase their production capacity and undertake new mergers and acquisitions, while reducing their dependency on the banks. The banks, more cautious and, in general, loyal to monetary orthodoxy, ended up weakened: between 1913 and 1924, the nine big Berlin banks lost 43% of their equity capital and 50% of their reserves, the bulk of these losses however, having, been endured during the war and the two first post-war years.[89] But the balance of power, largely in favour of the big banks before 1914, shifted towards large industrial groups. The weakness of the former inevitably had repercussions on Berlin's position as an international financial centre, which had always tended to be identified with the weight of the big banks and their influence on the German economy.

Just like their French counterparts, the German banks at that time found themselves far behind the British clearing banks in terms of size. Furthermore, their sphere of activity outside Germany had been con-siderably reduced by the confiscation or sale of a large part of their foreign assets. Deutsche Bank, for example, lost all its investments in oil and railways in Mosul and in Syria, but succeeded in transferring its interests in the Anatolian railways to the Bank für Orientalische Eisen-bahnen in Zurich; it also had to sell the Deutsche Überseeische Elektricitäts-Gesellschaft, transferred in 1920 to a Spanish banking consortium.[90] Inflation also led to capital flight, which reached huge proportions with the transition to hyperinflation, estimates of German foreign assets at the end of 1922 varying from 2 to 6 billion gold marks.[91] The big banks were fully involved in this capital outflow. Between 1920 and 1923, while the share of German Treasury Bonds fell from 48.3% to 2.2% of their assets, deposits in foreign banks – the main item on their balance sheets – grew from 7.3% to 30.9%, part of these deposits being invested directly in the subsidiaries that German banks had set up abroad, mainly in Amsterdam, to manage their currency transactions.[92] Although it weakened the Berlin market, inflation, among other opportunities, was particularly conducive to foreign exchange activities, which, in Berlin as in London and Paris, henceforth held a prime place in banking business. Between 1919 and 1924, 867 banks were founded in Germany, including 293 in Berlin, mainly to capture a slice of this market. The big banks also saw their business expand, the number of accounts opened at Deutsche Bank going, for example, from 290,000 in 1913 to 600,000 in 1919 and the number of salaried employees from 9,587 in 1913 to 37,000 in 1923. Inflation also encouraged the trend towards concentration in the sector, with the small regional banks, which lacked equity capital, finding themselves forced to sell up to avoid bankruptcy. The nine large Berlin banks acquired a total of 279 banks between 1918 and 1925, including 62 for Deutsche Bank and 36 for the Disconto-Gesellschaft.[93] The big banks continued to strengthen their position within the German banking system. Their share of the resources of commercial banks, which had been 39% before the war, went from 50% in 1925 to 70% in 1930. They were also more present in the Berlin Börse, whose membership in 1929 was nearly one and a half times higher than in 1914, and they far outnumbered the independent stockbrokers.[94]

The weight of the German big banks.   More than ever, therefore, the big banks constituted the cornerstone of a Berlin financial centre that was once more called upon to play a not insignificant role in international capital flows during the second part of the twenties. But this role was no longer the same as it had been before 1914, since Germany was from then on a capital-importing country. By 1938 German foreign assets represented a mere $700 million compared with $5,800 million in 1913 – which placed the country far behind Britain, the United States and France, not to mention small economies like the Netherlands, Switzerland and Belgium – whereas its liabilities increased by $4.2 billion for the 1924–30 period alone.[95] Another noteworthy difference with the pre-war period was that more than half the German external debt comprised short-term loans and that the bulk of imported funds was in fact used to pay reparations.

The influence of the private banks and of their networks of relationships should not be underestimated. However, the most important of these were no longer in Berlin. Mendelssohn was unquestionably still a leading banking house, particularly in foreign exchange transactions and loans to the government. Its Amsterdam branch played a key role in this, under the leadership of Fritz Mannheimer, 'probably the most gifted and certainly the most colourful of the international speculators of the 1920s'.[96] Yet Bleichröder, the other big name in Berlin's banking aristocracy, continued its irreversible decline. The most prominent firm of the day was M. M. Warburg & Co., from Hamburg, which took full advantage of its connections in the United States and acted, among other things, as the International Acceptance Bank's agent in Europe.[97] It was thus particularly well placed to facilitate the inflows of foreign capital to Germany and to obtain funds both for public and private institutions. Moreover, its national stature led it to open a representative office in Berlin in 1927.[98]

The big commercial banks, and to a certain extent the best-known private banks too, were institutions through which capital transfers were made. Their role was not purely a passive one, especially as far as the use of these funds on the national market was concerned. The big banks borrowed on a short-term basis abroad and then lent on a long-term basis to German companies, a risky strategy in the event of the influx of foreign capital coming to a stop. Furthermore, they had to deal with competition from foreign banks, above all American, which granted credit directly to German companies and took charge of issuing securities on their behalf on the New York market. The influx of foreign capital into the commercial banks complicated the Reichsbank's task, but the bank managed, nevertheless, to maintain the stability of the currency and prices. Independent from the government since 1922, it was chaired from 1924 to 1930 by Hjalmar Schacht, a former commercial bank manager whose contacts abroad, particularly with Montagu Norman, governor of the Bank of England, helped to enhance the prestige of the German central bank and of the Berlin market.[99]

The profits of the neutrals

The international financial position of the nations that had stayed neutral during the First World War, particularly the Netherlands, Sweden and Switzerland, strengthened after the end of the hostilities. These three countries benefited from stable currencies after their exchange rates had returned to their pre-war parity and they had become linked to gold from 1925. Foreign capital, which they attracted during periods of political and monetary turbulence, strengthened the capacity of their financial centres, especially those of Amsterdam and Zurich.

Amsterdam.   After London and Paris, Amsterdam probably established itself as the third European financial centre after the war, with its significance, at the beginning in any case, stemming from its relationships with its big neighbour across the Rhine. Indeed, Amsterdam was described as Germany's financial centre during the years of inflation and hyperinflation.[100] All the major German banks set up there immediately after the war,[101] while the industrialists, for example Thyssen who founded the Bank voor Handel en Scheepvaart, were not to be outdone. They were, of course, trying to protect their assets from the ravages of inflation and, above all, were active on the foreign exchange market, whose turnover is said to have reached £5 million per day in 1920, an amount higher than London's according to some estimates. But they were also active in Amsterdam's own financial activities. While they had been permanently refused admittance to the stock exchange in 1922, they were eventually allowed to take part in the discount market – the bills that they accepted being discountable from 1926 with the De Nederlandsche Bank, the Netherlands' central bank – as well as in foreign issues.

Encouraged by the Dutch monetary authorities, eager to enhance Amsterdam's status as an international centre, the acceptance market, for the most part made up of German drafts, experienced spectacular growth and quickly established itself as the foremost in continental Europe, its outstanding liabilities going from some 36 million florins ($24 million) in 1922–23 to 799 million ($535 million) in 1929–30;[102] in other words, more than twice the Parisian market's but only a quarter of London's. However, it was a rather local market, in view of the weak demand for these bills on the part of banks not established in the Netherlands.[103] As for the capital market, loans amounting to 1.4 billion florins – $936 million – were issued between 1924 and 1929 on behalf of foreign governments and companies;[104] that is to say, 42% of the total number of issues in the Netherlands, a percentage not far off London's and definitely higher than in Paris or New York. Moreover, few loans were taken out in the main international centres without the participation, even symbolic, of Amsterdam, which often also provided leadership for loans on a smaller scale, issued jointly with Switzerland and Sweden.[105]

The Swiss financial centre.   Switzerland played a more limited role than Amsterdam in the field of foreign issues and the discount market, the Swiss National Bank only rediscounting Swiss paper. It was the same in terms of foreign banks in the country's main financial centres, with only Lloyds Bank in Geneva in 1919 and American Express in Zurich in 1921 coming to join those already present in Switzerland. Basel's significance as a financial centre was enhanced by the decision to establish the Bank for International Settlements (BIS) there, a choice dictated by the need to reach a compromise among the powers, Britain refusing French preferences (Paris or Brussels) and

France refusing British preferences (London or Amsterdam).[106] All the same, the Swiss financial centre showed great vitality. On the capital market, 56 issues for a total of Fr.1.1 billion ($210 million), were placed in Switzerland – generally together with other centres – between 1924 and 1931;[107] in other words, about a quarter of that of the Netherlands'. Furthermore, the big banks and the cantonal banks traded foreign bills even in the absence of rediscount facilities at the National Bank. Also, a foreign exchange market, particularly for the currencies of central and eastern European countries, developed from the beginning of the twenties.[108]

Switzerland's speciality mainly consisted in attracting foreign capital and redirecting it to other financial centres, through both bank loans and wealth management activities. It is difficult, however, to estimate precisely the supply of capital inflows into the country. At the end of 1929, Gottlieb Bachmann, chairman of the Swiss National Bank, put the value of foreign accounts in Switzerland at between Fr.1 billion and Fr.1.3 billion ($200–250 million),[109] that is to say, 6% of total bank deposits but 15% of those of the big banks that attracted most of these funds. A significant part, but difficult to estimate precisely, of this capital, especially of French origin, was re-exported, generally in the form of short-term investments and chiefly with German debtors. It was this type of transaction that accounted for the very rapid growth during the twenties of the eight big Swiss banks,[110] whose total assets increased by 71% between 1918 and 1928, going from Fr.4.2 to Fr.7.2 billion. It even more than doubled for the Comptoir d'escompte, the Eidgenössische Bank and the Union Bank of Switzerland.[111]

The spectacular rise of the big banks was not without an impact on the Swiss banking system.[112] For the first time, they overtook the cantonal banks, far less involved in international business, to the extent that by 1930 their total assets represented 41% of those of all Swiss banks, compared with 36% for the cantonal banks and 23% for the other categories such as local banks, savings banks or mortgage banks. On the international level, the two largest Swiss banks – the Swiss Bank Corporation and the Crédit Suisse – grew nearer in size to the big French and German banks, but they still fell far short of the British banks.[113] On the other hand, their presence abroad remained weak, the two London branches of the Swiss Bank Corporation being the only remaining foreign branches of Swiss banks, no others having been opened after the war.

Nevertheless, the big banks took part in international issue syndicates, occasionally even as leading managers. In 1927, for example, the Crédit Suisse took charge of placing a significant instalment of the foreign loan of SwFr.150 million ($29 million) to the French national railways, the largest foreign loan ever handled by this bank, which considerably enhanced its international prestige.[114] But it was the loans across the Rhine that made up the largest part of the big Swiss banks' international credit activities. By 1930 Switzerland was Germany's fourth creditor, with 13% of the capital loaned, behind the United States (30%), the Netherlands (18%) and Britain (15%). Far riskier, German debtors gathered the bulk of the big banks' foreign credit. By 1929 they represented 24% of the Swiss Bank Corporation's liabilities, way ahead of the United States, in third position with 8%, and of Britain and France, each with 6%. Similar or higher proportions were to be found in other banks, since in 1933 Germany absorbed half the investment abroad of the Crédit Suisse and the Basler Handelsbank.[115] In this respect, the Swiss financial centre seemed less like a hub for international investment than a narrow canal transporting it to not very diversified destinations.

Another typical activity of the Swiss financial centre, wealth management, expanded dramatically from the twenties onwards. Here too, figures are lacking, especially as far as private bankers and the share of funds coming from abroad is concerned. It was probably during this period that the big banks overtook, in absolute value, the main private banks for the amount of funds managed off balance sheet. At the Swiss Bank Corporation, this went from Fr.436 million, 85% of the total assets, in 1910 to Fr.3.3 billions, twice the total assets, in 1930, a year in which the amounts managed on behalf of clients by the Crédit Suisse exceeded Fr.5 billion, that is to say, nearly three times this bank's total assets. The proportion of funds under management to the balance sheet total was even higher with private bankers. There are no figures available for the twenties, but in 1935, for example, MM. Pictet & Cie in Geneva managed on behalf of third parties a total amount of approximately Fr.300 million, which reached Fr.470 million in 1945, a sum that was more than ten times higher than its assets at that time. Geneva's role in wealth management was not, however, limited to the private bankers' share – by 1929 the Swiss Bank Corporation managed 20% of such funds from this city, compared with 39% from its headquarters in Basle and 31% in Zurich.[116]

Finance companies, the other Swiss speciality,[117] should not be overlooked either. Many of these, usually small, developed to attract capital in search of a haven during the troubled years immediately following the war.[118] Holding companies enabled foreign firms to develop a part of their financial activities from Switzerland, notably the German chemical giant IG Farben,[119] or continued to act as intermediaries for financing new industries abroad, oil activities taking over from electricity after the war.[120]

Faced with the problems posed by international capital flows, the young National Bank took its first difficult steps to try and limit this influx and its possible impact on prices in Switzerland. On a conceptual level, its commitment to gold and its endeavours at the end of the twenties to replace some of the banknotes in circulation with gold coins – an attempt at limiting the banks' power to create money – amazed even the high priest of monetary orthodoxy, Montagu Norman, governor of the Bank of England.[121] On a practical level, it drew its inspiration from the British model and in 1927 concluded a gentlemen's agreement with the big banks, which promised to refer the matter to the National Bank before issuing new foreign loans, subscribed above all by non-residents.[122] The formula was to be of limited success, but it would be widely adopted again during subsequent decades.

The years of crisis

The Roaring Twenties came to a close with the Wall Street Crash of October 1929, an eminently financial event, directly linked with the activities of the most dynamic financial centre of the day, New York. And yet, however significant the financial aspects were, it should not be forgotten that the depression of the thirties constituted a phenomenon on a far greater scale, on account of its duration and its effects, than the stock-market, banking and monetary crises that marked the period. In the industrialised countries, the first symptoms of the crisis – falling industrial production and employment indices – were visible in 1928. The reversal of economic circumstances thus preceded the stock-market crash, which was in fact itself partly caused by investors' fears about the state of the American economy. But such a violent shock inevitably made matters worse, if only by temporarily paralysing the credit mechanism.

The Wall Street Crash

People have long wondered about the causes of the Wall Street Crash, a legendary event in the chronicles of the twentieth century. Should it be seen as the quintessence of the New York market in the twenties, characterised by the euphoria of growth, speculative fever, inexperience and also, at times, fraud? More than anyone else, John Kenneth Galbraith popularised this interpretation in a book that is still famous fifty years after it was first published.[123] According to him, the raging bull market from early 1928 was conditioned by a popular belief in the market's perpetual rise – encouraged by the optimistic pronouncements of political and economic leaders, by the forming of investment trusts and holding companies, and by the tremendous leverage caused by the increasingly widespread practice of margin buying.

While the explanation contains a good deal of truth, Wall Street at that time could not be considered a vast casino plagued by a speculative orgy. On the whole, New York fulfilled its new role of 'world's banker' properly. Issues were certainly more costly than in London, but this was due to the need to offer higher interest to attract an American public that was still distrustful of foreign securities – all the more so because, with the sudden rise in shares, funds spurned foreign bonds, whose issues fell from $1,338 million to $673 million between 1927 and 1929,[124] in favour of short-term loans to brokers. In any case, and whatever the international context, the crash was primarily an American phenomenon, even if the foreign banks lent to brokers, and a number of foreign investors, especially British, speculated openly on the New York Stock Exchange. Furthermore, recent research has confirmed that black Thursday could not be attributed to external shocks, such as the downturn of European stock exchanges, particularly those of London and Berlin, which for the most part developed independently from New York's, and whose waning influence in late 1928 and early 1929 seemed more like a consequence of New York's rapid rise than a cause of the crash of October 1929.[125]

To what should this collapse be attributed? Whatever the excesses of the period, the boom of the years 1925–29 can be explained mainly by the increased prosperity of large American companies, following the rationalisation of production and the introduction of new management methods. The 'leaders' of the day, like RCA (Radio Corporation of America) or General Motors, reflected the profitability and the growth prospects of these companies. However, Eugene White's analyses suggest that a bubble had indeed formed from 1928 onwards, due essentially to the difficulty in evaluating the fundamentals – in other words, the proper relation between the spot rate of the share and a firm's capacity to maintain the level of its dividend for long enough. This evaluation is always delicate with new technologies, in which future prospects may seem brilliant even before the companies have earned sufficient profit. Indeed, it was these securities, with those of the public utilities, which at the time seemed the most overvalued. Moreover, the excessive level of stock prices did not escape the notice of contemporaries, judging by the strong increase in 1929 of the interest rates on loans pledged on securities that the brokers granted to their clients, the value of the pledge seeming less and less certain.[126]

Public confidence began to be shaken during the summer of 1929 due to the increasingly clear harbingers of a recession, and prices fell at the beginning of October. Brokers were quickly overwhelmed by the large increase in the volume of sales, margin calls became more frequent, and the ticker tape lagged further and further behind. Without any ongoing information on price levels, investors lost track of their positions and panic seized the stock exchange first on Thursday, 24 October, then on Tuesday, 29 October, after the attempts by the market's main players to stabilise share prices.[127] The New York banks, supported by the Federal Reserve of New York, quickly increased their loans and managed to prevent a widespread lack of liquidity and a series of bank bankruptcies. After having lost 30% since its height in August, the New York Stock Exchange stabilised in the first months of 1930, as did the production and employment indices. Similarly, issues of foreign loans took off again both in the United States – a little over $1 billion in 1930, compared with $705 million in 1929[128] – and at world level, thanks in particular to the Young Loan[129] of $300 million, issued on several markets in June 1930 as part of the rescheduling of German reparations and the founding of the Bank for International Settlements. But the economic crisis, aggravated by the Federal Reserve Board's imminent restrictive policy, would plunge the country into a slump and handicap the New York market during the thirties.

The effects of the crisis

The Great Depression of the early 1930s represented, should one need reminding, the most serious economic crisis of the twentieth century; the slump in production, the collapse in world trade and the dramatic rise in unemployment were its most striking characteristics. World industrial output dropped by 36% between 1929 and 1932, world trade by 25% in volume and 48% in value, the price of manufactured goods fell by 26% and that of raw materials by 56%.[130] Between 1930 and 1933, the average unemployment rate was 34.2% in Germany and 28.4% in the United States, the two countries most affected by the depression.[131]

Berlin and the banking crisis.   The effects of the stock-market crash were soon felt by financial institutions. The big Italian banks[132] went through serious difficulties in 1930, and in May 1931 the Credit-Anstalt in Vienna went bankrupt. Of the main international financial centres, Berlin was the first and most severely hit by the crisis affecting the German big banks.[133] On 13 July 1931 the Danat Bank, weakened by the collapse of the large textile company Nordwolle, closed its doors. This provoked a run of depositors on the other banks, which decided to pay only 20% of the sums that their clients wanted to withdraw; in other words, to suspend their payments. The German banks were initially penalised by the interruption, following the crash, of the foreign capital inflows into Germany on which the entire credit mechanism hinged. Then, as the crisis persisted, due above all to Chancellor Brüning's deflationary policy and to international tensions, especially surrounding the payment of reparations, they had to contend with massive withdrawals of foreign funds. Finally, in July 1931 they were no longer able to obtain refinancing from the Reichsbank, whose gold and currency reserves shrank constantly after it had failed, faced with conditions imposed by France, in its attempts to replenish them by means of a foreign loan, making gold cover for banknotes drop below its statutory minimum.

The intervention of the German government put an end to the panic. It ordered the immediate closure of all banks for two days, during which the Dresdner Bank also declared itself bankrupt, and introduced exchange controls on 15 July. Thus Germany was the first country to leave *de facto* the gold standard; the parity of the Reichsmark was admittedly maintained, but it was protected by imposing restrictions on the free movement of capital, gold and currencies. But state intervention went further. With state backing, the Reichsbank set up the Akzept- und Garantiebank to obtain credit for commercial banks and savings banks. Furthermore, the government undertook major restructuring, which boiled down to the near nationalisation of the big banks, forcing the Dresdner Bank and the Danat Bank to merge into a new institution, 91% held by the state and the Reichsbank. At the same time, the authorities ended up owning more than 50% of the Commerzbank's equity capital and approximately 35% of that of the Deutsche Bank und Disconto-Gesellschaft, created from the merger of the two banks two years earlier.[134] Of the big Berlin banks, only the Berliner Handels-Gesellschaft passed through the crisis without incident. All this had the effect of marginalising Berlin as a financial centre and cutting it off from the large international financial circuits, a situation that would hardly improve with the Third Reich's autarchic policy and its increased control over the national credit system, despite the re-privatisation of the big banks.

London and the end of the gold standard.   From Berlin, the crisis moved to London. It was not the City's big banks that were in danger.

They held out well and, unlike in other financial centres, no major British bank had to close its doors during this period. The merchant banks, on the other hand, were hit harder; with the contraction in international trade, the value of bills of exchange on the London discount market fell from £365 million to £134 million between 1929 and 1933. The introduction of exchange control in Germany dealt them an even more severe blow. Negotiations with the Weimar government led in September 1931 to an agreement stipulating that interest on German commercial debts would be paid in convertible currencies but the principal would be frozen. Other agreements would follow until August 1939, setting up mechanisms to reimburse a part of the acceptances in Reichsmarks; but the bills would not really be repaid before the fifties. As in 1914, the most vulnerable banking houses were those that were the most involved in financing German trade and that found themselves with sizeable sums of unconvertible acceptances – by 1936, £9.3 million for Kleinworts – three times the firm's capital – and £4.9 million for Schröders.[135] While these two large houses extricated themselves by drawing on their reserves and by borrowing from the Westminster Bank, smaller ones, which had in fact never fully recovered from the effects of the First World War, like Fedk. Huth & Co. and Goschen & Cunliffe, disappeared from the scene.

But the City's real crisis was that of the pound sterling, and it undermined for good the foundations that had underpinned its dominant position for more than a century.[136] Pressure on the pound had been almost constant since its return to the gold standard in 1925, but it intensified from 1929, owing to a loss of confidence in a British currency generally considered overvalued, with the Bank of England having to face increasingly frequent withdrawals of gold. The situation worsened during the summer of 1931 under the triple effect of, first, the German crisis and the anxieties that it gave rise to regarding the creditworthiness of British banks involved in Germany; second, the publication on 13 July of the report of the Macmillan Committee, revealing the huge gap between foreign short-term claims on London and the British gold and currency reserves; and, third and most important, the appearance on 31 July of the findings of the May Committee's inquiry into the state of public finances, which showed the extent of the budget deficit – insignificant nowadays but worrying for contemporaries – and recommended drastic savings. The crisis then took on a political dimension. The Labour government resigned on 24 August in the face of demands from the Bank of England for spending constraints – in particular a big reduction in unemployment benefit, recommended by the May report – in order to be able to obtain two loans, totalling £80 million, from the

United States and France. It was replaced by a government of national unity, still chaired by Labour Prime Minister Ramsay MacDonald. The announcement of a new budget on 10 September did not soothe anxieties, which on the contrary were exacerbated by news of a mutiny in the Royal Navy. Withdrawals of funds continued, especially following a bank bankruptcy in Amsterdam, and on 21 September 1931 the British government suspended the pound's gold convertibility, which henceforth floated in relation to the main currencies. In addition, twenty-five countries followed the trend, primarily those belonging to the British Empire (with the exception of Canada and South Africa), Scandinavia and eastern Europe, as well as Britain's key trading partners, Argentina and Portugal.

The abandonment of the gold standard marked a decisive turning point in the history of London as a financial centre. Confidence in 'impregnable' sterling was shaken for good. And even if the City was not greatly affected for the time being and suffered more from the collapse of international trade, its prestige and influence would never be the same again. To begin with, its position seemed shaky in comparison with that of New York and above all Paris. Even if the latter did not contribute to the fall in the pound, the size of its gold reserves and its foreign assets strengthened its position and made London pale. For many French commentators, Paris's time had come: 'At present, Paris seems to be winning the struggle for financial supremacy', wrote Pierre Coste in February 1932 in a book devoted to the top three financial centres, even though he was aware that 'this situation, which is due at least as much to exceptional international circumstances as to France's power and prestige, could well change if subsequent developments are unfavourable to our country'.[137]

Paris and New York in turmoil.   This is, indeed, what happened. The devaluation of the pound accentuated the effects of a crisis that deepened in France from 1931. The banks were not spared. Between October 1929 and September 1937, 670 French banks became insolvent, the vast majority of them small local and regional banks.[138] In Paris, the Banque Nationale de Crédit (BNC), the country's fourth deposit bank, collapsed in 1931 and was built up again the following year, with help from the state, under the name of Banque Nationale pour le Commerce et l'Industrie (BNCI).[139] The Banque de l'Union Parisienne, one of the main *banques d'affaires* shaken by the crises in Germany and central Europe, experienced serious difficulties that brought it to the brink of bankruptcy in 1932; but it was saved by the joint intervention of the Banque de France and the main Parisian banks.[140] On the other hand, attempts at setting up a money market in Paris came to nothing from 1931, the volume of acceptances of the Banque Française d'Acceptations falling from Fr.565 million in 1930 to Fr.53 million in 1934. As regards foreign issues, which had not really taken off on the Parisian market in the twenties, they ceased almost completely.[141] From 1933 there was growing pressure on the franc, which the monetary authorities, along with those of the other gold-block countries such as Belgium, the Netherlands and Switzerland, were determined not to devalue, preferring to opt for a deflationary policy that plunged the country even deeper into recession. The decision to devalue was eventually taken by the Front Populaire government on 26 September 1936, in an economic and political climate far from conducive to nurturing an international financial centre.[142]

The pound's devaluation also made itself felt in the United States. Pressure on the dollar and the gold losses recorded by the Federal Reserve led it to raise its discount rate considerably in October 1931 and to embark on a deflationary policy that deepened the recession even further. Bank bankruptcies were on the increase throughout the country, more than 10,000 banks closing their doors up until 1933.[143] The capital market was also shaken, issues on behalf of companies going from $8,000 million in 1929 to $160 million in 1933.[144] The decision to devalue the dollar, taken on 19 April 1933 by the new president, Franklin Roosevelt, gave the economy a bit of a boost. But New York saw its role as an international financial centre, which it had assumed during the twenties, shrivel; foreign loans, which had been its speciality, fell to less than $300 million in 1931 – less than the issues offered in London – and to less than $100 million in 1932 and 1933.

The thirties in Zurich and Geneva.   Nor did the crisis spare the secondary financial centres, among others the Swiss financial world. In 1932 German debt to Switzerland was estimated at 2.7 billion Reichsmarks, including 1.1 billion short-term bank credits and 296 million long-term credits.[145] As for Germany's other creditors – above all, American and British – short-term debt would be subjected to successive clearing agreements that would extend until 1945, with Switzerland consolidating an ever-larger proportion of short-term debt in long-term investments.[146] In view of the importance of their trans-actions with foreign countries, it was obviously the eight big banks that were hardest hit, their assets halving and their profits dropping by more than two-thirds between 1930 and 1935.[147] All the banks, except for the two largest – the Swiss Bank Corporation and the Crédit Suisse – had to agree to major reductions in equity capital; the Schweizerische

Volksbank, which had its headquarters in Bern and which had over-expanded in the twenties, especially because of loans to Germany, was rescued by the Confederation.[148] The bank situation was aggravated by pressure exerted on the Swiss franc following the devaluations of the pound in 1931, then of the dollar in 1933, the markets anticipating the imminent devaluation of the gold-block currencies, including the Swiss currency. The influx of capital into Switzerland, which had marked the beginning of the 1930s following, in particular, Germany's political and economic difficulties and international instability, turned from 1933 into an exodus that would only be stemmed, then turned back, with the devaluation by 30% of the Swiss franc on 26 September 1936.

The banking crisis was particularly severe in Geneva, where it led to the disappearance of the city's main commercial banks. The first to be hit was the Banque de Genève, a bank of a semi-public nature, which had been set up by the Radical government of 1848 and had renounced its issuing right in 1899.[149] Since then it had developed its commercial banking activities, particularly abroad, by tending to venture into risky deals. From the beginning of 1931, the difficulties confronting it were made public, then stirred up by the Socialist opposition and its leader, Léon Nicole. Finally, the Banque de Genève had to close its doors on 11 July 1931, in a tense political atmosphere. This bankruptcy did not help matters much at the Comptoir d'escompte, the city's main commercial bank, which since 1914 had ranked among the country's eight big banks. Weakened by the bank crisis in Germany, where it was deeply involved, various measures were taken to bolster it by the Confederation, which in August 1931 led to its merger with the Union Financière de Genève and to a capital contribution of Fr.30 million, jointly provided by the Swiss Bank Corporation and the Crédit Suisse. Despite these measures, it found itself in such serious difficulty at the beginning of 1933 that it required new aid from the federal government, before in May having to merge with the Banque de Dépôts et de Crédit (created by Genevan private bankers back in 1902) to form the Banque d'Escompte Suisse. The situation then improved for a time, but the crisis of confidence provoked by the election of a government with a Socialist majority in the cantonal elections of November 1933 caused another run on the bank. Faced with the cantonal authorities' refusal to inject new funds, the Banque d'Escompte Suisse had to close its doors on 30 April 1934.[150] From then on, the big Swiss banks would strengthen their foothold in the Genevan market, alongside the private bankers who specialised almost exclusively in wealth management, the foreign banks and the specialised banks of a local nature, like the Caisse Hypothécaire and the Caisse d'Epargne.

Regulation and retreat

In this period of economic stagnation, serial bankruptcies and isolationism, governments tended to intervene more actively in economic affairs, whereas the main financial centres were induced to fall back on their domestic market, whether national or colonial, to revive their activities. The bank bankruptcies and the crisis of confidence in financial institutions were the main reasons for the state intervening to regulate the banks and stock exchanges, and thus ensure the stability of both the economy and the financial system. But the prevailing ideology and growing distrust towards market mechanisms in all the industrialised countries should not be underestimated. Two issues dominated discussions in the thirties: relations between commercial banking and investment banking activities; and the rules governing how the financial markets functioned.

The New Deal reforms. The United States was the first to legislate and it was also the country that went furthest in this field. In the summer of 1932, at the height of the crisis, President Herbert Hoover launched an inquiry into how the securities market operated[151] that lasted two years. The revelations of incompetence and fraud on the part of some of the most prominent financiers were hardly flattering for Wall Street and left a strong negative impression on public opinion. Charles Mitchell, chairman of the National City Bank, had to resign during the hearings, following allegations of breaches of ethics verging on criminality. Some spectacular trials also took place, including that of Richard Whitney, former chairman of the New York Stock Exchange, sentenced and imprisoned for having systematically embezzled the funds of his clients, and that of Andrew Mellon, former secretary to the Treasury, eventually acquitted of accusations of tax evasion.

It was in this climate that radical reforms to the American financial market were introduced within the framework of the New Deal.[152] Two laws were passed in 1933, one on the capital market (the Securities Act) and the other on banks (the Banking Act, better known under the name of its two promoters as the Glass–Steagall Act). The first contained various provisions aimed at improving the quality of information about the securities offered and traded on the stock exchange. The second decreed the complete separation of commercial banking activities (taking deposits and making loans) from investment banking activities (issuing, distributing and trading securities), including if these activities were shared between parent companies and subsidiaries or through either the cross-holding of shares or overlapping directorships. In practice, the commercial banks parted from their subsidiaries involved in securities transactions, whereas the vast majority of private banks opted for investment banking. The major exception was J. P. Morgan & Co., Wall Street's most famous bank, which chose to become a commercial bank, a decision that led several partners to resign and to found an investment bank, Morgan, Stanley & Co. The Glass–Steagall Act also introduced federal deposit insurance, compulsory for banks that were members of the Federal Reserve System, but optional and conditional for the others. The insured institutions paid a premium based on a percentage of their total assets, as a contribution to a guarantee fund intended to pay the depositors of a bankrupt bank. Six months after voting on the law, 14,000 banks had already decided to insure their clients, for a maximum sum of $5,000 per deposit. Another federal regulation – Regulation Q – set a maximum interest rate that the banks could pay on savings deposits. As Richard Sylla has argued, the Glass–Steagall Act was ideological rather than pragmatic and could not simply be seen as an antidote to abuses and financial speculation or as a solution to the conflicts of interest between commercial banking and investment banking. It was rooted in Americans' instinctive distrust of financial concentration and power, already denounced by the Pujo Commission of Enquiry at the beginning of the century.[153] Subsequently, other laws – especially that of 1934 founding the Securities and Exchange Commission (SEC) – completed this New Deal legislation, which would profoundly influence how the New York market operated after 1945.

Banking legislation in continental Europe. Similar measures were taken in a number of European countries. This was notably the case in Belgium, where an initial decree on 22 August 1934 obliged mixed banks to carry out their deposit banking duties separately from their investment banking activities. From then on, the Société Générale de Belgique concentrated all its commercial banking activities in a new institution, the Banque de la Société Générale, later known by the name of Générale de Banque. A second decree on 9 July 1935 confirmed the abolition of mixed banking and, among other things, subjected all institutions having banking status to control by a new body, the *Commission bancaire*. Tellingly, these measures were largely inspired by the bankers themselves, who were anxious to restore confidence.[154]

The universal bank, however, survived in Germany. Even so, owing to the particularly close links between banking and industry, its abolition was debated in a tense mood marked by populist anti-capitalism, rampant anti-Semitism and politicians' paranoid fear of banking power. Moreover, at the time of the July 1931 crisis, Chancellor Brüning 'purged' the top management of the big banks, and a supervisory body was set up in the same year. The banking law of December 1934, enacted under the Nazis, attributed the crisis to individual failings rather than to any shortcoming of the system; it made do with strengthening bank supervision and introducing some restrictions on long-term deposits and on banks' representation on the supervisory boards of other companies. But even though universal banking survived, the government considerably strengthened its hold over institutions whose role in the economy grew weaker as a result of state subsidies granted to companies, the expansion of the savings banks – which became the dominant element in the German banking system, with some 45% of total assets by 1938, compared with 15% for the commercial banks – and the more or less automatic financing of growing public deficits through bank deposits. All this helped to marginalise the big banks, which in any case had never been in favour under the Nazi regime.[155]

Other laws, of a more sinister nature, also helped transform the banking landscape in Germany – those aimed at excluding Jews from economic life. Their departure took place at an unsteady rate. While most Jewish managers of big banks left their posts in 1933 and 1934 (for example, at Deutsche Bank, Oscar Wassermann, Theodor Frank and Georg Solmssen, even though the latter had been christened), some remained on boards of directors until 1938 (such as Hans Fürstenberg at the Berliner Handels-Gesellschaft).[156] The most prominent private banks did not seem too threatened so long as Schacht, who saw them as essential owing to their networks of relationships abroad, remained finance minister; in other words, until September 1937. The Aryanisation of Jewish companies took on renewed vigour in 1938 and became compulsory after the *Kristallnacht* pogroms of 9 and 10 November of the same year. Some banks, such as Mendelssohn & Co., taken over by Deutsche Bank in August 1938, decided to put themselves up for sale. Others chose to continue, transferring property and management into Aryan hands, like MM. Warburg & Co., which took the name of its two new managers, Brinkmann, Wirz & Co., and in which the Warburg family retained 25% of the capital.[157]

In Switzerland, the federal banking law of 1934 did not abolish universal banking, and its only effect was the Confederation's very mild interference in banking affairs.[158] Instead, it set fairly general rules relating to the authorisation to carry on business (including establishing foreign banks), emphasised the responsibility of senior management, contained provisions on liquid assets, imposed a minimum ratio between equity capital and deposits, and entrusted supervision of the system to an independent commission, the Federal Banking

Commission. The law of 1934 was above all famous for its article 47 relating to banking secrecy, which would play a role – whose significance is difficult to quantify but certainly by no means negligible – in the subsequent development of the Swiss financial centre.[159] This article made those who were subject to it – bank employees, managers, directors, auditors and supervisors – liable to fines or up to six months' imprisonment if they divulged business information and, above all, the names of a bank's clients.[160] Banking secrecy had been part of Swiss banking practice since the end of the nineteenth century, but it was only in force in some cantons and came under civil law. Its introduction in the law of 1934 extended its validity to the whole country and gave it a criminal character. The change can be explained mainly by the historical context within which the banking law was drawn up. Article 47 was not the subject of long parliamentary debates, but it was important for the Swiss banks. On the one hand, it prevented any information transmitted to the supervisory bodies from being leaked, which the Swiss banks dreaded at the time. On the other hand, it strengthened the protection offered to foreign depositors by guaranteeing their anonymity *vis-à-vis* foreign countries and, therefore, the capacity for attracting foreign capital – one of Switzerland's main competitive advantages as a financial centre – at a time when the German and French authorities were introducing an exchange control directed at outflows of capital and intensifying their struggle against tax evasion, including by spying and taking reprisals against Swiss banks.

An oral tradition prevailing in Swiss banking circles frequently referred to Gestapo agents who allegedly induced bank employees to divulge the names of some German clients, subsequently heavily sentenced beyond the Rhine – hence the introduction of numbered accounts, the identity of whose holder was only known by the bank management. Recent historical research tends to show that this factor was far from being the main reason why banking secrecy was introduced. Nevertheless, this tradition is undoubtedly a fairly accurate reflection of a widespread fear in Swiss banks and among their foreign clients at that time.

Britain, for its part, steered clear of the trend towards greater regulation of the banks, probably because there had not been any bank bankruptcies during the thirties, as well as because the financial system was more specialised than elsewhere and the Bank of England effectively monitored it to ensure that it was working properly. France, too, left things as they were until 1941, when the Vichy government introduced a law, upheld and completed in 1944, which controlled and regulated banking activities that until then had been open to any newcomers.

Henceforth, banks had to be registered according to their type of activity. The law made a clear distinction between an investment bank and a deposit bank. It also defined a number of specialised institutions, according to their operations or clientele, including finance companies and discount houses.[161]

The reorientation of capital flows.   Banking legislation was not really responsible for the collapse of international financial business in the thirties. The economic slump was first and foremost due to the continuation of the recession, the reduction in foreign trade, economic nationalism – with recourse to competitive devaluations and the introduction, in all the relevant countries, of protectionist tariffs – and the failure of attempts at reviving international cooperation. In such a climate, the activity of the main financial centres naturally took on a much more domestic character. This change did not represent a real break for New York, whose role as an international financial centre was relatively recent and had remained subordinate, throughout the twenties, to its tasks of financing the American economy. Nor was it a break for Berlin, the financial capital of an economic area that had become increasingly autarchic.

Things were different for London, whose prosperity had always largely depended on its international activities – to the point that it gave rise to a lively debate about its responsibility for the country's industrial problems. During the thirties, the City's retreat was initially a retreat to the economic area represented by the British Empire, which enabled it to continue to play, within the framework of the sterling zone, the role that it had previously played at world level. The sterling area was actually made up of a certain number of economies with political and/or economic ties to Britain whose governments decided to maintain a fixed exchange rate with the pound, even at the cost of exchange control. At the outset, it comprised the Commonwealth countries (except for Canada), which were joined in 1933 by the Scandinavian countries and Siam, as well as by associate members like Argentina, Bolivia, Greece, Japan and Yugoslavia. The sterling area also constituted a trade block after Britain's changeover to protectionism at the end of 1931 and the adoption of a preferential imperial tariff in 1932. Its significance and that of the empire for the City was evident in the field of issues. Whereas foreign loans outside the empire ceased almost completely after September 1931,[162] imperial issues continued throughout the decade, to reach £186.7 million in all; that is to say, 17% of the total amount of issues placed in London between 1932 and 1938.[163] The fact remains that the number of foreign issues as a whole, including in the empire, dropped considerably in the thirties, forcing the merchant banks who were mainly dependent on them for a living to show a greater interest in the national economy.

Short-term capital flows did not stop during the Great Depression and subsequent years, but they took a very different form and direction from what had been the norm before 1914 or even between 1920 and 1931. They no longer started out from the traditional capital-exporting countries and ended up in the less developed economies or, as in the twenties, in central Europe; instead, they followed the opposite trend, partly due to the economic situation, which drove creditor countries to repatriate their assets, and partly due to political troubles, which brought about capital flight in numerous countries. These funds were transferred above all to the United States, which saw $5.5 billion worth of short-term capital flood in between 1934 and 1937; to the United Kingdom, where this trend had started somewhat earlier and which received about $4 billion between 1931 and 1937; and to the small neutral countries, Switzerland and the Netherlands, which received some $340 million and $290 million respectively during this period. The bulk of the funds came from France (where the inflow of capital after the stabilisation of the franc in 1926 turned into an outflow after the devaluation of the pound, the forming of the gold block and the coming to power of the Front Populaire in 1936), from Germany and also, to a lesser extent, from Belgium.[164]

The Second World War

For the international financial centres, the Second World War was both similar to and different from the First. It was similar because, in both cases, war meant a decline in business, the mobilisation of financial resources to support it and renewed state intervention in economic life – in addition, of course, to departures to the front, deaths, injuries and material damage. Yet it was different too. First, because it had been expected and the outbreak of hostilities was not followed by crises and panic like those that had occurred in all the main financial centres in the summer of 1914. Second, because the state's hold over the economy was stronger than it had been during the Great War and because the opportunities for bankers and financiers to take part in the large financial transactions needed to run a modern armed conflict were far fewer, not to say non-existent. Finally, because the course of the operations made itself physically felt in most of the major markets, whether through the German occupation of Paris, Amsterdam and Brussels or the bombing of London and Berlin.

Capital transfers

Capital transfers did not cease during the conflict, far from it. But they took place mainly within each of the two camps and consisted of state-to-state transactions; they were thus taken care of by public bodies. On the Allied side, the United States was by far the coalition's biggest sponsor, and no bank or group of banks played a role comparable to that of J. P. Morgan & Co. between 1914 and 1917. Furthermore, American aid did not take the form of loans or credit, but consisted of providing, without reimbursement terms, to countries at war with Germany and Italy, then with Japan, the goods and services needed for their military effort. This programme, adopted in 1941 to ensure the United States' national defence, was known as lend-lease. At the end of the war, these transfers amounted to nearly $50 billion gross, from which thirty-eight countries, including the Soviet Union, benefited, but with two-thirds going to Britain. The latter was also granted credits by other countries, mainly those belonging to the sterling area. It actually paid the bulk of its imports by means of pounds credited to these countries' accounts and frozen in London. These were the sterling balances, which exceeded £3 billion ($12 billion) in 1945, of which a little over £1,000 million were for India, £300 million for Australia, New Zealand and South Africa, and around £100 million for Argentina. They enabled Britain to finance its war effort with far greater resources than it itself had, without the risk of bankruptcy and without jeopardising the pound's international status; they would prove to be a heavy burden for a long time after the war.[165]

Among the Axis powers, the Third Reich made extensive use of resources from the occupied territories. Discussion here will confine itself to financial transfers, the most significant of which were made up of the occupation costs that the countries conquered by Germany had to pay to it and which amounted to some 40% of German tax revenue during the war. The largest contribution was paid by France; this came to an average of 20 million Reichsmarks per day, an amount that, at the highly overvalued rate of 20 francs to the mark, was way above the cost of maintaining German troops in the country. Between 1940 and 1944, the occupation expenses paid by France exceeded 600 billion francs in total[166] – or in francs at the current rate, approximately $12.5 billion, a quarter of the total amount of American lend-lease credit during the war!

Finally, transfers were made via the neutral countries, particularly Switzerland, owing to the status of its currency, which throughout the war remained the only European currency freely convertible to gold by foreign central banks. As such, the Swiss franc was in great demand within the framework of certain international transactions. Of these, the most important were the gold sales undertaken by Germany in Switzerland in order to obtain francs to pay for the purchase of products needed for its war effort, such as oil or wolfram, that it had made from other neutral countries – Spain, Portugal, Romania or Turkey. Not wishing to keep more reserves in francs than necessary, they eventually asked Switzerland to deliver to them gold to pay the surplus balance that they indirectly had with it. The Swiss franc was thus a particularly convenient means of payment, especially as there were doubts at the time about the origin of the Reichsbank's gold, a part of which was suspected of having been plundered from the central banks of the occupied countries, first and foremost Belgium and the Netherlands. Many people have seen this as serving to launder the gold stolen by the Nazis. At the beginning of the war, the Germans sold gold directly in bars and in coins on the Swiss open market, but from October 1941 the Swiss National Bank centralised all gold transactions. From then on, the Reichsbank could no longer deal with the Swiss commercial banks,[167] so it could sell only Fr.101.2 million worth of gold through the latter between 1940 and 1944. At the same time, however, the National Bank accumulated Fr.1,231 million ($286 million). This sum may seem derisory compared with the forced transfers to which the occupied countries were subjected, but the strategic importance of this trade for Germany should not be underestimated. It also bought Fr.2,977 million worth (nearly $700 million) of gold from the Allies, an amount higher than the German purchases, partly to cover the Swiss trade surplus vis-à-vis their economies, but above all to cover the surplus earnings from Swiss investments frozen in the United States.[168]

Adapting to the war economy

These fund movements did little to revive business in the main financial centres, whose international activities, particularly foreign issues, had already slowed down considerably since the end of the twenties and in which the state henceforth held a central position.

For Wall Street, the war and the reduction in international activity meant that the relative influence of the New York Federal Reserve and its chairman dwindled, while the authority of the Board in Washington grew substantially. The latter, continuing the monetary policy that it had followed since 1937, kept its discount rate at 1% throughout the war; that is to say, at an extremely low level that allowed the federal government to finance, under the best conditions, a public debt that went from $48 to $260 billions between 1941 and 1945. The investment banks certainly took part in selling securities when the Treasury issued seven war loans, but they made no profit from it, and their expenses were not reimbursed. At the same time, issues on behalf of private companies fell by half between 1941 and 1943, before picking up again during the last two years of the war.[169] Commercial banking activities focused on financing the war effort, 90% of their new outstanding debt being in the form of American government bonds.[170]

The stock exchange, still under the shock of the Great Depression, also suffered, especially at the beginning of the war. On the New York Stock Exchange, the drop in the number of listed companies and the restrictions on margin buying by the Federal Reserve pushed down the volume of transactions, which remained below its level in the depths of the depression, but which went up again markedly at the end of the war.[171] As for prices, they fluctuated according to the news. They rose by 10% in September 1939, sellers hoping to see the profits of American companies inflated by orders for French and British arms, fell by 20% in May–June 1940 and then continuously until mid-April 1942, when they were 40% lower than before the war. On 28 April 1942 one of President Roosevelt's fireside chats, announcing the introduction of rationing and widespread price-fixing, made them pick up again, investors seeing the threat of inflation similar to that of the First World War recede. The New York Stock Exchange then got its colour back, and share prices had doubled by September 1945.

In London, the war strengthened the Treasury's political authority and decision-making power, the Bank of England acting mainly as an enforcer and an intermediary with the City, first and foremost with the commercial banks.[172] As during the First World War, the merchant banks were hit hard, whether in their acceptance, exchange or issue activities, following the diminution in the volume of business (international trade and foreign currency dealing) and increased state intervention (direct purchasing by the government from the Dominions, lend-lease and public loans).[173] The commercial banks came through better despite, if not because of, intervention by a state that supervised them while being their biggest client; they received precise instructions concerning the use of their resources which, as elsewhere, were used to finance the war effort. At the Midland Bank, for example, government paper represented 82% of deposits in August 1945.[174] On the London Stock Exchange, the volume of business dropped by 80% during the first two years of the war, then picked up again from 1942 onwards. In spite of the huge increase in public debt, which swelled from £7.1 to £21.1 billion between 1939 and 1945, government securities did not make up the most active sector of the stock-exchange list, the British government trying to bypass the stock exchange and address the public directly – a public whose preference clearly lay with shares. Share prices hit rock bottom in 1940, when the Blitz left nearly a third of the City's surface area in ruins; they then climbed steadily from June 1941, the *Financial News*'s industrial share index going from 79.7 at the end of 1941 to 93.7 twelve months later and to 103.1 on 31 December 1943, so that by the end of the war it had gained nearly 60% on its lowest level.[175]

In Paris, the Banque de France handled the transfer of occupation costs to Germany through the account that it had opened on behalf of the Reichskreditkasse and into which the Treasury paid Fr.4 billion every ten days. Its governor, Yves de Boisanger, tried to reduce these payments within the framework of discussions with Germany, but without challenging the state's policy on monetary cooperation. Besides, these negotiations were no longer his responsibility after Laval's return in April 1942, and the Banque de France granted all the requests for advances made by the government, despite its concern for controlling inflation.[176] On the Bourse, where forward transactions were prohibited, operations, supplied by the abundance of liquid assets, rocketed from 1941 – with prices almost tripling that year – and from the end of the year regained, in nominal value and measured in terms of commissions, their 1936 level.[177] As for the big banks, business slackened off; exchange operations plummeted, overseas trade financing grew scarce and the practice of cash payment became widespread to the detriment of discounting. As elsewhere, their assets included increasing numbers of Treasury bonds – for example, nearly 90% of the securities held by the Crédit Lyonnais in 1945. Profits took a nosedive in inflation-adjusted francs,[178] in spite of rising commissions earned in the context of public and private issues, which at that time reached levels unequalled since the early thirties.[179] Even the conclusion of a certain number of operations with the occupier (especially the liquidation of French holdings in central Europe and the Balkans, credits granted to French enterprises working for Germany, and the creation of Franco-German companies) did not fully compensate for the loss in earnings.[180] As far as the private banks were concerned, it was the Jewish houses that were the main victims of German occupation and of the Vichy government's anti-Semitic policy. In 1940, 30 banks out of 542 were identified as Jewish by the Comité d'Organisation des Banques. Most were wound up, including Lazard Frères, others were 'Aryanised', and the Rothschilds' property was confiscated by the French state. Of these, twenty-three nevertheless managed to survive during these dark years – often thanks to non-Jewish temporary partners – and were still officially registered as banks at the time of the Liberation.[181]

In Berlin, the state's power over the banks, firmly established since the beginning of Hitler's dictatorship, strengthened during the war, banks being reduced to mere administrative units transferring private savings into state coffers. From 1942 a campaign was launched to restrict their power. Among other things, banks were forced to cut the number of their branches throughout the country and to limit their representation on the supervisory boards of other companies. The big banks were, it is true, involved in German economic imperialism, but their conspicuous expansion in occupied Europe was usually dictated by political rather than economic logic. As Harold James has written, bankers, who were increasingly marginalised within the regime, took refuge in the comfortable certitudes of their economic rationality and did not look beyond their own business; they too thereby participated in Germany's moral disaster.[182]

In Switzerland also, the war years were marked by increased state intervention in financial matters. Alongside the suppression of free trade in gold, the banks saw their trade financing activities diminish, with most of the country's overseas trade being managed by the Office Suisse de Compensation.[183] Like elsewhere, their main activity at the time was financing state needs, Confederation bonds soon becoming the major share of their assets. The effect of this slump in business was obviously a considerable drop in profits,[184] even though the banks granted credits to German enterprises, including banks – the Crédit Suisse had close links with Deutsche Bank and the Swiss Bank Corporation with the Dresdner Bank – and manufacturing companies, including IG Farben.[185] Furthermore, the banks were hit hard by their assets being blocked in Britain and above all in the United States, by the indirect freeze on wealth management activities entailed by obstacles to the free movement of both people and mail, and by the proliferation of state controls introduced almost everywhere. Transactions on the Swiss stock exchanges were affected, their level in 1940 falling by 50% compared with what it had been in 1938; and even if it picked up somewhat in subsequent years, it would only return to its pre-war level in 1946.

It was the Second World War that brought the nineteenth century world economic order, centred on Britain, to an end for good. The Great War and the devaluation of the pound sterling in 1931 had already dealt a heavy blow to the City of London. The second worldwide conflict consolidated the United States' economic and financial supremacy and placed New York at the top of the hierarchy of

international financial centres. But crises and war had left their mark.
For politicians, growth and full employment now prevailed over market
liberalisation and capital flows. It was only with time that the large
international financial centres freed themselves from the straitjacket of
state controls and of regulations set up during these gloomy years.

5   Growth and regulation, 1945–1980

The thirty years that followed the Second World War were Europe's 'Golden Age'; commonly known in France as 'les Trentes Glorieuses'. At that time, the countries of Western Europe were experiencing the fastest growth rates in their history. Between 1950 and 1973, their GDP per capita grew at an average rate of 3.8% per year, compared with 1% between 1913 and 1950 and less than 2% throughout the twentieth century. Expansion was pronounced in Germany (5%), somewhat less so in France (4%) and considerably less so in the United Kingdom (2.5%) – where, however, the level of income was higher than in the major countries of continental Europe at the start of the period.[1] In one generation, Europe managed, if not to catch up with, then at least to draw closer to the United States, where growth, admittedly strong (2.2%), was bound to be slower. A European's average income, which barely exceeded half an American's in 1950, was getting on for three-quarters in 1973.[2] Europe had definitely entered the age of plenty and mass consumption. Economic development was even more spectacular in Japan which, thanks to average growth of 8% per year, became the second world economic power by 1973. By then its GDP was one and a half times higher than Germany's, despite having been only in sixth place, behind Italy, in 1950.[3]

What should this outstanding post-war expansion be attributed to? The international context was certainly conducive; it was marked by political stability, in spite of the Cold War; by cooperation among states, with the founding of the United Nations in 1945 and the setting up of a series of multilateral organisations; by the opening up of borders, especially in the field of international trade once the GATT had come into force in 1947. Moreover, for Europe, the establishment of the European Coal and Steel Community (ECSC) in 1951, then the Common Market in 1958, played a not insignificant role in this process. Yet, in the final analysis, this long phase of vigorous expansion can best be explained by the dilapidated state in which Europe and Japan found themselves in 1945, which gave them great potential for catching up with the world leader, namely the United States. It was, moreover, the weakening of this potential – whatever the role played at the same time by other factors, including the two oil crises – that largely explains why this growth slowed down to regain its age-old rhythm after 1973.

The banks and, more generally, the financial sector naturally helped the post-war economies to expand, and benefited from this in return. But until the sixties, or in some cases the seventies, the international financial centres' business remained mostly confined within national borders; the golden age of economic growth in Europe and Japan was not accompanied by intense international movements of private capital. Between 1955 and 1962, foreign issues floated in New York barely reached $4.2 billion – a feeble sum compared with the $126.5 billion for national issues and, above all, with the $98 billion in economic and military aid granted by the United States to foreign countries between 1945 and 1952.[4] Unlike in the twenties, reverting to the pre-war order was no longer acceptable. The largest capital transfers were not left to the private sector, but were undertaken by governments, state bodies and, to a lesser extent, multilateral agencies like the International Monetary Fund or the World Bank.

State intervention was in fact the main feature of this period. Disillusionment with *laissez-faire*, considered incapable of averting mass unemployment, and the experience of interventionism during the war, or in the thirties already, led all the industrialised countries to adopt Keynesian economic policies, favouring growth and full employment, through countercyclical government action. The state's weight and responsibilities, of course, varied from country to country, being of a highly interventionist nature in France, Italy and Japan, a little less so in Britain and the Scandinavian countries, but far more liberal in the United States, Germany and Switzerland. This trend was, however, common to all market economies and would not be reversed until the end of the seventies and, particularly, the beginning of the eighties.

State invervention takes various forms. In the financial field, it might mean directly managing operations formerly undertaken by private firms, like granting loans or other fund transfers. It might also mean several sets of regulations intended to improve the way that the capital markets function, to ensure their transparency or to protect them from embezzlement. This was the purpose of the banking laws introduced in the interwar period, and their effects continued to be felt during the fifties and sixties. It might also mean takeovers of private institutions, usually by nationalising them. At the time of the Liberation, France nationalised, along with the main banks and insurance companies, its central bank, whose statutes had already been made more democratic by the Front Populaire government in 1936.[5] In Britain, the Bank of England met the same fate in 1946, but without its management structures being fundamentally altered,[6] whereas the commercial banks remained private yet lost a great deal of their automomy. Finally, the state can intervene by introducing controls, restrictions and other directives of a more or less temporary nature within the framework of its overall economic policy objectives. The measure whose effects were most directly felt on the financial centres' international business was, of course, exchange control. With the exception of the United States and Switzerland, the main countries only re-established free convertibility on current account at the end of December 1958, even though controls had been relaxed on a number of occasions before this date, especially in Britain and Germany. For capital transfers, this convertibility would in the end only be full and complete in the late seventies or, depending on the country, during the following decade.

Ultimately, financial centres' prosperity is dependent upon the international monetary system in place. The exchange rate regime set up in 1944 attempted to re-establish the monetary stability that had been the characteristic feature of the gold standard by avoiding reproducing the rigidities that had brought it to a standstill and had made economic problems worse during the interwar period. The Bretton Woods Agreements made the dollar, a currency convertible to gold at the rate of $35 to the ounce, the system's reference currency against which the other currencies defined their parity. Exchange rates were fixed (with a fluctuation margin of ±1%) but adaptable in the event of a fundamental imbalance in the balance of payments. And the International Monetary Fund – the IMF – was established to make it easier for the system to function properly by providing support to currencies whose parity with the dollar might be endangered by temporary external payments difficulties.

The Bretton Woods regime did not work in a very satisfactory way, even though its years of existence coincided with a period of unprecedented economic growth. It only really came into force in January 1959, after the European currencies' return to convertibility; in other words, ten years after the deadline initially set. Almost immediately, it was confronted by growing American balance-of-payments deficits leading to a glut of dollars in the world, which came to swell the reserves of the central European banks and threatened to destabilise the system. Faced with these risks, various forms of monetary cooperation were devised in the early sixties under the aegis of the United States, in particular the *gold pool* to stabilise the price of gold at $35 per ounce, the *swap network* to quickly bring the collective assistance of the central banks to any bank that found itself short of currency reserves, and the *General Arrangements to Borrow* through which ten countries (which would later form the Group of Ten and which Switzerland would join *de facto*) made additional medium-term resources available to the IMF in the event of an emergency. In 1967 the latter created a new international reserve unit, the SDR (*Special Drawing Right*), which was supposed to act partially as a substitute for the dollar.[7]

Despite these efforts to prop it up, the regime would not survive. The British pound – which made up the system's second reserve currency due, among other things, to its role in the sterling area – came under constant pressure and, in the end, had to be devalued in November 1967, thus losing in a few years a good part of its status as an international currency. This precarious balance was lost in the early seventies. The dollar's gold convertibility was suspended on 15 August 1971, and the greenback was devalued *de facto* in December through a revaluation, at different rates, of the other main currencies. The attempt to maintain fixed exchange rates came to an end in March 1973, when currencies started to float, ushering in a new era in international monetary and financial relations.

These failures in the monetary system resulted in major financial innovations. The overabundance of dollars and American regulations gave rise, in the late fifties and early sixties, to the Eurodollar and Eurobond markets, which found a natural home in London. Their remarkable development in the seventies, sustained by the income from oil-exporting countries, coincided with a period of gradual deregulation, a floating exchange rate regime and an increase in international capital movements, opening up the way to a new era of globalisation for the world economy.

The development of the international financial centres beween 1945 and 1980 did not follow exactly the same path as general economic and political progress. New York's position, for example, was never entirely proportional to the United States' power and to the dollar's supremacy. The City certainly suffered from the decline of the pound, but in the end it largely overcame this handicap and continued to play a role out of all proportion to the size and fairly lacklustre performance of the British economy during this period. The Swiss financial centre, on the other hand, benefited fully from the national currency's strength, while increasingly playing the role of hub in the international circulation of capital, also in this case, out of all proportion to the real size of the domestic economy. The rise of Frankfurt, which replaced Berlin as Germany's financial centre, and that of Tokyo, were connected with Germany's and Japan's growing economic power, but they remained limited on an international level during this entire period. The most pronounced retreat was that of Paris, especially as regards the international status that the French capital had enjoyed until the early thirties, in spite of the French economy's excellent performance.

The difficult return to convertibility 1945–58

The history of the leading international centres should not be confused with that of the international monetary system; but the system's operating terms could have a considerable influence, for good or for bad, on the nature of activities, the volume of business and the strategic choices of the main players in the financial world. Between 1945 and 1958, it was the inconvertibility of European currencies that severely constrained international financial activities. This did not mean, far from it, that such activities were non-existent. Yet changes in the world hierarchy of the main centres, their relations of competition and cooperation, the connection between their national and international operations and the development of institutions took place in a context that was greatly influenced by the international payments regime.

New York's pre-eminence

Just after the Second World War, New York was indisputably the world's leading financial centre, a position that it had been unable to reach at the end of the First. But the balance of power on the international level had been profoundly altered in less than thirty years. More than at any other time in its history, New York's position reflected the economic superpower of the United States, which in 1946 provided approximately 50% of the world's industrial output and whose GDP in 1950 was more than double that of Britain, France and West Germany combined. Its supremacy was even more striking in the financial field, on account of the importance of American aid for European reconstruction needs. The problem of the shortage of dollars needed to import raw materials and capital goods from across the Atlantic was only solved thanks to the $13 billion worth of donations, mainly in kind, that the Marshall Plan transferred to Europe between 1948 and 1952.[8]

New York's financial centre reached maturity in the fifties.[9] Its position relied first and foremost, as had been the case for London before 1914, on the role that the national currency played as an international reserve currency and as a payment instrument between economies. This status was even more solid, since at that time the dollar was the only major currency that was fully convertible – the use of the

Swiss franc was inevitably more limited – and America could call on huge gold reserves. New York's position also hinged on the influence exerted both nationally and internationally by its financial institutions. In the first place, there was the Federal Reserve Bank of New York, which played a key role in international finance. It was the correspondent bank in the United States for the main foreign central banks and governments, from which it received deposits, to which it granted loans and for which it undertook various securities buying and selling operations. It also carried out exchange and transfer operations abroad both for the American Treasury and for other Federal Reserve Banks.

New York's commercial banks[10] had, as a group, become the world's largest, with total resources amounting to $32.3 billion in 1954 (compared with $19.8 billion for their London counterparts) for a total equity capital of $2.1 billion.[11] All large banks had well-organised departments for their international business – currency purchases and sales, trade financing and loans to foreign banks – and maintained correspondent relationships with banks worldwide. Most of them had a presence overseas; in 1955 seven American banks, mainly from New York, had a total of 106 branches.[12] In return and not including correspondent banks, twenty-one foreign banks belonging to twelve different countries had 'licenced agencies' in New York in 1954,[13] on top of which there were numerous subsidiaries of foreign banks registered as banks or trust companies in the state of New York. They were mainly involved in financing commercial and other financial transactions, particularly currency trading, usually in association with their country of origin, while investing the funds that had been entrusted to them by their parent company on the American money market.

New York also had an extensive range of specialist firms, typical of a large international financial centre: brokers and foreign exchange dealers, factoring companies (especially for managing accounts linked to foreign trade), customs brokers, shipping and import-export representatives, as well as discount and accepting houses, although the latter were less developed than in London. And, of course, there were the investment banks.[14] Forming the heart of New York's financial centre on the eve of the First World War, they continued to dominate the stage in the twenties, before more or less falling back into line following the crisis, competition from commercial banks and the New Deal regulations.[15] Finally, in addition to the investment banks, there were numerous brokers, with more or less close connections to them, who specialised in trading securities.

The New York Stock Exchange picked up again during the phase of economic expansion in the fifties. The Dow Jones rose from 260 in

September 1953 to 386 in December 1954, exceeding for the first time its peak of August 1929, then to 650 at the end of 1960 – that is to say, a rise of 240%. The volume of transactions also increased considerably, from an average of 312 million securities purchased per year at the end of the forties to 667 million in 1959. The minimum commission rule set by the New York Stock Exchange prevented any competition among brokers on price. On the other hand, the quality of their services could vary; the most prominent houses, for example Merrill Lynch, Paine Webber or Dean Witter, began to produce increasingly sophisticated research on securities and markets for their clients – a sign of competence that enhanced their professional status.[16] As prices rose, the stock exchange continued its process of democratisation, initiated after the Great War, with the number of individual shareholders doubling in the course of the fifties, even if their share – around 55% – in the total amount of transactions on the New York Stock Exchange remained just about stable whereas that of institutional investors increased, albeit moderately, from 20% to 25%.[17]

As in previous eras, including the twenties, the New York Stock Exchange was still a market where mostly American stocks were traded but in which traders from all over the world took part, giving it a truly international dimension. Foreign issues were in fact expensive and remained relatively limited. On the one hand, between 1941 and 1958, a large number of American capital transfers abroad were carried out through governmental and international agencies. On the other hand, the bulk of private capital exported – $5.4 billion between 1950 and 1954 – was made up of direct investment. The fifties actually saw a new wave of expansion in American multinationals, several of which, like General Electric, Standard Oil Co. of New Jersey (later EXXON), or IBM, were constituent parts of New York's financial centre where their registered offices were located. Foreign loans denominated in dollars were, nonetheless, issued on Wall Street on behalf of large enterprises, foreign governments[18] and multinational institutions, like the European Coal and Steel Community (ECSC), so that New York ranked top for foreign issues, well ahead of London, Zurich, Brussels and Amsterdam (see Table 5.1).

Even at its peak as the world's foremost financial centre, New York's influence was far more limited than London's had been half a century earlier. In the first place, there was the fact that New York's pre-eminence corresponded to a period in which international capital flows were far smaller than before 1931 or after 1960 and, above all, 1980. Next, there were regulations on banking and financial activities that limited the field of possibilities. In the fifties, commercial banks found it

Table 5.1. *International issues in the main financial centres, 1955–62*

	Millions of dollars
New York	4,171
London	1,064
Zurich	882
Brussels	393
Amsterdam	298
Frankfurt	163

Source: J. Mensbrugghe, 'Foreign issues in Europe', *International Monetary Fund Staff Papers*, 11, 1964, pp. 327–35.

more and more difficult to attract the funds needed to match the credit opportunities offered by the growth in the American economy. Their problem was both simple and complex. Growth in the demand for loans, doubling during the decade, was in fact much faster than that for their deposits, which only increased by 50%. One of the reasons for this gap was Regulation Q, which prevented them from paying a high enough interest on deposits during a phase in which rates were on an upward trend, the Federal Reserve increasing its discount rate substantially in 1956. This rise in non-banking money market rates drove companies to reduce the credit balances on their current accounts, which hardly yielded anything, and to invest their surplus of liquid assets in negotiable securities or Treasury Bonds. It was for this reason that New York's commercial banks, keen to increase their deposits at almost any cost, embarked from the mid-fifties on a vast merger movement. Wholesale banks (working mainly with businesses), needing to increase their resources to meet demand from their clients, merged with retail banks that had large branch networks in the state of New York and that were seeking to use their excess deposits coming from households. This was how Chase National Bank, belonging to the first group, joined up with the Bank of Manhattan in 1955, and the National City Bank with the First National Bank in the same year; J. P. Morgan with the Guarantee Trust, in 1959; and the Central Hanover Bank with the Manufacturers Trust, in 1961.[19]

The largest American banks thus become the world's largest (see Table 5.2), without however completely solving the problem of their funding squeeze.[20] Opportunities for them to expand in New York were not limitless, and American legislation prohibited them from spreading to other states in the Union. Other solutions were, on the one hand, making better use of existing facilities – like the interbank market that allowed them to share almost instantly any lack or excess of liquidity

Table 5.2. *The main commercial banks in the leading financial centres*

	Total assets in millions of dollars	
	1953	1960
United States		
Bank of America	7,022[a]	11,200
First National City Bank	6,026	8,160
Chase Manhattan Bank	5,574	8,420
Great Britain		
Barclays Bank[b]	6,064	7,463
Midland Bank	4,264	5,103
Lloyds Bank	3,745	5,033
France		
Crédit Lyonnais	1,243	2,616
Société Générale	1,068	2,285
BNCI	1,041	1,730
Germany		
Deutsche Bank	1,295	2,690
Dresdner Bank	–	1,905
Commerzbank	381	1,640
Switzerland		
Swiss Bank Corporation	690	1,192
Crédit Suisse	634	1,138
Belgium		
Générale de Banque	678	990
Banque de Bruxelles	456	813
Netherlands		
Nederlandsche Handel-Maatschappij	539[c]	605
Amsterdamsche Bank	446[c]	658

Notes: [a] 1951; [b] Including Barclays DCO (Dominion, Colonial and Overseas); [c] 1955.
Source: Bankers' Almanac.

among the banks – and, on the other hand and above all, finding funds on the money market thanks to new financial instruments. The major innovation here was the certificate of deposit, launched in 1961 by the First National City Bank, which would have a major impact on banking practice. What was new was the fact that the certificate was negotiable on a secondary market, created in advance by its promoters. By paying interest close to that of the market for fixed-term deposits and by making other instruments negotiable, the banks were able to augment their resources in a more flexible way and thereby manage not only their assets but also their liabilities.[21] A third solution to the American banks' financing problems would be, during the 1960s, internationalising and obtaining additional funds from Europe.

The persistence of the City

In second place, behind New York, and still the world leader in numerous markets, the City of London had not abandoned its international ambitions, in spite of far less favourable conditions than after the First World War. There were two problems, closely linked to each other. First, the British economy was increasingly struggling to support a financial centre of world dimensions, supplied by capital exports and reliant on an international reserve and exchange currency, on account of the difficulties that it had in showing an adequate external surplus, or even in simply stabilising its balance of payments. Slumps in the pound, which led to the devaluations of 1949 and 1967, to say nothing of its repeated dips in between, were evidence of these difficulties. Second, the City's financial business was hampered by the regulations that it was subjected to, not only exchange controls and restrictions on the movement of capital but also the highly interventionist policy of the Treasury, which controlled the distribution of credit via directives channelled through the Bank of England to the clearing banks. This is alleged to have made Keynes say that it was not necessary to nationalise these banks, seeing that in actual fact they already had been. For Lord Franks, chairman of Lloyds Bank from 1954 to 1962, 'it was like driving a powerful car at twenty miles an hour'.[22]

For despite everything, the institutions, mechanisms and expertise were still in place, whatever the physical damage inflicted on the City by German bombing. When the war was over, the Midland Bank was still the world's largest bank, ahead of the Bank of America. And while the top three British banks ended up being overtaken by the top three American banks in the fifties, they remained well ahead of their main rivals from continental Europe (Table 5.2). It is true that size is an imperfect indicator of banks' competiveness and often results from cartel agreements or protecting the national market. Nevertheless, it shows the Big Five's vast financial capacity and weight, even if this was mainly brought to bear on the domestic economy.

For all that, the City had a unique international banking network. The number of branches of overseas banks continued to grow and went from 2,315 in 1938 to 3,612 in 1955,[23] more than three-quarters of them were in Australia, New Zealand and South Africa, most of the others being in Asia, Latin America and Africa. The top British multinational bank, Barclays Bank DCO, had 997 foreign branches in 1955 – far more than the National City Bank's 55 branches. London had 69 branches and representative offices of foreign banks in 1955 and 80 in 1960 – many more than any other international financial centre.[24] The merchant banks had certainly begun to engage in domestic finance during the interwar depression, but they were still mainly looking to finance international trade. Acceptances still represented the main source of income for Schroders: 30% between 1946 and 1953, then 25% between 1954 and 1958.[25] For the merchant banks as a whole, the acceptance business took off again as world trade grew, outstanding debt going from £95 million in 1954 to £137 million in 1956. Unlike during the pre-1914 period or even during the twenties, it was increasingly linked to financing British foreign trade; whereas more than 70% of bills of exchange were drawn abroad at the end of the twenties, this proportion fell to 37% by the early fifties.[26]

Thus, in spite of its obvious decline, London nonetheless preserved its predominance in the field of international trade financing, a success that can be explained by the City's traditions and by the fact that, despite the dollar's supremacy, half of all international trade – that within the sterling area – continued to be denominated in pounds. The same went for the numerous markets that had been based in the City for more than a century and that, following their forced closure during the war years and in the immediate post-war period, reopened one after the other – rubber from 1946, tin in 1949, cocoa in 1951, lead in 1952, zinc, copper and wool in 1953 and, finally, coffee in 1958. They partly, and with varying fortunes, recovered their international influence – thanks mainly to the exemptions that they were granted in relation to exchange control. Their operations were, nevertheless, hampered by the restrictions that many governments imposed on free trade in raw materials considered essential and by the establishment of large, vertically integrated groups that were able to do without the markets. Competition also became tougher both from producing countries and from other financial centres. The London Metal Exchange held out fairly well against competition from New York, but the wool market moved to Sydney and the rubber market to the Far East, whereas the Baltic Exchange abandoned cereals to focus on freighting ships, in which it easily maintained its dominance.[27] The gold market, which reopened in 1954 and quickly recaptured top place at New York's and Zurich's expense, perhaps symbolised more than any other the City's enduring international influence.

On the international level, London also retained strong positions in the field of insurance, especially and above all compared with New York. A little over half the insurance premiums paid in Britain[28] came from abroad – a little over 10% for life insurance, but 60% to 70% for fire, accident and marine insurance. Lloyd's, which was a market not an insurance company,[29] continued to hold a prime place, notably in reinsuring risks in the United States, which was its largest overseas market, as well as being the insurance companies' biggest market. In all these services, which were more or less connected with international trade, the City managed, in a rather hostile environment, to retain its lead over the other big centres of the day, such as New York and to a lesser extent Zurich or even Paris. Where it lost ground, and in an even more obvious way than in the twenties, was in the field of foreign issues (see Table 5.1). While foreign loans had reached an annual average of nearly £200 million before the First World War and exceeded £150 million at the end of the twenties, they collapsed during the slump of the thirties – on average £31 million from 1933 to 1938 – to experience just a modest recovery after 1945, achieving an annual average of £61 million between 1950 and 1958. These foreign issues represented barely 6% of the total amount of new issues floated in Britain in 1961,[30] a clear sign of the national retreat made by the City after the Second World War, which was due mostly to the country's weak creditor position. However, the growing share of direct investment and transfers made by government agencies in international capital flows during this period should not be overlooked, as indeed in New York's case.

This retreat was also evident on the London Stock Exchange.[31] At the end of the 1940s, British government securities represented more than half the stocks quoted on the London Stock Exchange and 85% of the volume of transactions. Many British shares, especially in the railways and public utilities, disappeared from the stock exchange list following nationalisations, and trading in foreign stocks, including on behalf of non-resident traders, was severely handicapped by exchange control. The stock exchange was not only tightly regulated by the authorities, but its dealings were regarded with suspicion and deemed to be of little significance for the country's prosperity. The futures market only took off again in December 1946, but without the possibility of carry-over transactions, which in the end were only authorised in March 1949. Options, considered highly speculative, were only reintroduced in May 1958 after an interruption of nineteen years. Furthermore, the revival of international capital flows in the late 1950s was not very profitable for brokers and jobbers, since the City's banking houses – above all, the merchant banks and, even more so, the foreign brokers, chiefly from New York, established there – tended to do without their services and deal directly with foreign stock exchanges. It was the stock exchange's own regulations, especially the perpetuation of fixed commissions, far more than regulations imposed on it by the Bank of England and the Treasury, that were responsible for this state of affairs. In effect, the London Stock Exchange set itself up as the regulator of the securities market, with all the caution and conservatism that that implies. And yet the London Stock Exchange was not totally marginalised as a market, since its international decline was partly offset on a national level. Indeed, it became the market where above all British commercial and industrial stocks were traded[32] – and whose prices thrived owing to the public's appetite for shares, which were better able to withstand inflation. The FT 30-Share Index, which was around 120 in 1951 and passed the 300 mark by the end of the decade, was a clear reflection of this development.[33]

More than a national retreat, the City in fact refocused on the Commonwealth and, in particular, on the sterling area. This now included the Crown colonies and twelve independent states[34] and worked on the following principles: a fixed exchange rate among the various currencies; a common exchange control *vis-à-vis* the outside world; free circulation of capital among the countries in the area; and the pooling of exchange reserves. Britain stood at the heart of this system, ensuring that it worked properly by supplying long-term capital to all the countries in the area and absorbing their exports without any restraints.[35] So it comes as no surprise that the foreign loans issued in London during the fifties were almost exclusively reserved to member countries, where exchange control, which even if it was quickly relaxed for commercial transactions was still strict for capital flows, did not apply. The sterling area was certainly not enough to make full use of the issuing capacity of the merchant banks and other institutions involved in this type of activity, but its role in City business during this period should not be underestimated. The question of the costs and benefits of this system gave rise to a fair amount of debate in the fifties and sixties. Recent work makes it clear that this area did not check Britain's economic growth,[36] since the sterling balances did not represent a handicap in this respect. From the City's point of view, it represented, at least until the mid-fifties, the chance to remain a leading international financial centre because of its part in international trade and the pound's role as the system's anchor currency. Somewhat like Amsterdam in the first half of the nineteenth century, the Commonwealth and the sterling area enabled the City and the British currency to resume, in a more limited way, the role they had played on the world stage prior to 1914 and, to a lesser extent in the twenties – that is to say, offering a wide range of financial services in the case of the City and fulfilling the function of an international reserve and trading currency in the case of the pound.

Retreating to the sterling area was not, however, seen as a long-term option by the British authorities, for whom restoring their currency to full gold convertibility remained a priority. In 1962 Lord Cromer, the governor of the Bank of England, did not rule out reopening the London market to sterling-denominated foreign issues fairly quickly.[37] By this time, Britain was turning increasingly to Europe, and the City did not take long to recover its world calling – to the advantage of the Euromarkets.[38]

Paris's retreat

The development of Paris and London had some similarities in the second half of the twentieth century; to a greater or lesser extent, both had to give up their world ambitions, retreat to the national market and operate in a tightly regulated environment. This trend was, however, far more pronounced in the case of Paris, whose international influence after 1945 was a mere shadow of what it had been only some thirty years earlier. France ended up far more weakened than Britain by the years of crisis and war, with a GDP in 1945 nearly half the size of its 1938 level, whereas it was 15% higher across the Channel. Priority was given to efforts to rebuild the country and renew its industry rather than to enhancing Paris's international influence, whose benefits for the French economy had always mattered less than those provided to the British economy by the City. State intervention played a key role in this process – in terms less of nationalisations, which were fairly comparable in the two countries, than of political elites taking on responsibilities in the economic sphere, especially through the Ministry of Finance and its networks in the banks and nationalised industrial enterprises.

Most of the French financial sector came under state control after Liberation, except for the *banques d'affaires*, including the Banque de Paris et des Pays-Bas – commonly known as Paribas – and the members of the *haute banque*, which remained in private hands chiefly because of their international role. But the four big deposit banks,[39] thirty-four insurance companies,[40] the Banque de France and the Banque de l'Algérie were nationalised. These institutions joined an already unwieldy public and semi-public sector,[41] so that the state controlled 58% of the banking sector and, either directly or indirectly, more than half the financing for investment in France between 1945 and 1970.

Much more than in Britain, the state's grip ended up stifling Paris' capital market, not only when it came to foreign issues, practically nil during this period, but also issues by French companies, which only reached 3.5% of GDP in the fifties, compared with 5% in about 1900 and 11% around 1913.[42] As far as foreign issues were concerned, the franc area was far smaller than the sterling area, and investment there, fairly weak in the French colonial empire, was mostly of a public nature. As for companies, apart from self-financing, they initially found medium- and long-term credit from the Treasury, then from banks, thanks to the latters' refinancing possibilities with the central bank, which automatically rediscounted the credit, even medium-term, issued by French exporters.[43]

Consequently, the Paris Bourse was pretty sluggish. Having lost two-thirds of the nominal value of its securities through nationalisations, it went through a 'long depression' that lasted until the 1980s.[44] On top of the shortfall in issues came the weakness of institutional investors and the archaic organisation of trade, especially the persistent *agents de changes'* monopoly, which perpetuated the lack of dealers in the market. On the international level, even though the number of foreign securities quoted in Paris dropped by half between 1913 and 1950, it rose again to 266 by 1957; in other words, ten times higher than on the New York Stock Exchange. But since most of these stocks dated back to before 1914, they had become totally inactive, and the bulk of the transactions involved only a few of them, including South African gold mines, American companies like AT&T or Du Pont de Nemours, and oil companies like Royal Dutch Shell, approximately a quarter of which, mainly through the Rothschilds, was in French hands. In the sixties, foreign paper represented a mere 10% of the Parisian market's nominal capitalisation.

Paris nevertheless retained some attributes of an international financial centre, mostly of an institutional nature, which kept it near the top of international rankings based mainly on criteria such as domestic banks' expansion abroad or the presence of foreign banks in the centre. In spite of Paris's retreat into the national economy, the French banks, behind the British banks but ahead of the American ones, had the second largest network of foreign branches in the world at their disposal – a network that was not only inherited from the past but which continued to spread in the fifties. In 1963, for example, the Crédit Lyonnais controlled 85 foreign branches directly and 113 through its subsidiaries and through the banks with which it was associated, shared between Africa, Latin America, the Middle East and Western Europe.[45] Similarly Paris, with 32 branches of foreign banks and 41 representative offices in 1960, was only outmatched in this field by London and New York;[46] their aim was to establish relationships with French economic and financial circles and to transmit information between the Parisian centre and their country of origin.

Two other factors helped open up Paris to the world. First, there were the *banques d'affaires*,[47] which, having only very little room for manoeuvre in a domestic market controlled by the big nationalised banks, were forced to exploit certain niches or to innovate. This was the case for Paribas, which specialised in issues placed outside France on behalf of French and foreign businesses – a field of activity in which the nationalised banks were not very involved – and which also launched a medium-term financing plan, in the form of export credits, during the period of dollar shortage which followed the war.[48] Second, there was the establishment of the Common Market in 1958, which coincided with the restoration of the main European currencies' external convertibility and within whose framework a progressive liberation of capital movements was envisaged. Things would progress slowly, however, and only take shape during the decades to come. Yet Paris's European calling was already emerging, following on from its historical tradition and in contrast to the City.

From Berlin to Frankfurt

While London and Paris experienced a decline, to varying degrees, after 1945, Berlin was wiped off the map of international financial centres for obvious reasons; the German defeat and the Soviet presence in the city deprived the Reich's former capital of any hope of preserving its role as Germany's financial centre.[49] The measures taken by the Soviet authorities even before Western troops arrived in Berlin practically put an end to the centre's banking activities; a temporary stoppage, which would turn out to be permanent, was declared on 28 April 1945 by the supreme commander, General Nikolaï Bersarin. The Reichsbank's headquarters were transformed into the Berlin City Bank – Berlin Stadtbank – into which the other banks had to pay their liquid assets. And in January 1946, with the agreement of the Western powers, the headquarters of the big banks, which had continued to provide various services, had to close for good, the Americans and British having other plans for the German banking system. For their part, the banks had anticipated the move and began to transfer senior managers and their funds to the West. At the beginning of April 1945, Deutsche Bank set up an executive committee in Hamburg, and the Commerzbank likewise transferred the responsibilities of its Berlin headquarters there – its second largest office and city of origin. The Hanseatic city seemed destined to take over from Berlin as Germany's financial capital.

As it happens, Hamburg was particularly well equipped for this task – certainly better than any other German city. From before the war, it had made its mark as the second financial centre in Germany and after 1945 it unquestionably held top rank. It had the most banks, whether big German banks or major private banks,[50] as well as the overwhelming proportion of branches of foreign banks in Germany. The volume of stock-market transactions was distinctly higher there than elsewhere, as were payments to foreign countries. The city had traditionally held a strong position in insurance with 80% of West German companies' headquarters; it possessed a large port, and it formed the hub of German foreign trade. By way of comparison, Frankfurt had been relegated to the rank of a centre of purely local significance, whose international reputation was just a memory dating back to the Rothschild era. Even Cologne seemed better placed with its banking and finance traditions, and its position as the main business centre of the Ruhr and Germany's most populous *Land*.

All the same, Frankfurt has made a considerable name for itself; first as the German financial capital, and then as one of the largest centres in Europe and in the world. It is tempting to attribute this success to the city's financial traditions. Its causes are in fact more political in nature and were due, above all, to the decision taken in 1948 by the Anglo-American military authorities to establish the headquarters of the central bank there – the Bank deutscher Länder, which would become the Bundesbank in 1958. The city's best qualification at the time was to be the administrative centre of the *Bizone* – formed at the beginning of 1947 by amalgamating the American and British military occupation zones – and as such the potential capital of the future West German state. Frankfurt was basically the Americans' choice – from the start, the British had been in favour instead of Hamburg – for reasons that are not entirely clear. It apparently fell within the framework of a plan intended to decentralise the German banking system by splitting up the central bank and the big banks into regional units and by putting the Bank deutscher Länder, modelled on the Federal Reserve in Washington, close to the political power. Under British influence, the latter was transformed into a centralised institution on the European model[51] and, under pressure from Konrad Adenauer, Bonn was turned into the political capital. But Frankfurt kept the central bank, along with the advantages ensuing from it; that is to say, the concentration of the main German financial business on the banks of the Main.

Nevertheless, this concentration occurred gradually and would never be as high as in London, Paris or New York. If the number of people employed in the financial sector is taken as an indicator, Hamburg had the upper hand until the 1980s – thanks, it is true, to its strong position in insurance, which was moreover more fiercely contested by Munich and Cologne than by the Hessian city. It is in the banking field that Frankfurt really emerged in the fifties – a trend that intensified in the following decades.[52] The concentration of banking activities in Frankfurt was, above all, the consequence of reunifying the three big German banks – Deutsche Bank, the Dresdner Bank and the Commerzbank – that had been split up into regional banks immediately following the Nazi defeat. Deutsche Bank, for example, had been succeeded by ten separate institutions; the largest, the Rheinisch-Westphälische Bank with its registered office in Dusseldorf and assets of 891 million German marks in 1950, came way ahead of the next one, the Südwestbank with assets of 327 million marks and whose headquarters were shared between Stuttgart and Mannheim. These dismantling measures, largely inspired by the Americans, clearly ran counter to European banking traditions and came up against strong opposition from the German business world from the outset. From 1949 bank representatives made proposals along the lines of regrouping banks on a broader regional basis, making the most of the disagreement between the British and Americans on this issue, as well as of the favourable conditions offered by the cold war. From 1952 the ten regional institutions were reduced to only three – the Norddeutsche Bank, the Rheinisch-Westfälische Bank and the Süddeutsche Bank, in the case of Deutsche Bank. Full and complete reunification took place in 1957 for Deutsche Bank and the Dresdner Bank, which set up their main headquarters in Frankfurt, and in 1958 for the Commerzbank, which originally opted for Dusseldorf and moved its headquarters to the banks of the Main a few years later.[53]

These changes in the German financial sector still had only a limited international impact in the fifties, during which time Frankfurt developed in a primarily West German context in which the banking sector, focused entirely on financing reconstruction, brought together the best part of the operations that had formerly been run from Berlin. Its international influence would come later as the Federal Republic and its currency grew in importance.

The rise of the Swiss financial centre

The years that followed the Second World War opened up an unprecedented period for the Swiss centres, above all Zurich, one of the rare financial markets, along with New York, to strengthen its international position. Immediately following the world conflict, Switzerland's economic situation was advantageous, with a trade surplus, notably with the United States, and both public debt and the level of inflation under control. These made the Swiss franc the only currency convertible with the dollar and one of the strongest currencies in the world. All these conditions encouraged the rise of an international financial centre, especially in a Europe regulated by exchange controls. Switzerland could quickly pick up again and develop its role as a hub for accommodating and investing foreign capital. The Washington Agreements, signed on 25 May 1946 by the United States, Britain and France, enabled Swiss assets in dollars to be released and, from spring 1947, income from Swiss assets in the United States to be freely transferred. Foreign issues took off again in May 1947, with a loan of Fr.50 million at 4% on behalf of the Régie des Téléphones et Télégraphes in Brussels.[54]

These issuing activities continued during the fifties, totalling Fr.2.4 billion – $550 million – between 1950 and 1959.[55] They made Zurich, where the vast majority of them were placed, the second centre for foreign loan issues, far behind New York, which was still the great world purveyor of funds, and just about on a par with London, their respective positions varying according to the reference years (see Table 5.1). While they served as outlets for foreign capital placed in Switzerland, these issues were still partly dependent on gentlemen's agreements[56] often made between the National Bank and the Swiss banks to contain capital inflows judged at times to be excessive. This resulted in them stopping almost entirely from July 1956 to June 1958.

Foreign bond issues thus emerged in the 1950s as one of the Swiss financial centre's specialities and were where its strength lay on the international level, alongside other niches like foreign exchange transactions, trade in precious metals and wealth management. The latter remained the prerogative of private bankers, especially Genevan ones,[57] with the big banks – the Union Bank of Switzerland, the Swiss Bank Corporation and the Crédit Suisse – and foreign banks in Switzerland only really starting to engage in this activity from the 1960s onwards. Zurich, on the other hand, established itself as the main market for gold immediately following the Second World War, taking advantage of the closure of London's gold market until 1954, at the same time as benefiting from the lack of exchange control and the desires of the Swiss banks' rich, cosmopolitan clientele. While the London gold market quickly regained its pre-eminence, Zurich nonetheless continued to play a key role in this sphere, more than two-thirds of the metal delivered to London being regularly redirected to the banks of the Limmat. Being smaller, Geneva remained a more cosmopolitan centre than Zurich in many respects, in particular because of the large number of foreign banks that had been set up there. Long-established banks, such as Paribas, the Crédit Lyonnais or Lloyds Bank, were joined by new ones like the American Express Company, also present in Zurich, the First National City Bank or the Banque de l'Indochine, while other foreign institutions, especially Middle Eastern ones, set up affiliated banks under Swiss law.[58] Numerous international trading companies, also often with links to the Middle East, set up shop there too. Moreover, the city was to become the second European centre, behind London, for trade in certain raw materials, especially oil, cereals and cotton.

The Swiss financial centre's new international dimension nevertheless came up against some limits that reflected both the international context of the time and Swiss banking traditions. Swiss banks still had weak representation abroad, with only twelve branches in 1962, and foreign banks – about fifteen, not counting the representative offices – had a weak presence in Switzerland. The Swiss banking system continued to be dominated by the cantonal banks until around 1960,[59] but the big banks strengthened their position thanks to their international business: interbank deposits and loans both to companies and individuals outside Switzerland. By 1962 their foreign assets had reached Fr.7.1 billion, or 29% of their total assets, compared with 16% for the banking system as a whole.[60] That year, for the first time since 1930, their total assets exceeded those of the cantonal banks, as a result of internationalisation that would increase dramatically in scale in the decades to come.

The birth and development of the Euromarkets 1958–73

At the end of the 1950s and the beginning of the 1960s, the emergence of the Euromarkets – for Eurodollars, then for Eurobonds and Eurocredits – represented a turning point in the history of international finance. As genuine international capital markets that circumvented the various national regulations, they gave a new impetus to capital flows and brought about a realignment of the hierarchy of international financial centres, from which the leading beneficiary was the City of London.

The emergence of Eurodollars

Eurodollars are dollars held outside the United States, free of American regulations. Their origin dates back to the beginning of the 1950s, when, for various reasons, dollar deposits started to accumulate in European banks, especially in London. The cold war played a role in this process, the Soviet Union and the eastern European countries preferring to deposit their assets in American currency in Europe, for fear of having them frozen in the United States if tension in the international climate were to mount. The first deposit of this type was allegedly that made in Paris by the Banque commerciale pour l'Europe du Nord, a Russian bank whose telegraphic address was Eurobank – hence the name Eurodollars. There was also, and above all, American investment, mainly by multinational enterprises, in addition to civil aid and the military presence abroad, as well as the growing American balance-of-payments deficit. But the influx of dollars into Europe was also a consequence of Regulation Q, limiting the interest rates paid on bank deposits within the United States. British banks, which were able to offer higher interest, particularly because of the high interest rates prevailing at the time in Britain, managed to attract funds to London, mainly from American multinationals abroad, that they could then use in various national and international operations.

The first bank to make the most of this opportunity – and the one credited with introducing this major innovation – appears to have been the Midland. In June 1955 it offered an interest rate of $1\frac{7}{8}$% on 30-day deposits denominated in dollars, whereas the maximum payable in the United States was 1%. The bank, which in fact needed to increase its sterling deposits, put these funds to domestic use, selling the dollars for pounds sterling cash and repurchasing them forward, all at a rate below the Bank of England's discount rate.[61] As Catherine Schenk has pointed out, the Midland Bank's innovation started out as arbitrage on interest rates.[62] But it would be taken up again for other purposes. The ban on using sterling instruments to finance third-country trade, brought in by the British government to counter downward pressure on the pound that intensified in 1957, led the City's banks – which did not want to lose their clients – to use dollars instead. The initiative was taken by the merchant banks, including Kleinworts, Samuel Montagu and Warburgs, and by the overseas banks, first and foremost the Bank of London and South America at the instigation of its chairman, Sir George Bolton – a keen advocate of replacing the pound by the dollar for certain types of international transactions carried out in the City.[63]

Table 5.3. *The growth of the Euromarkets, 1958–73 (in millions of dollars)*

	1958	1963	1968	1973
Eurodollars[a]	1,500	9,000	25,000	132,000
Eurobonds	–	258	3,942	4,209
Syndicated Eurocredits	–	–	–	20,826

Note: [a] Net market, with the exception of double entries coming from interbank deposits.
Source: International Capital Markets Statistics, 1950–1995, Paris, OCDE, 1996, BIS; Annual Reports.

With the European currencies' return to external convertibility in December 1958 and, from the early sixties, the gradual relaxing of controls on capital flows, the Eurodollar market expanded rapidly. It was supplied mainly by American multinationals and by European central banks, either directly or through the Bank for International Settlements. It provided credit on a worldwide scale in hitherto unprecedented proportions. This credit mainly provided interbank deposits and financed international trade and other short-term loans – transactions involving extremely large sums. From approximately $1.5 billion when it started in 1958, this market reached $25 billion ten years later and more than $130 billion in 1973 (see Table 5.3).

Eurobond issues

The Eurodollar market quickly gave rise to the Eurobond market. The idea of using funds deposited in this way not only for bank loans but also for issuing dollar-denominated bonds, in London rather than in New York, did not take long to form in City bankers' minds. Foreign issues in the United States aroused little interest among the American public and yielded a far better return to American banks than to European ones, even though it was the European banks that mainly took charge of placing securities with their clients. The time thus seemed right to relaunch these issues – one of the City's historical specialities – and the Bank of England gave its consent in July 1962. The first Eurobond is generally attributed to Siegmund Warburg, who in January 1963 concluded an agreement with Autostrade Italiane, a subsidiary of IRI, for a loan of $15 million at $5\frac{1}{2}$% over six years that was finally issued on 1 July 1963.[64] It was not, however, the very first issue. In fact, a few weeks earlier in mid-May, the merchant bank Samuel Montagu had already succeeded in placing a loan of $20 million at 5% on behalf of the Belgian government. This, bought at par by a banking consortium, was not allotted to the public, which explains why it did not attract as much attention.

Come what may, the advance was now under way and received a huge incentive with the introduction, from 18 July 1963, of the Interest Equalization Tax – a tax on foreign loans issued in the United States. This measure, intended to curb the export of American capital, increased the cost of foreign bond issues in the United States and made that of Eurobonds even more attractive. Five years after their launch, Eurobonds had already reached $4 billion per year (see Table 5.3), catching up with classic foreign loans – issued in local currency on behalf of a non-resident borrower – and overtook them for good from the 1980s onwards. Eurobonds indeed afforded advantages to all parties. For borrowers, they were not very demanding as regards prospectuses and information, since they were not subject to the jurisdiction of any specific country. For investors – in the 1960s mainly individuals – they were issued to bearer, so were anonymous and exempt from withholding tax, and they were particularly convenient for the legendary Belgian dentist or for the somewhat more real clients of Swiss banks.[65] Lastly, for the banks responsible for the issue, the simplicity and stability of the commission structure were appealing: 2.5%, shared between the lead banks (0.5%), the underwriters (0.5%) and those who placed it with the public (1.5%) – one bank quite easily being able to accumulate the three types of return.[66]

Eurocredits

A third form of Eurocredit – medium term this time, lasting from three to ten years – developed in the mid-sixties, between short-term, mainly interbank, deposits, which formed the Eurocurrency market proper, and long-term Eurobonds. These were international bank loans wholly financed by resources in Eurodollars and generally granted on the basis of floating interest rates, which made the borrower carry any risks associated with interest rate fluctuations – a vital transfer of responsibility for the banks that financed these medium-term loans with very short-term deposits or even with demand deposits.[67] But the borrower found this a more flexible source of funding than a bond issue. Medium-term Eurocredits really took off with the issue in May 1966 of the first certificates of deposit in Eurodollars, introduced in London by their American creator, the First National City Bank.[68] Towards the late sixties, in view of the growing demand for these loans and the size of the amounts required, the banks organised syndicated loans bringing several of them together. Among the first syndicated Eurocredits was a loan for

$15 million organised in June 1968 by the Bank of London and South America, and another for $100 million to Austria, orchestrated by Lehman Brothers and Bankers Trust International.[69] From barely $2 billion in 1968, Eurocredits quickly swelled to exceed $20 billion in 1973 – or more than four times the amount of Eurobonds (see Table 5.3). In this respect, and quantitatively speaking at least, Eurocredits, rather than Eurobonds, represented the main financial innovation of the 1970s.

The City's rebirth

The emergence of the Euromarkets, which quickly made London their natural home, was a clear sign that the City was once more among the highest-ranking international financial centres, but under conditions that were very different from those that had prevailed before 1914 or even in the 1920s. Why and how did the City come to accommodate these markets? Mainly for three reasons: London's financial traditions, the attitude of both the British and European monetary authorities, and the impact of American banking regulations.

There is little doubt that London was well equipped for taking charge of this type of operation. Its bankers' age-old experience, their expertise in international financial matters, the diversity and complementarity of its institutions and markets, its critical mass as far as material and people were concerned – all of these elements were still present on the banks of the Thames. In 1965 nearly 130,000 people were employed in the City, including 50,000 in the banking sector, nearly as many in insurance and the rest in the stock exchange and commodity markets.[70] In other words, the centre's mechanisms, checked by sterling's weakness, were just waiting to be reactivated, and the first transactions in Eurodollars were, of course, the preserve of the City's bankers. As Humphrey Mynors, one of the Bank of England's executive directors, wrote in 1963: 'It is par excellence an example of the kind of business which London ought to be able to do both well and profitably. That is why we, at the Bank, have never seen any reason to place any obstacles in the way of London taking its full and increasing share. If we were to stop the business here, it would move to other centres with a consequent loss of earnings for London.'[71]

This positive attitude on the part of the British monetary authorities played a decisive role in the success of the Eurodollar market in London. It was clearly dictated by the intention of promoting the City's position as an international financial centre – a goal that overrode any fears aroused by this new product, especially the volatility risks associated with such transactions, the possible inflationary effects of these capital inflows and the larger difficulties that these might pose to the conduct of monetary policy. Their choice in fact meant differentiating between domestic financial activities denominated in sterling, which were tightly regulated, and international activities in foreign currencies on behalf of non-residents, who enjoyed far greater freedoms. This choice contrasted with that of the monetary authorities of other continental European countries, which were far more suspicious of capital considered speculative. Measures intended to discourage foreign deposits were taken at the beginning of the 1960s in France,[72] Switzerland, Italy and Germany. From then on, London was able to capture most of the Eurodollar market and once more became the centre of international banking transactions. As Walter Wriston, head of the Overseas Division and future chairman of Citibank, explained: 'The Eurodollar market exists in London because people believe that the British government is not about to close it down.'[73]

The first sign of the City's rebirth was the attraction that it held for banks throughout the world. There was nothing new about this, since foreign banks had set up branches there since before 1914 and, for the most part, had kept them. Yet this was now on a quite different scale; indeed, the number of foreign banks represented in London went from 69 in 1955 to 159 in 1970 and to 243 in 1975,[74] that is to say, nearly twice the corresponding number for New York.[75] Participation in the Eurodollar market was now added to their traditional activities of financing international trade and foreign exchange operations: by the late sixties, 80% of Eurofunds were being borrowed through London.

A new type of bank also made its appearance in the City, adding further to its internationalism: the banking consortia.[76] These were institutions – not simple associations – set up by groups of banks of different nationalities within the framework of strategic alliances. Such arrangements were not new; before 1914, for example, numerous European banks had founded joint subsidiaries, usually in order to break into new and uncertain markets abroad. In the sixties and seventies, banking consortia were set up by banks that were reluctant to venture alone on to the Euromarkets – at that time considered new, uncertain and risky. The initiative fell to the Midland Bank, which in 1964 founded the Midland and International Banks Limited, jointly with the Toronto Dominion Bank, the Standard Bank and the Commonwealth Bank of Australia. Many others followed – among them, the Orion Bank in 1970, which became the most important consortium.[77] Their profusion coincided with the rise of syndicated Eurocredits – their main field of activity, for which they held 20% of the market in 1973, compared with 8% for Eurocurrency loans maturing in less than one year.[78] Most of them would disappear in the 1980s, victims of their parent companies' differing goals.

However, the City's openness to the world and the resulting invisible income that it brought came at a price: increased competition for the British banks and, on the Euromarkets, the dominating influence of the London branches of foreign banks. Whereas the British banks, irrespective of type, controlled two-thirds of the Eurodollar market in 1958, this share fell to about one-third ten years later, that of the clearing banks dropping from 22% to less than 2%, while the merchant banks and overseas banks – traditionally more focused on this type of business – managed to retain 10% and 20% of the market respectively until the end of the sixties.[79] The situation was similar in Eurobond issues, in which only three British firms – Warburgs, Rothschilds and Hambros – appeared in the list of the top twenty lead banks or joint lead banks of issue syndicates between 1963 and 1972.[80] Nevertheless, the effects of this international competition were by and large positive.[81] The arrival of the American banks forced the British banks out of their torpor, making them improve their practices and diversify their products. Certificates of deposit in sterling, for example, were introduced in 1968, and the hundred-year-old discount houses renewed themselves by making them their secondary market. Parallel money markets developed, especially those for interbank deposits in sterling, which experienced a boom in the 1960s. Finally, the national capital market, supplied by the wave of mergers and acquisitions that started in 1961, took on a new dimension and allowed the merchant banks to dominate the field of corporate finance.

The City's rebirth occurred even though the pound was coming increasingly under pressure, which was often interpreted – particularly outside Britain – as a sign of the London centre weakening. The pound's devaluation in November 1967 was a traumatic time for the City, not only for reasons of national pride but also because most of its leading lights continued to think that international financial centre status was linked to the strength of the national currency. But times had changed and, even if the phenomenon was still not noticeable to everybody, the City's destinies were in the process of parting more and more from those of the British economy and its currency.

The American challenge

To some extent, the City's rebirth meant that New York's international role waned somewhat in the sixties. American banking legislation and the various measures taken to curb the export of American capital had played a decisive role in this. Did they penalise New York in favour of London and bring about a reversal in the roles of the two rival centres? It would be tempting but superficial to reply in the affirmative. First, because the New York banks, and American banks more generally, kept supreme control over international finance, irrespective of the financial centre in which operations were carried out. Next, because international business had traditionally only made up a small part of Wall Street's activities and because major developments were taking place in tandem on the American capital market. More than ever, New York was the world's most important financial centre because it was the financial capital of the United States.

Indeed, the sixties marked the start of the American banks' huge multinational expansion, after an initial short-lived wave in the early twenties. They went from having 131 branches abroad in 1950 to having 899, in addition to their 860 foreign subidiaries, in 1986.[82] Moreover, this network of branches was far more dynamic than that of the British overseas banks, since it was more concentrated in industrialised countries and in international financial centres, including offshore ones. Europe was the preferred destination; by 1975 the eight largest American banks had set up 113 branches and 29 representative offices there, London alone having 58 of them.

While London bankers were the founders of the Euromarkets, American banks quickly followed the trend. From November 1959 the First National City Bank used its London branch to collect deposits that were then transferred to New York to finance its loans in the United States. For, as Richard Sylla has argued, American banks' expansion at that time was not so much an invasion of Europe, as lamented by some people, as flight from the United States and from its complex and restrictive banking regulations. The situation did not improve during the sixties, with restrictions being placed on direct investment by multinationals in 1965 and official interest rates being raised, notably in 1966 and 1969, even though Regulation Q remained in force.[83] It was not long before American banks appropriated – one might be tempted to say reappropriated – the Eurodollar market; after all, these were transactions carried out in their national currency. Their share of the Eurocurrency market, over three-quarters of which comprised dollar deposits, went from 17% in 1958 to 54% in 1969 – their maximum level. After the introduction of the Interest Equalization Tax in 1963 and the Voluntary Foreign Credit Restraint Programme in 1965,[84] which closed the New York capital market to foreign issues, American banks increasingly used their branches in London and Europe to carry out this type of operation. They occupied a prominent position in the Eurobond market where, between 1963 and 1972, eight of them ranked among this market's top twenty intermediaries. Not only did they invade the Euromarkets but they gave these markets a boost that they would never otherwise have had. While American banking legislation thus strengthened London's international role to the detriment of New York's, American banks took full advantage of the situation, dominating the Euromarkets and integrating them into their global strategy.

Between 1962 and 1973, the American economy underwent a very long expansion, interrupted only by a short recession in 1969–70, the Dow Jones going from 650 at the beginning of 1960 to 1,020 at the end of 1972. The capital market, which formed Wall Street's basic structure, was extremely active, since it benefited from the third wave of mergers in United States history, after the 1890s and the Roaring Twenties.[85] This wave resulted from the more pronounced diversification strategy adopted by large American enterprises[86] and, above all, from the widespread forming of conglomerates.[87] These conglomerates were characterised by their diversification into activities that were completely unrelated to each other, the underlying idea being that such diversification would shield them from the economic ups and downs in a particular sector and thus increase their profitability. Further profit came from selling some of the conglomerates' constituent parts.[88] In this way, International Telegraph and Telephone (ITT), probably the best known among them, acquired 163 companies in the fifties and sixties. By lavishing advice on enterprises, Wall Street's investment banks – particularly Morgan Stanley, Goldman Sachs and Lazard Frères[89] – were directly involved in this merger and acquisition trend, as well as in the ensuing sales of companies, the number of which increased substantially at the turn of the 1970s.

Banks or markets in Europe?

Continental Europe's main centres – Frankfurt, Paris and Zurich – also gained from the revival in international financial business from the end of the fifties. It was, however, the established financial intermediaries, primarily the banks, that were the foremost beneficiaries, whereas the development of their markets remained limited, both on the national level, in contrast to New York, and on the international level, in contrast to London. This situation can be explained partly by the culture of capital control that prevailed in central Europe and, to a lesser extent, in France, where the state played a dominant role, and partly by the suspicion aroused by Eurodollars in their early days.

Luxembourg. The exception to this was Luxembourg, one of the main beneficiaries of the Eurobond market since 1963, both for loan issues, in which it held second place behind London, and for the secondary market, where they were traded once they had been issued.[90] The number of bond issues quoted on the Luxembourg Stock Exchange went from 117 in 1962 to 717 in 1970, including 552 Eurobonds – a success that can be explained, above all, by the absence of duty on transactions, very low commissions and greatly simplified formalities. Holding companies were another of Luxembourg's specialities. Benefiting from legislation, dating back to 1929, on accommodating foreign capital, which exempted it from any tax on profits and from capital gains tax, they numbered 119 in 1968. Numerous foreign banks also set up, in successive waves, in the Grand Duchy. The first of these, from the early 1960s, comprised German banks trying to avoid the exceedingly large compulsory reserves laid down by the Bundesbank. They were followed, ten years later, by Swiss banks that came to take advantage of the Euromarket and the presence of German banks; then, at the end of the 1970s, by American banks keen to profit from the absence of withholding tax, and by Scandinavian banks wishing to circumvent the ban on lending in foreign currencies in their country of origin.

Luxembourg was the most important of the offshore centres that, in connection with the expansion in Eurocurrencies and thanks to the tax advantages they offered, developed from the 1960s onwards. Ten years later, there were about twenty of them, of which the Bahamas, the Cayman Islands, Bahrain and Jersey are the best known.[91] Regardless of their importance on the international financial circuits, they did not belong to the group of leading international financial centres that are of particular interest to us here.

Frankfurt. In many respects, Frankfurt was a more serious candidate than London to host the Eurobond market. While the German financial centre admittedly did not have the City's experience, expertise and international networks, it could count on much more abundant savings, powerful institutions and the almost total absence of exchange control. But this freedom of exchange made the German authorities fear the pernicious effects that international activities might have on their monetary policy and prompted them to control issues tightly, whereas, paradoxically, the exchange control in force enabled Britain to delink its domestic market from the international market and to liberalise the latter completely.[92] A 25% withholding tax on the total amount of bond coupons paid to non-residents was thus introduced in 1965. This was a defensive measure intended to curb the inflow of foreign capital into Germany and to lower the upward pressure that it exerted on the mark, but it represented a very serious handicap for the German bond market. Similarly, the Bundesbank insisted that the banks maintain relatively large reserves – a minimum of nearly 15% for deposits on current accounts – whereas this cover obligation, unknown in Britain, did not exist for deposits in Eurocurrencies.[93] As a result, the big German banks developed their international business from other financial centres, particularly London, and Luxembourg which then really took off.

Between 1960 and 1980, Frankfurt thus remained a centre of national rather than international dimension, despite the mark's growing international role, which overtook that of the pound during the sixties. The German currency, which quickly acquired the reputation of being a strong currency, was sought after by international traders, but mark-denominated issues on behalf of foreign borrowers remained limited, totalling barely 5 billion marks, compared with 135 billion for domestic issues, between 1958 and 1967. In the face of growing demand for the former, the Bundesbank signed a gentleman's agreement in 1968 with the main banks that dealt in issuing loans in marks for non-resident debtors. Henceforth, these had to have a German bank as the lead bank, which undertook to take into account the market's ability to absorb funds and to respect the issue schedule drawn up by a committee representing the German banking system.[94] All this took place under the watchful eye of the Bundesbank that, furthermore, reached informal agreements within the framework of the Bank for International Settlements with other central banks, especially the Bank of England, to ban issues abroad of bonds denominated in marks and in this way to prevent the German currency from becoming an international reserve currency. Nevertheless, the appeal of the mark strengthened the big German banks based in Frankfurt, which collected directly in deposits any funds wishing to be placed in marks. This enabled them to play an active role on the Euromarkets – first by placing Eurobonds, then by joining issue syndicates. Headed by Deutsche Bank, they would not take long to occupy the top places in international rankings of lead banks for issues of foreign bonds and Eurobonds, mainly on account of their position in those denominated, since 1968, in marks.[95]

Paris. France's situation was different due to the closure of Paris' international capital market, which penalised both the Parisian financial centre, where foreign loans were banned, and French banks, which could not place bonds, issued in London or elsewhere, with their domestic clientele. Nevertheless, the big banks endeavoured to take part in the Eurobond market from the outset.[96] Paribas succeeded from 1964, thanks to its alliances in New York (with Lehman Brothers and Kuhn Loeb) and in London (with Warburgs) and to its Geneva subsidiary's placing capacity, in taking part in several issue syndicates and even in assuming the lead role in some. In the course of the sixties, it managed to work its way up to the top ten of lead or co-lead banks in international issues. The Crédit Lyonnais, which strove to regain its pre-1914 role, found it more difficult to make a name for itself – even though it too, like all the main French banks, including private houses such as Rothschilds or Lazards, succeeded in gaining a prominent place in issue syndicates. As a deposit bank, its competitive advantage lay mainly in its placing capacity, and the opening up of the French market would considerably strengthen its position in negotiations with its European partners. The liberalisation of the French capital market, advocated by the banks, was on the agenda by the mid-sixties, even if things occurred in a somewhat haphazard manner and at a slower pace than the banks had hoped. Liberalisation measures were considered from 1965 by successive finance ministers, thereby showing that France set greater store by hosting a leading international financial centre than did Germany. The re-establishment of the country's creditor position and the franc's recent strong currency status rekindled ambitions of seeing Paris once more hold its own against London and, above all, present itself as the financial capital of the European Community – which seemed to be its immediate concern. The time seemed right, especially as the pound was experiencing severe difficulties and Britain had still not joined the Common Market. The Treasury nevertheless proceeded cautiously, since the advantages of liberalising the Parisian market – capital inflows, increased efficiency, prestige and profits from financial operations – seemed to it to be offset by the dangers, especially increased dependency on foreign countries and the loss of autonomy in conducting monetary policy.[97]

In November 1966 certain measures were indeed taken to liberalise the Paris market. The issue of international loans on the French market was authorised for national or foreign debtors. Not only were banks granted the right to place foreign bonds with their clientele, but stocks were henceforth allowed to be quoted in Paris. Finally, companies were permitted to borrow abroad, thus giving French banks more opportunities to act as lead banks for these issues. With the lifting of exchange control in December 1966, these outward-looking measures were thus fairly sweeping. The Ministry of Finance was nevertheless still able to set the total amount and timing of foreign issues, and it did not seem to have a very clear vision of the outward-looking policy to follow.

It remained especially doubtful about foreign loan issues in francs on the Paris market and about international issues in francs, but seemed to develop a more positive attitude, authorising among other things an international issue on behalf of the French subsidiary of British Petroleum in February 1968. However, the events of May 1968 and the subsequent re-establishment of exchange control put an abrupt end to these efforts – the most ambitious since the end of the twenties – to promote Paris as an international financial centre.

European cooperation. The European response to competition from American banks came from institutions rather than from markets. To make the most of all the opportunities offered by the development of the Euromarkets, the big European banks adopted an alliance strategy in the spirit of European construction getting underway at the time. In actual fact, the Treaty of Rome signed in March 1957, which gave rise to the European Community,[98] did not make provision for creating a European monetary area, merely recommending that monetary policies be coordinated. Furthermore, the Old World's most important international financial centres – London and Zurich – were outside the Community. And the chances of achieving genuine European financial integration by allowing a dominant centre to emerge seemed highly remote, even with the prospect of Britain joining the Common Market, which eventually took place in 1973.[99]

Two other more immediate developments brought European banks closer together. The first was the possibility of monetary union that emerged at the end of the 1960s; the Werner Report,[100] made public in 1971, actually anticipated Europe's monetary union within the space of ten years, and banks tried to get into an advantageous position in case the project succeeded. The second, as in the case of the banking consortia mentioned earlier, was the banks' tendency to join forces in order to confront competition on new ground. These strategic alliances, in which British banks participated, took the form of 'banking clubs'. Unlike consortia, registered as companies, the clubs were coalitions among big commercial banks in which each preserved its full and complete independence. Their primary goal was to enable their members to offer their services in different European countries without having to be represented there directly.[101] Their cooperation took many different forms, including creating banking consortia to intervene on the Euromarkets. Four main clubs were set up in the course of the 1960s, bringing together most of the big European banks, with in principle no more than one per country: ABECOR,[102] EBIC,[103] Europartners[104] and Inter Alpha.[105]

EBIC, one of the oldest and most dynamic, is a good example of how these banking clubs worked.[106] Its origins date back to 1959, when the *Club des Célibataires* was founded by Deutsche Bank, the Amsterdamsche Bank and the Belgian Générale de Banque. The choice of name clearly indicated what kind of cooperation existed among the members – everything could be shared except their independence. The Midland Bank joined them in 1963, and then the club took the name of the European Advisory Committee. Together, the four banks launched several joint ventures in Europe and in the United States, and for that purpose set up joint subsidiaries, including the Banque Européenne de crédit à moyen terme (BEC) in Brussels in 1967[107] and the European American Banking Corporation (EAB) in New York in 1968.[108] In 1970 they decided to strengthen the institutional framework of their cooperation and founded the European Banks' International Company (EBIC), with a capital of $2 million and registered offices in Brussels. Several EBIC companies were set up to develop joint banking operations and financial products.[109] When the Société Générale and the Creditanstalt-Bankverein in Vienna joined in 1971, followed two years later by the Banca Commerciale Italiana, this strengthened the group, as did the creation in 1973 of the European Banking Company (EBC) in London to operate in the field of international investment banking.

EBIC's achievements, like those of the other banking clubs, were thus far from insignificant. And yet, from the mid-1970s, cracks began to appear, and these various cooperative structures collapsed at the beginning of the 1980s, one of the members of the club usually buying up its partners' shares in their joint subsidiary. Several factors explain the failure of this first move towards banking integration in Europe. First, there was the monetary instability that followed the collapse of the Bretton Woods system and the abandonment, for an unspecified period, of the plan for European monetary union. Conflicts of interest also arose among the members, particularly concerning the original agreement not to intervene in one's own name in the country of one of the other members of the group. Finally, and this was the main reason for failure, there was the desire of various members to build their own network of branches abroad and to be represented directly in the main international financial centres.

Switzerland's golden age

Switzerland's position in these years was more favourable than that of the other continental European centres, to the exent that it combined the development of its financial institutions, first and foremost its big banks, with that of its markets. Foreign capital flowed into the country and was then redirected abroad, Switzerland fully playing its role as a financial hub. In 1975, for example, capital inflows amounted to Fr.40 billion and outflows to Fr.47 billion, the Fr.7 billion difference coming from Swiss residents' surplus savings; Fr.20 billion worth of outgoing capital flows were invested in the form of bank deposits abroad, including the increase in foreign currency reserves at the National Bank; Fr.4 billion in credit granted by Swiss banks to non-banking non-residents; Fr.10 billion in the form of bonds in Swiss francs from foreign debtors; and, finally, Fr.13 billion in Eurobonds and other stocks denominated in a currency other than the Swiss franc.[110]

In the early 1960s, Switzerland was second behind the United States for foreign issues. Taking all currencies into account, these amounted to $627 million between 1961 and 1964, compared with $4 billion for the United States but just over $200 billion each for the Netherlands and Germany, with Britain, France and Italy trailing far behind. But the growth in Eurobonds from 1963 onwards put the Swiss capital market in an awkward position, since the Swiss authorities decided to ban international issues in foreign currencies in Switzerland – a ban made permanent in 1971 with the introduction of stamp duty on these operations, eliminating any chance of Zurich being competitive in this field. Similarly, the Swiss National Bank, following the example of the Bundesbank, endeavoured through agreements with other central banks to prevent loans in Swiss francs from being issued abroad, out of fear of excessive pressure on the franc and the uncontrolled internationalisation of the Swiss currency.[111] Switzerland thus remained on the sidelines as Eurobonds developed, by preventing them from being issued on its territory or from being issued in its currency on a foreign market. On the other hand, foreign bonds in Swiss francs issued in one of the country's financial centres were a lasting success. Their amount was far from insignificant, in spite of the overall success of Eurobonds: in 1974 they represented 11.3% of the total amount of international loans.[112] It is also significant that they regularly exceeded foreign bonds in dollars, the market for which had been closed in the United States after the introduction of the Interest Equalization Tax in 1963, before opening again in the mid-1970s.

For their part, the Swiss banks, including banks in foreign hands under Swiss law, held a number of aces. In the national market, they enjoyed a monopoly in bond issues in Swiss francs regardless of the borrower's origin (national or foreign) and character (government, international organisation or private enterprise). In the Eurobond market outside Switzerland, they had a vast placing capacity, which strengthened their position in international syndicates. In the mid-sixties, more than half of all Euro-issues were probably placed through Swiss banks. It is undoubtedly for these reasons that the latter played only a fairly passive role in the market until the end of the decade, making do with collecting their 1.5% commission for placing these papers. It was only from the 1970s that the three big banks – the Union Bank of Switzerland, the Swiss Bank Corporation and the Crédit Suisse – appeared regularly in the top ten places in the rankings of lead banks for international issues.

Between 1950 and 1970, Switzerland thus became one of the world's most important financial centres, probably in third place behind New York and London. Besides the issuing business, its position was also strong in the money market; Switzerland held third place in international banking operations in 1965, with 8.3% of the foreign assets of commercial banks, and fourth in 1975, with 8.4%.[113] These international operations were managed above all by the three big banks, which underwent a huge expansion during this period; between 1963 and 1973, their foreign assets increased sixfold and their foreign liabilities fivefold, whereas national operations, on both sides of their balance sheet, only increased by 2.5.[114]

Nevertheless, the balance-sheet total reflected only one part of Swiss banking business – and not the most important one at that. Wealth management, the Swiss financial centre's other great speciality, can only be gauged roughly, as precise data are not available, whether as to the overall amount of funds being managed or their distribution by type of bank or by city. But pointers are not deceptive. Fiduciary accounts, for example, were basically off-balance-sheet operations.[115] They came to Fr.41 billion at the end of 1973, an amount representing 15% of Swiss banks' balance-sheet total – Fr.277 billion – compared with less than 1% twelve or so years earlier.[116] It was the same for stock-market transactions, Swiss banks managing on behalf of their private clientele securities whose overall value probably exceeded Fr.100 billion and which, in view of the narrowness of the domestic market, were mostly traded abroad. The main Swiss stock exchanges (Zurich, Geneva and Basel) were, nonetheless, welcoming to international stocks: 123 foreign shares and 109 Swiss shares were, for example, quoted on the Geneva Stock Exchange. Foreign exchange transactions should not be overlooked either, nor trade in precious metals, especially Zurich's role as the main physical gold market from 1968 onwards, with the creation by the three big banks of a gold pool that absorbed the bulk of South Africa's and the Soviet Union's output.

The rise of the Swiss financial centre attracted foreign banks far more than in the past; 99 had established themselves there by 1973 – of

which 84 were organised under Swiss law and 15 were subsidiaries of
foreign banks – and represented more than 11% of the total assets of
banks in Switzerland. They were especially active in international credit
operations (with a 28% share, compared with the big banks' 63%),
transactions in securities and currencies, and, increasingly, wealth
management. For their part, the Swiss banks strengthened their presence abroad, the number of their branches going from twelve in 1962
to twenty-two in 1972, mostly in the large international financial
centres.[117]

Swiss financial circles were aware of the Swiss financial centre's new
international importance. It was not without some pride that, at the end
of the sixties, Max Iklé, former general director of the National Bank,
estimated that the income from this centre (Fr.2.14 billion) was only
just below that of the City of London (Fr.2.7 billion), the difference
coming mainly from insurance, in which Switzerland nevertheless held a
strong international position.[118] Irrespective of these figures' validity,
the Swiss financial centre's performance during this period was astonishing, bearing in mind the country's size. The legacy of war, the dividend of neutrality and banking secrecy certainly contributed to this, as
did the strength of the Swiss franc and interest rates that were lower
than elsewhere. While its prosperity would be maintained in decades to
come, it would be much more difficult to retain its relative position.

The dawn of globalisation 1973–80

The end of the fixed exchange rate system in 1973 gave a new impetus
to international capital flows. Even if there was not yet any talk of globalisation – the phenomenon only picked up from the 1980s – the first
signs were nevertheless visible. The resumption of capital exports can
mainly be explained by what is known, following Robert Mundell, as the
Impossible Trinity – in other words, the impossibility of carrying out an
economic policy combining more than two of the three following elements: free circulation of capital, fixed exchange rates and an independent monetary policy.[119] The abandonment of fixed exchange rates
thus opened the way for transferring capital without losing any autonomy in the conducting of monetary policy, which contrasted with the
situation prior to 1914, when capital circulated throughout the world
with fixed parities but national monetary policy was dictated by the
automatic functioning of the gold standard. The analytical framework is
appealing, even if it is inevitably somewhat oversimplified. The process of
opening up to the world that had got underway in the late fifties, as
European currencies returned to convertibility, really gathered speed

in the seventies. Euromarkets – the symbols and instruments of this openness – expanded once again. Between 1974 and 1980, the Euro-currency market went from $177 billion to $575 billion,[120] the Eurobond market from $3.4 to $20.4 billion and the syndicated Eurocredit market from $28.5 to $78 billion.[121] New financial instruments reinforced this expansion, especially the introduction from 1970 of convertible bonds and stock warrants.[122]

The 'recycling of petrodollars'

Another event occurring in 1973 made a decisive contribution to this growth: the decision taken in October by the OPEC countries to double the price of oil, then to double it again two months later. Oil-exporting countries' revenue thus went from $24 billion before the crisis to $117 billion afterwards. Between 1974 and 1980, these countries accumulated $383 billion in liquid assets, half of which was invested as short-term bank deposits with the biggest American and European banks. These deposits had all the characteristics of Eurodollars – mobility and an absence of control by a national authority – and swelled the already existing pool of Eurodollars. The question of the risks that this influx of money posed to international financial stability was widely debated in the wake of the first oil shock, particularly in the United States. Before long, a solution for placing or 'recycling' these new Eurodollars, dubbed 'petrodollars', needed to be found. From the outset, the main banks involved, above all Citibank from New York, envisaged lending these funds to developing countries, whose public and trade deficits increased sharply following the oil price hike, with the at least tacit approval of Western monetary authorities.

Henceforth, up to the early 1980s, international capital movements were dominated by commercial bank credit to third world countries. These were the largest international bank loans, increasing in amount from about $40 billion in 1975 to $160 billion in 1980.[123] As for emerging countries' foreign debt, it went from $126 billion in 1975 to $455 billion in 1982, with the share of private debt, mostly made up of bank loans, growing at the same time from 43% to 56% of the total.[124] Resorting directly to the capital market thus temporarily became less important; bank loans, usually in the form of syndicated floating-rate Eurocredits,[125] clearly had the edge over international issues. This was a new way of transferring capital to sovereign states. Until then, and especially before 1914, banks had served as inter-mediaries between the borrowing state and the public, making the latter bear the risk of any possible default; Russian loans, considered safe investments, were a classic example. This time it was the banks that were on the front line.

They lived to regret it in 1982, when Mexico unilaterally declared a three months' moratorium on paying the principal on its debt, unleashing a debt crisis that lasted throughout the eighties. Poor risk assessment? Lack of historical knowledge? Loans 'imposed' on Third World countries? The banks were accused of all these evils, after having been commended by national and international monetary authorities for so skilfully solving the problem of international imbalances caused by the oil price hike. It is clear that mistakes were made, although to varying degrees. Although all the banks followed the trend, they were not all exposed in the same way; the big American banks led the field in dubious loans, followed by British banks, with the Swiss banks lagging far behind.

Towards market liberalisation

One of the causes of this infatuation with loans to the third world was undeniably the herd instinct, or the fear of missing the boat – a fear reinforced by lenders gathering in a few large-scale financial centres. Tellingly, this resurgence in international bank flows did not disrupt the organisation and hierarchy of the main centres. It was as if previous developments were being consolidated, especially the transformations caused by the emergence of the Euromarkets ten to fifteen years earlier. This continuation naturally opened the way up for the deregulation of the financial markets that would leave its mark on the late twentieth century.

London remained the Euromarket centre; arrangements for syndicated Eurocredits to developing countries were quite similar operations to Eurobond issues that at the same time were still going at full tilt. They required the same networks and were led by bankers with the same socio-professional profiles: 'a special coterie of cosmopolitan younger bankers ... [who] enjoyed a social world of their own: finance ministers treated them as old friends; they entertained each other lavishly; the final signing of a loan was celebrated with a huge banquet at the Ritz or the Berkeley'.[126] The number of foreign banks in the City continued to increase and reached 328 in 1979. Deutsche Bank, among others, reopened a branch in 1976 – the one that had been established in 1871 and closed during the Great War – from which it conducted a growing share of its operations on the Euromarkets. The British banks held out better against foreign competition and more or less retained their market shares. This time, the 'Big Four',[127] traditionally on the sidelines of big international business, and the overseas banks, became very heavily involved in syndicated Eurocredits – far more so than the merchant banks, which still specialised in market operations. In continental Europe, the growth and international expansion of the big banks were more significant than the development of their financial markets. The German, Swiss, French, Belgian and Dutch banks strengthened their positions in issue syndicates and kept up their international cooperation in clubs and banking consortia, while expanding their own networks of international branches. In Switzerland, wealth management continued its advance,[128] while foreign bond issues in Swiss francs, particularly sought after, proliferated from the late 1970s.[129]

The most significant changes took place in New York, which regained ground after its first steps in liberalising its financial sector. In the capital market, the abolition of the Interest Equalization Tax revived foreign bond issues, which went from $3.6 to $10.8 billion between 1974 and 1976.[130] On the stock exchange, the abolition by the SEC of fixed commissions from 1 May 1975 made competition there even keener. This measure, made necessary by the growing part played by institutional investors in stock-market transactions, notably led to numerous small brokers disappearing and the largest of them,[131] along with investment banks which henceforth had far greater equity capital at their disposal, being transformed into joint-stock companies. A little earlier, the introduction of an automated listing system in 1971 brought about a dramatic rise in the volume of trade, paving the way for a real revolution on Wall Street.[132]

Tokyo's arrival

The major event of the seventies was the rise of Tokyo, which in twenty years went from being a regional financial centre, with its influence limited to South-East Asia, to a centre of world dimensions, ranked among the top in the international hierarchy. Such growth was even more remarkable since Tokyo had only taken the lead among Asian centres from Hong Kong during the fifties.[133] Yet this growth was no more remarkable than that of the Japanese economy during the same period. The Tokyo centre's arrival was, above all, due to Japan's rise to the rank of economic superpower, as had been the case for Berlin in the 1880s and for New York at the turn of the twentieth century. And even more than these two centres, Tokyo had managed to translate the impact of the phenomenal Japanese industrial growth into financial terms.

The Japanese capital city becoming a global financial centre also resulted from steps taken by the Japanese monetary authorities to open

Japan up to the world at the end of the 1970s. Until then, the country's financial resources had been entirely devoted to the reconstruction effort and to fostering national economic growth, through a banking system that was almost autarchic and was tightly regulated by the Ministry of Finance and the Bank of Japan. Indeed, the Japanese banking system, reformed immediately after the Second World War, was largely inspired by the American model of differentiating among financial institutions according to their type of operation. The former *zaibatsu*, family-owned conglomerates that encompassed some of the biggest banks in the country, were abolished. A law passed in 1948 prohibited commercial banks from holding industrial and commercial shares or from putting them on the market, a possibility reserved exclusively for investment banks, which became increasingly important from the 1980s.[134] The commercial banks' position was nevertheless very strong during the post-war years, owing to strong demand for credit from companies that were unable to self-finance their rapid expansion or to go elsewhere due to the very weak development of the Japanese capital market.[135] Moreover, from 1952, when Japan formally regained independence, the law changed and banks were allowed to hold industrial shares up to a limit of 10% (reduced to 5% in 1977), which intensified the practice of cross-shareholding.[136]

In a financial system that was strongly dominated by bank loans, to a far greater extent than in the United States, Britain or Germany, the Bank of Japan carried out its monetary policy by making good use of its discount rate and the volume of its loans to commercial banks. Open-market operations played practically no role, given the lack of government bonds due to the state practising a budget-balancing policy during these years. For their loans to businesses, commercial banks were heavily dependent on advances and, above all, on advice in the form of the famous *window guidance* from the central bank. By reducing its advances to commercial banks, the Bank of Japan was also able to control the volume of their loans and thereby all economic activity. Furthermore, capital flows entering and leaving the country were tightly controlled. Almost all transactions were subject to approval by the government, in particular the acquisition of Japanese stocks by non-residents, foreign bond issues in Japan and borrowing abroad by Japanese enterprises. Banking activities on the Eurodollar market were also subject to controls, as were inflows of short-term bank funds, by placing restrictions on converting the yen.[137] All these measures kept the country out of the international financial system. In 1975 less than 1% of international bonds were denominated in yen, compared with 51% in dollars, 17% in Swiss francs and 16% in marks.[138]

The state of the economy in the 1970s, marked by inflation, the end of the fixed exchange rate regime and the slowdown in economic growth, practically forced the Japanese authorities to open Tokyo up to the world. This was brought about by the simultaneous development of the Tokyo capital market and the liberalisation of international financial operations.

The capital market grew up principally around government bonds that the authorities began to issue from 1975 to finance a budget deficit that was rising sharply under pressure from the oil crisis and the economic recession. The volume of government bonds in circulation increased eightfold, going from 7% to 32% of GDP between 1975 and 1982.[139] For their part, businesses increasingly turned to what the Japanese call direct financing, that is to say the capital market, but the special relationship between banks and industry, characteristic of the Japanese system, was not fundamentally called into question.[140] Besides, companies' share of bonds represented less than 10% of the total bonds in circulation in the early eighties.

This expansion of the capital market was accompanied by the liberalisation of existing markets, particularly the market for *Gensaki* – that is, repurchase agreements of short-term monetary papers – and the appearance of new financial instruments. In 1979 banks were authorised to, among other things, issue certificates of deposit, for which a secondary market was created the following year. Capital movements too were liberalised, but the monetary authorities' standpoint was still influenced by the evolution of the foreign exchange market. The fall in the yen in 1973 and 1974 led the government to encourage the inflow of capital on the one hand – by removing limits placed on buying Japanese stocks by non-residents and by raising the ceiling on loans that Japanese companies could take out abroad – and to discourage outflows of funds on the other hand – by prohibiting foreign yen issues in Japan. Conversely, with the yen's recovery between 1976 and 1978, it was capital outflows that were encouraged, the authorities lifting restrictions on residents buying foreign stocks, while giving banks more leeway in lending abroad. The general trend continued to be towards greater liberalisation. In 1979 granting authorisation to non-residents to take part in the market for *Gensaki* and in that for certificates of deposit opened the way for the Japanese money market to be integrated into the world market.[141]

By volume of national transactions, Tokyo was unquestionably the world's second financial centre at the end of the 1970s, reflecting the country's size and economic dynamism. Domestic issues on the Japanese capital market, for example, amounted to $161 billion in

1980 – admittedly behind the United States ($272 billion), but ahead of Germany ($79 billion) and Britain ($36 billion). The Tokyo Stock Exchange was the world's second, in terms of market capitalisation, in 1981 ($418 billion) – behind New York ($1,100 billion), but way ahead of London ($190 billion) and Frankfurt ($56 billion). Above all, its influence started to make itself felt on the international level. Japanese capital outflows went from an average of some $5.1 billion per year between 1973 and 1977 to $18.4 billion between 1978 and 1982; inflows went from $1.5 to $8.9 billion. The percentage of yen-denominated issues exceeded 5% of total foreign issues in 1980, the number of branches of non-Japanese banks in Tokyo increased from forty-five to seventy-six between 1970 and 1980, and the country's five big commercial banks all came among the top twenty in the world in 1980. Henceforth, Tokyo – with New York and London – belonged among the three international financial centres of truly world dimensions and would thus play a decisive role in accelerating the process of globalisation that left its mark on the last two decades of the twentieth century.

6   Globalisation and financial innovations, 1980–2005

The temptation to compare the last twenty-five years with the situation prevailing a century ago is a strong one, and many commentators have given in to it. Owing to its open economy, the turn of the twenty-first century is surprisingly like that of the twentieth. Measured by the freedom and intensity of capital flows, the degree of globalisation reached on the eve of the First World War was not surpassed before the nineties. For us, the main difference is of course our inability to anticipate how the current process will evolve in the future. Instead of trying, in vain, to use history for predictive purposes, we are better served by placing the changes of the last quarter of a century in a historical perspective. For while there is some continuity with the previous period, globalisation having started in the 1960s, there was unquestionably a break around 1980. Rather than a single event, it was a series of changes, both quantitative (volume of transactions) and qualitative (the kind of financial instruments), that launched this new phase that still endured twenty-five years later. For all that, the specificities of the late twentieth century characterised in particular by the end of the cold war and the arrival of the post-industrial society, should not be overlooked.

The new world economy

On an economic and financial level, three major characteristics, closely linked to each other, define this new era: globalisation, deregulation and innovation. The first has been hotly debated since the early 1990s. Some people embrace it with enthusiasm, others accept it anxiously and a minority reject it by rebelling against it. This is because this phenomenon, whose nature is essentially financial even if its industrial and commercial aspects should not be underestimated, has taken on a social, political and cultural dimension that goes way beyond the microcosm of finance. Apart from questioning the repercussions of capital transfers for both rich and poor countries, there is the matter of national and cultural identity in a world where domination by a superpower, the United States, seems limitless owing to the end of large antagonistic blocks and in spite of efforts at European integration.

Globalisation

The current phase of globalisation reveals both similarities to and differences from the one that preceded it by a century and that we have characterised by five elements: free movement of people; enhanced transport facilities; faster communications; increased trade; and capital flows on a massive scale. We find them again today, in various forms and to different degrees, except for one – the movement of people. Nowadays, it is clear that freedom of movement is far from widespread among all the inhabitants of this planet. For many, travelling is far from unimpeded, while immigration to rich countries comes up against all sorts of obstacles. In general, shifts in population are distinctly smaller, in relative and absolute terms, than they were before 1914, in spite of the amazing progress made in transport – above all, the development and democratisation of private cars – over the last century. In particular, the ever more widespread use of jets, allowing people physically to reach any part of the world in less than twenty-four hours, is synonymous with a reduction in distance that was unimaginable a hundred years ago and which makes the notion of globalisation very concrete. The financial centres have benefited hugely from this, by making personal contacts between one centre and another, however far away, commonplace – yet without being put at a disadvantage by the general slowdown in population shifts. On the contrary, bankers and financiers, of all levels of expertise and responsibility, make up an extremely mobile workforce whose top talent is ever on the look-out for the opportunities offered by the most dynamic centres.

Although it plays a central role in the current globalisation process, the speeding-up of communications represents a less fundamental break with the end of the nineteenth century. Before 1914 it was in fact already possible to communicate almost instantaneously, thanks to the telegraph, wireless telegraphy and the telephone, even if in the case of the latter the earliest intercontinental connections were only established after the Great War. It is the quantity, quality, variety and accessibility of the means of communication that differ, on a truly vast scale, between the two periods. If there is a break, it is in information technologies, which offer the possibility of storing almost limitless volumes of information that can be processed in ever more sophisticated ways and be disseminated instantly thanks to the new telecommunications net-works.[1] These developments lie at the root of the major innovations that have transformed financial techniques and instruments over the last twenty years – and without which globalisation, even supposing that it could have occurred in their absence, would have looked entirely different.

Just as during the period prior to 1914, it was international capital flows that formed the heart of globalisation. According to a recent estimate, the supply of capital invested abroad reached some \$29,000 billion in 2000, increasing tenfold in twenty years, since it was only \$2,800 billion in 1980, and nearly doubling in five years (\$15,500 billion in 1995). Even more significantly, foreign assets represented 92% of world GDP in 2000, compared with 62% in 1995, 25% in 1980 and barely 6% in 1960.[2] Even if these figures are somewhat overestimated, this is an unprecedented level of globalization. At the end of the twentieth century, the United States was – as indeed it had been since the end of the Second World War – the largest holder of capital outside its territory, ahead of Britain, Japan, Germany and France (Table 6.1). While the order of importance has altered and a newcomer, Japan, has worked its way up into the leading group, we find the same countries as before 1914. Once again it is noticeable that they are the ones hosting the main international financial centres. As for the borrowers or the beneficiaries of these savings flows, differences from the first phase of globalisation are more pronounced. Then, it was the colonies and new countries that received the bulk of these transfers; today, it is the rich countries of Europe and North America that, with Japan, absorb more than 80% of foreign investment.[3] This is a major change, fraught with consequences both for those left out of globalisation and for the international financial centres' field of action and their reciprocal interaction.

Deregulation

The upsurge in capital exports was directly linked to the second major aspect of the period, the progressive liberalisation of the financial markets. Alongside the phenomenon of globalisation, this rapid dismantling of restrictive economic and financial measures was also part of a much broader trend, of which it was both the cause and the consequence – the growing influence, first in the Anglo-Saxon countries, and then elsewhere in the world, of a neo-liberal view of the economy and of society. In this respect, at least symbolically, the coming to power of Margaret Thatcher in the United Kingdom in 1979 and Ronald Reagan in the

Table 6.1. *Stock of foreign investment, 2000 (in billions of dollars)*

		(%)
Foreign assets		
United States	7,350	*(26)*
Great Britain	4,450	*(15)*
Japan	2,970	*(10)*
Germany	2,600	*(9)*
France	2,430	*(8)*
Miscellaneous	9,184	*(32)*
Total	28,984	*(100)*
Foreign liabilities		
Europe	14,509	*(48)*
North America	9,611	*(32)*
Japan	1,810	*(6)*
Oceania	494	*(2)*
Developing countries	3,595	*(12)*
Total	30,020	*(100)*

Source: M. Obstfeld and A. M. Taylor, *Global Capital Markets. Integration, Crisis and Growth*, Cambridge, 2004, p. 53.

United States in 1981 marked the beginning of this new vogue. Some resistance has certainly been encountered, attitudes have shifted and policies have changed over the following decades; but the fundamental economic dispensation – the smaller state and the strengthening of market mechanisms – has not really been challenged, least of all in the financial sphere.

The first step towards market liberalisation, the return to external currency convertibility in 1958, had not removed all the constraints upon the free movement of capital. While various factors, including the easing of regulations and the ingenuity of initiatives taken to circumvent them, eroded the impact of existing restrictions from 1960, most countries did not dismantle their exchange controls before the eighties. As for capital outflows, the United States, without ever setting up any formal control, introduced, as we have seen, measures intended to curb the export of American capital between 1963 and 1974. Britain, which after 1958 had kept tight control over international capital flows in pounds, abolished exchange control after the Conservatives returned to power in 1979 – ironically to the great surprise of the City.[4] France would wait more than ten years before following the European Community's directive and liberalising capital movements from 1 July 1990. Fund outflows have never been controlled in Switzerland and they have been almost free since 1958 in Germany, where the last remnants of exchange control were eliminated in 1981.

But there were also obstacles to capital inflows, particularly in countries whose balance of payments was in surplus, like Germany, Japan or Switzerland. They too were gradually eliminated. From the beginning of the eighties, Switzerland dismantled measures – such as the negative interest rate on non-residents' bank deposits – limiting the inflow of foreign funds. In 1984 Germany did away with the 25% withholding tax on income from bonds held by non-residents that had been introduced nearly twenty years earlier. In the same year, Japan, continuing its moves towards liberalisation started in the seventies, relaxed regulations on yen issues, especially on behalf of foreigners; and from 1990 there were no longer any official restrictions on importing or exporting capital, at least not for institutional investors.

The deregulation of the financial markets occurred more slowly, each financial centre proceeding at its own pace. More than any other, one event fired people's imagination – the 'Big Bang' that took place in the City of London on 27 October 1986.[5] Rather than being a starting point, it seemed more like a culmination – namely of a series of transformations that had started more than twenty years earlier as the Euromarkets emerged. But it was the abolition of exchange control in 1979 that, by giving a new boost to capital exports and foreign issues denominated in sterling, formed its pivot.[6] This resulted in far greater interaction between national and international activities in the City, which quickly revealed inadequacies, especially on the part of London brokers and jobbers, who were less and less competitive in a market that had become global.

For the 'Big Bang' was in fact a reform of the London Stock Exchange. It was the result of an agreement in 1983 between the government and the exchange, copying what had been done in New York in 1975, and abolishing by the end of 1986 fixed commissions and also the separation, unique to the London Stock Exchange, between the functions of brokers and jobbers. It was also decided to open up the stock exchange to the outside world by permitting banks to buy member firms, hitherto banned. This brought about the disappearance of almost all the leading brokerage houses – the major exception being Cazenove – which were simultaneously faced with soaring computing costs and tempted by extremely enticing offers. They were taken over by merchant banks, as well as by the main commercial banks, both British and foreign. Beyond the individual destinies and the successes or failures particular to each firm, the 'Big Bang' contributed towards modernising the City – thanks to massive investment in information technologies – thus strengthening the London financial sector's international competitiveness and increasing its lead over its European competitors.

Paris was confronted, on a larger scale and after some delay, with the same fundamental problem as the City, namely that of its international competitiveness. What is more, Paris had to revive, then internationalise, a market that had played only a marginal role in financing the French economy since the Second World War. In the end, this objective, which went back to the sixties, would only be carried out in the mid-eighties under the pressure of market globalisation. Furthermore, the liberalisation measures taken in 1984–85 – the Paris 'Big Bang' – enabled new short-term financial instruments to be introduced. These included negotiable certificates of deposit and Treasury bills, for which a secondary market quickly developed; the near complete elimination of fixed commissions for bond issues and for brokerage involving large sums; and finally, from 1992 the abolition of the stockbrokers' monopoly.[7]

The competitiveness of its financial markets was also an issue for Germany. In 1984–85, the Bundesbank, despite its distrust of financial innovation, authorised certificates of deposit and floating-rate issues, the development of which nevertheless remained limited in the ten years that followed. It also allowed the subsidiaries of foreign banks to act as lead banks for foreign issues in marks. The banks' obligation to keep unpaid minimal reserves at the central bank was however maintained, even though it did not exist for Eurocurrencies, and even a considerable reduction in liquidity ratios in 1992 was not enough to prevent a number of banking businesses from being diverted to London and Luxembourg.[8] At the Frankfurt Börse, dominated by the big banks, tax on transactions (0.25% on shares and 0.1% on bonds) was finally eliminated in 1991.

The Swiss monetary authorities found themselves faced with a similar situation; but the preservation of stamp duty affecting all issues drove them to maintain protectionist rules for foreign bonds in Swiss francs, the more so as this business was flourishing.[9] Taking advantage of an informal agreement within the framework of the Bank for International Settlements, it continued to insist that only banks domiciled in Switzerland could take part in an issue syndicate or a credit consortium for operations in Swiss francs from Switzerland. It was only after the stamp duty reform and the ban on brokerage agreements between banks that, from 1992, the National Bank authorised non-resident banks to participate in, then to lead manage, these issues – interest in which had, in any case, dropped substantially with the Japanese stock-market crash at the beginning of the nineties.[10]

The United States, which had made the first move by reforming the stock exchange in 1975, took much longer to relax its still very restrictive banking legislation. While Regulation Q was done away with for good in

1982, it was not until 1994 and the Riegle-Neal Interstate Banking and Efficiency Act that the banks were able to set up networks of branches throughout the country. Finally, in 1999 the Glass-Steagall Act of 1933 was abolished with the arrival of Financial Modernisation Act. It had been *de facto* emptied of its substance after the American cartel authorities had in 1998 ratified the merger, under the name of Citigroup, of Citicorp and Travelers, an insurance company owning Salomon Smith Barney, an investment bank. In so doing, they let the largest financial group in the world come into being, partly because the development of new financial instruments justified a trend towards greater concentration among the various intermediaries in the world of finance.

As the markets liberalised, new regulatory frameworks were set up to ensure that they functioned properly.[11] The withdrawal, partial or total, of state control over financial activities gave way to a series of ground rules for players and protective measures for consumers of the new financial products freely available on the market. Mainly worked out at national level, some regulations were also subject to international conventions – like the Basel Accords on banks' solvability ratios[12] or the plan, currently at a standstill, for European regulation of financial markets that got underway following the Lisbon Summit in 2000. These new regulatory frameworks, often seen as adding to administrative constraints, played an increasing role in enhancing the competitiveness of the international financial centres.

Innovation

The almost constant arrival of new financial products since the mid-seventies has been an unprecedented phenomenon in financial history. Until then, practices, services and activity, without being entirely static, had not fundamentally changed from one generation to the next. In this respect, innovation has been the most original aspect of recent times, especially because of its impact on the international financial centres' role.

Theory and practice. A turning point was reached when the Euromarkets emerged, which was an opportunity for complex arrangements to be made, taking clients' needs and legal and regulatory constraints into account. But it was from the mid-seventies and, especially the eighties, that innovation really became an integral part of financial activity. Three main factors account for this development. First, there was monetary instability, due to inflation and to newly floating currencies that, although providing dealers with new earning opportunities, meant that there was a need to hedge against fluctuations in interest rates and in foreign exchange rates. Next, there was the incredible progress made in computing, without which the new financial products would never have been able to reach the degree of sophistication that they have nowadays. Finally, there was the application to the markets of what could be called fundamental research, in other words theoretical advances made by a certain number of economists in the fifties and sixties. One thinks in particular of the works by Markowitz and Sharpe on the efficient portfolio that links risks and return; by Modigliani and Miller on the conditions under which the value of a firm is independent of its leverage ratio; by Fama on the efficient market where prices reflect perfectly the information available; and by Black, Scholes and Merton on calculating the value of derivatives.[13] On a more applied level, the move of numerous mathematicians, physicians and engineers over to finance from the eighties onwards, and especially from 1990 – a trend known as *Econophysics* – is part of the same process.[14]

Financial innovation at the end of the twentieth century affected financial markets far more than banking business, one of the main characteristics of the period being financial de-intermediation. To obtain funding, corporate borrowers resorted less and less to intermediaries, particularly to loans from traditional banks, and instead went directly to the market by issuing securities, whether certificates of deposit to meet their cash needs, initial public offerings or rights issues. From then on, it was agents specialising in issue activities and those operating in the secondary markets where these securities were traded that were the real orchestrators of financing mechanisms. The change is visible from the employment figures on Wall Street where, over twenty-five years, the number of people employed by commercial banks has dropped sharply, whereas those engaged in the securities industry has increased considerably.[15] This change, particularly pronounced in the United States, can be explained above all by stock-market performance, whose trend, even if it went through the occasional rough patch, was almost continually upward during the eighties and nineties – making investment in stocks and shares, whatever the associated risks, infinitely more profitable than bank deposits. It can also be explained by the growing influence of institutional investors – pension funds, insurance companies and investment companies – over the financial markets, as well as by the very effect of financial innovation and the proliferation of new negotiable instruments.

Derivatives.   Derivatives are indeed the most important financial innovation of the late twentieth century and a true symbol of the triumphant market. These are contracts whose value 'derives' from an underlying asset. There are two main types:[16] futures – standardised forward contracts – and options. There is certainly nothing new about forward contracts, since those relating to the price of raw materials have commonly been traded on the large commodity markets since the last quarter of the nineteenth century, and those relating to shares are as old as the stock exchanges themselves. In this field, the recent innovation is on a different level. On the one hand, futures are listed continuously on a secondary market, which limits the risks for the brokers;[17] on the other hand, along with currencies, they increasingly focus on synthetic financial assets, such as notional interest rates or the various stock-market indices, called financial futures.[18] The second main type of derivative – options – which have been around for a long time on various stock exchanges, have made outstanding progress – first on individual shares in the United States, then on almost all other financial assets, including futures.

Modern derivatives came into being in Chicago, the United States' second financial centre and the world leader in forward markets thanks to its two large commodity markets – the Chicago Board of Trade and the Chicago Mercantile Exchange. In 1972 the latter launched the first futures market in the world, the International Monetary Market, where currency contracts were traded – an initiative taken immediately after the collapse of the Bretton Woods system to provide an opportunity for hedging against foreign exchange fluctuations. The following year, its great rival founded the Chicago Board Options Exchange, where options were traded on shares. In 1975 the International Monetary Market introduced futures on American Treasury Bills – the first based on interest rates.

Notwithstanding the reaction in New York, where the American Stock Exchange launched its own financial futures contracts in the mid-seventies and where in 1980 the New York Stock Exchange created the New York Futures Exchange, Chicago held on to its lead. Competition from the European financial centres would become tougher. It began in London, where in 1982 LIFFE (London International Financial Futures Exchange) was inaugurated – an initiative taken neither by the London Stock Exchange which, unlike its New York counterpart, had decided not to get involved in this business, nor by the commodity markets despite their historical experience of forward operations, but by various players in the City.[19] Paris followed a few years later by setting up, on the state's initiative, MATIF (Marché à Terme des Instruments Financiers, later to become the Marché à Terme International de France) in 1986.[20] SOFFEX (Swiss Options and Financial Futures

Exchange) opened its doors in Zurich in 1986, followed in early 1990 by DTB (Deutsche Termin Börse), a subsidiary of the Frankfurt Börse. These last two stock exchanges merged under the name of Eurex in 1998.

Despite a degree of specialisation (like the contract on the government reference – notional – local bond) and their obvious complementarity, competition among these derivatives markets was fierce, even though they followed the trend towards regrouping and rationalising the financial markets. In Europe, LIFFE initially went into the lead, was caught up by MATIF, then broke away again to take second place in the world ranking, between the two Chicago markets, in the late nineties.[21] Eurex, benefiting from an efficient electronic trading system, as opposed to the auction abandoned belatedly in London, then broke away in turn to become the world's leading market by 2003. This competition was accompanied by cooperation agreements, such as those signed in 2000 between LIFFE and the Chicago Mercantile Exchange or between Eurex and the Chicago Board of Trade, and by acquisitions, such as the buyout of LIFFE by Euronext[22] in 2002, which allowed an intitial regrouping around the new electronic trading platform developed by the former.

Derivatives were also combined with a new investment medium: alternative management funds, much better known as hedge funds, which appeared during the eighties. While they do not easily fit a single definition, they display a certain number of characteristics: a domicile in an offshore centre; a predilection for short positions, through derivatives or forward operations; frequent use of leverage; and ongoing control of risks taken. They are often organised in the form of unregulated investment pools or closed funds with rather limited exit possibilities. Finally, their managers earn high bonuses[23] and, as a rule, invest their own funds alongside those of their clients. Hedge funds experienced incredible growth during the nineties: between 1990 and 2003, their number grew from approximately 2,000 to nearly 8,000, and the funds managed from $60 billion to $750 billion. It was a development somewhat reminiscent of the investment trusts in Britain in the 1880s and in the United States in the 1920s, with which in their early stages they shared a reputation that was uncertain to say the least – they, too, being considered highly risky, if only owing to their very high leverage.

In the course of their short history, hedge funds have experienced spectacular successes and resounding defeats. George Soros, reputed to have earned more than a $1 billion in 1993, undoubtedly best personifies the former, the yield from his Quantum Fund exceeding 100% that year. But others also made headlines in the financial press by working their way up to the top of the earnings league on Wall Street in the nineties.[24] The most spectacular bankruptcy was of course that of Long-Term Capital Management (LCTM). Founded in 1994 by John Meriwether, a former star trader with Salomon Brothers, LCTM was one of the most important hedge funds and the most prestigious with, among others, Merton and Scholes, both winners of the Nobel Prize in Economics, among its directors. After three extremely profitable years, it was hit with full force by the Russian government's default on part of its debt and was on the brink of bankruptcy in September 1998. It was only saved by the New York Federal Reserve which, fearing the disastrous effects that its bankruptcy might have on the markets and on other financial institutions, set up a consortium of Wall Street's main banks that invested $3.65 billion in exchange for 90% of its capital. Since the early 2000s, hedge funds have nevertheless been taken up by much more conservative portfolio managers. Their average debt ratio has, it is true, dropped considerably – from ten times equity capital in 1998 (and twenty-eight times in LCTM's case) to two to four times in 2005 – as has their annual return, which has recently been around 8% to 10%, compared with two- or three-figure returns ten years ago.

The Euro.   All the same, the most memorable new development of the period has been in an entirely different sphere. This was the advent of the euro on 1 January 1999.[25] The creation of the new European currency, shared by eleven sovereign countries,[26] was a historical first; neither the gold-standard system, nor regional currency unions such as the Latin Monetary Union, nor even national monetary unions such as the one that gave rise to the German mark in 1876, could be compared with it. Regardless of economic logic, in keeping with the adoption of the Single European Act in 1987,[27] or of expected gains, resulting mainly from eliminating exchange risks and from lowering transaction costs, there was nothing automatic or spontaneous about the advent of the euro. It was above all a political decision, arising both from the wish to give a boost to European construction in the late eighties and from the international context following the fall of the Berlin Wall and German reunification in October 1990. The first attempt at monetary union, envisaged in the Werner Report, had come up against the monetary upheavals of the early seventies and was politically premature. The Delors Report,[28] made public in April 1989, relaunched the plan with improved chances of success. This was much more precise concerning the three stages that were supposed to lead to monetary union and, among other things, made provision for setting up a European Monetary Institute, intended to strengthen cooperation among national central banks and to pave the way for a European Central Bank to be established. Conditions were also much more favourable. On an economic level, inflation, which had left its mark on the two previous decades, by this time seemed under control. On a political level, the French president, François Mitterrand, pushed very hard for economic and monetary union, judging that abandoning the mark, the strongest European currency, would more firmly anchor Germany in Europe.

The process then got underway. The Treaty of Maastricht, signed in February 1992, set 1 January 1999 as the date on which the European Union member countries that met five precise convergence criteria[29] would automatically form a single monetary area, others joining whenever they fulfilled the criteria. Moreover, a protocol allowed the United Kingdom and Denmark to remain outside the union – an offer that these two countries, as well as Sweden, took up. This preparatory phase exercised minds a great deal in the main European centres. The currency crisis of September 1992, which will be discussed below, did not undermine the wish to succeed, despite persistent doubts in Britain and the United States. On the contrary, the single currency provided European financial centres with new opportunities that they had to seize. While the plan was above all political, financial circles were aware of the advantages, especially in terms of international influence, that a currency able to hold its own against the dollar, or even replace it as the main reserve currency, would bring them. They also detected the possibility of creating a genuine European capital market and, therefore, of meeting the financial needs of a much larger geographical area. But at the same time, the single currency stirred up rivalry among the financial centres and presented them with a number of challenges. Would Frankfurt and Paris be able to take advantage of Britain's non-participation to supplant London in Europe? Choosing the former to host the headquarters of the European Central Bank seemed to go in the Hessian metropolis' favour, while financial institutions everywhere set to work to take up the twin technological and competitive challenge triggered by this colossal change.

The advent of the euro was undeniably a success technically speaking, even if the European Central Bank's management of monetary policy continues to be rather problematic. And yet, six years after coming into force, its impact on the international financial centres remains limited. The European currency has not supplanted the dollar; a truly integrated European capital market has still not been established; and London, in spite of Frankfurt and Paris, has held on to its top place in the hierarchy of European financial centres.

Business trends

The world of finance has, on the whole, lived through exceptional times over the last twenty-five years. This is an obvious fact, even if it is still too soon for us to pass final judgement, as we can for the period 1890–1914 for example, if we are to continue comparing the two great eras of globalisation.

Crises and slowdowns.   Quite naturally for a prosperous period, business expansion and the rise in stock-market prices experienced over the last quarter of a century have, to a great extent, prevailed over the inevitable slowdowns and crises that have interrupted it without lasting repercussions. In 1982, when Mexico announced a moratorium on its foreign debt interest payments, the third world debt crisis put an end to the euphoria of petrodollar recycling that had marked the years 1974–80. It dealt a blow to the big commercial banks, in the first place the American banks, which from then marked time, and above all to debtor countries, whose burden represented by debt servicing had grown tremendously and which would take more than ten years to ease with the help of the International Monetary Fund, the Club of Paris and the United States. In an entirely different field, people were shaken by the stock-market crash of October 1987. The Dow Jones lost 500 points on 19 October – that is to say, a drop of 20%, the sharpest ever registered in a single day, and invoking comparisons with 1929, but there were no major effects, merely temporary ones. Yet another kind of crisis, the European Monetary System crisis of September 1992, drove the pound and the lira – the latter momentarily – to leave the exchange-rate mechanism and the peseta to devalue by 5%, while striking fear into the French franc. But it did not check the process of monetary union in Europe.

Then in 1997 the markets were shaken by the financial crisis in the countries of South-East Asia, due to the excessive inflow of foreign funds in domestic investments that were less and less financially viable and at foreign exchange rates that were hard to sustain. From July the Thai, Malaysian, Indonesian, Philippine and, finally, South Korean currencies depreciated sharply against the main currencies, leading to stock-market collapses, bank bankruptcies and massive capital withdrawals in these countries. Shares also plunged in Hong Kong and Japan, where several banks went bankrupt. In August 1998 the crisis affected Russia, with the devaluation of the rouble and the Russian government defaulting on part of its debt, before spreading to Latin America, where the markets' jitteriness triggered off capital flight. In the

West, stock-market prices, after a drastic correction – the notorious hedge fund LTCM was the main victim of this turbulence – picked up again and continued to surge until the technology stock bubble burst in spring 2000. The markets then slowed markedly to recover somewhat from 2003; it had been a financial rather than economic phenomenon and it did not cause a deep recession. Between 1980 and 2005, no crisis really jeopardised business prosperity or challenged the globalisation of the world economy.

Financial operations. For the banking and financial sector, this prosperity found expression in an impressive increase in the number and amount of international transactions, as can be seen in Table 6.2. Foreign exchange transactions rose sharply after fixed exchange rates were abandoned, going from a daily average of some $15 billion at the beginning of the seventies to $60 billion in 1982, then exploded to reach a volume of $1,490 billion per day in 1998, before slowing down somewhat following the introduction of the euro and then rebounding to $1,880 billion in 2004. Derivatives took off as well, the amounts in circulation (traded on the markets and over the counter) going from $3,500 billion in 1991 to $184,000 billion in 2004.[30] The strong acceleration in capital movements in the seventies and their dramatic rise from the 1980s onwards, mentioned a little earlier, led to a phenomenal growth in the international money market – the total amount of Eurocurrency bank lending increasing from $983 to $9,900 billion between 1982 and 2004 – and in international bonds (Eurobonds and ordinary foreign bonds), issues of which went from $82 billion in 1982 to $1,560 billion in 2004.[31]

Mergers and acquisitions. The eighties were also the years when corporate finance – that is to say all the activities relating to organising and financing mergers and acquisitions – really took off. Underlying this trend was the conviction – widespread in the United States by the late seventies, particularly because of conglomerates' disappointing performance – that the interests of company shareholders were not always well served by their salaried managers. From this viewpoint, a takeover bid, if necessary unfriendly and addressed directly to shareholders, seemed to be the best penalty for poor management and the threat of such an action the best way of compelling management to remain vigilant. A wave of buying and selling businesses, and of mergers and demergers followed. The latter were often friendly and guided by real strategies aimed, for example, at refocusing a firm's activities on its most profitable trade. At other times, they were hostile and undertaken with the sole aim

Table 6.2. *International financial operations, 1982–2004 (in billions of dollars)*

	1982	1990	1997	2004
Eurocurrency bank loans	983	3,870	5,695	9,883
International bonds	82	226	595	1,560
Derivatives[a]	n.a.	3,450[b]	29,035	183,503
Foreign exchange market (av. per day)	60	590	1,490[c]	1,880

Notes: [a] Including credit default swaps and equity derivatives; [b] 1991; [c] 1998.

Sources: R. Roberts, *Inside International Finance,* London, 1998; BIS; International Swaps and Derivatives Association.

of taking advantage of out-and-out dealing in companies, notably by using their assets for the benefit of the operation's promoters and shareholders. While hostile takeover bids were few in number, in value they represented nearly a quarter of the total and were by far the most spectacular. It was the era of the great Wall Street raiders,[32] who henceforth took on very large enterprises – RJR Nabisco was purchased for $25 billion in 1985 – and their acquisitions were financed to a great extent through leveraged buyouts.[33]

A growing part of this debt was made up of junk bonds, popularised by Michael Milken, one of the managers at the Drexel Burnham Lambert bank. These were bonds that were held in low esteem by the big credit-rating agencies owing to their high risk, which barred large institutional investors in the United States from buying them.[34] Milken and his firm's innovation was to have created both a primary and a secondary market for these lowly rated, but high-yielding, bonds. Junk bonds provided financing opportunities to businesses that would not have had any otherwise; but they tended to be used increasingly to finance acquisitions at very high prices and levels of debt. In the late eighties, this technique fell into disuse and Michael Milken into disgrace, following his sentencing for fraud and insider trading.

The merger and acquisition trend quickly spread to Britain, thus giving rise to the term 'Anglo-Saxon capitalism', meaning dominated by market forces. The raiders were also present in the City, personified in the extreme by Lord Hanson, who in 1986 acquired the Imperial Group, one of the ten largest British companies, and in 1989 acquired Consolidated Goldfields, one of the largest mining groups in the world, before being thwarted in 1991 in the face of his ultimate prey, the chemical giant ICI.[35] But it was the Thatcher government's privatisations that more than anything characterised the eighties in Britain. Assets in excess of £40 billion ($75 billion) were put on the market between 1981 and 1991, more than half of which belonged to public utilities (telephone, gas, water and electricity), ushering in a new form of popular capitalism. By the end of the process, Britain had more than 8.5 million individual investors – that is to say, one fifth of the adult population – compared with 3 million at the start. Privatisations were more limited in France – they brought the state in some Fr. 70 billion (approximately $13 billion) between 1986 and 1988 – and affected enterprises in the competitive sector (Saint-Gobain, CGE, Paribas and others), mostly nationalised a few years earlier and over which the authorities continued to exert control by forming hard cores of stockholders interlinking these enterprises among themselves through cross-holdings.

The wave of mergers became even more intense during the nineties. In the United States, the trend got underway relentlessly again from 1994, with the total amount of mergers and acquisitions reaching more than $1,600 billion in 1998, compared with just over $200 billion in 1989. In early 2000 the purchase of Time Warner by AOL for more than $180 billion surpassed all previous transactions, including the mergers between Citicorp and Travelers, or Exxon and Mobil. Foreign enterprises participated widely in this trend, notably with the buyout of Chrysler by Daimler Benz and that of the Bankers Trust by Deutsche Bank. Hostile takeovers and stock-market battles began to hit continental Europe; in France, the BNP acquired Paribas, even though it had been coveted by the Société Générale; in Germany, Mannesmann, the country's second industrial group in the process of reconverting from metallurgy to telecommunications, fell under attack from the British mobile telephone operator Vodafone, after a battle that shook the very foundations of the Rhineland model of capitalism, distinguished by the dominating role of the banks and the pre-eminence of management over shareholders.

These operations took place in the large financial centres, first and foremost New York and London, and were orchestrated by the main investment banks, where large American firms held sway (see Table 6.4). Goldman Sachs, Merrill Lynch and Morgan Stanley stood out in the nineties, followed by Crédit Suisse First Boston, J. P. Morgan, Citigroup, Deutsche Bank, UBS, Lehman Brothers and several others, in a ranking that varied slightly from year to year but remained relatively stable as far as the fifteen or twenty main players were concerned – among which were also Paribas, Lazard, Dresdner Bank, Nomura and some others. The City's merchant banks, actively involved in the British privatisations of the eighties, subsequently lost ground. Bought out, for the most part, by big American and European banks, they usually formed the base from which the latter developed their market activities in London. This was notably the case with Warburgs, the most competitive in this field, taken over by the Swiss Bank Corporation in 1995 and subsequently incorporated into the UBS group.[36] The investment banks were supported in these activities by large accountancy firms   (PricewaterhouseCooper, KPMG and Deloitte Touche Tohmatsu) and the large specialised law firms   (Clifford Chance, Baker & McKenzie and Freshfield, Bruckhaus Deringer) – two sectors that have also regrouped on a vast scale at world level over the last two decades.

The Stock Market's meteoric rise.   Finally, and above all, the exceptional nature of this period comes from the almost continually bullish stock market, particularly for technology securities. During the first fifteen years, except for the crash of October 1987, the stock market's rise was initially quite regular and saw the main indices increase about 4.5-fold. Then from 1995, its increase accelerated suddenly, zigzagging along in the wake of the Asian and Russian crises, before soaring away in a typical bubble between autumn 1999 and March 2000. At their absolute peak, American and British shares were fourteen times more expensive than in 1980, and French, German and Swiss ones some sixteen times.[37] The increase in the NASDAQ, the market for new technologies, was even more impressive, since prices rose by 33.4 in twenty years.[38] Japan, of course, was the exception. The Nikkei 225 experienced a spectacular sudden rise in the eighties, rocketing from 6,570 in January 1980 to 38,916 by December 1989. It then suffered a sharp and sustained slump that made it fall below 8,000 by spring 2003, before embarking on a slow recovery, to fluctuate, during the first half of 2005, around the same level as in 1984; that is to say, 70% below its absolute peak. This crisis affected Tokyo's international standing. Meanwhile, the new technology bubble, especially in Internet securities, burst in spring 2000, dispelling stock-market euphoria in Europe and in the United States. Prices fell back sharply – a trend aggravated by the tragedy of 11 September 2001 and the accounting fraud scandals discovered in summer 2002. In September of that year, American indices were at their lowest, whereas European stock exchanges, fearing repercussions from the United States' impending intervention in Iraq, continued to drop until winter 2003.[39] There was then a recovery in all the markets, fairly pronounced at first, then slower until spring 2005, by which time most of the indices were only at the level that they had been at in 1997.

The stock-market reversal of the early twenty-first century was associated with some spectacular bankruptcies and scandals, first and foremost in the United States. These tarnished the image of the Anglo-Saxon capitalist model, centred on stock-market performance, whose dynamism had held much appeal during the previous decade. The bankruptcies of the energy group Enron in 2001 and of the telecommunications operator WorldCom the following year were undoubtedly the ones to which most attention was paid, owing to the size of the enterprises concerned[40] and especially to the scale of the fraud perpetuated by their managers. What is more, these two companies' accounts had been audited by one of the main international auditing companies, Arthur Andersen, which did not survive the accusations of incompetence or complicity that were levelled at it. These and numerous other scandals led some people to wonder whether morality was declining in the world of finance, due to the arrival of new elites that were less scrupulous as far as ethics and corporate governance were concerned. This looks questionable. Embezzlement has been a fact of life throughout the history of the international financial centres. What is new is that, for thirty years or so, such behaviour has been typical of members of the boards of large enterprises, rather than of lone adventurers.

The new financial elites

The dramatic rise in and transformation of financial business have inevitably been accompanied by adjustments to the established socio-professional order.[41] This change can be explained mainly by the new business opportunities that have arisen in the main international centres, as well as by the setting up of organisational structures and administrative hierarchies to meet the strategic and technological challenges of a sector in perpetual motion. Nor should the generation effect, which always makes itself felt more strongly during phases of transformation, be overlooked. Four major features characterised the financial elites at the end of the twentieth century, providing evidence of modifications, as well as continuity, in a distinct circle within the world of big business.

First, the most influential personalities in the world of banking and finance are nowadays almost all found at the head of large, indeed very large, enterprises, organised in the form of joint-stock companies: banks, insurance companies, investment companies and their specialised subsidiaries. This phenomenon is not new but spread after the Second World War. It presents a striking contrast with the *Belle Epoque* or even the 1920s, when the City's merchant bankers and Wall Street's investment bankers, all partners of relatively modestly sized private houses, were still capable of influencing the course of events. The situation persisted, although in a less and less pronounced way, until the 1960s, by which time the merchant banks, which had gradually disappeared from 1990 onwards, and the investment banks, which are still very much alive today, could no longer be considered private institutions. In other financial centres, private banks as a group had, since the interwar period, ceased to play a significant role on the national or international level. The exception is Geneva – the only centre of any importance that has retained some bankers of international calibre in the field of wealth management, at least as far as the two largest banking houses are concerned: Pictet on the one hand, and Lombard, Odier, Darier, Hentsch on the other.

The second feature, more specific to the current period, is the broadening of the group belonging to the financial elites. The notion of elites – in the sense of those who have reached the top of their respective field of activity – necessarily is arbitrary. At which point can one be said to have reached the top? If one considers that it is a matter of boards of directors and management, then elites have become distinctly more numerous, since the membership of these bodies has increased. While, in the early twentieth century, a big bank's management included a general manager and one or two deputy managers, a modern bank's top management is much larger and more complex. From the sixties onwards, the big banks reorganised themselves, often with the help of consultancies, first and foremost McKinseys. Citibank adopted a divisional structure from 1967, and the National Westminster Bank from 1970. In 2005 the governing bodies of the UBS, one of the main multinational banks, based in Switzerland, was made up of a board of directors with ten members, a group executive board of eight members and a group managing board of more than fifty members.[42] Similar structures can be found in all big banks. The senior management of Citigroup, the largest banking group in the world, was made up of a management committee of fifty-seven people, including the group's chairman and vice-chairman.

The third characteristic of the new financial elites is their level of pay, which definitely outstrips that in other sectors. Here too, the phenomenon is not entirely new. Finance, and in particular international finance, has from time immemorial lain at the root of some of the largest fortunes. And disparities in income and wealth have grown, to various degrees, in all advanced industrial societies from the eighties onwards. The world of finance nevertheless holds a special place, owing to the total amount of salaries, bonuses and stock options distributed, to the number of individuals benefiting from such pay – at least 1,000 millionaires worked in the City of London in the mid-nineties[43] – and finally to the fact that salaried managers and traders, and no longer only self-employed entrepreneurs, can henceforth make their fortune. This complicates the question of how financial elites are made up, to the extent that these huge earnings are not the prerogative of members of the governing bodies of big financial institutions alone.

Lastly, the new financial elites are distinguished by their cosmopolitanism and their mobility. The first feature is fairly typical in the world of finance, whether one thinks, for example, of the Parisian *haute banque* and the City's merchant banks at the beginning of the nineteenth century or, one hundred years later, of New York's investment banks. But this was due to foreign bankers and financiers immigrating for good to more promising markets, and it tended to become less marked as they became assimilated into the local elites from the second generation onwards, even if the international networks continued to operate. Today's cosmopolitanism is based on a much more transient migration – that of the senior management of big multinational banks, who move from one financial centre to another according to the responsibilities that they are called upon to assume. Becoming integrated into the national elites is no longer a requirement for gaining access to the highest responsibilities, and the management of the big financial institutions has become much more international: to date, four of the eight members of the UBS' executive board are foreigners, the chairman of Deutsche Bank's executive board is Swiss and of Barclays Bank is Canadian. Expansion abroad, carried out by purchasing major banks, especially in the United States and Britain, has contributed greatly to this development. However, it is not unique to the world of finance but is an increasingly typical feature of multinational enterprises as a whole. It often leads to a loss of identity, due to the lack of a local base and lack of involvement in community life, so businesses often make up for this by setting up cultural or educational programmes in city centres.

The leading financial centres at the dawn of the twenty-first century

The opening up of the world economy has unquestionably revitalised the main international financial centres. Even more revealing of the recent period is that this revitalisation has coincided, in advanced countries, with the transition to a post-industrial economy dominated by tertiary activities, within which financial services hold a prime place. One may prefer the concept of third industrial revolution to that of post-industrial economy and society, since the borderline between industry and services is increasingly blurred – in high-tech sectors in any case. In particular, the links between these sectors, first and foremost information technologies and financial activities, are constantly growing stronger.

Furthermore, the weight carried by finance has increased considerably over a generation. In economic, political and academic circles, financial intermediation is no longer simply considered to be a backup for the 'real' economy, a means of financing industrial growth, but a source of wealth in itself, which has to be encouraged and developed. Dissenting voices are certainly making themselves heard, denouncing the excessive power of the financial markets and proposing restrictive measures – like the famous Tobin tax on international monetary transactions, aimed at curbing speculation in this field, notably in the foreign exchange market. But for the time being, due to the concentration of financial activities in specific urban spaces, financial centres are arousing ever-growing interest, especially among politicians, who are striving to promote their development at national, regional and international level. For the most important centres, the wish to strengthen their position is stronger than ever, rekindling long-standing rivalries and creating new ones.

These rivalries are, however, different from those that had pitted London against Paris in the mid-nineteenth century or London against New York in the 1920s. First, because they have affected *all* the large centres: New York, Tokyo, London, Frankfurt, Paris, Zurich, Hong Kong and Singapore – and not only two or three of them. Second, because, even if Tokyo toyed momentarily with the ambition of becoming number one in the eighties, New York's world leadership has not really been challenged, given the United States' overwhelming economic superiority. And third, because of the existence of a major centre in each of the main time zones – New York in North America, London in Europe and Tokyo in Asia.

Competition has been more open on each continent taken separately, particularly in Europe, where Paris and Frankfurt have been endeavouring for fifteen years or so to supplant London, while also competing against each other. The creation of 'Paris Europlace' in 1993 and 'Finanzplatz Deutschland' in 1996, organisations each aiming to promote its centre of origin, were signs of that determination. In Asia, both Hong Kong, itself challenged by its return to China and by the rise of Shanghai, and more recently Singapore, have been trying to take advantage of Japanese deflation to compete with Tokyo.

Rivalries are also strong when it comes to more specific activities within the sector. London ranks top in most of these, except for American domestic business, in which New York's position is untouchable. Competition tends to be tough in some markets, like the stock markets, derivatives or asset management, while there is a division of labour and cooperation on the international level. But the separation, new in history, between the main financial centre for direct international transactions, namely London, and the dominant economy, the United States, has inevitably given rise to new ambitions among a greater number of candidates.

The international order has not altered in the course of the last twenty-five years. It has become even more hierarchical, with three global centres – New York, London and Tokyo – at the top, followed by five other international centres, of which three are in Europe – Frankfurt, Paris and Zurich – and two in Asia – Hong Kong and Singapore. These are themselves followed by centres on a lesser scale, but whose importance should not be underestimated, including Amsterdam, Chicago, Geneva, Hamburg, Luxembourg, Toronto and Sydney.

New York

Of the three global centres, the top place has to go to New York, even if London has the edge in direct international activities. This reflects a historical difference between the financial centres of the two Anglo-Saxon cities. Even if New York has become far more international since the fifties, the weight of the American economy dominates the way that its financial institutions operate, as well as the activity and turnover of its markets, which thus almost effortlessly outperform the City. For, in any case, it is New York that sets the tone in international financial business, if only because of the might of the American banks, mostly in New York, and moreover on which a great deal of London's international influence depends.

The two biggest American banks, Citigroup and J. P. Morgan Chase, have their registered offices in New York. Although they both came into being in the nineteenth century, in their current form they are the fruit of huge mergers in the nineties, following the relaxation of banking regulations. Alongside Citigroup, J. P. Morgan Chase resulted from the grouping together of several big banks, culminating in 1999 in the merger between J. P. Morgan (heir to the famous dynasty) and Chase Manhattan (which had itself acquired Chemical and Manufacturers Hanover – two of the main New York banks). In 2004 the new group bought out Bank One, the sixth American bank, based in Chicago, and it too was the result of numerous mergers. But, more than the commercial banks, it is the investment banks that, for about twenty years, have again symbolised the United States' immense financial power. At world level, they largely dominate all operations connected with mergers and acquisitions, activities in which six American banks ranked among the top ten in 2001, with the three biggest, Goldman Sachs, Merrill Lynch and Morgan Stanley, taking the top three places (Table 6.4). In this field, the clients are primarily Americans, so business connected with the United States represents more than half of all operations, not only for the New York investment banks but also for foreign banks involved in this area of specialisation.[44] Furthermore, to do this, the foreign banks use domestic banks that they have bought up and whose management remains American.[45]

Of the four main indicators most often used to gauge the importance of international financial centres (international banking transactions, asset management, the capital market and other markets, including the foreign exchange market),[46] New York comes top, but with a large lead in only one of them: the capital market. The capitalisation of the New York Stock Exchange is more than five times higher than that of the next ones, whether London or Tokyo.[47] It is certainly a matter of chiefly domestic markets, but their international influence is considerable, in view of the number of foreigners holding or dealing in American securities, and so they form a cornerstone in the running of a financial centre such as Wall Street. Moreover, the number of foreign companies listed on the banks of the Hudson is constantly increasing thanks to the existence of ADRs – American Depositary Receipts – which guarantee that a foreign firm's securities have been deposited in the United States, authorising them to be traded on American soil.[48]

In portfolio management, the amounts managed in the United States are easily the largest in the world. Yet New York, the largest manager at domestic level, does not rank top in the world, since in the United States it has to share this business with other centres. Boston, San Francisco, Los Angeles, Philadelphia and Denver in fact all come in the top ten cities for fund management (with London, Tokyo, Paris and Zurich). As for other activities, Wall Street is surpassed by the City in the foreign exchange market and by Chicago in the derivatives market.

All this makes New York the most impressive financial centre in the world – and for many the symbol of the American economic superpower and of a globalised economy under American domination. The terrorist attacks on 11 September 2001 demonstrated this in the most dramatic way. Besides their political and financial impact, they also contributed towards speeding up the transfer of activities within and around the city. Less and less dependent on the physical proximity of the trading floor, many players in the New York financial world, investment banks in particular, had already left the vicinity of Wall Street to settle in Midtown. The destruction of the World Trade Center obviously reinforced this trend. And the shift continues, since many hedge funds, one of the big new areas of specialisation on the New York market, are getting up and leaving the city to set up shop, often for tax reasons, around

Greenwich, Connecticut, which is becoming a satellite town of New York, while being fully integrated into its financial world.

London

Such a shift outwards is also noticeable in London,[49] the centre that is following hot on Wall Street's heels. Employment in its financial sector – apart from retail banking – gives a fairly good idea of a centre's size: in 2004 the respective figures were 314,000 people in New York and 311,000 in the City. This is a remarkable figure for the financial centre of a medium-sized economic power, which can only be explained by London's massive specialisation in international financial business. In this respect, the London metropolis clearly outstrips Tokyo (around 172,000 employed), Frankfurt (90,000), Hong Kong (approximately 80,000) and Paris (65,000).[50]

The policy of opening up to the world, instigated by the City and backed up by the British authorities when the Euromarkets were established in the late 1950s, has been kept up relentlessly. And it has borne fruit, for the City's record of international achievements is impressive indeed. At the turn of the twenty-first century, London comes top in five of the main fields of international financial business: cross-border bank lending, with 19.5% of the market, ahead of Tokyo (11.5%); foreign currency transactions (32%), ahead of New York (18%); asset management with $2,600 billion, just over New York's $2,400 billion; the number of foreign banks and representative offices (481), ahead of New York (287); and Eurobond issues, 60% of which take place in London and which represent 90% of all international issues. Furthermore, London holds second place, behind Chicago, in the derivatives futures markets, but first place in over-the-counter (OTC) transactions with 36% of the market; and third place, behind New York and Tokyo, in equity market capitalisation; but first in foreign securities trading (45%), ahead of New York (22%).[51] Of course, these figures change from year to year, partly because of exchange rate fluctuations, and a place can be temporarily or even permanently lost.[52] But by and large, London has held top place in international financial business since the sixties and, in forty years, it has even increased its lead, especially by capturing new markets.[53]

The causes of the City's rebirth in the sixties are well known. It was due principally to historical traditions, the flexibility of Common Law and the British authorities' standpoint, especially through their pragmatic approach – liberal, yet strict at the same time – to monitoring markets. Its lead over its European competitors then enabled the City to benefit from external economies of scale. Firms come and set up in a large centre for the numerous advantages that they find there and that are often lacking in smaller centres: more liquid and more efficient markets; a plentiful and well-qualified workforce; business concentration; the quality, diversity and complementary nature of the services available; opportunities for high-level meetings; and the capacity for innovation. London has been able to cultivate all these advantages, in addition to which it has the English language, the world's lingua franca and, above all, the language of the American bankers who have been revitalising the London market since the sixties. While tougher competition for the British banks has helped bring about this revitalisation, the challenge of maintaining the leadership thus built up on the international level has been accompanied, from the mid-eighties, by foreign banks' growing influence over activities. Nothing is more indicative of this state of affairs than the recent disappearance of the merchant banks.[54]

Both on a social and a professional level, merchant banks used to represent the City's aristocracy. For nearly two centuries, they dominated big business there, in particular foreign issues and, from the 1960s, activities connected with corporate finance, into which they had partly moved. Still fairly modest in size, they faced increasingly keen competition from American investment banks and big European universal banks, which bolstered their presence in London from the beginning of the nineties. The former were attracted by the prospects that Europe's economic and monetary union seemed to offer, while the latter wished to strengthen and diversify their international activities in various types of markets. After the first mergers at the end of the eighties,[55] it was Baring Brothers' bankruptcy in February 1995 that sparked off a widespread buyout trend. Like other merchant banks, and in the image of the American investment banks, the City's venerable banking house had gone into transactions on its own account in order to offset its shrinking margins. Things took a nasty turn when losses caused by speculating on derivatives on the part of its rogue trader in Singapore, Nick Leeson, exceeded £800 million – in other words, the bank's entire capital. It was bought up for the symbolic sum of £1 by the Dutch bank ING.[56] Ten years later, only N. M. Rothschild and Lazard Brothers were still independent.

Meanwhile, the big British commercial banks still rank among the largest in the world. The HSBC group, heir to the Hongkong and Shanghai Banking Corporation and the Midland Bank, which it purchased in 1991, was the world's second bank in terms of market capitalisation, behind Citigroup in 2001. The Royal Bank of Scotland,

Table 6.3. *The 20 largest commercial banks, 2001 (in millions of dollars)*

	Market capitalisation
1. Citigroup (United States)	250,143
2. HSBC (United Kingdom)	140,693
3. J. P. Morgan Chase (United States)	103.113
4. Wells Fargo (United States)	89,251
5. Bank of America (United States)	82,745
6. UBS (Switzerland)	73,673
7. Royal Bank of Scotland (United Kingdom)	62,865
8. Lloyds TSB (United Kingdom)	60,663
9. Crédit Suisse (Switzerland)	55,719
10. Barclays (United Kingdom)	53,630
11. Deutsche Bank (Germany)	51,047
12. BSCH (Spain)	48,311
13. Bank of Tokyo-Mitsubishi (Japan)	46,986
14. BBV Argentaria (Spain)	46,774
15. Bank One (United States)	46,395
16. Fleetboston Financial (United States)	46,022
17. Bank of New York (United States)	41,466
18. Fortis (Belgium/Netherlands)	39,368
19. BNP Paribas (France)	38,367
20. ABN Amro (Netherlands)	35,370

Source: Financial Times.

which took over the National Westminster Bank in 2000, was in seventh place, Lloyds TSB in eighth place and Barclays in eleventh place worldwide (Table 6.3). But these banks have not managed to replace the merchant banks in the field of merchant banking and corporate finance.[57]

How much importance should be given to this eclipse of British financial institutions, that some people have called a financial Wimbledon, alluding to the fact that this tournament, famous the world over, is habitually won by foreign players? Many British commentators are very pleased about the London market's economic success without worrying unduly about its dependence on foreign banks. They are probably right; but some voices have the good sense to warn against the fragility of such a position and the risks of some business retreating to other centres, first and foremost New York, should there be a protracted bear market.[58] Come what may, the City has never had, and still does not really have, any choice. It could only become, and can only remain, a global financial centre in the same vein as New York and Tokyo by being completely internationalised. The alternative is a financial centre commensurate with the British economy – that is to say, bearing in mind a number of competitive advantages, slightly larger than Paris or Frankfurt.

Tokyo

The possibility that Tokyo might overtake New York and become the world's leading financial centre did not seem entirely far-fetched at the end of the eighties. At that time, the 'Japanese model' was at its height, and the United States was showing signs of decline and was putting off modernising its antiquated banking system. Japanese banks comprised the top ten, measured by total assets, in the ranking of leading world banks. By 1987 the profits of Nomura Securities, the brokerage company and investment bank, had outstripped those of Citibank and Merrill Lynch, and in spring of that year Tokyo's market capitalisation at last exceeded that of the New York Stock Exchange.[59] Long-term analyses were indicating that the world's financial leadership was in the process of switching from New York to Tokyo, just as it had started to switch from London to New York at the beginning of the twentieth century.[60] Such judgements were far too hasty. First, the strength of the yen skewed rankings and international comparisons expressed in dollars in Japan's favour, a bias boosted still further by the overvaluation of land prices and of Japanese shares. Next, the American economy, far from declining as some people had expected, on the contrary experienced spectacular growth in the nineties, whereas the Japanese economy went into a long slump, confirming for the time being the victory of Anglo-Saxon capitalism and the all-powerful market.

This reversal of the situation had severe repercussions on Tokyo's international position, even if it did not collapse from one day to the next. As the financial capital of the world's second economic power, Tokyo continued to play a far from insignificant role in international financial relations. The yen remained the third international currency after the dollar and the euro, the Tokyo Stock Exchange the second after New York in terms of capitalisation, and Japanese bank loans overseas were still impressive, putting them in second or third place worldwide depending on the year. But the erosion suffered by Tokyo had, after all, been one of the most serious ever observed in such a short time – less than ten years – and during a period of peace. The use of the yen – its share of world currency turnover going from 13.5% to 10.5% between 1989 and 1998 – dropped sharply, market capitalisation fell by half and the presence of foreign banks in Tokyo decreased, some having considerably scaled back their activities and others having completely

Table 6.4. *The top 10 investment banks, 2001 (billions of dollars)*

	Worldwide merges and acquisitions; value of deals
1. Goldman Sachs (United States)	594
2. Merril Lynch (United States)	475
3. Morgan Stanley (United States)	445
4. Crédit Suisse First Boston (Switzerland/United States)	387
5. J. P. Morgan (United States)	383
6. Citigroup/Salomon Smith Barney (United States)	262
7. Deutsche Bank (Germany)	221
8. UBS Warburg (Switzerland)	211
9. Lehman Brothers (United States)	125
10. Dresdner Kleinwort Wasserstein (Germany)	120

Source: Financial Times.

abandoned their operations in Japan. Furthermore, the steady level of bank credit to non-residents was apparent rather than real. While such credit remained substantial in amount, it was no longer of a truly international nature, since it was almost entirely made up of loans to the subsidiaries of Japanese enterprises established abroad, mainly in Asia.

But it was Japanese banks in particular that withdrew *en masse* from the international markets. Besides their losses in operations connected with the bursting of the stock-market and real-estate bubbles in the early nineties, they had indirectly been victims of the Basel Accords. These agreements, adopted in 1987 among the monitoring authorities of developed countries with the aim of creating a level playing field for competition among international banks, required them to hold equity capital equivalent to some 8% of their liabilities. It just so happened that, at the time, the declared capital of Japanese banks often only made up 2% of their balance sheets. But these banks had buffers in the form of shares in other companies, valued at purchasing price, that is to say, way below the prevailing market rate. Not without some recklessness, the Japanese authorities at that time authorised their banks to consider these unrealised stock-market earnings to be equity capital, so that they could adhere without any problem to the ratio of 8% the moment that the Basle Accords came into force at the end of the eighties. As soon as the bubble had burst, the banks' situation deteriorated, their capital thus defined melting away. Many had reduced their loans to lighten their balance sheets, which made the economic and financial crisis even worse. And most of the big banks had discontinued their international operations in order once again to become purely domestic banks, for which a ratio of only 4% of equity capital was needed.

This disappearance of numerous international players in fact greatly contributed to reducing the activity and, above all, international influence of Tokyo. Under these conditions, it came as no surprise that the Japanese authorities tried to reverse the trend. In 1997, determined to strengthen Tokyo's competititiveness against New York and London, they took a series of measures dubbed the 'Big Bang' and implemented between 1998 and 2001. They had three goals: to liberalise a financial system still highly regulated either explicitly by the law or implicitly by entrenched habit; to entice domestic savers, who had taken refuge in bank deposits, back to the financial market; and to lift the last remaining exchange control to encourage internationalisation and, above all, a fall in the yen, which had just been through an acute phase of overvaluation between 1994 and 1997. To do this, they abolished, among other things, barriers separating banking activities, securities transactions and insurance; liberalised foreign exchange transactions; brought the accounting system into line with international standards; strengthened the powers of the bodies monitoring the financial system; and granted more autonomy to the Bank of Japan.

Will this slow liberalisation process bear fruit? Will Tokyo's financial centre recover its prestige of the eighties? In one sense, yes, in another sense, no. Yes, because paradoxically the slump of the 1990s enabled Japan to modernise its financial sector and especially its banking sector that, until then, had been overly cartelised. The Japanese banks, particularly the big ones, have been stabilised and become solid institutions once more – in the image of Mitsubishi Tokyo or Sumitomo Mitsui Financial Group – ready to come back in force in the international banking markets. Japan is in fact still the main capital exporter and, after the extraordinary period when capital was almost entirely invested by the monetary authorities, the Japanese banks will have an important role to play in this redistribution in the future. No, because it is likely that international market activities will take a long time to regain their exuberance of the 1980s. Tokyo thus has everything it needs to be Asia's leading centre for a long time to come – but a centre that is basically dependent on the domestic economy, like New York or, on a smaller scale, Frankfurt.

Frankfurt

For Frankfurt, the ambition of supplanting London as the main financial centre in Europe was born and then became keener in the nineties.

Forecasts were being made at breakneck speed. In 1995 a survey conducted by the American television channel CNBC announced that Frankfurt would supplant London as the main European financial centre by 2005. Frankfurt financiers, without exactly making this prediction their motto, were optimistic: 'How quickly the mood can swing ... the shift in Frankfurt's favour is remarkable', the banker Friedrich von Metzler[61] wrote at the end of 1998, while admitting that 'Frankfurt's path to the head of Europe is not assured'.[62]

Three factors accounted for such optimism. The first was the decision taken in 1992 to establish the headquarters of the new European Central Bank in Frankfurt. In actual fact, this decision was not very controversial; Germany pointed out that only if Frankfurt were selected could the German population be convinced to accept the Maastricht Treaty and give up the mark. France agreed to make this concession to Germany and, in any case, Europe's monetary union still seemed both a long way off and uncertain.[63] The consequences of this choice, especially for Frankfurt and London, began to be the subject of more serious debate as the euro's introduction, scheduled for 1 January 1999, took shape. There were some who thought that the European Central Bank would give Frankfurt a definite edge over London, notably by attracting a much higher number of banks and financiers to the banks of the Main. The second cause of optimism was the faith that Frankfurt's financial circles had in the German capital market's development capabilities. In 1996 market capitalisation represented 30% of German GNP, compared with 130% for Britain, as a result of the banks' traditional influence over financing the German economy and, perhaps, of the absence of large pension funds as institutional investors. There was, therefore, huge growth potential, which obviously depended on a change in structures and mentalities making people resort more systematically to the capital markets, especially on the part of small- and medium-sized enterprises (the famous *Mittlestand*); in other words, on the transition to Anglo-Saxon type capitalism. The creation of the *Neue Markt* in 1997 and other market-strengthening measures were steps in this direction. Lastly, the third reason was the new political climate after the fall of Communism. German unification, then the European Union's and the Euro zone's enlargement to the east, seemed bound to allow Germany to regain its natural sway over Central and Eastern Europe and thus to extend the influence exerted internationally by Frankfurt.

But in practice Frankfurt has neither caught up with nor overtaken London – and it is unlikely to do so any time soon, even if its potential is still far from being fully exploited. With a population of 650,000 inhabitants, the city is not large enough to host a global financial centre employing more than 300,000 salaried workers, even by including the surrounding area and its 1.6 million residents. It also appears to be too tied to the Rhine and not cosmopolitan enough to attract the world of international high finance, to say nothing of the language barrier. The fall of the German economic model has also been detrimental to its interests. Nevertheless, in spite of everything, Frankfurt is still the world's fourth financial centre, with a relatively strong position in the derivatives markets but a relatively weak one in the field of asset management. German financial circles are now less preoccupied by rivalry with London than by Frankfurt's cooperation, complementarity and influence in continental Europe.[64]

Paris

What place for Paris? The French capital succeeded in maintaining a certain international financial standing – thanks to the presence of foreign banks, for example – even at the height of interventionism in the post-war period. Although surpassed by Frankfurt from the nineties, it is the lost time in relation to the Anglo-Saxon financial centres that really matters for the French elite and that it is worried about making up. The reforms introduced in the eighties have borne fruit, particularly by strengthening the role of the financial market, starved for three decades during which the economy was financed by the state or the banks. The ratio of market capitalisation to nominal GDP, still very modest at the end of the eighties, has developed considerably over the last decade, going from 35% in 1989 to 65% in 2004, after having reached one point above 100% in 1999–2000, thus far exceeding that of Germany (40%), while still lagging way behind that of Britain (125%).[65]

However, this increase concerns primarily French companies. The international activity of the Parisian market remains weak, with barely $10 billion worth of transactions on foreign shares in 1998; that is to say, five times less than in Frankfurt and, above all, 120 times less than in London.[66] Few foreign firms are actually listed on the Paris Bourse, whereas, on the contrary, numerous foreigners – American investment funds among others – are investing more and more in French companies, to the point where they hold 35% of French market capitalisation. This admittedly growing but still inadequate internationalisation probably represents the main handicap for Parisian finance. From abroad, Paris is still not seen as a truly international centre and it continues to be associated with the image of a government that remains fundamentally interventionist.[67]

Paris nevertheless holds some important aces, even if it does not dominate any of the main international fields of activity. Its strong points include asset management, in second place in Europe after London, as well as the bond market and derivatives. Moreover, the founding of Euronext in 2000 offers Paris some strategic prospects within the potential grouping of European stock exchanges. Finally, the city's appeal and the quality of life that it can offer should not be underestimated. In this area, which matters at a time when financial centres are increasingly turning into places where big business is discussed and built up, Paris is the only European city that can hold its own with London.

All the same, there is little chance that it will succeed in rivalling the City. In the mid-nineteenth century, Paris' handicap in relation to London was mainly due to the French economy's lesser development. In the early twenty-first century, it is mainly due to Paris' lesser internationalisation. Besides the considerable lead that London has in this, it is not at all certain that the French authorities and financial circles wish to go so far in this direction. In Europe on the other hand, Paris, which is getting ahead of Frankfurt in numerous markets, should be able to recover the 'brilliant second' place that it held before 1914.

Zurich and Geneva

Ranked sixth in the world at the dawn of the twenty-first century, the Swiss financial centre – chiefly Zurich and Geneva – still held an enviable position, even though it had dropped back slightly since the beginnings of globalisation. As restrictions on capital flows were eased, it became practically impossible for Switzerland to compete, in quantitative terms, with the financial centres of the large industrialised countries. And in the nineties, falling inflation and the growing stability of the main European currencies, culminating in the introduction of the euro, made the Swiss franc lose one of its traditional attractions.

Even so, Switzerland remains a hub in the world of finance, attracting foreign capital and reinvesting it outside the country, which enables it still to play a major role in international banking business. In 2000 Swiss banks held 7.2% of banks' foreign liabilities, which ranked them fourth in the world,[68] without of course counting funds managed off balance sheet. Likewise, Switzerland holds fourth place in banks' foreign assets, with 8.9% of the world's total.[69] It is obvious that Switzerland cannot play a comparable role in the money and financial markets, whether in shares, currencies or derivatives, in which it hovers in around seventh or eighth place. Nevertheless, the franc remains the fifth international currency, after the dollar, the euro, the yen and the pound, and Switzerland hosted 148 foreign banks in 2003, 67 of which were in Zurich and 50 in Geneva.

Even if it is still competitive in most markets, the Swiss financial centre's strength continues to lie in a few niches, the most important of which is wealth management, especially for private clients. Indeed, while Zurich ranks eighth in the world in the management of both private and institutional assets, the Swiss financial centre manages about 35% of the world's private offshore wealth (ahead of Britain with 21% and the United States with 12%). Geneva in particular is widely seen as the world's capital of private banking; numerous foreign banks have made it their centre for this sort of activity and the two big Swiss banks manage their largest sums there. Private bankers admittedly retain relatively small market shares, but their business continues to develop and the most important houses are banks that matter in their area of specialisation. Moreover, they are extending their services to institutional management and are offering new products to their private clientele, such as the Family Office, intended for families with considerable wealth and having complex needs when it comes to succession management.

The Swiss financial centre's competitiveness stems from several factors, including the country's banking traditions, highly qualified workforce, technical expertise, political stability and the strength of its currency. All these elements are increasingly typical of both industrialised and emerging economies. And yet, a far from insignificant part of these countries' wealth, including that of neighbouring countries, continues to be managed from Switzerland, where there is still apparently a surfeit of security. Banking secrecy, which guarantees the confidentiality of information held by the banks on their clients, undoubtedly has something to do with this phenomenon. Subject to fierce controversy in the sixties and seventies, it has been made more flexible over the last twenty years, especially as far as international cooperation within the framework of criminal activities is concerned, on which Swiss legislation is extremely strict. On the other hand, banking secrecy fully plays its role in the field of taxation where avoidance, perfectly legal in Switzerland, is distinguished from evasion and even more so from fraud – whence the opposition that it provokes abroad, particularly on the part of the European Union. Defended in the name of the principle of the inviolability of private life, banking secrecy continues to be one of the Helvetian centre's main competitive advantages.

The Swiss financial centre is dominated by the big banks. Their share of the Swiss banks' total assets grew from half in 1980 to two-thirds in 2003, whereas they fell from five to two in number, with the Crédit Suisse's takeover of the Bank Leu in 1990 and of the Swiss Volksbank in 1993, and then the merger between the Union Bank of Switzerland and the Swiss Bank Corporation in 1998. But at the same time, the two big banks are multinational banks; in terms of market capitalisation, the UBS ranked sixth and Crédit Suisse twentieth in the world in the banking sector in 2004.[70] Such a development can be explained not only by their international operations run from Switzerland but also by their presence abroad, where they are involved primarily in New York and London, mainly in investment banking and asset management. This international influence is, however, not necessarily to the Swiss financial centre's advantage, should these two banks become increasingly cosmopolitan, especially with the growth in opportunities presented by Asia's rapid development.

Hong Kong and Singapore

One of the most striking differences between globalisation prior to 1914 and at the turn of the twenty-first century is the rise of the Asia-Pacific centres to become centres of truly international calibre, whereas they had been confined previously to Western Europe and North America. Tokyo's arrival in the seventies reflected Japan's new economic superpower status at that time; the arrival of Singapore and Hong Kong in the eighties was connected to the emergence of newly industrialised countries in South-East Asia.[71]

Singapore's and Hong Kong's boom was not due to chance, even if their development took different paths. In fact, the two cities had various attributes that are considered conducive to the emergence of an international financial centre. First, they were not starting from scratch. In the twenties both of them, with Shanghai, were already among the region's main financial centres and they continued to play this role after 1945. They have solid banking institutions dating from the nineteenth century and heirs to the British overseas banks, especially the Hongkong and Shanghai Banking Corporation. They also enjoy an advantageous geographical location, with lively ports, as well as being linked to the rest of the world by excellent transport, particularly air transport, and telecommunications networks. Finally, their political regimes are stable, despite the troubles that plagued Hong Kong during the Chinese Cultural Revolution at the end of the sixties and the uncertainty relating to its return to its big neighbour in 1997.[72]

In spite of these favourable conditions, there was nothing spontaneous about Singapore's development, which preceded that of Hong Kong. On the contrary, it was the result of a systematic effort made on the part of the authorities, immediately upon the country's independence in 1965, to turn it into an international financial centre. The first step was taken in 1968, when they authorised the Bank of America to open an Asian currency unit to carry out foreign currency operations; in other words, to collect deposits and grant loans in dollars to Asian clients. Thus, the Eurodollar market came into being in Asia; it was known as the Asian dollar market, and from the outset established itself in Singapore. Like London's, basically comprising interbank loans, this market expanded quickly to reach $86 billion in 1982, helped by a whole series of government measures and orchestrated by the Monetary Authority of Singapore, Singapore's central bank, established in 1971.[73] The government also intervened more directly to encourage the emergence of a bond market. The first issue of Asian dollar bonds took place in Singapore in 1971 – US $10 million on behalf of the Development Bank of Singapore, a publicly owned bank – followed in 1972 by an issue for $100 million on behalf of the Republic of Singapore.

Singapore's financial markets only really took on an international dimension from the eighties. This was notably the case for the Asian dollar market, which went from $86 million in 1982 to more than $350 million in 1990. The foreign exchange market grew in its wake, from a daily average of some $12 billion in 1985 to $139 billion in 1998 – fourth position in the world behind London, New York and Tokyo. Derivatives have been traded since 1984, when the first organised market in Asia, the SIMEX (Singapore International Monetary Exchange), was founded, modelled on the Chicago Mercantile Exchange to which it is linked by a mutual clearing arrangement. The effect of this dynamism has been an increase in the number of foreign banks setting up there, from 145 in 1981 to 185 in 1995 and joined by 75 investment banks (39 in 1981), still called merchant banks in the very British terminology current in Singapore.[74] With its aces, Singapore's financial centre doubtless has a bright future ahead of it – in the middle of an expanding region, surrounded by a solid economy with a huge current account surplus and a stable political regime – even if the development of its market activities might be slightly hampered by the narrowness of its economic base and by interventionism that is rather too heavy-handed for them. But the banks' soundness and the good managerial conditions should allow Singapore's financial centre to excel in banking business and wealth management, somewhat in the image of Switzerland.

While Singapore was making a name for itself as the main centre in Asia for the Eurodollar and Eurobond markets, syndicated Eurocredits found a home in Hong Kong. At the end of the sixties, the government of the British colony actually maintained a 15% withholding tax on the interest on foreign currency deposits, thus leaving Singapore a clear field in the Asian dollar market. But these Eurocurrencies were redirected outside, particularly to Hong Kong, which used them to set up syndicated Eurocredit operations on behalf of enterprises and governments in the region's main economies: Japan, Taiwan, South Korea and even Australia and New Zealand, joined by Thailand, the Philippines and, above all, China. In the space of about twelve years, Hong Kong established itself as the world's third centre for Eurocredits, behind London and New York, thanks to the competitive advantage gained from its geographical proximity to the borrowing countries and to a much more liberal standpoint than Singapore when it comes to hosting foreign bankers and businessmen on its territory. This has brought it crucial expertise in this field.[75] Unlike Singapore, Hong Kong does not owe its rise to deliberate government policy. On the contrary, the authorities have adopted a non-interventionist stance; this is one of the centre's main competitive advantages, at the same time creating conditions that are conducive to developing financial activities, notably a favourable tax system and modern infrastructure. On top of this, there was an absence of exchange control, as well as free circulation of capital, a robust legal system, the existence of the rule of law and, above all, its position as the door for a China that began to open up to the world at the end of the seventies.

A few years later, Hong Kong made up for lost time and overtook Singapore. In particular, the decision in 1983 by its monetary authorities to tie its currency to the US dollar at a fixed rate – the famous peg – and then the success of this policy, greatly contributed towards reassuring international traders as to the Territory's financial soundness after the severe crisis that its currency underwent at the time of the second oil crisis. Its share of international banking business, gauged in terms of foreign assets held by commercial banks, went from 1.6% in 1975 to 5.6% in 1987, and that of its Asian rival from 1.9% to 4.4%. By 1998 the two centres ranked fifth and eighth in the world respectively for international bank loans.[76] Hong Kong focused also on activities that were underdeveloped in Singapore, such as the gold market, in which it worked its way up to fourth place in the world behind London, New York and Zurich, as well as, but to a lesser extent, portfolio management. In terms of market capitalisation, its financial market was for a long time second in Asia – it was outstripped by Taiwan in

2004 – behind Tokyo but far ahead of Singapore. It served in particular as a financing bridge for the whole region, first and foremost for China, on account of the numerous Chinese securities that were, and still are, listed there – even though this specialisation is challenged by the opening up of the Chinese market. On the other hand, its share of the bond market, in which Singapore retains its leadership, is smaller. Perhaps more than any other indicator, Hong Kong's international status is mirrored in the presence of foreign banks, numbering 357 in 1995, that is to say, more than in any other financial centre except for London.[77]

Hong Kong's destiny is inextricably linked to developments in China. The founding of the People's Republic in 1949 strengthened its role at the regional level by closing down the Shanghai market. China's reopening to the outside world at the end of the seventies enabled it to work its way up to the rank of international financial centre. Will China's accession to the rank of economic superpower in the course of the twenty-first century make it a truly global financial centre, in the same way as New York, London or Tokyo? There is little doubt that China, like the United States and Japan before it, will sooner or later have a centre on such a scale. But where will it be located? Hong Kong should be able to keep its ranking over the next fifteen or twenty years, thanks to its established strengths, in particular the convertibility of its currency and its legal system. But Shanghai, which is undergoing phenomenal growth and is in favour with the Chinese authorities, could well gain the upper hand in the long term. Whatever the outcome of this rivalry, the galaxy of the main international financial centres has already anticipated the new influence of the Asia Pacific over the world economy in the twenty-first century.

Conclusion

How can the rise and decline of the international financial centres be explained? Contemporary economic and financial literature has identified conditions that are necessary, if not sufficient, for their development. The most important and most frequently debated of these include: stability of political institutions; strength of the currency; sufficient savings that can readily be invested abroad; powerful financial institutions; firm, but not intrusive, state supervision; a light tax burden; a highly skilled workforce; efficient means of communication; and plentiful, reliable and widely accessible information. This list may not be exhaustive, yet it is hard to refute it. We have seen that these various elements, or most of them, can be found in the centres that, at one time or another in history, have held a dominant position in the international hierarchy. Conversely, those centres that have seen their international influence fade lack one or several of these elements.

Another analytical grid, or at the very least a different departure point, nevertheless seems more apt for understanding the changes in fortune of the capitals of capital over more than two centuries. In the final analysis, the elements of explanation most commonly put forward appear to be short- and medium-term consequences rather than the *underlying* causes of the relative success or failure of the main international financial centres.

Staying power and change

A first conclusion prompted by long-term historical analysis is that the rise of a major centre is closely linked to the economic power of the country that hosts it. This may seem an obvious thing, yet it is often overlooked. Each of the three cities (Amsterdam, London and New York) successively ranked top in world finance since the end of the eighteenth century has at the same time been the financial centre of the dominant national economy of the day – and for New York, this is obviously still the case. The same goes for Berlin's emergence in the last

279

third of the nineteenth century, as well as for Tokyo's and Frankfurt's one hundred years later, as Germany and Japan in turn acquired an economic standing that gave their respective financial centres an international dimension. Even Hong Kong owes, indirectly at least, its recent rise to the growing weight of a China that is opening up to the world economy. Nor is it by chance that in 1913 London, Paris, New York and Berlin were the four leading international financial centres and that today the five leading centres are New York, London, Tokyo, Frankfurt and Paris. They happen to be the financial capitals of the four largest economic powers in 1913 and the five largest in 2005. The ranking of the centres and that of the economies do not match exactly, since the emergence of a major international financial centre follows, with some degree of time-lag, a nation's rise to being a great economic power. Britain had already overtaken the Netherlands when London replaced Amsterdam as the world's financial centre at the turn of the nineteenth century, while the United States was largely ahead of Britain when New York began to supplant London in the 1920s. Similarly, it took Tokyo about twenty years to transfer the feats performed by Japanese industry in the post-war period on to the level of international finance. This time-lag can be explained in terms of stages of economic development, of industry's gradual transition to services and finance, or simply of the force of inertia of entrenched positions.

As usual, there are exceptions that prove the rule; consider three. There is Switzerland from the 1950s to the 1990s, during which time the financial sector held a position in the hierarchy of international financial centres – probably third – that was out of all proportion to the size of the country. This position was due to exceptional circumstances arising from its neutrality during the war, capital inflows and the role of refuge currency played by the Swiss franc, as well as to the relatively weak activity of other financial centres in continental Europe – especially Paris and Frankfurt – prior to the early 1980s. Since then, while remaining a centre of considerable importance, Switzerland has retreated somewhat. There is Singapore, able to take advantage of the emerging Asian dollar market from the late 1960s and of the absence of a major financial centre in South-East Asia, but now likely to be threatened by the development of new centres in the region. And, of course, there is London. The City's rebirth in the 1960s and its current rank of leading financial centre for international activities are out of all proportion to Britain's economic weight in the world. Nor can this be considered, at least not in 2005, as resulting from its role as Europe's financial centre, even if its location in the European time zone has something to do with it. This success can be explained by its still recent world pre-eminence and by its unrivalled international openness. Yet one should not forget that, although London holds top ranking for international financial activities, it drops back to third place, behind New York and Tokyo, if national financial activities are included.

A further conclusion is that the fall of an international financial centre is usually triggered off by a military cataclysm – irrespective of the outcome, whether victory or defeat. Amsterdam's demise at the turn of the eighteenth century is probably the classic example of such a path, but there are others. After the 1870 defeat, Paris marked time before beginning its long decline after the First World War, aggravated by the 1940 defeat and German occupation. The City came out of the First World War weakened, and its decline seemed irreversible after the Second. A variation on this theme, owing to its mainly national dimension, was Frankfurt's eclipse following Austria's defeat by Prussia in 1866. As for Berlin's fall, this was a direct consequence of the German defeat in 1945.

A final conclusion concerns the remarkable longevity of the leading international financial centres, in spite of the phases of boom and bust in the course of their existence. Once established, they kept up with the front-runners, or caught them up again after being left behind – even though the internal ranking within the group changed and there were significant differences among the leading centres. The exception here is Berlin. This can be explained by the unique circumstances surrounding the collapse of the Third Reich and was offset by the path followed by Frankfurt, which returned to the limelight after some eighty years of obscurity. Brussels certainly lost a fair amount of ground, but Amsterdam regained an appropriate position during the course of the twentieth century. Staying power through changes in the world economy, as well as the traditions of the cities of finance, have played a role here.

A crucial contributory factor in the financial centres' development over the last two centuries, and even longer, is the arrival of new talent to replenish their energy and their capacity to innovate. It is not a one-sided relationship. A centre needs to be dynamic enough to attract foreign bankers and financiers, but in return it benefits enormously from this intake. Such immigration, chiefly of German and Swiss origin, decisively shaped the Parisian *haute banque* in the first half of the nineteenth century. More cosmopolitan in London, immigration swelled the ranks of international finance, traditionally separated from banking activity proper, throughout the nineteenth century. In New York, an entire area of investment banking was built up by German Jewish immigrants during the second half of the nineteenth century.

These migrations carried on during the twentieth century. The most dynamic centres continued to exert their appeal, as the anti-Semitism of the Nazi regime made numerous Jewish bankers from Germany and central Europe leave, bound mainly for New York and London. The small centres had their intakes too, particularly Brussels in the nineteenth century and Geneva after 1945 – to say nothing, of course, of the Huguenot refugees in the sixteenth and seventeenth centuries. We have seen the role played by the Rothschilds in Paris and London, Junius Spencer Morgan in London, Jacob Schiff in New York before 1914, and Siegmund Warburg in London and André Meyer in New York after 1945, to mention just a few of the best-known personalities. These migratory shifts have changed in nature since the 1960s, but without disappearing, and typically involve foreign bank managers settling in the main centres. Their presence is more short lived and more impersonal, whatever their impact on business life.

These are the more *long-term* foundations underpinning the financial centres' evolution that have now come to light. What, then, is to be made of the development factors so frequently touched on and cited above? Inasmuch as they provide explanations that are valid mainly in the short or medium term, taking them into account serves to compensate for the possibly simplistic aspects of the long-term approach, which risks being deterministic. Doing so undoubtedly leads to a better understanding of the phases of boom and bust that have marked the main centres' existence. At the same time, the longer historical perspective allows the role of these factors in a given spatial and temporal context to be assessed, and their degree of universality thereby to be tested. Two of them in particular demand a closer look: the strength of the currency and the extent of state regulation.

The monetary factor

National currency status is an interesting case. There are various ways of conveying a status widely regarded as favourable, which can be described under the generic label of a strong currency. It can be a stable currency or a convertible currency. It can be a reserve currency, which works as an instrument of exchange and a unit of reserve on the international level. Finally, it can be the leading currency at world level, namely the pound sterling until 1914 or even until 1931 and the dollar since 1945. Each of these statuses has its advantages – occasionally disadvantages – varying according to the period, or more precisely to the monetary regime and financial centre. During the classic age of the gold standard between 1880 and 1914, the criterion of the stability of the currency was hardly applicable insofar as exchange rates were fixed and it seemed inconceivable that one of the main currencies might one day devalue. As far as a reserve currency is concerned, it can boost an international financial centre's activities, as shown by the contribution of the franc and the mark to the rise of Paris and Berlin. As for the distinction of being a leading currency, this meant a critical advantage for London's financial centre. A stable currency represents an ace in a period of monetary instability – a period that can exist even under a fixed exchange rate system as in the 1920s. Centres like Zurich, Geneva or Amsterdam took advantage of this, unlike Paris (until 1926) or Berlin. The City continued after 1914 to benefit from the pound sterling's status as a world currency, but at the same time it was put at a disadvantage by the difficulties that the British economy had in preserving this status.

For London, this situation continued but with difficulties mounting in the 1950s and 1960s, during which time the pound's status was reduced to that of a reserve currency. At that time, New York fully enjoyed the advantages accorded to it by the dollar's status as the leading currency. The Swiss franc's strength was undoubtedly an asset for the Swiss financial centre, strengthening its appeal and its role as refuge. The strength of the mark and the yen, on the other hand, did not play such a crucial role for Frankfurt and Tokyo. Their international development remained slow, considering the weight of the German and Japanese economies – a gap that can be explained partly by these countries' leaders opting to give priority to the expansion of the national economy. From the 1960s an international financial centre's activity became less linked to the status of the currency of the country hosting it. The City's rebirth and then its formidable rise, based on transactions in dollars and in other foreign currencies far more than in pounds, was of course the most obvious example of this new order of things; but examples abound elsewhere, primarily in the offshore centres. The fact that there was no longer any connection between the leading currency and the leading financial centre, reflecting the globalisation of capital under a floating exchange rate system, offered development opportunities to the main international financial centres, while relieving them of the burden that a reserve currency might represent.

State and finance

More than any other factor, state intervention and the regulatory framework have been put forward to explain the performance of financial centres. The assertion that the state should limit its interference to guaranteeing conditions that allow the market to function properly is nowadays commonly acknowledged in the financial literature. There are countless examples showing that state interference harms financial markets' competitiveness – even without taking wars, when economic activities everywhere were subject to far tighter control, or interventionist measures, such as credit control or nationalisations, into account. One only need think of the various measures intended to channel or limit international movements of capital: the need for a green light from the political authorities to list a foreign security on the Paris and Berlin stock exchanges before 1914; the embargo on foreign issues in London in the early 1920s; exchange controls in post-war Europe; the introduction of the Interest Equalization Tax in the United States in 1963; measures aimed at curbing the development of Euromarkets in continental Europe in the 1960s, and so on.

As we know, all these measures were more or less detrimental to the financial centres of the nations that introduced them, and they benefited rival centres. Two questions should thus be considered: Were there any other options? What damage did these measures actually inflict on the financial centres? The answer to the first question is that, in almost every case, another option could theoretically have been envisaged, but it was practically and, above all, politically hard to achieve. Yet, and this answers the second question, it is doubtful whether another non-interventionist path would have made any difference at all to the medium- and long-term development of the financial centres concerned.

The political authorities' meddling in the international capital market in Paris and Berlin before 1914 did not have any real repercussions on their role as international financial centres. Paris remained the 'brilliant second' and could not aspire to any other role; nor could Berlin, whose leanings were in any case national rather than international. Great store has been set by the American regulations that led to international finance's centre of gravity shifting from New York to London in the 1960s. These were political decisions whose justification or even economic effectiveness in limiting capital outflows is open to debate. It is a fact, nevertheless, that these measures barely penalised American banks' international activities and did not really jeopardise New York's position as a financial centre, where domestic activities had traditionally prevailed and which had always had the ability to recover at least part of its lost international business. Would Paris or Frankfurt have been able to accommodate the Euromarkets and experience development comparable to London's from the 1960s onwards if the monetary authorities had shown more flexibility? That seems highly improbable.

All this does not mean that state intervention in financial matters has no effect, but it rarely determines the destinies of international financial centres in a lasting or fundamental way. It is more likely to accentuate conditions that already exist – and it is on this level that political decisions become all-important. The British authorities' firm stand on Eurodollars greatly contributed towards the City's recovery, but London was much better equipped than any other centre to take charge of these operations. In Switzerland, banking secrecy, introduced in 1934, strengthened the competitive advantage, if only through its neutrality, that the country already had when it came to accommodating foreign capital. The Singapore government's effort to turn the city into an international centre was far more directive, but Singapore was not lacking in financial traditions and, at that time, conditions were particularly favourable in South-East Asia.

It is the same for the regulatory frameworks set up over the last twenty-five years as state intervention has become less direct. It is widely acknowledged that, with the Financial Services Authority, founded in 2000, London has a regulatory environment that is superior to that of its main competitors, especially New York, Frankfurt and Paris. This is certainly an appreciable advantage, but it is undoubtedly as much the consequence as the cause of the City's international pre-eminence – and the big banks will not leave London at the first signs of change.

Furthermore, the regulatory options as regards financial matters have been strongly conditioned by the institutional framework prevailing in each country. Banking systems, which have taken shape since the eighteenth century or even earlier in a specific politico-economic context, play a key role here. There have been endless discussions about the respective merits of systems dominated by the banks and those orchestrated by the capital market. Determining the superiority of one system over the other is arguably an act of faith rather than one of economic analysis. Even so, it seems that the rise of the main international financial centres has depended more on developing their markets than their financial institutions. It is, nevertheless, a fact that the authorities' room for manoeuvre has been limited, especially since their decisions have also been influenced by the ideological preferences of the day. The regulations enacted in the 1930s and immediately following the Second World War were inspired by a distrust of market mechanisms that was very widespread at the time and was accentuated by the Great Depression. Similarly, the deregulations of the 1980s and 1990s showed that the pendulum was swinging back and that the *Zeitgeist* was much better disposed towards neo-liberal solutions.

Past, present and future

For more than two centuries, the international financial centres' contribution to the wealth of nations has been incalculable, whether in terms of their role in developing the world economy, their efforts to make the national economy grow, or even the advantages enjoyed by the cities of finance. The fact is hard to refute, despite arguments, not entirely without foundation, relating to the price paid for this success – whether by domestic industry, considered by some, particularly in Britain, to have been sacrificed on the altar of finance, or by peripheral countries through colonialism or the economic domination of 'neo-imperialism'. The international financial centres have experienced an unprecedented rise for twenty-five years with the globalisation of the world economy, and the advent in Western countries of a post-industrial society has made their services even more valuable. Will their future be as rosy? It is not for the historian to answer, but he is perhaps better placed than others to detect long-term trends.

The financial centres will first have to confront the criticism, muddled and not always well founded but felt by many people, that they are responsible for the most harmful effects of globalisation, especially the excessive pay of some individuals, job losses attributed to relocations and the exploitation of the third world. Their success in the medium and long term will, however, depend less on their ability to respond to these criticisms than on maintaining the world economy's openness. No one can predict when globalisation will end, but at some point there is likely to be a reversal of the trend on a more or less large scale. Even on a limited scale, such a setback would hit the financial centres hard, in terms of income, profits and jobs, but it would probably not disrupt their hierarchical order, even if certain niches, such as wealth management, should be able to cope better than general activities, such as international fund transfers; on the other hand, the emergence of a new large centre, logically in China, would probably be delayed.

All the same, one may speculate whether the real risk that the international financial centres are running is that of becoming obsolete. This spectre has often been raised, and one is aware of both the reasons potentially hastening their disappearance – amazing progress in long-distance communications enabling firms to access information and execute transactions from anywhere in the world – and those so far ensuring their survival – external economies, the effect of emulation and the importance of personal connections and networks of relationships. The arguments in favour of their survival are more plausible. While there is a noticeable historical trend towards change in the hierarchy of the main centres, it is more difficult to discern any trend leading to their disappearance. The telecommunications revolution may certainly seem like a phenomenon without precedent, but the cities of finance have continually had to grapple with transformations in ways of exchange. These cities' layout, their functions and their organisation have ended up vastly altered. Tomorrow's financial centres will reveal a different face, which will require new efforts of adaptation; but as the nerve centres of international financial activity, they remain hard to replace.

Glossary

This glossary contains some of the more frequently used financial and economic terms in the book. In the following definitions, terms marked by an asterisk are defined as keywords in the glossary.

Acceptance. Contractal agreement guaranteeing the beneficiary of a bill* repayment of a debt upon maturity if the drawer of the bill is unable to do so. In most cases, the acceptance is made by the drawee backing a bill of exchange* prior to maturity, thereby guaranteeing payment by the drawee itself or by a commercial bank* designated by the drawee. Originally, the drawee was almost always a merchant banker*, who was more familiar than the local banks with its trading partners' financial soundness. Acceptances have thus been used from an early stage in financing the international trade of goods, particularly in London.

Arbitrage. Taking advantage of the spread between two prices quoted simultaneously for the same entities – securities, commodities, currencies – in two different locations. Unlike the speculator*, the arbitrageur cannot go wrong as both prices are known to him.

Balance of payments. Total value of all transactions conducted in a year between one country and the rest of the world; each transaction results in payments being made (imports) or received (exports) in a currency other than that of the country in question. The balance of payments is traditionally made up of the current account*, which covers actual physical transactions, and the capital account*.

Bank. A financial institution that collects funds in order to lend them with interest or use them to buy other financial instruments. In principle, bank account holders are free to withdraw their funds unconditionally upon maturity, unlike insurance policyholders. Banks can be divided into various types on the basis of their ownership structure, e.g. public or state bank, private bank*, joint-stock bank*, mutual or cooperative bank. They can also be classified according to their main specialisation: note-issuing bank or central bank*, commercial bank*, savings bank specialising in small deposits, investment bank*, asset management bank, and mixed or universal bank*.

Bank loan. The main assets-generating activity of banks, particularly commercial banks*. These may grant unsecured credit – often overdraft facilities – or, more usually, collateral-backed loans. Apart from mortgages, three types of secured loans played an important role in the past and are still used to a greater or lesser extent today. First there is the discount credit, on which interest is paid up-front by the debtor, who agrees to repay the sum borrowed at par upon maturity and pledges a guaranteed bill* for the same amount and with the same maturity as the loan. Then there is the securities-backed loan – also known as a Lombard credit – for which the collateral comprises securities held by the borrower, with the bank advancing funds only up to a certain percentage of the value of the pledged securities to protect itself from price variations. Another form of loan against pledged securities, commonly used today in the money market*, is the repurchase agreement (or repo), wherein the borrower sells securities to the lender and agrees to buy them back at par on a specified date in the future.

Banque d'affaires. See Investment bank*.

Bill, or draft. A written pledge by an issuer – called the drawer – to pay a certain amount at a certain place. These documents may be payable at sight or within a short-term maturity date (less than one year) and made out to a specified beneficiary or to bearer. Different types of bill exist, such as a cheque, which is an order to a bank to pay the specified amount upon presentation, a promissory note and other such pledges to pay a given amount at a given place and time, and a bill of exchange, which is an order addressed from the drawer to a third party – the drawee – to pay a certain amount at a given place and time. The drawee may accept* the bill before maturity and thereby take responsibility for payment. When such bills are adequately guaranteed by the creditworthiness of the drawer or the acceptor, they are perfect instruments for securing a loan in the form of a discount credit*, as the bank advancing the funds is sure of being reimbursed at par upon maturity.

Bimetallism. See exchange rate regime*.

Bonds. Loans issued by a private or public entity in the form of paper providing a coupon – a fixed sum of money determined upon issuance – generally paid every six months or every year. There are numerous different types of bonds, some of which have fallen into disuse. Bonds may be divided into perpetual bonds, which are non-redeemable and pay their coupon indefinitely, and fixed-maturity bonds – the most common type today – which the debtor promises to redeem on a specific date. Another distinction can be made between domestic bonds, which are issued on the market by a local borrower and denominated in the local currency, and international bonds, issued by a debtor not residing in the country of issuance. As a rule, the latter are denominated in the currency used at the place of issuance, although, for thirty years now, Eurobonds have been denominated in another convertible currency than that used at the place of issuance, particularly in dollars. A further subdivision of bonds is into simple bonds, redeemed in legal tender, and convertible bonds, which are generally traded upon maturity, though sometimes beforehand, against shares* or share options* in the debtor company.

Broker, or stockbroker. A financial intermediary that trades in securities either on its own behalf or on behalf of its clients, to whom it often lends either money or securities so as to enable them to take speculative* positions. The broker is associated with or has a seat on an exchange* on which it intervenes either directly, as is usually the case with an electronic trading system*, or indirectly via an agent trading directly on the floor.

Capital account. Net flow of capital between one country and the rest of the world. This flow is divided into direct investments*, on the one hand, and financial investments – which cover banking as well as portfolio transactions, particularly the buying and selling of securities – between one country and the rest of the world, on the other.

Capital market. A place for trading financial instruments such as shares* or bonds*. A distinction is made between the primary market, where new securities are issued, and the secondary market, where existing instruments are traded, with the dealing usually taking place on an exchange*.

Central bank. An institution – nowadays publicly held – which is in charge of issuing currency. As central banks originally only printed notes that were wholly or partially covered by gold or silver, they traditionally hold a country's foreign reserves, i.e. gold, silver, convertible currencies. Legal tender is issued by crediting the accounts of banks or the state at the central bank whenever the latter grants them a loan or buys from them either securities on the secondary market* – open-market transactions – or currencies on the foreign exchange market. The central bank regulates the amount of legal tender in circulation by varying its lending or discount rate, its level of open-market transactions or by means of unsterilised currency intervention.

Clearing. The act of offsetting payables with receivables without any exchange of money. Given the circular nature of exchanges and therefore of payment orders, a properly run commercial bank* processes almost as many outgoing payment orders on any given day as it does incoming payments from other banks on the same marketplace (or country in the case of an integrated monetary system). In order to avoid the large-scale movement of currency that would exist if each order resulted in a physical payment, the banks – usually under the aegis of the central bank* – create an organisation called a clearing house, where orders to be cleared offset each other to such an extent that only the final balances actually have to be paid.

Commercial bank. A bank that accepts short-term deposits from the public – repayable at par on demand or within a relatively short maturity – on which it may or may not pay interest, and then uses these funds as short-term loans to businesses and other economic agents (the state, households, non-residents). As the deposits are used for making payments, for instance by means of cheques, a commercial bank has to be able to participate in the interbank clearing* mechanism in order to fulfil its role. As such establishments perform the most classical banking function, they are often simply referred to as banks.

Current account. The net flow of goods, services and factor incomes between one country and the rest of the world. It consists of the trade balance, which covers the exchange of merchandise, the balance of services, which lists spending in tourism, fees and commissions, and the balance of factor incomes, which takes account of incomes earned by a country's residents on their investments and work abroad (interest, dividends, fees, etc.) less similar incomes earned by non-residents in the country in question. Sometimes the term balance of goods and services is used to mean the sum of the trade balance and the balance of services as defined above.

Deposit bank. Synonym of commercial bank*.

Direct investment. Capital flows accruing from the partial purchase or takeover of property, means of production or a firm in a foreign country by non-residents – business enterprises in general – of that country. Direct investment is intended primarily for controlling the company in which it is made. The notion of control (absolute majority of capital, blocking minority or simply a significant holding) has been the subject of much debate, but the IMF considers that owning 25% of the company's capital is enough to control it. In this respect, the notion of direct investment is synonymous with that of a multinational corporation.

Discount credit. See Bank loan*.

Draft. See Bill*.

Electronic trading system. See Exchange*.

Equities. See Shares*.

Euro-issues. See Euromarket*.

Euromarket. The market for depositing, lending and trading financial instruments denominated in a currency other than that of the country in which the transactions are made. Generally known as Eurocurrencies and Eurocredits, these are large deposits and bank loans, the latter often in consortia, generally denominated in dollars in a bank in London. Euro-issues refer to the issuance of bonds, called Eurobonds, which meet the general definition of Euromarkets.

Exchange. A marketplace for trading homogeneous goods (in the case of a commodity exchange) or securities (stock exchange), usually through an agreement between dealers and brokers of a particular location. The term also refers to the place at which the transactions are conducted, although this is increasingly being replaced by computers and a telecommunications network forming an electronic trading system, as the bidding system and the associated shouting and gesturing of pit traders is fast becoming obsolete. Each exchange is organised differently. When forward transactions* or buying on margin are allowed, a settlement day is set aside, usually once a month or fortnight, to settle these contracts or carry them forward to the next settlement day, subject to a commission and the agreement of the counterparty (carry-over transactions).

Exchange rate regime. A set of rules defining the exchange policy of a country or economic zone. These can be divided into fixed regimes, where the rate for the national currency is fixed at a certain parity and held at this level through the systematic intervention of the central bank, and floating regimes, where the exchange rate is determined on the free market. Two countries under a metallic monetary regime* have, by definition, a fixed exchange rate if they are using the same standard or if one of them is bimetallist. A fiduciary monetary regime* requires an exchange-rate rule. Most major currencies are now free-floating, with the exception of those pegged to the dollar or the euro.

Financial market. See Capital market*.

Forward transaction. A commercial or financial transaction wherein both parties – by mutual consent and at the time the contract is signed – agree on the subsequent date on which the item will be delivered and on the price that will be paid for this purchase. This transaction provides a good opportunity for speculation* as the buyer does not have to have the amount needed for its purchase immediately and the seller does not have to be in possession of the item in question before the specific date.

Gold standard, or gold exchange standard. See Exchange rate regime*.

Haute banque. See Private bank*.

Holding, or trust company. A partnership or limited liability company set up to hold a stake – either directly or through the purchase of a share package providing a certain degree of control – in firms, usually within the same economic sector. Such companies are very similar to the closed-end investment funds*, except for the control they have over the companies in which they have invested.

Investment bank, also referred to as banque d'affaires in the text. A bank that purchases properties on its own behalf or takes a controlling share in a business. Such holdings may be long term, although most are usually short term nowadays. In fact, issues* have become the principal activity of such establishments, sometimes in association with company mergers or acquisitions – another special field of investment banks' activities – for which they negotiate the conditions in detail.

Investment trust, or investment fund. A pool of funds put together by numerous investors for the purpose of buying a certain class of financial instruments or securities, most often shares* or bonds*, of a specific type (e.g., same country, same sector or same ratings). It enables small- to medium-scale savers to mitigate their risk by spreading it among a range of different debtors or companies. Such a fund can be either an open-end fund (also called a unit trust, or a mutual fund in the USA) where the number of units or shares varies according to the fund's level of inflows and outflows, a partially open-end fund where the rules with respect to inflows and, more particularly, outflows are clearly defined (outflows are usually subject to a deadline and a penalty), or a closed-end fund (also known as investment company) where the number of units is fixed.

Issuance. The act of issuing securities – usually shares* or bonds* – for a fee and distributing them to potential investors. To do this, banks and other institutions usually set up an issue syndicate*, which underwrites all the new securities created – guaranteeing to pay the issuer a certain amount in return for his new securities – before placing these with interested investors, who may be other financial intermediaries, institutions or the public.

Issue syndicate, or underwriting consortium. A consortium of banks and other financial intermediaries, including insurance companies, set up to place new securities issued by companies or the state among a relatively large group of investors. The consortium is headed by one or two lead managers, who are in charge of organising and following through the transaction, and its members place the securities with their clients or the general public. In the case of Euro-issues*, the syndicate members are usually divided into guaranteeing members – the group that underwrites the issue and which automatically includes the lead managers – and regular members, who agree only to place the issue in proportion to the number of requests they receive.

Joint-stock bank. A bank organised in the form of a limited liability company, the most common legal status for banks today due to the ease with which this structure can be used to raise capital or fresh funds.

Leverage. Borrowing by pledging part or all of the assets held by a borrower – securities, property, etc. – in order to buy more such assets. The leveraged investor hopes that the value of his assets will be higher upon maturity of the credit, thus generating enough profit to pay the interest and reimburse the loan. Inversely, if the value of his assets drops, he will suffer heavy losses and could even be pushed into bankruptcy.

Lombard credit. A loan against pledged securities. See Bank loan*.

Merchant bank. The UK term for investment bank*. See also Merchant banker*.

Merchant banker. Originally, merchant bankers were international merchants based in London who issued acceptances* for bills* of exchange drawn on them by their trading partners abroad and gradually evolved into acceptance houses and subsequently banks*, usually investment banks*.

Mixed bank. Synonym of universal bank*.

Monetary regime. The set of rules governing legal tender – the currency authorised by law to settle debts – and how it is defined. This regime can be either metallic or fiduciary. In the former, the currency is defined as a certain weight of a precious metal – gold or silver.

Therefore, the banknotes in circulation, convertible on sight into metal, have to be covered in whole or in part by the metallic reserves of the central bank*. The best-known monetary regimes are the gold standard, the silver standard and gold/silver bimetallism, where the rate of exchange between the two metals is set by law. In the fiduciary regime, the monetary unit of a country or economic zone is defined by law without any reference to precious metals, and bank notes are not redeemable at the issuing institution. All modern monetary schemes are fiduciary nowadays. A hybrid system, which prevailed between 1945 and 1971, was the Gold Exchange Standard in which the currency was defined in terms of either gold or another currency defined in terms of gold, normally the dollar, at $35 for an ounce of gold.

Money market. A place for trading money-market paper, i.e. short-term securities, or loans between banks participating in the clearing* system. Also known as the interbank market, most transactions here are conducted on a day-to-day or call basis, i.e. with a 24-hour maturity.

Options. The right to buy (call) or to sell (put) a financial instrument on a certain date and at a price that is fixed in advance, called the strike price. The buyer of the option pays the seller a premium for having the right to exercise this option as and when required. Options are bought either on a specialist exchange or directly from the seller (OTC – over the counter), which is usually a bank.

Overseas bank, formerly known also as colonial and foreign bank. A bank that has its headquarters or a major office in the centre of a formal or informal empire and which conducts the bulk of its activities – acceptances, foreign exchange, loans and deposits, issues – in a particular region of this empire. Many such banks continued trading after the colonies were granted independence.

Primary market. See Capital market*.

Private bank. A bank organised in the form of a partnership in which the partners share unlimited liability with respect to their own wealth. Originally, the only banks that existed were private banks, owned by wealthy financiers who provided the firm's equity. This was the origin of the term *haute banque*, referring to both the social background of their owners as well as the prestige and longevity of such banking houses themselves.

Private banking. See Wealth management*.

Regime. See Monetary regime* or Exchange-rate regime*.

Repurchase agreement. See Bank loan*.

Secondary market. See Capital market*.

Shares, also called equities or stocks (US). Securities representing part-ownership in a limited liability company which entitle the holder to receive a dividend and which, as a rule, are not redeemable. In the case of bankruptcy, shareholders' losses are limited to the value of the shares they hold.

Speculation. The practice of betting on a discrepancy in prices or rates over time. A speculator obviously takes a risk as this price upon maturity cannot be known in advance.

Spot transaction. A commercial or financial transaction wherein the item sold is deliverable and payable immediately in accordance with local practice.

Stocks. See Shares*.

Stock exchange. See Exchange*.

Syndicate. See Issue syndicate*.

Trust. See Holding*.

Underwriting consortium. See Issue syndicate*.

Universal bank. A financial institution that conducts all or almost all types of banking and financial transactions, including those of an investment bank*, those of a wealth manager and also often those of a broker*. These banks, common in Germany and central Europe, used to be banned in many countries due to the high risk of collusion and multiple conflicts of interest. Nowadays, they tend to be authorised provided that they observe the strict limits set by the various banking and trading supervisory authorities.

Wealth management. The management of all or some of the assets of an individual or institution, which remains the owner of the assets and assumes the risk incurred in the management decisions, provided that the manager complies with the instructions given, the rules and regulations in place and the standard practice in the profession. In the case of private investors, the manager generally only accepts clients whose fortune exceeds a certain sum and with whom a relationship of trust will be built, which is why this business is now generally called private banking.

Notes

INTRODUCTION

1 See Saskia Sassen's analyses on this topic, especially *The Global City. New York, London, Tokyo*, Princeton, 2001.
2 C. Kindleberger, 'The formation of financial centers', *Princeton Studies in International Finance*, 36, 1974, pp. 1–78.
3 D. Scholey, 'Essential features of international financial centres', in Swiss Bankers' Association, *International Financial Centres: Structure, Achievements and Prospects*, Proceedings of the 40th International Summer School, Interlaken/Basle, 1987, p. 12.
4 H. C. Reed, *The Preeminence of International Financial Centers*, New York, 1981.
5 G. Jones, 'International financial centres in Asia, the Middle East and Australia: a historical perspective', in Y. Cassis (ed.), *Finance and Financiers in European History 1880–1960*, Cambridge, 1992, pp. 405–6.
6 R. Roberts, 'The economics of cities of finance', in H. A. Diedericks and D. Reeder (eds.), *Cities of Finance*, Amsterdam, 1996, pp. 7–19.
7 G. Dufey and I. H. Giddy, *The International Money Market*, Prentice-Hall, 1978.
8 Additional information can be found in R. Roberts (ed.), *International Financial Centres*, 4 vols., Aldershot, 1994.

1. THE AGE OF PRIVATE BANKERS, 1780–1840

1 S. R. Cope, *Walter Boyd. A Merchant Banker in the Age of Napoleon*, London, 1983.
2 See the classic work by Eric Hobsbawm, *The Age of Revolution*, London, 1962.
3 N. Crafts, *British Economic Growth during the Industrial Revolution*, Oxford, 1985.
4 A. Mayer, *The Persistence of the Old Regime*, London, 1981.
5 See J. de Vries and A. van der Woude, *The First Modern Economy. Success, Failure, and Perseverance of the Dutch Economy, 1500–1815*, Cambridge, 1997.
6 A. Maddison, *Dynamic Forces in Economic Development*, Oxford, 1991, pp. 30–5.
7 C. Wilson, *Anglo-Dutch Commerce and Finance in the Eighteenth Century*, Cambridge, 1941, pp. 16–27.
8 J. Jonker and K. Sluyterman, *At Home on the World Markets. Dutch International Trading Companies from the 16th Century until the Present*, The Hague, 2000, pp. 124–5.

9 J. C. Riley, *International Government Finance and the Amsterdam Capital Market, 1740–1815*, Cambridge, 1980.

10 M. G. Buist, *At spes non fracta. Hope & Co. 1770–1815, Merchant Bankers and Diplomats at Work*, The Hague, 1974.

11 de Vries and van der Woude, *First Modern Economy*, p. 146.

12 The following paragraphs are mainly based on the book by J. Jonker, *Merchants, Bankers, Middlemen. The Amsterdam Money Market During the First Half of the 19th Century*, Amsterdam, 1996.

13 Ibid., p. 154.

14 Ibid., p. 156.

15 The first to immigrate were Julius Königswärter in 1817, S. Raphael & Co. in 1818 and L. R. Bischoffsheim in 1820, with Sichel, Oppenheim, Stern and Rindskopff arriving at about the same time.

16 Jonker, *Merchants, Bankers, Middlemen*, pp. 249–50.

17 Ibid., pp. 90–2.

18 Hope & Co., D. Crommelin & Son and Van Eeghen & Co. Note that the notion of capital was not well defined at the time in the case of private bankers. It could refer either to equity capital or to equity capital plus other contributions, such as the reserves or personal assets of partners and members of their families.

19 Jonker, *Merchants, Bankers, Middlemen*, p. 228.

20 Ibid., pp. 70–1.

21 Ibid., p. 40.

22 Ibid., pp. 41–4.

23 Jonker and Sluyterman, *At home on the World Markets*, pp. 167–8.

24 See, in particular, P. G. M. Dickson, *The Financial Revolution in England. A Study in the Development of Public Credit, 1688–1756*, London, 1967; L. Neal, *The Rise of Financial Capitalism. International Capital Markets in the Age of Reason*, Cambridge, 1990.

25 This system was based on the centralisation of tax collection and above all on the institutionalisation of the public debt, with official recognition and partial securitisation of the debt, to which was added a redemption plan controlled by Parliament.

26 J. M. Price, 'What did merchants do? Reflections on British overseas trade, 1660–1790', *Journal of Economic History*, 49, 2, 1989, pp. 267–84.

27 D. Kynaston, *The City of London. Volume I: A World of its Own 1815–1890*, London, 1994, p. 10.

28 See D. E. W. Gibb, *Lloyd's of London. A Study in Individualism*, London, 1957; C. Wright and C. E. Fayle, *A History of Lloyd's*, London, 1928.

29 B. Supple, *The Royal Exchange Assurance. A History of British Insurance 1720–1970*, Cambridge, 1970.

30 D. M. Joslin, 'London private bankers, 1720–1785', *Economic History Review*, 7, 1954.

31 They included houses like Barclay & Co., Barnett, Hoare & Co., Glyn, Mills & Co., Martin & Co., Smith and Payne & Smiths in their ranks.

32 S. Chapman, *The Rise of Merchant Banking*, London, 1984, pp. 5–9.

33 H. Thornton, *An Inquiry into Paper Credit*, London, 1802, p. 59.

34 Chapman, *Rise of Merchant Banking*, pp. 105–6.

35 Ibid., p. 39.

36 Cope, *Walter Boyd*, pp. 47–8.

37 A French colony until 1763, Louisiana then passed into Spanish hands, before returning to France in 1800 – which did not exactly delight the Americans. Jefferson sent an emissary to Paris to find out whether France would be willing to sell part of this territory. Napoleon, who was not very interested in Louisiana and was in need of money, agreed to cede the whole territory for $15 million minus $3.75 million in American accounts receivable from France; in other words, $11.25 million, which at that time represented Fr. 52 million.

38 P. Ziegler, *The Sixth Great Power. Barings, 1762–1929*, London, 1988, pp. 70–1.

39 R. Roberts, *Schroders. Merchants & Bankers*, Basingstoke and London, 1992, pp. 28–30.

40 They included, in particular, Horstman & Co., founded in 1802, William Brandt Sons & Co. in 1805, Frederick Huth & Co. in 1809 and Frühling & Goschen in 1814.

41 N. Ferguson, *The World's Banker. The History of the House of Rothschild*, London, 1998, pp. 50–63, 95–102.

42 Neal, *Rise of Financial Capitalism*, pp. 88–90.

43 Ferguson, *World's Banker*, pp. 135–6.

44 R. Michie, *The London Stock Exchange. A History*, Oxford, 1999, p. 53.

45 Some other banking houses, mainly involved in minor South American issues, such as B. A. Goldschmidt & Co., Irving, Reid & Co. and Thomas Wilson & Co., were also members of this group.

46 Among them could be mentioned Barclay, Tritton, Bevan & Co., Smith Payne & Smiths, Glyn, Hallifax, Mills & Co. and Jones, Loyd & Co. In London in 1810 there was a total of eighty-three private bankers, who were then at their apogee.

47 W. Bagehot, *Lombard Street. A Description of the Money Market*, London, 1910, p. 214.

48 Thellusson, Necker & Cie, Tourton & Baur and Lecouteulx & Cie.

49 H. Lüthy, *La banque protestante en France de la Révocation de l'Edit de Nantes à la Révolution française*, 2 vols., Paris, 1959–61, vol. II, p. 142.

50 Cited in P. Vilar, *Or et monnaie dans l'histoire*, Paris, 1974, p. 342.

51 P. Hoffman, G. Postel-Vinay and J.-L. Rosenthal, *Des marchés sans prix. Une économie politique du crédit à Paris, 1660–1870*, Paris 2001.

52 A. Plessis, 'Le développement des activités financières à Paris au XIXème siècle', in H. A. Diederiks and D. Reeder (eds.), *Cities of Finance*, Amsterdam, 1996, pp. 167–79.

53 M. Lévy-Leboyer, *Les banques européennes et l'industrialisation internationale dans la première moitié du XIXe siècle*, Paris, 1964, pp. 427–8.

54 A. Plessis, 'La création de la Banque de France et la genèse des banques nationales d'émission en Europe au XIXe siècle', in O. Feiertag and M. Margairaz (eds.), *Politiques et pratiques des banques d'émission en Europe (XVIIe–XXe siècle)*, Paris, 2003, pp. 25–51; F. Crouzet, 'Politics and banking in revolutionary and Napoleonic France', in R. Sylla, R. Tilly and

G. Tortella (eds.), *The State, the Financial System and Economic Modernization*, Cambridge, 1999, pp. 20–52.

55 L. Bergeron, *Banquiers, négociants et manufacturiers parisiens du Directoire à l'Empire*, Paris, 1978, p. 45.

56 L. Bergeron, *Les Rothschild et les autres . . . La gloire des banquiers*, Paris, 1991, pp. 36–7.

57 Others followed during the early years of the nineteenth century; Michel-Frédéric Pillet-Will left his partners in Lausanne and in 1811 settled in Paris, where he formed a partnership with Charles Vernes. In 1812 Henri Hentsch sent his partner Jean-Antoine Blanc from Geneva to Paris, where he joined him one year later; in 1821 Jean Ador and Auguste Dassier founded the banking house Ador, Vernes & Dassier; Barthélemy Paccard followed in 1825, joined two years later by his colleague Louis Dufour.

58 Bergeron, *Rothschild*, p. 46; M. Stürmer, G. Teichmann and W. Treue, *Wägen und Wagen. Sal. Oppenhein jr. & Cie. Geschichte einer Bank und einer Familie*, Munich and Zurich, 1989, p. 41.

59 Even though they stayed in Cologne, where they had been the first Jews to settle in 1798, the Oppenheims founded, in partnership with Berr-Léon Fould, the bank B. L. Fould & Fould-Oppenheim in Paris in 1813, forging a solid and lasting alliance between the two families, consolidated by the marriage in the same year of Hélène Oppenheim to Benedict Fould, son of Berr-Léon. The settlement of the Habers, from Karlsruhe, was more direct. Maurice Haber (1798–1874), son of Salomon (banker to the Baden and Prussian courts since 1794, which earned him the title of baron of Baden in 1829), arrived in Paris in 1822, equipped with a share from his father, and formed a partnership with Felix Worms from Romilly. Another distinguished personality of German origin in the Parisian *haute banque* was Adolphe d'Eichthal, son of Aron-Elias Seligman, banker to the king of Bavaria and made Baron d'Eichthal in 1814 for services rendered as a supplier during the Napoleonic Wars.

60 Lévy-Leboyer, *Les banques européennes*, pp. 437–40.

61 Ibid., pp. 441–2.

62 Greffulhe, Baguenault, Hottinguer and Laffitte.

63 B. Gille, *La banque et le crédit en France de 1815 à 1848*, Paris, 1959, pp. 227–9.

64 Ibid., p. 260–1.

65 Along with Bethmann and Metzler, Goll, Ohlenschalger or Neufville could be mentioned. See C.-L. Holtfrerich, *Frankfurt as a Financial Centre. From Medieval Trade Fair to European Banking Centre*, Munich, 1999, pp. 93–4.

66 This was particularly so in the case of the Erlangers, Goldschmidts, Seligmanns, Speyers and Sterns.

67 B. S. Chlepner, *Le marché financier belge depuis cent ans*, Brussels, 1930, p. 10.

68 K. Veraghtert, 'Bruxelles éclipse Anvers. Le centre boursier belge se déplace, 1800–1840', in G. de Clercq (ed.), *A la Bourse. Histoire du marché des valeurs en Belgique de 1300 à 1990*, Louvain-la-Neuve, 1992, p. 173.

69 The city indeed suffered damage; the Escaut was closed to shipping, and between 1830 and 1835 Antwerp saw a good half of its fleet change its port of registry and go over to the Netherlands.

70 Germain Cassel, who was related to Bischoffsheim, is believed to have arrived in Belgium just after independence. He founded a firm under the name of Banque Cassel et Cie in April 1839, after a stay in London. J. G. Mettenius, who settled in Brussels in 1797 at the age of 20, also originated from Frankfurt. Through Adolphe Oppenheim, who was born in Frankfurt in 1793 and arrived in Brussels in 1809, it was the Salomon Oppenheim banking house from Cologne that entered the Brussels financial centre after independence.

71 See S. Tilman, 'Portrait collectif des grands banquiers belges Bruxelles–Liège–Anvers (1830–1935): Contribution à une histoire des élites', doctoral thesis, Université Libre de Bruxelles, 2003–04, vol. II, pp. 348–84.

72 Veraghtert, 'Bruxelles éclipse Anvers', pp. 177–8.

73 Chlepner, Le marché financier belge, p. 49.

74 Lüthy, La banque protestante en France, vol. II, p. 80.

75 Lullin, Masbou, Aubert & Cie, Bontemps, Mallet & Cie, two days after the homonymous banking house in Paris, and Passavant, Bertrand & Cie. Lévy-Leboyer, Les banques européennes, p. 424.

76 After several name changes, Ferrier, Darier & Cie became Ferrier, Lullin & Cie in 1908, Henri Hentsch & Cie became Hentsch & Cie in 1835, J. G. Lombard & J. J. Lullin took the name of Lombard, Odier & Cie in 1830 and, also after several changes, de Candolle, Mallet & Cie adopted the corporate name Pictet & Cie in 1926.

77 Lévy Leboyer, Les banques européennes, p. 425; J. Seitz, Histoire de la banque à Genève, Geneva, 1931, pp. 20–1; L. H. Mottet, Regards sur l'histoire des banques et banquiers genevois, Geneva, 1982, pp. 135–6, 142.

78 Lévy-Leboyer, Les banques européennes, p. 429.

79 B. Gille, Histoire de la maison Rothschild, vol. I, Des origines à 1848, Geneva, 1965, p. 62.

80 D. M. Paccard & Cie in 1819, Louis Pictet & Cie in 1829, F. Bonna & Cie in 1830 and Chaponnière & Cie in 1837.

81 Pictet & Cie 1805–1955, 1955, Geneva, pp. 23–8.

82 Kynaston, City of London, vol. I, pp. 36–43.

83 Huskisson Papers, British Library, Add Ms 38,741, cited by Kynaston, City of London, vol. I, p. 37.

84 See Stürmer, Teichmann and Treue, Wägen und Wagen; F. Barbier, Finance et politique. La dynastie des Fould XVIIIe–XXe siècle, Paris, 1991.

85 See G. Kurgan-van Hentenrijk, S. Jaumain and V. Montens (eds.), Dictionnaire des patrons en Belgique. Les hommes, les entreprises, les réseaux, Brussels, 1996.

86 Ferguson, World's Banker, pp. 391–4, 574–7.

87 Ibid., pp. 302–3.

88 Kurgan-van Hentenrijk et al. (eds.), Dictionnaire des patrons en Belgique, p. 409.

89 Roberts, Schroders, pp. 21–3.

90 C. A. Jones, *International Business in the Nineteenth Century. The Rise and Fall of a Cosmopolitan Bourgeosie*, New York, 1987.

2. THE CONCENTRATION OF CAPITAL, 1840–1875

1 In Great Britain 1856–62, in France 1863–67 and in Germany 1870.
2 M. Obstfeld and A. Taylor, 'Globalization and capital markets', in M. Bordo, A. Taylor and J. Williamson (eds.), *Globalization in Historical Perspective*, Chicago, 2003, pp. 141–2.
3 The National Provincial Bank of England was founded in 1833, the London and Westminster Bank in 1834, the London and County Banking Company and the London Joint Stock Bank in 1836, and the Union Bank of London in 1839.
4 The Birmingham and Midland Bank, in particular, founded in 1836.
5 W. F. Crick and J. E. Wadsworth, *A Hundred Years of Joint Stock Banking*, London, 1936, p. 22.
6 W. Bagehot, *Lombard Street. A Description of the Money Market*, London, 1873, pp. 252–3.
7 The first were founded in Australia, with the Bank of Australasia (1835) and the Union Bank of Australia (1837); in the West Indies, with the Colonial Bank (1836); in Canada, with the Bank of British North America (1836); in India and the Far East with the Chartered Bank of India, Australia and China (1854); and in South Africa with the Standard Bank of South Africa (1862).
8 The London and River Plate Bank and the London and Brazilian Bank were both established in 1862, and the Anglo-Egyptian Bank in 1864, but this is not an exhaustive list.
9 G. Jones, *British Multinational Banking 1830–1990*, Oxford, 1993, pp. 393–5.
10 The London and Brazilian Bank, for example, was founded by a group that included the House of E. Johnston & Co., one of the most important firms involved in the coffee trade, the merchant banks Robert Benson & Co. and Bischoffsheim & Goldschmidt, and the famous private bank Glyn, Mills & Co. Moreover, Glyn, Mills stood at the centre of a network of several banks, including the Bank of Egypt, founded in 1855, the Ottoman Bank in 1856 and the Anglo-Austrian Bank in 1863. See D. Joslin, *A Century of Banking in Latin America*, London, 1963, pp. 64–5; P. L. Cottrell, 'A cluster of corporate international banks, 1855–75', *Business History*, 33, 3, 1991, pp. 31–52.
11 H. van der Wee and M. van der Wee-Verbreyt, 'Belgian banking in the nineteenth and twentieth centuries: the Société Générale and the Générale de Banque (1822–1997)', in R. Sylla, R. Tilly and G. Tortella (eds.), *The State, the Financial System and Economic Modernization*, Cambridge, 1999, p. 61.
12 H. Houtman-De Smedt, 'Société Générale from 1822 to 1848. From "Bank of the Crown Lands" to "mixed-type bank" ', in H. van der Wee (ed.), *The Generale Bank 1822–1897*, Tielt, 1997, p. 49.
13 See G. Kurgan-van Hentenryk, 'Société Générale, 1850–1934', in van der Wee, *Generale Bank*.

14 G. Kurgan-van Hentenryk, *Gouverner la Générale de Belgique. Essai de biographie collective*, Brussels, 1996, p. 15.

15 Jacques Laffitte also became prime minister in 1830–31, but saw his bank collapse at the same time.

16 At that time, the Banque de France's capital amounted to a mere Fr. 67.9 million.

17 See B. Gille, *La banque et le crédit en France de 1815 à 1848*, Paris, 1959, pp. 109–17.

18 Amongst these was the Comptoir Général du Commerce, founded in 1842 by Hippolyte Ganneron, a notable tradesman from Paris, with a nominal capital of Fr. 20 million, as well as the Caisse Commerciale de Paris, created in 1845 by transforming the private bank Béchet, Dethomas & Cie. The Caisse Générale du Commerce et des Chemins de Fer, established in 1846 by two former receivers general, Baudon and Saint-Albin, had a nominal capital of Fr. 25 million at its disposal. See Gille, *La banque et le crédit en France*, pp. 120–1.

19 F. Torres, *Banquiers d'avenir. Des comptoirs d'escompte à la naissance de BNP Paribas*, Paris, 2000, pp. 12–19.

20 In India (Calcutta in 1860 and Bombay in 1862), in China (Shanghai in 1860 and Hong Kong in 1862), in Yokohama in 1867, in Alexandria in 1869 and, finally, in London in 1869.

21 H. Bonin, 'L'outre-mer, marché pour la banque commerciale de 1875 à 1985?', in J. Marseilles (ed.), *La France et l'outre-mer. Un siècle de relations monétaires et financières*, Paris, 1998, pp. 437–83.

22 The decree authorising this was signed by Emperor Napoleon III on 15 November.

23 Among the main publications on this topic, see D. Landes, 'Vieille banque et banque nouvelle: la révolution bancaire du XIXe siècle', *Revue d'histoire moderne et contemporaine*, 3, 1956, pp. 204–22; B. Gille, *Histoire de la Maison Rothschild*, vol. II: *1848–1870*, Geneva, 1967; J. Autin, *Les frères Pereire. Le bonheur d'entreprendre*, Paris, 1984; E. Chadeau, *L'économie du risque. Les entrepreneurs 1850–1980*, Paris, 1988.

24 In the autumn of 1852, they founded the Compagnie des Chemins de Fer du Midi, followed one year later by the Grand Central, another railway company; in 1854 they created a real-estate company, the Société Anonyme de l'Hôtel et des Immeubles de la Rue de Rivoli; and in 1855 they established successively the Compagnie Générale Maritime (the future Compagnie Générale Transatlantique), the Compagnie Générale des Omnibus de Paris, the Compagnie du Grand Hôtel Saint Honoré and, finally, the Compagnie Parisienne d'Eclairage et de Chauffage par le Gaz.

25 Frankfurt, Paris, London, Vienna and Naples.

26 The Banque de France in fact succeeded in blocking the last way out available to the Pereires in 1860, when Savoy was incorporated into France. Savoy had its own central bank, the Banque de Savoie, which the Savoyards hoped to keep, and the Pereires, who favoured the existence of several issuing banks, signed a convention with its directors in September 1863. This was a waste of effort, since less than two years later Napoleon III

decided to dissolve the Banque de Savoie and integrate it into the Banque de France.

27 They were led by William Gladstone, from the London firm Thomson, Bonar & Co. The introduction of the cheque by the CIC in France is attributed to Armand Donon, directly inspired by British and American practice. N. Stoskopf, *Banquiers et financiers parisiens*, vol. VII in the series *Les patrons du Second Empire*, Paris, 2002, pp. 143–4.

28 See J. Bouvier, *Le Crédit Lyonnais de 1863 à 1882. Les années de formation d'une banque de dépôts*, 2 vols., Paris, 1961.

29 The railway magnates François Bartholony and Paulin Talabot, the English banker Edward Blount, as well as various members of the *haute banque*.

30 E. Bussière, *Paribas, 1872–1992. L'Europe et le monde*, Antwerp, 1992, pp. 19–27; Stoskopf, *Banquiers et financiers*, pp. 44–8, 302–5.

31 Jacques Laffitte took the first initiatives from the 1820s and 1830s.

32 Among others, Gustav Mevissen and Abraham Oppenheim, who had failed, owing to opposition from the authorities, in their attempt to create a big joint-stock bank in Cologne and then in Frankfurt.

33 In particular, Mendelssohn, Bleichröder and Warschauer from Berlin, as well as Mevissen and Oppenheim from Cologne.

34 The Allgemeine Deutsche Credit-Anstalt in Leipzig, the Norddeutsche Bank in Hamburg and the Mitteldeutsche Creditbank in Meiningen, Saxony.

35 L. Gall *et al.*, *The Deutsche Bank 1870–1975*, London, 1995, pp. 3–10.

36 R. Rosenbaum and A. J. Sherman, *M. M. Warburg & Co., 1798–1938. Merchant Bankers of Hamburg*, London, 1979, p. 91.

37 *Neue Deutsche Biographie*; W. E. Mosse, *Jews in the German Economy. The German–Jewish Economic Elite 1820–1935*, Oxford, 1987, p. 225.

38 The Disconto-Gesellschaft and the Berliner Handels-Gesellschaft.

39 J. Seitz, *Histoire de la banque à Genève*, Geneva, 1931, pp. 34–5; L.-H. Mottet, *Regards sur l'histoire des banques et banquiers genevois*, Geneva, 1982, p. 164.

40 Figures calculated on the basis of F. Ritzmann, *Die Schweizer Banken. Geschichte, Theorie, Statistik*, Bern and Stuttgart, 1973, Table 1.

41 R. Sylla, 'Shaping the U.S. financial system, 1690–1913: the dominant role of public finance', in R. Sylla, R. Tilly and G. Tortella (eds.), *The State, the Financial System and Economic Modernization*, pp. 249–70.

42 By setting up a system for collecting indirect taxes; establishing a modern national debt, as a result of consolidating on the federal level the various debts incurred during the War of Independence.

43 The notes were henceforth printed and supplied by the Treasury.

44 The link between Liverpool and Manchester was finished in 1830. In France, the line between Saint Etienne and Lyons was opened to travellers in 1832, and the line between Nuremberg and Fürth in Bavaria came into service in 1835. In the United States, the first line between Baltimore and Ellicott's Mills was inaugurated in 1830.

45 T. Gourvish, *Railways and the British Economy 1830–1914*, London and Basingstoke, 1980, pp. 9–13.

46 R. Fremdling, 'Railroads and German economic growth: A leading sector analysis with a comparison to the United States and Great Britain', *Journal of Economic History*, 37, 3, 1977, p. 585.

47 All the figures are in national currency. Converted into dollars, this makes some $3 billion for Britain; from more than $200 million in 1852 to more than $1.5 billion in 1870 for France; and from $22 million at the beginning of the 1850s to $125 million at the end of the 1870s for Germany – in other words, an accrued sum of about $2.5 billion.

48 The very first line, between Stockton and Darlington, was above all a Quaker affair, both on account of its promoters, Edward Pease and Jonathan Backhouse, and its financing, obtained through the family network of the Society of Friends that operated at local and national level. Most of the capital for the line between Manchester and Liverpool came from Lancashire. M. W. Kirby, *Men of Business and Politics. The Rise and Fall of the Quaker Peace Dynasty of North-East England, 1700–1943*, London, 1984, pp. 11–12.

49 His personal inclinations and his business sense led Glyn to become involved in founding the London and Birmingham, of which he was a member of the board of directors when it was set up in 1833. He became its chairman in 1837, a post that he held for fifteen years, and played a major role in the successive mergers that in 1846 produced the London and North Western Railway Company, one of the four large companies (with the Midland, the Great Western and the North Eastern) that already dominated the British network. R. Fulford, *Glyn's 1753–1953. Six Generations in Lombard Street*, London, 1953, pp. 120–7.

50 In particular, Masterman, Peters & Mildred, working in England and abroad and having links to the entrepreneurs Thomas Brassey and Samuel Peto. D. Kynaston, *The City of London, vol. I: A World of its Own, 1815–1890*, London, 1994, p. 152.

51 R. Michie, *The London Stock Exchange. A History*, Oxford, 1999, pp. 63–6.

52 Kynaston, *City of London*, vol. I, p. 174.

53 D. R. Adler, *British Investment in American Railways, 1834–1898*, Charlottesville, 1970.

54 M. Wilkins, *The History of Foreign Investment in the United States to 1914*, Cambridge, Mass., 1989, pp. 113–23.

55 With the lines from Strasburg to Basle and from Paris to Orléans, both granted in 1838.

56 G. Ribeill, *La révolution ferroviaire. La formation des compagnies de chemins de fer en France (1823–1870)*, Paris, 1993, pp. 97–102.

57 Supported, among others, by Sanson Davillier, Adolphe d'Eichthal and Francis Lefebvre.

58 Charles Laffitte was the nephew of Jacques Laffitte, and Edward Blount was a Scottish banker settled in France and very actively involved in promoting the railways. They were partners from 1834 to 1848 in the bank Laffitte, Blount & Cie.

59 Formed mainly of houses of Genevan and Swiss origin, including Pillet-Will (ousted in 1839), André & Cottier, Paccard, Dufour & Cie and Adolphe de Waru.

60 See Ribeill, *Révolution ferroviaire*, pp. 112–15.
61 The Nord, the Paris–Strasbourg, the Paris–Lyon, the Lyon–Avigon and the Midi.
62 Rothschilds, d'Eichthal, Thurneyssen, Laffitte-Blount, Bartholony, Hottinguer, Mallet, Fould-Oppenheim and Gouin.
63 Ribeill, *Révolution ferroviaire*, p. 113.
64 The first project, the Grand Central, formed in 1853 under the aegis of Morny, the emperor's half-brother, was intended to link Paris to the Compagnie du Midi, controlled by the Pereires, by sliding between the Paris–Orléans, controlled by Bartholony, and the Talabots' future Paris–Lyon–Méditerranée (PLM). It disappeared in 1857, when Morny left the Pereire clan, and its remains were shared between its two competitors. The second project, which consisted in extending the Compagnie du Midi, which linked Bordeaux to Sète, as far as Marseilles, was rejected by the public authorities in 1863.
65 See Gille, *Histoire de la Maison Rothschild, vol. II*, R. Cameron, *France and the Economic Development of Europe, 1800–1914*, Princeton, 1961.
66 In particular, S. Oppenheim, A. Schaaffhausen, J. H. Stein and I. D. Herstatt.
67 A. Oppenhein would be its *de facto* managing director between 1837 and 1844, then its vice-chairman.
68 See M. Stürmer, G. Teichmann and W. Treue, *Wägen und Wagen. Sal. Oppenheim jr. & Co. Geschichte einer Bank und einer Familie*, Munich/Zurich, 1989.
69 Mosse, *Jews in the German Economy*, pp. 111–15.
70 Including the private banks Bleichröder and Warschauer, as well as the big banks Disconto-Gesellschaft and Berliner Handels-Gesellschaft.
71 F. Stern, *Gold and Iron. Bismarck, Bleichröder and the Building of the German Empire*, New York, 1977, p. 62.
72 Jay Cooke had exclusive control over placing the company's securities; acting as a tax officer, he could appoint two of its directors and two members of its executive committee and was responsible for purchasing its equipment. In return, he received securities equivalent at their nominal value to some 80% of the company's capital, which at that time had reached $100 million, the remaining shares being paid to him as a bonus, at a rate of $200 for $1,000 of bonds sold. Cooke intended to place his securities in Europe, with the support of European bankers, and in the United States, through an aggressive sales campaign. He failed, due to the distrust of European bankers, including the Rothschilds, and to the difficult conditions of the American market following the Wall Street collapse on 24 September 1869.
73 V. Carosso, *Investment Banking in America. A History*, Cambridge, Mass., 1970, pp. 12, 23–5.
74 F. Crouzet, *L'économie de la Grande-Bretagne victorienne*, Paris, 1978, p. 22; P. Bairoch, 'La place de la France sur les marchés internationaux', in M. Lévy-Leboyer (ed.), *La position internationale de la France. Aspects économiques et sociaux XIXe–XXe siècles*, Paris, 1977, p. 38.

75 *Financial News*, 22 January 1934, Fiftieth Anniversary Number, *The City 1884–1934*, p. 25.
76 Tea, sugar, coffee, tobacco, indigo and other tropical products.
77 R. Michie, *The City of London. Continuity and Change, 1850–1990*, Basingstoke and London, 1990; Kynaston, *City of London*, vol. I.
78 Along with Paris, these two ports provided 47% of French customs receipts.
79 See L. Girard, *La politique des travaux publics sous le Second Empire*, Paris, 1952.
80 In 1860, they founded the Compagnie des Entrepôts et Magasins Généraux, which took over what was left of the Napoleon Docks and absorbed other smaller firms, and then considered merging the Paris Docks and those of Marseilles, with the goal of making Paris continental Europe's greatest emporium. Autin, *Les frères Pereire*, pp. 94, 255.
81 A. Plessis, Preface to Y. Cassis, *La City de Londres, 1870–1914*, Paris, 1987, p. 9.
82 N. Ferguson, *The World's Banker. The History of the House of Rothschild*, London, 1998; P. Ziegler, *The Sixth Great Power, Barings, 1762–1929*, London, 1988; A. Plessis, *Régents et gouverneurs de la Banque de France sous le Second Empire*, Geneva, 1985.
83 Michie, *London Stock Exchange*, p. 88; A. Dupont-Ferrier, *Le marché financier de Paris sous le Second Empire*, Paris, 1925, p. 185.
84 Estimations based on A. Imlah, 'British balance of payments and the export of capital, 1816–1913', *Economic History Review*, 2nd ser., 2, 1952, pp. 235–6; M. Lévy-Leboyer, 'La balance des paiements et l'exportation des capitaux français', in Lévy-Leboyer (ed.), *La position internationale de la France*, pp. 119–20.
85 French investments in Europe were distributed as follows: Italy, Spain and Portugal 36%, central Europe (Austria-Hungary, Germany and Switzerland) 19%, eastern Europe (Russia, Romania, Greece and Serbia) 9% and north-western Europe (Benelux, United Kingdom, Scandinavia) 4%.
86 For France, the figures come from R. Cameron, *France and the Economic Development of Europe 1800–1914*, Princeton, 1961, p. 88. For England, the percentages have been calculated on the basis of M. Simon, 'The pattern of new British portfolio foreign investment, 1865–1914', in A. R. Hall (ed.), *The Export of Capital from Britain, 1870–1914*, London, 1968, pp. 39–40.
87 Its geographical distribution is not known before this date.
88 Apart from in Europe, the only French investment of any significance was in the Middle East (23% of the total), the colonial empire accounting for 4.3%, which left just a little over 5% for the rest of the world, including North and South America; on the other hand, these received 41% of British investment (28% for North America and 13% for South America), the rest flowing to Asia (13%), Australia (11%) and Africa (6%).
89 These concerned primarily loans to foreign governments in Europe, whose share would be slightly higher for Britain if figures were available for the fifties and the beginning of the sixties, and in the Middle East, where British capital is known to have been abundant during this period, before gradually diminishing.

90 Cameron, *France and the Economic Development of Europe*, pp. 438–40; B. Bramsen and K. Wain, *The Hambros 1779–1979*, London, 1979, pp. 263–72.

91 *Des emprunts d'Etat*, 19 May 1865, Archives nationales, Papiers Rouher, 45 AP, carton 20, 2, cited by L. Einaudi, *Money and Politics. European Monetary Unification and the International Gold Standard (1865–1873)*, Cambridge, 2001, pp. 43–4.

92 Dupont-Ferrier, *Le marché financier de Paris*, pp. 187–9.

93 Einaudi, *Money and Politics*, pp. 43–4.

94 Austria-Hungary, Belgium, Spain, Italy and Switzerland.

95 M. Flandreau, 'The economics and politics of monetary unions: a reassessment of the Latin Monetary Union, 1865–1871', *Financial History Review*, 7, 1, 2000, pp. 34–7.

96 Ibid. See also A. Plessis, *La politique de la Banque de France de 1851 à 1870*, Geneva, 1985.

97 Bagehot, *Lombard Street*, pp. 32–3.

98 These currencies, including the Italian lira, all had the same nominal value.

99 The ecu was struck with a fineness of 900/1,000, whereas an alloy of 835/1,000 was adopted for lower-denomination silver coins.

100 Flandreau, 'Economics and politics of monetary unions', pp. 28–32.

101 On this topic, see Einaudi, *Money and Politics*. The following paragraphs are based on this book.

102 Here, it was thinking of countries that could easily be integrated into a franc zone, like Greece, Spain, the Papal States or Austria-Hungary.

103 A £1 sterling coin.

104 Furthermore, delegates agreed to recommend that the proportion of gold contained in the coins total 9/10, that these coins have a value of Fr. 5 or be multiples of five and that they be legal tender in the signatory countries to the convention.

105 A lawyer, a deputy, for a time a minister, then a member of the State Council, of which he was vice-chairman from 1855 to 1870, Parieu was a great expert on international monetary matters.

106 A report, however, indicated the excessive debasement of nearly one third of the gold coins in circulation.

107 Georges J. Goschen, a Liberal MP, was a former merchant banker and a director of the Bank of England.

108 The balance would have been Fr. 967 million in 1871, Fr. 1,939 million in 1872 and Fr. 1,554 million in 1873 if the German indemnity had not been deducted. Lévy-Leboyer, 'La balance des paiements', p. 120

109 Respectively, Fr. 5.9 billion for Britain and Fr. 2.6 million for France between 1874 and 1880 according to Lévy-Leboyer, 'La balance des paiements', p. 120, and Imlah, 'British balance of payments', p. 237.

110 Cited by J. Bouvier, *Les Rothschild*, Paris, 1963, pp. 213–14.

111 Fould, Sellière, Hottinguer, Mallet, André & Marcuard and Pillet-Will.

112 See J. Jonker, *Merchants, Bankers, Middlemen. The Amsterdam Money Market during the First Half of the 19th Century*, Amsterdam, 1996.

113 Wilkins, *History of Foreign Investment in the United States to 1914*, pp. 117–18.

114 B. S. Chlepner, *Le marché financier belge depuis cent ans*, Brussels, 1930, pp. 50–4.

115 H. van der Wee and M. Goossens, 'Belgium', in R. Cameron and V. I. Bovykin, *International Banking 1870–1914*, Oxford, 1991, p. 118.

116 Maurice de Hirsch, born in Munich, settled in Belgium from 1851, aged 20, and in 1855 married Clara, the daughter of Jonathan-Raphaël Bischoffsheim. A railway tycoon in central and eastern Europe, he is often described as one of the wealthiest Europeans of his time. Jacques Errera, the son of a rich Venetian banker, married one of Joseph Oppenheim's daughters in 1857. In 1871 he founded the Banque de Bruxelles with a group of Belgian financiers. Franz Philippson, originally from Magdeburg and destined for a brilliant career, learnt the ropes in the 1860s in the Banque Errera-Oppenheim.

117 S. Tilman, 'Portrait collectif de grands banquiers belges Bruxelles-Liège-Anvers (1830–1935): contribution à une histoire des élites', doctoral thesis, Université Libre de Bruxelles, 2003–2004, vol. II, pp. 348–84.

118 Henry Hentsch & Cie, Lombard, Odier & Cie, de Candolle, Turretini & Cie (currently the house of Pictet & Cie) and Louis Pictet & Cie.

119 With the banking houses Bonna & Cie, Paccard, Ador & Cie and Philippe Roget & fils, which were joined by Chenevière & Cie in 1866.

120 Seitz, *Histoire de la banque à Genève*, pp. 58–60; Mottet, *Regards sur l'histoire des banques et banquiers genevois*, pp. 148–9.

121 The private bankers Charles Hentsch and Constant Paccard, and the stockbroker Jean-David Lenoir.

122 Jean Bouvier, *Le Crédit Lyonnais de 1863 à 1882. Les années de formation d'une banque de dépôts*, 2 vols., Paris, 1961, vol. I, pp. 128–38, vol. II, pp. 602–3.

123 Bussière, *Paribas*, pp. 19–29.

124 Amalgamated since 1945 into the Union Bank of Switzerland.

125 Seitz, *Histoire de la banque à Genève*, pp. 35–9, Mottet, *Regards sur l'histoire des banques et banquiers genevois*, pp. 166.

126 The following paragraphs are mainly based on the book by C.-L. Holtfrerich, *Frankfurt as a Financial Centre. From Medieval Trade Fair to European Banking Centre*, Munich, 1999.

127 The Prussian General Vogel von Falckenstein had, however, argued in favour of Frankfurt as the capital, but to no avail; the Prussian authorities tried to prevent any strengthening of the commercial and financial metropolis.

128 The central bank was nonetheless a private body, its shareholders being represented by a central committee of fifteen members, nine of whom had to be resident in Berlin, which met each month to discuss the board of directors' report.

129 Wilhelm Carl Rothschild died in that year without leaving any male descendants, and the other members of the family – in London, Vienna and Paris – abandoned the idea of continuing to do business in their city of origin.

130 The building of the Erie Canal, approved in 1817 and completed in 1825, played a decisive role here. With a length of 584 kilometres, it linked New

York to Lake Erie and, for the first time, opened up an economical and fast route across the Appalachians from east to west, from the Atlantic to the Great Lakes.
131 See R. G. Albion, *The Rise of New York Port (1815–1860)*, New York, 1939; C. Kindleberger, 'The formation of financial centers', *Princeton Studies in International Finance*, 36, 1974, pp. 1–78.
132 See Sylla, 'Shaping the US financial system'.
133 See S. Bekert, *The Monied Metropolis. New York City and the Consolidation of the American Bourgeoisie 1850–1896*, Cambridge, 2001.

3. A GLOBALISED WORLD, 1875–1914

1 See L. Neal, 'Integration of international capital markets: quantitative evidence from the eighteenth to the twentieth centuries', *Journal of Economic History*, 45, 2, 1985, pp. 219–26; S. Homer and R. Sylla, *A History of Interest Rates*, 3rd edn, revised with a foreword by H. Kaufman, New Brunswick, 1996.
2 P. Bairoch, *Victoires et déboires. Histoire économique et sociale du monde du XVIe siècle à nos jours*, 3 vols., Paris, 1997, vol. II, pp. 175–9.
3 Ibid., p. 123.
4 Ibid., p. 127.
5 In 1900 the number of telegrams sent worldwide was of the order of 500 million per year. The financial centres were heavy users of them: 6.5 million telegrams, or one every 5 seconds, were exchanged between London and the rest of Europe in 1907, and 5,000 of them are believed to have been sent each day between London and New York alone, or nearly 1.5 million per year, on the eve of the first World War.
6 The telephone was invented in 1876 by Alexander Graham Bell, who set up the first network in New Haven less than two years later.
7 It was invented by, among others, the Italian Gugliemo Marconi, who emigrated to Great Britain in 1896 to develop his invention on a commercial basis.
8 P. Bairoch, *Commerce extérieur et développement économique de l'Europe au XIXe siècle*, Paris, 1976.
9 Simon, 'The pattern of new British portfolio investment, 1865–1914', in A. R. Hall (ed.), *The Export of Capital from Britain 1870–1914*, London, 1968, p. 23.
10 J. Marseille, *Empire colonial et capitalisme français. Histoire d'un divorce*, Paris, 1984, pp. 100–1.
11 A. Imlah, 'British balance of payments and the export of capital, 1816–1913', *Economic History Review*, 2nd ser., 2, 1952, pp. 237–9; M. Lévy-Leboyer, 'La balance des paiements et l'exportation des capitaux français', in Lévy-Leboyer (ed.), *La position internationale de la France. Aspects économiques et sociaux*, Paris, 1977, pp. 120–1.
12 On these issues, see G. Jones, *The Evolution of International Business*, London, 1996.
13 L. E. Davis and R. J. Cull, *International Capital Markets and American Economic Growth 1820–1914*, Cambridge, 1994, p. 81.

14 Jones, *Evolution of International Business*, p. 30.

15 M. Wilkins, 'The free-standing company, 1870–1914: an important type of British foreign direct investment', *Economic History Review*, 41, 2, 1988, pp. 259–85.

16 The Hongkong and Shanghai Banking Corporation, the Chartered Bank of India, Australia and China, the London and River Plate Bank, and many others.

17 On Great Britain's dominant position before 1914, see F. Crouzet, *L'économie de la Grande-Bretagne victorienne*, Paris, 1978, pp. 17–25.

18 In 1870 the United Kingdom's GDP, measured in dollars of 1985, came to $82 billion and that of the United States to $90 billion. In 1913 the figures were $184 and $472 billion respectively. Even in terms of per capita income, while Britain retained a small lead over the United States in 1870 ($2,610 compared with $2,247), this was no longer the case on the eve of the war ($4,024 to $4,854). A. Maddison, *Dynamic Forces in Capitalist Development*, Oxford, 1991, pp. 199, 6–7.

19 See S.B. Saul, *Studies in British Overseas Trade, 1870–1914*, Liverpool, 1960, and F. Crouzet, 'Commerce extérieur et empire: l'expérience britannique du libre-échange à la Première Guerre mondiale', *Annales E.S.C.*, 19, 2, 1964.

20 Barry Eichengreen and Marc Flandreau, 'The geography of the gold standard', in J. Braga de Macedo, B. Eichengreen and J. Reis (eds.), *Currency Convertibility. The Gold Standard and Beyond*, London, 1996, pp. 113–43.

21 At that time, the production of silver literally exploded thanks to electrolysis, which enabled this metal to be extracted from different ores that were more abundant in their natural state, such as copper.

22 If the automatic adjustment of balances of payment or the idea that the central banks followed the strict monetary 'rules of the game' are ruled out as explanations. See B. Eichengreen, *Globalizing Capital. A History of the International Monetary System*, Princeton, 1996.

23 *Journal of the Institute of Bankers*, 1904, p. 58.

24 R. Michie, *The City of London. Continuity and Change, 1850–1990*, Basingstoke and London, 1992, p. 14.

25 *The Economist*, 20 May 1911, p. 1059.

26 S. Chapman, *The Rise of Merchant Banking*, London, 1984, pp. 105–7, 209.

27 The Baring crisis is discussed below in this chapter.

28 Liabilities on acceptances: £14.4 million for the Dresdner Bank, £12.5 for the Disconto-Gesellschaft, £5.7 for the Crédit Lyonnais, £7.8 million for the London County and Westminster Bank and £5.8 million for the Union Bank of London. Chapman, *Rise of Merchant Banking*.

29 A.R. Hall, *The London Capital Market and Australia, 1870–1914*, Canberra, 1963, p. 72.

30 Chapman, *Rise of Merchant Banking*, p. 58; R. Roberts, 'What's in a name? Merchants, merchant bankers, accepting houses, issuing houses, industrial bankers and investment bankers', *Business History*, 35, 3, 1993, p. 25.

31 Y. Cassis, *City bankers, 1890–1914*, Cambridge, 1994, pp. 30–1.

32 Many were of foreign origin, including Seligman Brothers, also present in New York having arrived in London in 1864, Lazard Frères, founded in Paris in 1854, established in New York in 1859, then in London in 1877, and A. Rüffer & Co., which came from Lyons in 1872 – all members of the Accepting Houses Committee.

33 See N. Ferguson, *The World's Banker. The History of the House of Rothschild*, London, 1998.

34 It placed 28.7% of the issues floated by these railways with the merchant banks on the London market between 1865 and 1890. D. Adler, *British Investment in American Railways, 1834–1898*, Charlottesville, 1970, pp. 143–4.

35 See the section on the Bank of England further on in this chapter.

36 Most often with Morgan, Baring Brothers headed several issue syndicates in cooperation with the Banque de Paris et des Pays-Bas in Paris and with Deutsche Bank in Berlin.

37 See P. Ziegler, *The Sixth Great Power. Barings, 1762–1929*, London, 1988.

38 Initially a partner of George Peabody, Junius Spencer Morgan, a member of New England's business elite tempted by the prospects offered by the London market, succeeded him in 1864.

39 See K. Burk, *Morgan Grenfell 1838–1988. The Biography of a Merchant Bank*, Oxford, 1989.

40 Kleinworts' liabilities in acceptances were five times higher than its capital, and Schröders' were four times higher, whereas the norm for other firms was from three to four times higher. See R. Roberts, *Schroders. Merchants & Bankers*, Basingstoke and London, 1992; J. Wake, *Kleinwort Benson. The History of two Families in Banking*, Oxford, 1997.

41 Michie, *City of London*, p. 17.

42 Half the firms represented between 1870 and 1914 were merchant houses, a little over a third merchant banks, and 15% industrial firms. Y. Cassis, *La City de Londres, 1870–1914*, Paris, 1987, p. 93.

43 S. Chapman, *Merchant Enterprise in Britain*, Cambridge, 1992, pp. 209–11.

44 Michie, *City of London*, p. 39.

45 S. Chapman, 'British-based investment groups before 1914', *Economic History Review*, 38, 2, 1985, pp. 230–51.

46 This was particularly the case for Finlay & Co., which had a strong foothold in India, with interests in banking, textile manufacturing (cotton, jute and silk), coal mines, shipping companies and tea plantations; for Butterfield & Swire, involved primarily in China in docks, shipping companies and silk mills; while the interests of Balfour Williamson, who settled in the City in 1909, mainly centred on Latin America, but also concerned fields as diverse as cement, milling, the steel industry, coal mining and oil. Plenty of others could be mentioned, including Ralli Brothers in India, Knoop in Russia and Wernher Beit in South Africa.

47 Points of reference on the size of the largest European companies can be found in Y. Cassis, *Big Business. The European Experience in the Twentieth Century*, Oxford, 1997, pp. 3–11.

48 An international finance house that held, among others, stakes in the Swedish railways. It was the first opportunity for Cassel, who laid the foundations for his fortune by introducing the Gilchrist-Thomas process in the Swedish processing of iron ore in the early 1880s.

49 In particular, the Texas & Pacific, the New York, Ontario & Western and the Mexican Central.

50 The company's success remained limited and the plan to be involved, with Deutsche Bank, in financing the Baghdad railway to open up oil prospects in Mesopotamia came to nothing.

51 E. Halévy, *Histoire du peuple anglais au XIXe siècle*, epilogue II, *Vers la démocratie sociale et vers la guerre (1905–1914)*, Paris, 1932, pp. 550–4.

52 Lloyds Bank, for example, paid Barnetts, Hoare & Co. the equivalent of seven years' profit to buy it out in 1884, even though its manager, Howard Lloyd, considered that as a general rule five years constituted a perfectly fair upper limit. R. S. Sayers, *Lloyds Bank in the History of English Banking*, Oxford, 1957, p. 148.

53 The Birmingham and Midland Bank acquired the Central Bank of London for this purpose.

54 In 1904 the two largest advances granted by the London and County Bank were the £750,000 to the Hongkong and Shanghai Bank and the £500,000 to the London and River Plate Bank, which illustrated the importance of the interbank services provided by the City of London.

55 C.A.E. Goodhart, *The Business of Banking, 1891–1914*, London, 1972.

56 Parr's Bank took over the leadership of a consortium in charge of issuing a loan of £10 million to the Japanese government; the Midland Bank did likewise to issue £3.4 million worth of bonds on behalf of the Aramavir-Touapsé railway, backed by the Russian government; Lloyds Bank issued bonds for a value of £2 million for the municipality of Budapest, together with Neuman Luebeck & Co., a company recently founded with the fortune accumulated in South Africa by Sir Sigmund Neumann.

57 In 1913 the Midland Bank acted as the London agent for 156 foreign banks, compared with only 6 in 1892; the London County and Westminster Bank represented more than 200 foreign banks in London, compared with only seven for the London and County Bank in 1892, and apparently none for the London and Westminster Bank.

58 S. Battilossi, 'Financial innovation and the golden age of international banking: 1890–1931 and 1958–81', *Financial History Review*, 7, 2, 2000, pp. 150–1; M. Flandreau and F. Gallice, 'Paris, London and the international money market: lessons from Paribas, 1885–1913', in Y. Cassis and E. Bussière (eds.), *London and Paris as International Financial Centres in the Twentieth Century*, Oxford, 2005, pp. 79–106.

59 G. Jones, *British Multinational Banking 1830–1990*, Oxford, 1993, pp. 394–7.

60 Cassis, *La City de Londres*, p. 39.

61 The Chartered Bank of India, Australia and China, the Standard Bank of South Africa, the Bank of Australasia and the Union Bank of Australia, and the London and River Plate Bank.

62 The London and River Plate Bank, for example, issued only two loans on behalf of Argentina at the beginning of the 1890s; in other words, during the eclipse of Baring Brothers.

63 Jones, *British Multinational Banking*, pp. 119–30.

64 Cited by J. Bouvier, *Le Crédit Lyonnais de 1863 à 1882. Les années de formation d'une banque de dépôts*, 2 vols., Paris, 1961, vol. II, pp. 577–9.

65 The Crédit Lyonnais, the Société Générale, the Comptoir d'escompte and the CIC for the French; Deutsche Bank, the Dresdner Bank and the Disconto-Gesellschaft for the Germans. Until 1913 the American national banks were not authorised to open branches abroad and so were not present in the City. The trust companies, on the other hand, were not subject to this legislation, and six of them opened a branch there, the most important being the Guaranty Trust Company of New York.

66 *Bankers' Magazine*, 80, 1905, p. 19.

67 F. Gallice, 'Le Crédit Lyonnais à Londres 1870–1939', in B. Desjardins et al. (eds.), *Le Crédit Lyonnais (1863–1986)*, Geneva, 2003, pp. 499–519.

68 This was in the region of £15 million per annum between 1875 and 1904 and reached nearly £24 million during the decade preceding the First World War. See Imlah, 'British balance of payments', pp. 237–9.

69 B. Supple, 'Corporate growth and structural change in a service industry: insurance 1870–1914', in B. Supple (ed.), *Essays in British Business History*, Oxford, 1977, pp. 70–2.

70 B. Supple, *The Royal Exchange Assurance. A History of British Insurance 1720–1970*, Oxford, 1970, p. 295.

71 These changes implied that insurance companies were far more active on the stock exchange; 60% of their investment went through the London Stock Exchange in 1913, compared with 25% in 1880.

72 See Y. Cassis, 'The emergence of a new financial institution: investment trusts in Britain 1870–1939', in J.J. van Helten and Y. Cassis (eds.), *Capitalism in a Mature Economy. Financial Institutions, Capital Exports and British Industry*, Aldershot, 1990, pp. 139–58.

73 The issue leaflet from the Foreign and Colonial Government Trust claimed in 1868 that according to the plan it put forward: 'A capitalist who at any time within the last twenty or thirty years had invested, say £1,000,000 in 10 or 12 stocks selected with ordinary prudence, would, on the above plan, not only have received a high rate of interest, but by this time have received back his original capital by the action of the drawings and sinking fund, and held the greater part of his stock for nothing.' Cited by E.T. Powell, *The Evolution of the Money Market*, London, 1915, p. 467.

74 *Bankers' Magazine*, 56, 1893, pp. 165–73.

75 Y. Cassis, *City Bankers, 1890–1914*, Cambridge, 1994.

76 D. Kynaston, *The City of London*, vol. II, *Golden Age 1890–1914*, London, 1994, p. 21.

77 In the second half of the eighteenth century, their clientele comprised long-established colonial firms, like Hudson's Bay, shipping companies, like the Peninsular & Oriental Steam Navigation Company, banks and mining

companies in England and abroad, as well as the large insurance market, Lloyd's of London.

78 Under the name of McAuliffe, Davis, Bell & Co. As the auditor in London for the trading and investment company Harrison & Crosfield, McAuliffe, Davis & Hope extended its activities to the Far East and opened an office in Penang in 1909, another one in Singapore in 1912 and a third in Kota Bahru in 1915.

79 R. Michie, *The London Stock Exchange. A History*, Oxford, 1999, p. 88.

80 L. Davis and L. Neal, 'Micro rules and macro outcomes: the impact of micro structures on the efficiency of security exchanges, London, New York and Paris, 1800–1914', *American Economic Review*, 88, 2, 1998, pp. 40–5.

81 See Michie, *Stock Exchange*; D. Kynaston, 'The London Stock Exchange, 1870–1914: an institutional history', doctoral thesis, University of London, 1983.

82 The membership fee went, with successive increases, from 50 guineas in 1870 to 500 in 1901 (from £52.5 to £525), without the Committee for General Purposes raising any objections. Various attempts at reform were made between 1876 and 1914, with the underlying idea of making each member a shareholder, and in 1904 it was decided that each new member would have to acquire three shares, at that time worth between £150 and £250 for paid-in capital of £13.

83 Furthermore, 300 of the largest firms signed a petition against these new measures, but in vain, they would have to wait nearly 80 years to have their wishes granted.

84 The bid-asked spread was often far greater for less frequently traded stocks, mainly securities in British manufacturing companies, insofar as the jobber, who set the rates without knowing whether the broker was the buyer or the seller, did not know at which price he could procure or resell these securities.

85 Michie, *Stock Exchange*, pp. 133–5.

86 In fact, buying on the stock exchange was essentially done on the basis of loans, in a proportion that reached 80% in the mid-1890s and even 90% fifteen years later; so much so that at the beginning of August 1914, brokers and jobbers owed more than £80 million to the City's banks and other financial institutions.

87 W. T. C. King, *A History of the London Discount Market*, London, 1936, p. 282.

88 H. Withers, *The Meaning of Money*, London, 1910, p. 210.

89 R.S. Sayers, *The Bank of England 1891–1944*, Cambridge, 1976, pp. 37–43.

90 H. Bonin, 'Le Crédit Lyonnais, la Société générale et les autres: essai d'appréciation des rapports de force (1864–1966)', in B. Desjardins *et al.* (eds.), *Le Crédit Lyonnais, (1863–1986)*, Geneva, 2003, pp. 725–49.

91 Besides London, the Crédit Lyonnais was present in Geneva, Brussels, Alexandria, Cairo, Constantinople, Smyrna, Jerusalem, Madrid, Barcelona, Lisbon and St Petersburg. The Comptoir d'escompte was the only French deposit bank present in Australia and India – it had wound up its branches in China and Japan.

92 See, among others, A. Autheman, *La Banque impériale ottomane*, Paris, 1996; E. Eldem, *A History of the Ottoman Bank*, Istanbul, 1999.

93 Both a state bank (as well as its privilege of issuing Turkish paper money, it was in charge of all Treasury transactions on behalf of the Ottoman government) and a merchant bank (it held a very strong position in all Ottoman issues, which were mainly placed in the Paris centre), it was comparable in size to the main British overseas banks, with total assets worth slightly over £24 million sterling in 1913.

94 See M. Meuleau, *Des pionniers en Extrême-Orient: histoire de la Banque de l'Indochine (1875–1975)*, Paris, 1989.

95 See S. Saul, 'Banking alliances and international issues on the Paris capital market, 1890–1914', in Cassis and Bussière (eds.), *London and Paris as International Financial Centres*, pp. 119–50.

96 Paribas's investments went from Fr. 52 to Fr. 156 million between 1900 and 1913, a period during which it pulled out of eastern Europe, mainly in favour of Latin America. See E. Bussière, *Paribas 1872–1992. L'Europe et le monde*, Antwerp, 1992.

97 See H. Bonin, *La Banque de l'union parisienne (1874/1904–1974). Histoire de la deuxième grande banque d'affaires française*, Paris, 2001.

98 The Anglo-Egyptian Bank, the London and Brazilian Bank, the London and River Plate Bank and the Hongkong and Shanghai Banking Corporation all had branches in Paris.

99 In 1911 Lloyds Bank bought up the Armstrong & Cie bank in Paris, re-christened Lloyds Bank (France), and the Westminster Bank set up a subsidiary there in 1913, the Westminster Foreign Bank. Less involved in Paris's activities as an international financial centre, their main goal was to attract an Anglo-Saxon clientele residing in France.

100 E. Kaufmann, *La banque en France*, Paris, 1914, pp. 191–201; L. Dufourq-Lagelouse, *Les banques étrangères en France*, Paris, 1922.

101 Kaufmann, *La banque en France*, pp. 166–74. The corporate names were: de Rothschild Frères, Hottinguer & Cie, Mallet Frères, Vernes & Cie, Mirabaud & Cie, de Neuflize & Cie, Heine & Cie and Demachy & F. Seillière.

102 Ferguson, *World's Banker*, p. 1039. This was an absolutely enormous sum that the big banks only exceeded, thanks to their deposits, in the 1880s.

103 One of the most famous was the Chemin de Fer du Nord, in which they had five places on the board of directors in 1869 and six in 1933.

104 J. P. McKay, 'The House of Rothschild (Paris) as multinational industrial enterprise: 1875–1914', in A. Teichova, M. Lévy-Leboyer and H. Nussbaum (eds.), *Multinational Enterprise in Historical Perspective*, Cambridge, 1986, pp. 74–86. Peñarroya had silver and lead mines in Spain, Le Nickel oilfields in New Caledonia and the Société du Boléo copper mines in Mexico; BNITO is made up of the Russian initials of the oil company that the Rothschilds acquired in 1886 and sold in 1912 to Royal Dutch, in which they thus became the largest shareholders.

105 A. Plessis, 'La haute banque parisienne et l'économie internationale au XIX*e* siècle et au début du XX*e* siècle', paper presented at the colloquium 'The World of Private Banking', London, 22–23 May 1998.

106 In his survey on French banking at the beginning of the twentieth century, Eugen Kaufmann estimated the number of private banks in Paris at some 150, in addition to the banking houses of the *haute banque*. Kaufmann, *La banque en France*, p. 175.

107 This was the case for Lazard Frères, E. N. Raphaël, Seligmann Frères and A. J. Stern.

108 N. J. and S. Bardac were closely linked to the Imperial Ottoman Bank, I. Camondo & Cie, which came from Constantinople, to the Banque de Paris et des Pays-Bas, and Gans & Cie to Deutsche Bank, which was a limited partner in it.

109 M. Flandreau, 'Central bank cooperation in historical perspective: a sceptical view', *Economic History Review*, 50, 4, 1997, pp. 735–63.

110 Moreover, throughout this period, the Banque de France's rates were much more stable and, in general, lower than those of the Bank of England – a policy by which the French central bank set great store.

111 Robert Warschauer & Co., F. Mart Magnus and Gebrüder Schickler were among Berlin's other prominent banking houses.

112 Founded under the name of Königliche Giro- und Lehnbanco, it became the Preussiche Bank in 1846.

113 C.-L. Holtfrerich, 'The monetary unification process in 19th century Germany: relevance and lessons for Europe today', in M. de Cecco and A. Giovannini (eds.), *A European Central Bank? Perspectives on Monetary Unification after Ten Years of the EMS*, Cambridge, 1989, pp. 216–41.

114 F. Stern, *Gold and Iron. Bismarck, Bleichröder and the Building of the German Empire*, New York, 1977, pp. 180–1.

115 It is true that there was a shortage of gold in the world at that time and that a long period of deflation was about to begin. The new German monetary system nevertheless included a safety valve against the gold shortage, since banknotes in marks only had to be 40% covered by gold and not 100%, as was the case in England.

116 H. James, 'The Reichsbank 1876 1945', in Deutsche Bundesbank (ed.), *Fifty Years of the Deutsche Mark. Central Bank and the Currency in Germany since 1948*, Oxford, 1999, pp. 3–53.

117 R. Tilly, 'International aspects of the development of German Banking', in R. Cameron and V.I. Bovykin (eds.), *International Banking 1870–1914*, Oxford, 1991, p. 106.

118 R. Tilly, 'Berlin als preussiches und deutsches Finanzzentrum und seine Beziehungen zu den anderen Zentren in Ost und West', in W. Ribbe and J. Schmädeke (eds.), *Berlin in Europa der Neuzeit*, Berlin, New York, 1990, pp. 202–4.

119 J. Riesser, *Zur Entwicklung der deutschen Grossbanken mit besonderer Rücksicht auf die Konzentrationsbestrebungen*, Jena, 1906, p. 228.

120 This mixture of activities naturally brought the big banks closer to the country's large industrial firms. The extent of their influence, indeed their

power over these firms and thus even over the entire German economy, has stirred up considerable controversy ever since the publication in 1910 of the famous book by Rudolf Hilferding, *Das Finanzkapital*. It is not our intention to reopen this debate here, other than to point out that the latest research has shown that the weight of the big banks in the German economy has been largely overestimated in economic and political literature. See, in particular, V. Wellhöner, *Grossbanken und Grossindustrie im Kaiserreich*, Göttingen, 1989; J. Edwards and S. Ogilvie, 'Universal banks and German industrialization: a reappraisal', *Economic History Review*, 49, 3, 1996. For a dissenting voice, see P. Marguerat, 'Banques mixtes et grandes entreprises industrielles en Allemagne, 1880–1913: du mythe à l'antimythe', in P. Marguerat, L. Tissot and Y. Froidevaux (eds.), *Banques et entreprises industrielles en Europe de l'Ouest, XIXe–XXe siècles: aspects nationaux et régionaux*, Geneva, 2000, pp. 29–58.

121 See Stern, *Gold and Iron*, part II.

122 See W. Treue, 'Das Bankhaus Mendelssohn als Beispiel einer Privatbank im 19. und 20. Jahrhundert', in C. Lowenthal-Hensel, *Mendelssohn Studien. Beiträge zur neueren deutschen Kultur und Wirtschaftsgeschichte*, vol. I, Berlin, 1972; P. Emden, *Money Powers of Europe in the Nineteenth and Twentieth Centuries*, London, 1938.

123 P. Hertner, 'German banks abroad before 1914', in G. Jones (ed.), *Banks as Multinationals*, London, 1990.

124 Two other banks were founded to operate in Latin America, one in 1887 by the Disconto-Gesellschaft and its ally the Norddeutsche Bank (Brasilianische Bank für Deutschland), headquartered in Hamburg; the other in 1905 by the Dresdner Bank, the Schaafhausenscher Bankverein and the National Bank für Deutschland (Deutsch-Südamerikanische Bank).

125 The three main shareholders each acquired 550 shares out of a total of 5,000 issued. Moreover, in 1905 the Dresdner Bank, the Schaafhausenscher Bankverein and the National Bank für Deutschland founded the Deutsche Orientbank, active above all in the Maghreb and the Middle East.

126 None of the twenty-one others, including the Cologne, Munich or Düsseldorf stock exchanges, reached 2%. R. Gömmel, 'Entstehung und Entwicklung der Effektenbörse im 19. Jahrhundert bis 1914', in H. Pohl (ed.), *Deutsche Börsengeschichte*, Frankfurt am Main, 1992, pp. 135–210.

127 Ibid., pp. 170–9.

128 Germany's share of exports in world trade reached 13.1% in 1913, just behind England's 13.9%. S. Pollard, *Britain's Prime and Britain's Decline. The British Economy 1870–1914*, London, 1989, p. 6.

129 Sweden, Denmark, Romania, Italy and Austria-Hungary for example.

130 See, for example, G. Diouritch, *L'expansion des banques allemandes à l'étranger*, Paris, 1909.

131 See Davis and Cull, *International Capital*.

132 Drexel & Co. was one of the main American merchant banks, based in Philadelphia but also present in New York, London and Paris. From 1876

John Pierpont Morgan took over the leadership of the New York banking house that became Drexel, Morgan & Co.

133 See B. Supple, 'A business elite: German–Jewish financiers in nineteenth century New York', *Business History Review*, 31, 2, 1957, pp. 143–78.

134 Jacob Schiff belonged to a distinguished family of academics and businessmen from Frankfurt. Having disembarked in the United States in 1865, aged 18, he returned to Germany in 1872, before returning to settle permanently in the United States and being invited by Salomon Loeb, whose daughter he married, to join his bank.

135 J.B. de Long, 'Did J.P. Morgan's men add value? An economist's perspective on financial capitalism', in P. Temin (ed.), *Inside the Business Enterprise. Historical Perspectives on the Use of Information*, Chicago and London, 1991, pp. 205–36.

136 V. Carosso, *Investment Banking in America: A History*, Cambridge, Mass., 1970, p. 91.

137 Burk, *Morgan Grenfell*, p. 62.

138 Speyer & Co. in New York were linked to Speyer Brothers in London and Lazard Speyer-Ellisen in Frankfurt; and J. & W. Seligman & Co. in New York were linked to Seligman Brothers in London and Seligman Frères & Cie in Paris.

139 A member of the Baring family was a partner in Kidder Peabody, New York. Ziegler, *Sixth Great Power*, pp. 220–3.

140 One of the partners, Felix Warburg, married Jacob Schiff's daughter in 1895, and his brother Paul married one of Salomon Loeb's daughters six months later. R. Rosenbaum and A. J. Sherman, *M.M. Warburg & Co. 1798 1938. Merchant Bankers of Hamburg*, London, 1979; R. Chernow, *The Warburgs. A Family Saga*, London, 1993.

141 See, among others, E. White, *The Regulation and Reform of the American Banking System*, Princeton, 1983.

142 Percentage calculated from M. Myers, *The New York Money Market*, vol. I, *Origins and Development*, New York, 1931, p. 248.

143 James Stillman, chairman of the National City Bank from 1891 to 1911, became allied with Kuhn Loeb in particular, by offering him placing facilities within the framework of the reorganisation of the Union Pacific railway. His network of contacts included, among others, William Rockefeller, brother of James D. and chairman of the Standard Oil Company of New York. H. van B. Cleveland and T. Huertas, *Citibank 1812–1970*, Cambridge, Mass., 1985, pp. 32–53.

144 L. Neal, 'Trust companies and financial innovation, 1897–1914', *Business History Review*, 45, 1, 1971.

145 V. Carosso, *Investment Banking in America. A History*, Cambridge, Mass., 1970, pp. 47, 125.

146 R. Michie, *The London and New York Stock Exchanges*, London, 1987, pp. 168–70.

147 The effects of such a restricted intake immediately made themselves felt on the negotiated membership fee, which increased from $3,000 in 1862 to $10,000 in 1866 and fluctuated between $65,000 and $94,000

in 1910. Remember that the fee at the time was a little over $2,500 in London.

148 The London Stock Exchange, where up until the 1890s more American stocks were quoted than in New York, with the exception of railway company securities, should not be overlooked in this distribution of tasks.

149 Burk, *Morgan Grenfell*, pp. 111–23.

150 Granville Farquhar to Edward Hamilton, the permanent secretary to the British Treasury, in February 1901. *Edward Hamilton's Diary*, Add Mss 48,614, 6 February 1901, cited by Kynaston, *City of London*, vol. II, p. 222.

151 Carosso, *Investment Banking*, pp. 80–2.

152 The national banks could not actually own branches abroad, so the entire group of American banks had only 26 foreign branches in 1913, compared with nearly 1,400 for the British banks and around 500 for the French and German banks. M. Wilkins, 'Banks over borders: some evidence from their pre-1914 history', in G. Jones (ed.), *Banks as Multinationals*, London, 1990, p. 232.

153 The Chartered Bank, the Hongkong and Shanghai Banking Corporation, the London and River Plate Bank and the Standard Bank, just to mention the most important ones, the others operating in the Americas.

154 M. Wilkins, *The History of Foreign Investment in the United States to 1914*, Cambridge, Mass., 1989, pp. 453–69.

155 See M. Friedman and A. J. Schwartz, *A Monetary History of the United States 1867–1960*, Princeton, 1963, pp. 156–68.

156 Sayers, *Bank of England*, pp. 58–60.

157 Arsène Pujo, Democrat member of Congress for Louisiana, chaired the Commission of Enquiry.

158 See Carosso, *Investment Banking*, pp. 137–55.

159 G.D. Smith and R. Sylla, 'Capital markets', in S. Kutler *et al.* (eds.)., *Encyclopedia of the United States in the Twentieth Century*, New York, 1996, vol. III, pp. 1209–42.

160 Their geographical distribution reflects the socio-economic development of the United States at the time, with five banks on the east coast (Boston, New York, Philadelphia, Richmond and Atlanta), six in the mid-west (Cleveland, Chicago, Minneapolis, St Louis, Kansas and Dallas) and only one in the west (San Francisco). Note that the state of Missouri had two (in St Louis and Kansas City–Missouri), a concession made to obtain from the senators of this state the votes needed to pass the law.

161 By 1913 the Société Générale de Belgique's total assets came to £71.9 million sterling, compared with £32.2 million for the Swiss Bank Corporation, £21.6 million for the Crédit Suisse and £20.5 million for the Nederlandsche Handel-Maatschappij.

162 In the 1890s the Société Générale de Belgique acquired holdings in the Banque Russo-Chinoise, the Anglo-Argentine Bank and the Banque Française du Brésil. In 1902 it founded the Banque Sino-Belge, which formed the linchpin of its international expansion by becoming the Banque Belge pour l'Etranger in 1913. In 1911 it was involved in founding the Banque Brésilienne Italo-Belge, whose main shareholder was the Credito

Italiano and which took the name of Banque Italo-Belge in 1913. H. van der Wee, 'Belgium', in R. Cameron and V.I. Bovykin (eds.), *International Banking 1870–1914*, Oxford, 1991, p. 125; G. Kurgan-van Hentenryk, 'The Société Générale, 1850–1934', in H. van der Wee (ed.), *The Generale Bank 1822–1997*, Tielt, 1997, pp. 152–67.

163 On the functioning of these holding companies and their role in financing the power industry, see the Swiss case discussed below.

164 Originally created by the Banque de Bruxelles, the Banque de Paris et des Pays-Bas and the private banks Brugmann and Cassel, the Société Générale des Chemins de Fer Economiques absorbed in 1882 the Société Générale des Tramways, founded in 1874 and chiefly operating in Italy, whose main shareholders were the Banque de Bruxelles and its founder, the private banker Jacques Errera.

165 The Compagnie Générale des Chemins de Fer Secondaires was founded in 1880 by the Banque Centrale Anversoise, the private bank Philippson-Horwitz, the Empain group and a German group.

166 Gesfürel stands for Gesellschaft für elektrische Unternehmungen, and UEG for Union Elektricitäts Gesellschaft.

167 The Lamberts' family ties with the Rothschilds were strengthened with the marriage between Léon Lambert, the son of the bank's founder, and Lucie, the daughter of Gustave de Rothschild in 1882.

168 S. Tilman, 'Portrait collectif des grands banquiers belges Bruxelles-Liège-Anvers (1830–1935), Contribution à une histoire des élites', doctoral thesis, Université Libre de Bruxelles, 2003–4, vol. II, pp. 348–84.

169 The Banque de Paris et des Pays-Bas had had a foothold in Brussels since its foundation in 1872, the Crédit Lyonnais since 1888, the Société Générale since 1898 (through the Société française de Banque et de Dépôts), the Comptoir national d'escompte de Paris and the CIC since 1903 and, indirectly, the Crédit du Nord (through its contacts with the Société de Dépôts et de Crédit, founded in 1896).

170 M.-T. Bitsch, *La Belgique entre la France et l'Allemagne 1905–1914*, Paris, 1994, pp. 137–44.

171 G. Kurgan-van Hentenryk, 'Finance and financiers in Belgium, 1880–1914', in Y. Cassis (ed.), *Finance and Financiers in European History 1880–1960*, Cambridge, 1992, p. 322.

172 On the rise of the big banks, see the recent study by M. Mazbouri, *L'émergence de la place financière suisse*, Lausanne, 2005.

173 The Zurich banks were the Crédit Suisse, Leu & Co., the Eidgenössische Bank, which had transferred its headquarters from Bern to Zurich in 1892, and the Bank in Winterthur, which in 1912 became the Union Bank of Switzerland; the Basle banks were the Basler Handelsbank and the Swiss Bank Corporation, whereas Bern only had the Schweizerische Volksbank. Figures calculated from F. Ritzmann, *Die Schweizer Banken. Geschichte – Theorie – Statistik*, Bern, 1973, pp. 261ff.

174 R. Zimmermann, *Volksbank oder Aktienbank? Parlamantsdebatten, Referendum und zunehmende Verbandsmacht beim Streit um die Nationalbankgründung 1891–1905*, Zurich, 1987.

175 The chairman's department and the department responsible for both discount and transfer operations were located in Zurich, whereas the department responsible for issuing banknotes and for relations with the Federal Administration was in Bern. *Banque Nationale Suisse 1907–1957*, Bern, 1957, p. 36.

176 See Y. Cassis, 'Swiss international banking, 1900–1950', in Jones (ed.), *Banks as Multinationals*, pp. 160–72.

177 W.A. Jöhr, *Schweizerische Kreditanstalt 1856–1956*, Zurich, 1956, pp. 208–9; Wirtschaftsarchiv Basel, 623, Schweizerisch-Südamerikanische Bank.

178 With a capital of 20 million francs (of which 10 million were paid up), 75% held by the Crédit Suisse and 25% by the Eidgenössische Bank, this bank had its headquarters in Zurich, with branches in Lugano and Buenos Aires, where it shared its management with the Hypothekenbank.

179 It was opened at the initiative of its chairman, J. J. Schuster-Burckhardt, who like many of his European colleagues was determined to take advantage of the business opportunities offered by the City.

180 H. Bauer, *Société de Banque Suisse, 1872–1972*, Basle, 1972, pp. 131–8.

181 Moreover, Genevans held key posts at the helm of the bank, with two general managers out of three between 1872 and 1918: Charles Sautter from 1872 to 1892, and Albert Turrettini from 1908 to 1918. See E. Bussière, *Paribas. L'Europe et le monde, 1872–1992*, Antwerp, 1992.

182 Note that until 1935 the Genevan branch was a French regional branch within the organisational structure of the Crédit Lyonnais (in the same way as Marseilles, Nice or Grenoble) and not a foreign branch (like London, Alexandria, Constantinople and others).

183 See Y. Cassis, 'Le Crédit Lyonnais à Genève, 1876–2001', in B. Desjardins *et al.*, *Le Crédit Lyonnais*, pp. 619–20.

184 In the form of the discounting of commercial paper, loans for forward stock-exchange transactions and securities deposits (called Lombard loans in Switzerland and Germany).

185 The Société Belge de Crédit Industriel et Commercial et de Dépôts, the Banque d'Alsace et de Lorraine and the Banque Internationale de Petrograd in particular. L. Mottet, *Regards sur l'histoire des banques et banquiers genevois*, Geneva, 1982, p. 174.

186 The official corporate names were: Bonna & Cie, Chenevière & Cie, Darier & Cie, Ferrier, Lullin & Cie, Galopin, Forget & Cie, Hentsch & Cie, Lenoir, Poulin & Cie, Lombard, Odier & Cie, Mirabaud & Cie and Ernest Pictet & Cie.

187 The Banque nouvelle des chemins de fer had been established in Geneva in 1885 to succeed the Banque des Chemins de Fer, itself created in Basle in 1878 to take over the assets of the Chemin de Fer du Nord-est. Initially interested in financing the Simplon Tunnel, it abandoned this project to set up, with some Paris banks, two finance companies with stakes in Serbia and in the Ottoman Empire. Wound up in 1889 after the collapse of its main partner, the Comptoir d'escompte de Paris, it had to merge with the Association financière.

188 J. Seitz, *Histoire de la banque à Genève*, Geneva, 1931, pp. 86–7, Mottet, *Regards*, pp. 176–7.

189 These were investment companies specialising in one sector of industry or in a specific part of the world, the two often going hand in hand or, somewhat less frequently, practising far greater diversification in their investments, similar to the British investment trusts. See S. Paquier, 'Swiss holding companies from the mid-nineteenth century to the early 1930s: the forerunners and subsequent waves of creation', *Financial History Review*, 8, 2, 2001, pp. 163–82.

190 Several finance companies were founded in Geneva during this period, including the Société Financière Franco-Suisse in 1892 and the Société Financière pour Entreprises Electriques aux Etats-Unis in 1910. *Pictet & Cie 1805–1855*, Geneva, 1955, pp. 52–5.

191 S. Paquier, 'Banques, sociétés financières, industrie électrique de 1895 à 1914', in Y. Cassis and J. Tanner (eds.), *Banques et crédit en Suisse (1850–1930)*, Zurich, 1993, pp. 242–5. See also his *Histoire de l'électricité en Suisse: La dynamique d'un petit pays européen 1875–1939*, Geneva, 1998.

192 After five successive increases, its initial capital of 30 million francs reached 75 million on the eve of the First World War – in other words, as much as that of the Crédit Suisse – on top of which came Fr. 75 million worth of bonds.

193 The group included the Basler Handelsbank, the Leu & Cie bank and the Berlin private bank Warschauer & Co.

194 See Paquier, 'Banques, sociétés financières, industrie électrique' and P. Hertner, 'Les sociétés financières suisses et le développement de l'industrie électrique jusqu'à la Première Guerre mondiale', in F. Cardot (ed.), *1880–1980. Un siècle d'électricité dans le monde*, Paris, 1987, pp. 341–55.

195 This was particularly the case with regard to increases in share capital and securities trading (both could be undertaken without the firm's capital being fully paid up), to the opportunities that companies had to acquire their own shares, and to the fact that no limit was put on issuing bonds. The absence of stamp duty also made the cost of floating an issue in Switzerland attractive.

196 Between 1905 and 1908, Baring Brothers took part, with Kidder Peabody and other American investment banks, including J. P. Morgan and, on this occasion, Hope & Co. in Amsterdam, in the issue of more than $150 million worth of securities on behalf of American Telephone & Telegraph and of $70 million for its New York subsidiary between 1909 and 1912. J. Orbell, *Baring Brothers & Co. Limited. A History to 1939*, London, 1985, pp. 69–70.

197 The following paragraphs are largely inspired by R. Michie, *The London and New York Stock Exchanges 1870–1914*, London, 1987, pp. 34–98.

198 B. Barth, 'The financial history of the Anatolian and Baghdad railways, 1889–1914', *Financial History Review*, 5, 1998, pp. 115–37.

199 To aid comparison, the amounts of wealth estimated below are all given in dollars of that time. These figures have to be multiplied by fifty to obtain a rough estimation of today's value.

200 D. Augustine, *Patricians and Parvenus. Wealth and High Society in Wilhelmine Germany*, Oxford, 1994, p. 29.

201 The wealth of Baron Max von Goldschmidt-Rothschild was estimated at $39 million and that of Baroness Mathilde von Rothschild at $22 million (163 and 92 million marks respectively). R. Martin, *Das Jahrbuch der Millionäre Deutschlands*, Berlin, 1913.

202 For example, Hans von Bleichröder ($7 million), Paul von Schwabach ($5 million) and James von Bleichröder ($4.2 million) – all partners of the private bank S. Bleichröder.

203 W. D. Rubinstein, *Men of Property*, London, 1981, pp. 62–3.

204 In England, 172 bankers died between 1900 and 1939, with fortunes worth at least $2.5 million (£500,000). It can be roughly estimated that at least twice this number, or 344, were worth $1.5 million in 1911, compared with 136 in Germany, taking into account those who died before 1911, the pound's depreciation, the fortunes made during and after the Great War, the donations *inter vivos* and, finally, the increase in the size of the base as one goes down the wealth pyramid.

205 See A. Daumard, *Les fortunes françaises au XIXème siècle*, Paris, 1973.

206 A. Plessis, *Regents et gouverneurs de la Banque de France sous le Second Empire*, Geneva, 1985.

207 W. D. Rubinstein, 'Introduction' in Rubinstein (ed.), *Wealth and the Wealthy in the Modern World*, London, 1980, p. 19.

208 Ibid., p. 18.

209 S. Beckert, *The Monied Metropolis. New York City and the Consolidation of the American Bourgeoisie, 1850–1896*, Cambridge, 2001, p. 245.

210 The most sought-after clubs were the Carlton, the Reform, Brooks, the Athenaeum, the Travellers and Whites in London; the Jockey Club, the Cercle de l'Union and the Cercle de la Rue Royale in Paris; and the Union Club, the Union League, the Manhattan Club and the Knickerbocker Club in New York.

211 Traditionally referring to trade balance in the broader sense of the word, in other words excluding factor incomes.

212 S. Pollard, 'Capital exports, 1870–1914: harmful or beneficial?', *Economic History Review*, 38, 4, 1985, pp. 489–514.

213 Note that, while his point relating to the links between capital exports and the export of goods was valid for England, this was not, however, borne out for France.

214 See Lysis, *Contre l'oligarchie financière en France*, Paris, 1907 (which brings together his articles published in December 1906 and at the beginning of 1907 in *La Revue*); and Testis, *Le rôle des établissements de crédit en France*, Paris, 1907 (which brings together his articles published in 1907 in *La revue politique et parlementaire*).

215 See M. Flandreau, 'Le service des etudes financières sous Henri Germain (1871–1905): une macro-économie d'acteurs', in Desjardins *et al.* (eds.), *Le Crédit Lyonnais*, pp. 271–301.

216 M. Bordo and H. Rockoff, 'The gold standard as a "Good Housekeeping Seal of Approval"', *Journal of Economic History*, 56, 2, 1996, pp. 389–428.

217 N. Ferguson, 'The City of London and British imperialism: new light on an old question', in Cassis and Bussière (eds.), *London and Paris as International Financial Centres*, pp. 57–77.

218 M. Flandreau and D. Zumer, *The Making of Global Finance 1880–1913*, OECD, 2004.

219 P. J. Cain and A. G. Hopkins, *British Imperialism*, 2 vols., London, 1993.

220 Letter from Ferdinand de Rothschild to Sir Charles Dilke, 14 January 1885, cited by Ferguson, *World's Banker*, p. 849.

221 Kynaston, *City of London*, vol. II, pp. 194–5.

222 *Journal of the Institute of Bankers*, 33, 2, 1912, p. 82.

4. WARS AND DEPRESSION, 1914–1945

1 Cited in P. Ziegler, *The Sixth Great Power. Barings, 1762–1929*, London, 1988, p. 320.

2 E. Hobsbawm, *Age of Extremes. The Short Twentieth Century 1914–1991*, London, 1994.

3 R. Michie, *The London Stock Exchange. A History*, Oxford, 1999, p. 165.

4 See M. de Cecco, *Money and Empire. The International Gold Standard, 1890–1914*, Oxford, 1974.

5 J. Rivoire, *Le Crédit Lyonnais. Histoire d'une banque*, Paris, 1989, p. 106.

6 G. D. Feldman, *The Great Disorder. Politics, Economics, and Society in the German Inflation, 1914–1924*, Oxford, 1997, pp. 34–5.

7 These included Rothschilds, Barings, Morgan Grenfell, Schröders, Kleinworts, Hambros, Lazard and Fredk. Huth.

8 Figures calculated from data provided by Ziegler, *Sixth Great Power*, p. 377.

9 R. Roberts, *Schroders. Merchants & Bankers*, London, 1992, pp. 159–65.

10 D. Artaud, 'Les dettes de guerre de la France, 1919–1929', in M. Lévy-Leboyer (ed.), *La position internationale de la France. Aspects économique et financiers, XIXe–XXe siècles*, Paris, 1977, pp. 313–18.

11 In London, their situation was aggravated by the death of three partners, all aged over 70, in the space of three years. Moreover, the bank sustained heavy losses during the early years of the war – nearly £1.5 million in 1914 and more than £100,000 in 1915.

12 N. Ferguson, *The World's Banker. A History of the House of Rothschild*, London, 1998, pp. 982–3.

13 V. Carosso, *Investment Banking in America. A History*, Cambridge, Mass., 1970, p. 212.

14 K. Burk, *Morgan Grenfell 1838–1988. The Biography of a Merchant Bank*, Oxford, 1989, pp. 125–34.

15 R. Chernow, *The House of Morgan. An American Banking Dynasty and the Rise of Modern Finance*, London, 1990, p. 188.

16 Burk, *Morgan Grenfell*, pp. 268–9.

17 Morgan Grenfell's net profits reached £439,000 in 1915 and £185,000 on average each year for the rest of the war, whereas Barings' exceeded £1 million in 1915 and came up to an average of £589,000 between 1916 and 1918.

18 Baring Archive 204071.1, 'History of the Russian business of Barings 1914–1985'. I thank John Orbell, archivist at ING Barings, for having put this valuable summary, carefully prepared by him, at my disposal.

19 Its commission was usually 1/4%, which may seem low, but the sums were considerable and the transactions involved almost no risk. Barings notably received a commission of 1/16% on the large loan of £300 million contracted in 1915, followed by another loan of £150 million twelve months later, which earned it £281,000 in total.

20 A. R. Holmes and E. Green, *Midland, 150 Years of Banking Business*, London, 1986, p. 128.

21 Rivoire, *Le Crédit Lyonnais*, p. 108.

22 Holmes and Green, *Midland*, p. 128.

23 O. Feiertag, 'Le Crédit Lyonnais et le Trésor public dans l'entre-deux-guerres: les ressorts de l'économie d'endettement du XXe siècle', in B. Desjardins *et al.* (ed.), *Le Crédit Lyonnais 1863–1986*, Geneva, 2003, pp. 805–32; G. D. Feldman, 'The Deutsche Bank from world war to world economic crisis 1914–1933', in L. Gall *et al.*, *The Deutsche Bank 1870–1995*, London, 1995, p. 130.

24 Michie, *London Stock Exchange*, p. 184.

25 F.-W. Henning, 'Börsenkrisen und Börsengesetzgebung von 1914 bis 1945 in Deutschland', in H. Pohl (ed.), *Deutsche Börsengeschichte*, Frankfurt am Main, 1992.

26 A. Plessis, 'When Paris dreamt of competing with the City', in Y. Cassis and E. Bussière (eds.), *London and Paris as International Financial Centres in the Twentieth Century*, Oxford, 2005, pp. 42–54.

27 D. Kynaston, *The City of London, vol. III: Illusions of Gold 1914–1945*, London, 1999, p. 10.

28 A. J. Mayer, *The Persistence of the Old Regime. Europe to the Great War*, London, 1981.

29 C. Feinstein and K. Watson, 'Private international capital flows in Europe in the inter-war period', in C. Feinstein (ed.), *Banking, Currency and Finance in Europe Between the Wars*, Oxford, 1995, p. 98.

30 Between 1913 and 1919, wholesale prices multiplied by 2.0 in the United States, 2.5 in Britain, 3.5 in France and by more than 4.0 in Germany. The differences were of the same order of magnitude for consumer prices.

31 G. Hardach, *The First World War 1914–1918*, London, 1977, p. 172.

32 Charles Dawes, an American businessman and public servant, was the chairman of the Expert Commission in charge of examining the issue, and a Nobel Peace Prize winner in 1925.

33 Including fifty-five branches abroad for the National City Bank of New York alone, which adopted a strategy of global expansion very early on.

34 M. Wilkins, 'Cosmopolitan finance in the 1920s: New York's emergence as an international financial centre', in R. Sylla, R. Tilly and G. Tortella (eds.), *The State, the Financial System and Economic Modernization*, Cambridge, 1999.

35 Established in New York at the initiative of Paul Warburg, and with the participation of American and European investors, including Kuhn Loeb in New York, N. M. Rothschild and the National Provincial in London, the

Banque de Paris et des Pays-Bas, M. M. Warburg in Hamburg, the Banque de Bruxelles, the Crédit Suisse and the Swiss Bank Corporation. M. Wilkins, *The History of Foreign Investment in the United States, 1914–1945*, Cambridge, Mass., 2004, pp. 175–6.

36 B. H. Beckhart, *The New York Money Market*, vol. III, New York, 1932, pp. 310–19.
37 T. Balogh, *Studies in Financial Organization*, Cambridge, 1947, p. 167.
38 Beckhart, *The New York Money Market*, vol. III, pp. 322–5.
39 The foreign issues floated in New York and London amounted to $969 million and $592 million respectively in 1924, to $1,337 and $676 in 1927, and to $671 and $457 million in 1929. K. Burk, 'Money and power: the shift from Great Britain to the United States', in Y. Cassis (ed.), *Finance and Financiers in European History*, Cambridge, 1992, p. 364.
40 Carosso, *Investment Banking in America*, pp. 255–62.
41 H. van B. Cleveland and T. Huertas, *Citibank 1812–1970*, Cambridge, Mass., 1985, pp. 113–58.
42 L. V. Chandler, *Benjamin Strong, Central Banker*, Washington, DC, 1958; H. Clay, *Lord Norman*, London, 1957; B. Eichengreen, *Golden Fetters. The Gold Standard and the Great Depression 1919–1939*, Oxford, 1995; P. Roberts, 'Benjamin Strong, the Federal Reserve and the limits to interwar American nationalism', Federal Reserve Bank of Richmond, *Economic Quarterly*, 86, 2, 2000, pp. 61–98.
43 The figure was thirty-eight in 1923, its drop by the end of the decade mainly being due to the retreat of Polish, Romanian and Czech banks.
44 Wilkins, *Foreign Investment in the United States, 1914–1945*, pp. 274–80.
45 F. Torres, *Banquiers d'avenir. Des comptoirs d'escompte à la naissance de BNP Paribas*, Paris, 2000, p. 64.
46 Roberts, *Schroders*, pp. 214–37.
47 H. Bullock, *The Story of Investment Companies*, New York, 1959, p. 212.
48 In the twenties, foreign issues in New York fluctuated between 15% and 18% of the total amount of new issues, including domestic ones, with troughs of 10% in 1923 and 6% in 1929.
49 Carosso, *Investment Banking in America*, p. 248.
50 Cleveland and Huertas, *Citibank*, pp. 140–3.
51 Wilkins, *Foreign Investment in the United States, 1914–1945*, p. 184.
52 M. L. Jollife, *The United States as a Financial Centre 1919–1933*, Cardiff, 1935, p. 112.
53 L. H. Jenks, *The Migration of British Capital to 1875*, New York, 1927, p. 6.
54 On the pound's return to the gold standard, see also D. E. Moggridge, *British Monetary Policy, 1924–1931*, Cambridge, 1972; S. Howson, *Domestic Monetary Management in Britain, 1919–1939*, Cambridge, 1975; R. S. Sayers, *The Bank of England 1891–1944*, Cambridge, 1976; Eichengreen, *Golden Fetters*; Kynaston, *City of London*, vol. III.
55 See, for example, Sidney Pollard, 'Introduction', in Pollard (ed.), *The Gold Standard and Employment Policies between the Wars*, London, 1970.
56 Moreover, the governor of the Bank of England, Montagu Norman, played a crucial role in the so-called League of Nations loans, intended to stabilise the

economies of central Europe, issued simultaneously in several financial centres between 1922 and 1924, with the City being the financial centre of choice, even if the largest instalments of these loans were placed in New York.

57 P. L. Cottrell, 'Established connections and new opportunities. London as an international financial centre, 1914–1958', in Cassis and Bussière (eds.), *London and Paris as International Financial Centres*, pp. 161–4.

58 Balogh, *Studies in Financial Organization*, p. 167.

59 W. M. Scammel, *The London Discount Market*, London, 1968, pp. 192–219.

60 J. Wake, *Kleinwort Benson. The History of Two Families in Banking*, Oxford, 1997, pp. 213–16.

61 Michie, *London Stock Exchange*, pp. 245–56.

62 See Clay, *Lord Norman*; Sayers, *Bank of England*; Kynaston, *City of London*, vol. III.

63 In 1929 three subsidiaries belonging to four of the 'Big Five' – the Lloyds and National Provincial Foreign Bank, the Westminster Foreign Bank and Barclays Bank (France), the Midland Bank having bucked the trend – had forty-two branches in Europe, mainly in France. See G. Jones, 'Lombard Street on the Riviera: The British clearing banks and Europe, 1900–1960', *Business History*, 24, 1982, pp. 186–210.

64 M. Ackrill and L. Hannah, *Barclays. The Business of Banking 1690–1996*, Cambridge, 2001, pp. 79–85, 399.

65 The most important was the Bank of London and South America (BOLSA), formed in 1923 through the merger of the London and River Plate Bank and the London and Brazilian Bank, in which it had a holding of slightly over 50%. D. Joslin, *A Century of Banking in Latin America*, London, 1963.

66 The Chartered Bank of India, Australia and China; the Hongkong and Shanghai Banking Corporation; the Standard Bank of South Africa; the Bank of Australasia; the Union Bank of Australia; the BOLSA.

67 G. Jones, *British Multinational Banking 1830–1990*, Oxford, 1993.

68 See Ziegler, *Sixth Great Power*; Roberts, *Schroders*; Wake, *Kleinwort Benson*; Burk, *Morgan Grenfell*; Ferguson, *World's Banker*; B. Bramsen and K. Wain, *The Hambros 1779–1979*, London, 1979; Kynaston, *City of London*, vol. III.

69 S. A. Schuker, *The End of French Predominance in Europe. The Financial Crisis of 1924 and the Adoption of the Dawes Plan*, Chapel Hill, 1976; J.-N. Jeanneney, *L'argent caché. Milieux d'affaires et pouvoir politique dans la France du XXe siècle*, Paris, 1981; J. N. Jeanneney, *Leçon d'histoire pour une gauche au pouvoir. La faillite du Cartel 1926–1926*, Paris, 1977.

70 Plessis, 'When Paris dreamt of competing with the City...', in Cassis and Bussière (eds.), *London and Paris as International Financial Centres*, p. 47; A. Sauvy, *Histoire économique de la France entre les deux guerres*, Paris, 1984, vol. II, p. 173.

71 See M. Myers, *Paris as a Financial Centre*, London, 1936, pp. 141–3.

72 See O. Feiertag, 'La Banque de France et les problèmes monétaires européens de la Conférence de Gênes à la création de la B. R. I. (1922–1930)', in E. Bussière and M. Dumoulin (eds.), *Milieux économiques et intégration européenne en Europe occidentale au XXe siècle*, Arras, 1998.

73 E. Moreau, *Souvenirs d'un gouverneur de la Banque de France: Histoire de la stabilisation du franc (1926–1928)*, Paris, 1954, p. 603.

74 Myers, *Paris as a Financial Centre*, pp. 162–77; K. Mouré, *La politique du franc Poincaré (1926–1936)*, Paris, 1998, pp. 217–23.

75 Myers, *Paris as a Financial Centre*, p. 170.

76 One of the intended goals of the attempt to set up an international discount market in Paris was, moreover, to compensate for this decline in issues.

77 Myers, *Paris as a Financial Centre*, pp. 140–4.

78 Jolliffe, *The United States as a Financial Centre*, p. 106; Balogh, *Studies in Financial Organization*, pp. 249–50.

79 The example of the Crédit Lyonnais, the largest French bank, was typical in this respect. In inflation-adjusted francs, its balance sheet only exceeded its pre-war level at the beginning of the thirties and, even if it reached nearly Fr. 14 billion in 1929, this figure seems very low when compared with the in excess of Fr. 50 billion on the balance sheet of Lloyds Bank at the time.

80 B. Ambigapathi, 'La stratégie de cartellisation bancaire en France du Crédit Lyonnais entre 1919 et 1925', in Desjardins *et al.* (eds.), *Le Crédit Lyonnais*, pp. 851 66.

81 In 1930 the Crédit Lyonnais had forty-four foreign branches and subsidiaries abroad and in the colonial empire, while the Comptoir National d'Escompte de Paris had twenty-nine.

82 E. Bussière, 'The French "Banques d'affaires" in the interwar period: the case of the Banque de Paris et des Pays-Bas (Paribas)', in M. Kasuya (ed.), *Coping with Crisis. International Financial Institutions in the Interwar Period*, Oxford, 2003, pp. 114–21.

83 H. Bonin, *L'apogée de l'économie libérale bancaire française (1919–1935)*, Paris, 2000, pp. 204–7; L. Dufourcq-Lagelouse, *Les banques étrangères en France*, Paris, 1922.

84 J. Bouvier, *Les Rothschild*, Brussels, 1983, p. 309.

85 A. Sabouret, *MM Lazard Frères et Cie: Une Saga de la fortune*, Paris, 1987; H. Bonin, 'Les banques face au cas Citroën: Essai d'appréciation de la puissance bancaire', *Revue d'histoire moderne et contemporaine*, 32, 1985, pp. 74–98.

86 See O. Feiertag and P. Martin-Aceña, 'The delayed modernization of the central banks of France and Spain in the twentieth century', in C.-L. Holtfrerich, J. Reis and G. Toniolo (eds.), *The Emergence of Modern Central Banking from 1918 to the Present*, Aldershot, 1999, pp. 41–4.

87 Feiertag, 'La Banque de France et les problèmes monétaires européens'.

88 The classic work on this issue, covering its economic, social and political aspects, is G. D. Feldman, *The Great Disorder. Politics, Economy and Society in the German Inflation 1914–1924*, Oxford, 1997.

89 H. Wixforth, 'German banks and their business strategies in the Weimar Republic: new findings and preliminary results', in Kasuya (ed.), *Coping with Crisis*, p. 138.

90 Feldman, 'Deutsche Bank from world war to world economic crisis', pp. 181–2.

91 Figures cited in Feldman, *Great Disorder*, pp. 598–9.

92 Wixforth, 'German banks', p. 136.

93 H. James, 'Strukturwandel im Kriegs- und Kriszeiten 1914–1945', in
    H. Pohl (ed.), *Geschichte des Finanzplatzes Berlin*, Frankfurt, 2002, p. 162.
94 Henning, 'Börsenkrisen und Börsengeschichte von 1914 bis 1945'.
95 Feinstein and Watson, 'Private international capital flows in Europe',
    pp. 97, 110.
96 H. James, *The German Slump. Politics and Economics 1924–1936*, Oxford,
    1986, p. 145.
97 It was also involved in setting up other international finance companies,
    including the American and Continental Corporation in New York and the
    N. V. Nederlandsche Crediet-enFinanciering-Maatschappij in Amsterdam,
    together with Mendelssohn and the Nederlandsche Handels-Maatschappij.
98 E. Rosenbaum and A. J. Sherman, *M. M. Warburg and Co., 1798–1938:
    Merchant Bankers of Hamburg*, London, 1979, pp. 135–40.
99 See H. James, *The Reichsbank and Public Finance in Germany 1924–1933*,
    Frankfurt, 1985; T. Balderston, 'A comparison of British and German
    monetary policy 1919–1932', in Feinstein (ed.), *Banking, Currency and
    Finance in Europe between the Wars*.
100 J. Houwink ten Cate, 'Amsterdam als Finanzplatz Deutschlands
    (1919–1923)', in G. D. Feldman *et al.* (eds.), *Konsequenzen der Inflation*,
    Berlin, 1989, pp. 152–89.
101 In addition to Mendelssohn, mentioned above, Deutsche Bank and
    the Commerz- und Privat Bank opened a branch there; the Dresdner Bank
    did so by setting up a private bank, Proehl & Guttmann, and the Disconto-
    Gesellschaft did so by transferring its Antwerp branch, Albert de Pury & Co.
102 J. Jonker, 'Spoilt for choice? Banking concentration and the structure of the
    Dutch capital market, 1900–40', in Y. Cassis, G. D. Feldman and
    U. Olsson (eds.), *The Evolution of Financial Institutions and Markets in
    Twentieth Century Europe*, Aldershot, 1995, p. 203.
103 P. Einzig, *The Fight for Financial Supremacy*, London, 1931, p. 137.
104 Jonker, 'Spoilt for choice?', p. 203.
105 Einzig, *Fight for Financial Supremacy*, p. 138.
106 E. L. Dulles, *The Bank for International Settlements at Work*, New York,
    1932.
107 M. Worner, *La Suisse, centre financier européen*, Argenton, 1931, p. 111.
108 Einzig, *Fight for Financial Supremacy*, pp. 139–42.
109 Worner, *La Suisse, centre financier européen*, p. 101.
110 The Swiss Bank Corporation, the Crédit Suisse, the Schweizerische
    Volksbank, the Union Bank of Switzerland, the Eidgenössische Bank, the
    Basler Handelsbank, the Comptoir d'Escompte de Genève and Leu & Co.
111 F. Ritzmann, *Die Schweizer Banken. Geschichte, Theorie, Statistik*, Bern,
    1983, p. 267.
112 See Y. Cassis, 'Commercial banks in 20th century Switzerland', in Cassis,
    Feldman and Olsson (eds.), *Evolution of Financial Institutions and Markets*,
    pp. 64–77.
113 Each of them had total assets of Fr. 1.6 billion in 1930, compared with
    Fr. 2.8 billion for the Crédit Lyonnais, Fr. 3.6 billion for Deutsche Bank,
    but Fr. 11 billion for Lloyds Bank.

114 M. Perrenoud and R. Lopez, *Aspects des relations financières franco-suisses (1936–1946)*, Zurich, 2002, p. 42.

115 M. Fior, *Les banques suisses, le franc et l'Allemagne. Contribution à l'histoire de la place financière suisse (1924–1945)*, Geneva, 2002, pp. 198–9.

116 M. Perrenoud *et al.*, *La place financière et les banques suisses à l'époque du national-socialisme*, Zurich, 2002, pp. 87–98, 620–3.

117 Particularly the holding companies, discussed in chapter 3, in which Switzerland had enjoyed a significant competitive advantage before the war.

118 S. Paquier, 'Swiss holding companies from the mid-nineteenth century to the early 1930s: the forerunners and subsequent waves of creations', *Financial History Review*, 8, 2, 2001, 177–81.

119 M. König, *Interhandel. Die Schweizerische Holding der IG Farben und ihre Metamorphosen (1910–1999)*, Zurich, 2001.

120 The Société Réunie des Pétroles Fanto SA was founded in Geneva in 1920, jointly by the Union Bank of Switzerland and the Österreichische Bodenkreditanstalt, and held majority stakes in several oil companies in Austria, Hungary, Czechoslovakia and Poland. And, at the initiative of French and German interests, the International Petroleum Company was founded in Zurich in 1921, with a capital of Fr.220 million.

121 Y. Cassis, 'La place financière suisse et la City de Londres, 1890–1990', in P. Bairoch and M. Körner (eds.), *La Suisse dans l'économie mondiale (15ème–20ème siècle)*, Zurich, 1990, p. 348.

122 Y. Sancey, 'Place financière suisse et émergence d'une régulation para-étatique durant l'Entre-deux-guerres', in S. Guex *et al.* (eds.), *Krisen und Stabilisierung. Die Schweiz in der Zwischenkriegszeit*, Zurich, 1998, pp. 81–93.

123 J. K. Galbraith, *The Great Crash, 1929*, Boston, 1954.

124 E. White, 'The stock market boom and crash of 1929 revisited', *Journal of Economic Perspectives*, 4, 2, 1990, p. 76.

125 Ibid., pp. 79–80.

126 See P. Rappoport and E. White, 'Was the crash of 1929 expected?' *American Economic Review*, 84, 1, 1994, pp. 271–81.

127 White, 'Stock market boom and crash', p. 81.

128 Jolliffe, *The United States as a Financial Centre*, p. 106.

129 Owen P. Young, chairman of General Electric and of RCA, as well as chairman of the German Reparations Conference in 1929, which decided, among other things, to found the Bank for International Settlements.

130 Statistics from the League of Nations cited in C. H. Feinstein, P. Temin and G. Toniolo, *The European Economy between the Wars*, Oxford, 1997, pp. 104–7.

131 P. Bairoch, *Victoires et déboires*, vol. III, Paris, 1997, p. 80.

132 The Banca Commerciale Italiana, the Banca di Roma and the Credito Italiano.

133 The German banking crisis has caused a lot of ink to flow. In particular, see K. E. Born, *Die Deutsche Bankenkrise 1931*, Munich, 1967; H. James, 'The causes of the German banking crisis of 1931', *Economic History Review*, 38,

1984; T. Balderston, 'The banks and the gold standard in the German financial crisis of 1931', *Financial History Review*, 1, 1 1994.

134 These mergers were followed by the reduction of equity capital, that of the Dresdner & Danat falling from 220 to 150 million Reichsmarks and that of the Deutsche und Disconto-Gesellschaft from 285 to 144 million.

135 This situation brought about appreciable losses that reached £1.5 million for Schröders in 1931 and, probably, £3.3 million for Kleinworts in 1935. Roberts, *Schroders*, pp. 262–6; Wake, *Kleinwort Benson*, pp. 244–9.

136 See Sayers, *Bank of England*, pp. 387–415; A. Cairncross and B. Eichengreen, *Sterling in Decline: The Devaluations of 1931, 1949 and 1967*, Oxford, 1983; D. B. Kunz, *The Battle for Britain's Gold Standard in 1931*, London, 1987; P. Williamson, *National Crisis and National Government: British Politics, the Economy and Empire, 1926–1932*, Cambridge, 1992.

137 P. Coste, *La lutte pour la suprématie financière. Les grands marchés financiers. Paris, Londres, New York*, Paris, 1932, p. 10.

138 H. Laufenburger, *Les banques françaises*, Paris, 1940, p. 237.

139 H. Bonin, *La Banque nationale de crédit. Histoire de la quatrième banque de dépôts française en 1913–1932*, Paris, 2002.

140 H. Bonin, *La Banque de l'union parisienne (1874/1904–1974). Histoire de la deuxième grande banque d'affaires française*, Paris, 2001.

141 Myers, *Paris as a financial centre*, p. 168.

142 Belgium had already devalued in May 1935, whereas the Netherlands and Switzerland would soon follow France.

143 In the United States, the number of commercial banks dropped from 24,504 in June 1929 to 14,440 at the end of 1933, whereas their deposits shrank from $49 billion to $33 billion during the same period.

144 E. White, 'Banking and finance in the twentieth century', in S. L. Engerman and R. E. Gallman (eds.), *The Cambridge Economic History of the United States, Volume III, The Twentieth Century*, Cambridge, 2000, pp. 761–3.

145 P. Ehrsam, 'Die Bankenkrise der 30er Jahre in der Schweiz', in Eidgenössische Bankenkommission (ed.), *50 Jahre eidgenössische Bankenaufsicht*, Zurich, 1985, p. 87.

146 See Perrenoud *et al. La place financière et les banques suisses*, pp. 153–95.

147 Their total assets dropped between 1930 and 1935 from Fr. 8.6 to Fr. 4.1 billion and their net profits from Fr. 7.4 to 2.1 million.

148 In total, the losses sustained by the shareholders of the six big banks in trouble have been estimated at Fr. 1.4 billion. Ehrsam, 'Die Bankenkrise der 30er Jahre in der Schweiz'.

149 While the institution was independent, the canton of Geneva was one of its shareholders and delegated two members to its board of directors, which explains the violence of the political reactions that caused its difficulties.

150 D. Bodmer, *L'intervention de la Confédération dans l'économie bancaire suisse*, Basle, 1948, pp. 50–65.

151 It was known as the Gray–Pecora investigation, named after the two general counsels who led the two Senate sub-committees in charge of carrying it through to a successful conclusion.

152 See White, 'Banking and finance', pp. 764–9.

153 G. D. Smith and R. Sylla, 'Wall Street and the US. capital markets in the twentieth century', in *Financial Markets, Institutions and Instruments*, 1993.

154 G. Kurgan–van Hentenryk, 'Finance and financiers in Belgium', in Y. Cassis (ed.), *Finance and Financiers in European History 1880–1960*, Cambridge, 1992, p. 327.

155 H. James, 'Banks and bankers in the German interwar depression', in Cassis (ed.), *Finance and Financiers in European History*, pp. 277–9.

156 W. E. Mosse, *Jews in the German Economy. The German–Jewish Economic Elite 1820–1935*, Oxford, 1987, pp. 374–75; H. James, 'The Deutsche Bank and the dictatorship 1933–1945', in L. Gall *et al.*, *The Deutsche Bank 1870–1995*, London, 1995, pp. 293–8.

157 C. Kopper, *Zwischen Marktwirtschaft und Dirigismus. Bankenpolitik im 'Dritten Reich' 1933–1939*, Bonn, 1995, pp. 254–75.

158 See A. Hirsch, 'Les objectifs de la loi sur les banques', in Eidgenossische Bankenkommission (ed.), *50 Jahre eidgenossische Bankenaufsicht*, pp. 271–2.

159 On banking secrecy, see M. Aubert, J.-P. Kernen and H. Schönle, *Le secret bancaire suisse*, Bern, 1982; S. Guex, 'The origins of the Swiss banking secrecy law and its Repercussions for Swiss federal policy', *Business History Review*, 74, 2000, pp. 237–66; R. Vogler, 'The genesis of Swiss banking secrecy: political and economic environment', *Financial History Review*, 8, 1, 2001, pp. 73–84.

160 This prohibition was general and also applied to the public administration, including the tax authorities, but it could be lifted by a judge within the framework of a criminal procedure, the law not being intended to protect activities defined as criminal in Switzerland. Swiss law considers that concealment of assets is an administrative and not a criminal offence, which prevents a judge from lifting banking secrecy in this case. The fact remains that practice has varied considerably on this point and that recently the definition of concealment of assets has become narrower.

161 See C. Andrieu, *Les banques sous l'occupation. Paradoxes de l'histoire d'une profession*, Paris, 1990, pp. 201–37.

162 Foreign loans outside the empire added up to a mere £28.5 million between 1932 and 1938; that is to say, less than 3% of the total amount of issues in London.

163 Balogh, *Studies in Financial Organization*, p. 250.

164 Feinstein and Watson, 'Private international capital flows in Europe', pp. 116–18.

165 S. Pollard, *The Development of the British Economy, 1914–1980*, 3rd edn, London, 1983, pp. 216–23.

166 A. S. Milward, *War, Economy and Society, 1939–1945*, London, 1977, pp. 132–49.

167 The regulation was strengthened in December 1942, with the introduction by the Federal Council of a maximum price for coins and gold bars and the

requirement for an authorisation from the National Bank to be able to import and export the precious metal.

168 Commission Indépendante d'Experts Suisse–Seconde Guerre Mondiale, *La Suisse, le national-socialisme et la Seconde Guerre Mondiale. Rapport final*, Zurich, 2002, pp. 224–38.

169 C. R. Geisst, *Wall Street. A History*, Oxford, 1997, pp. 264–7.

170 In 1945 Treasury securities added up to $2.5 billion at the National City Bank; that is to say, 52% of this bank's assets.

171 White, 'Banking and finance in the twentieth century', pp. 773–4.

172 Kynaston, *City of London*, vol. III, pp. 462–507.

173 Roberts, *Schroders*, p. 274.

174 Holmes and Green, *Midland*, p. 208.

175 Kynaston, *City of London*, vol. III, pp. 463–507; Michie, *London Stock Exchange*, pp. 287–325.

176 M. Margairaz, 'La Banque de France et l'occupation', in M. Margairaz (ed.), *Banques, Banque de France et Seconde Guerre mondiale*, Paris, 2002, pp. 37–84.

177 Information kindly provided by Patrick Verley.

178 The profits of the Crédit Lyonnais fell in inflation-adjusted francs – 1938 value – from Fr. 82 to Fr. 49 million between 1939 and 1944.

179 A Plessis, 'Les grandes banques de dépôts et l'occupation', in Margairaz (ed.), *Banques, Banque de France et Seconde Guerre mondiale*, pp. 15–36.

180 P. Burrin, *La France à l'heure allemande 1940–1944*, Paris, 1995, pp. 267–82.

181 J.-M. Dreyfus, 'La spoliation des banques juives. Trois études de cas', in Margairaz (ed.), *Banques, Banque de France et Seconde Guerre mondiale*, pp. 130–51; Andrieu, *La banque sous l'occupation*, pp. 238–79.

182 James, 'Deutsche Bank and the dictatorship 1933–1945', pp. 338–54.

183 Perrenoud *et al.*, *La place financière et les banques suisses à l'époque du national-socialisme*, p. 144.

184 The actual profit of the Crédit Suisse, as well as that of the Swiss Bank Corporation, fell by 21% at current price between 1939 and 1945.

185 Commission Indépendante d'Experts, *La Suisse, le national-socialisme et la Seconde Guerre Mondiale*, pp. 249–51.

5. GROWTH AND REGULATION, 1945–1980

1 A. Maddison, *Dynamic Forces in Capitalist Development. A Long-Run Comparative View*, Oxford, 1991, p. 49; N. Crafts and G. Toniolo, 'Postwar growth: an overview', in N. Crafts and G. Toniolo (eds.), *Economic Growth in Europe since 1945*, Oxford, 1996, p. 2.

2 G. Toniolo, 'Europe's golden age, 1950–1973: speculations from a long-run perspective', *Economic History Review*, 51, 2, 1998, p. 256.

3 Maddison, *Dynamic Forces*, pp. 198–9.

4 M. Nadler, S. Heller and S. Shipman, 'New York as an international financial center', in *The Money Market and its Institutions*, New York, 1955, pp. 290–1; R. Orsingher, *Les banques dans le monde*, Paris, 1964, pp. 140–1.

5 The law of 24 July 1936 gave the authorities the means to intervene more directly in the Bank's management. The 15 *régents*, mainly representatives of the *haute banque* elected by the 200 largest shareholders, were replaced by 20 councillors, only two of whom were elected by the General Assembly. Most of the others, who represented various interest groups, were appointed by the government. Another new fact was that a councillor was henceforth elected by the employees.

6 The members of the board of directors, who were 16 in number including the governor and deputy governor, were henceforth nominated by the Treasury whereas they had been co-opted beforehand. In practice, the main merchant banks continued to be represented on it, but they no longer had any real influence when it came to conducting British monetary policy.

7 H. James, *International Monetary Cooperation since Bretton Woods*, New York and Oxford, 1996, pp. 148–74.

8 See, in particular, M. J. Hogan, *The Marshall Plan: America, Britain, and the Reconstruction of Western Europe, 1947–1952*, Cambridge, 1987; R. Girault and M. Lévy-Leboyer (eds.), *Le Plan Marshall et le relèvement économique de l'Europe*, Paris, 1993.

9 See Nadler, Heller and Shipman, 'New York as an international financial center'.

10 The leading banks were National City Bank, Chase National Bank, Manufacturers Trust, Central Hanover Bank, Chemical Trust and J. P. Morgan.

11 Nadler, Heller and Shipman, 'New York as an international financial center', pp. 294–5.

12 Including fifty-five in Latin America, seventeen in Europe and twenty in the Far East.

13 During the 1950s, neither New York State nor US federal law authorised foreign bank branches.

14 V. Carosso, *Investment Banking in America*, Cambridge, Mass., 1970, pp. 458–95.

15 Of these, seventeen, including Morgan Stanley, Kuhn Loeb, Dillon Read, Lehman Brothers, Goldman Sachs and First Boston, were subject to a complaint by the Ministry of Justice in 1947 and were accused in November 1950 of having monopolised the securities business. But the lawsuit was abandoned in 1953, and these firms came out of it with their reputation enhanced.

16 R. Roberts, *Wall Street*, London, 2002, pp. 32–3.

17 C. R. Geisst, *Wall Street. A History*, Oxford, 1997, p. 280.

18 Amongst these were Australia (thirteen loans), Norway (five), Belgium (four), New Zealand (three) and Denmark (two), as well as the Development Bank of Japan.

19 The first became Chase Manhattan Bank, the second First National City Bank and the last Manufacturers Hanover Trust, names that would dominate New York's banking centre until the wave of mergers in the nineties.

20 R. Sylla, 'United States banks and Europe: strategy and attitude', in S. Battilossi and Y. Cassis (eds.), *European Banks and the American Challenge. Competition and Cooperation in International Banking Under Bretton Woods*, Oxford, 2002, pp. 53–73.

21 See H. van B. Cleveland and T. Huertas, *Citibank 1812–1970*, Cambridge, Mass., 1985, pp. 254–7.

22 Cited in A. Sampson, *The Money Lenders*, London, 1981, p. 121.

23 G. Jones, *British Multinational Banking 1830–1990*, Oxford, 1993, pp. 400–1.

24 C. Schenk, 'International financial centres, 1958–1971: competitiveness and complementarity', in Battilossi and Cassis (eds.), *European Banks and the American Challenge*, p. 75.

25 R. Roberts, *Schroders. Merchants & Bankers*, London, 1992, p. 326.

26 W. M. Clarke, *The City's Invisible Earnings*, London, 1958, p. 21.

27 Ibid., pp. 66–74; R. Michie, *The City of London. Continuity and Change, 1850–1990*, Basingstoke and London, 1992, pp. 53–60; D. Kynaston, *The City of London*, vol. IV: *A Club No More, 1945–2000*, London, 2001, pp. 123–7.

28 They exceeded £1.5 billion per year – $4.2 billion – in the mid-fifties.

29 Lloyd's of London was an insurance market that, through brokers, brought together insurance buyers and insurers willing to underwrite the risk. Underwriting syndicates were led by insurance professionals but were mostly made up of Lloyd's members, commonly known as *Names*, who received a share of the syndicate's profits but who, in the event of bankruptcy, were liable with their entire fortune.

30 J. Mensbrugghe, 'Foreign issues in Europe', *International Monetary Fund Staff Papers*, 111, 1964, pp. 327–8.

31 See R. Michie, *The London Stock Exchange. A History*, Oxford, 1999, pp. 326–422.

32 Between 1950 and 1960, the proportion of shares in British companies in the total of quoted stocks went, in terms of market capitalisation, from 21% to 40%, and that of public securities from 57% to 33%.

33 G. Blakey, *The Post-War History of the London Stock Market*, London 2nd edn, 1994, pp. 30–8.

34 Australia, New Zealand, South Africa, India, Pakistan, Ceylon, Burma, Iceland, Iraq, Jordan, Libya and the Persian Gulf territoires.

35 C. Schenk, *Britain and the Sterling Area. From Devaluation to Convertibility in the 1950s*, London, 1994, p. 11.

36 See Catherine Schenk's statement, *Britain and the Sterling Area*, on this question.

37 G. Burn, 'The state, the City and the Euromarkets', *Review of International Political Economy*, 6, 2, 1999, p. 238.

38 The sterling area continued to function, albeit in an increasingly slack manner, especially after the pound's devaluation in 1967, until the abandonment of fixed exchange rates in 1972.

39 The Crédit Lyonnais, the Société Générale, the Comptoir National d'Escompte de Paris (CNEP) and the Banque Nationale pour le Commerce et l'Industrie (BNCI).

40 Among them were the three Compagnies d'Assurances Générales (accidents, life and fire), the four La Nationale companies, the two Le Phénix companies and the two L'Union companies.

41 It included the Caisse des Dépôts et Consignations (depositary of, among other things, the bulk of the savings banks' assets), the Crédit National (founded immediately after the First World War and specialising in medium- and long-term credit to enterprises), the Crédit Foncier, the Caisse Nationale de Crédit Agricole and the Banque Française du Commerce extérieur, founded in 1946.

42 F. Marnata, *La Bourse et le financement des investissements*, Paris, 1973, pp. 74, 80.

43 See A. Straus, 'Structures financiers et performances des entreprises industrielles en France dans la seconde moitié du XXe siècle', *Entreprises et Histoire*, 2, 1992, pp. 19–33.

44 See O. Feiertag, 'The international opening-up of the Paris Bourse: overdraft-economy curbs and market dynamics', in Y. Cassis and E. Bussière (eds.), *London and Paris as International Financial Centres in the Twentieth Century*, Oxford, 2005, pp. 229–46.

45 The other big French banks were present abroad too – the BNCI with fifty-six branches, the Société Générale with thirty-five and the CNEP with twenty-six.

46 Schenk, 'International financial centres', p. 75 ; Orsingher, *Les banques dans le monde*, pp. 36–8.

47 The Banque de Paris et des Pays-Bas (Paribas), the Banque de l'Union Parisienne and the Banque de l'Indochine, which remained private.

48 Eric Bussière, *Paribas. L'Europe et le monde, 1872–1992*, Antwerp, 1992.

49 This section is based on the work by C.-L. Holtfrerich, *Frankfurt as a Financial Centre. From Medieval Fair Trade to European Banking Centre*, Munich, 1999, pp. 220–38.

50 Like Brinckmann, Wirz & Co. (the former M. M. Warburg & Co. bank or Delbrück, Schickler & Co).

51 M. Dickhaus, 'Fostering "the bank that rules Europe": the Bank of England, the Allied Banking Commission and the Bank deutscher Länder, 1948–51', *Contemporary European History*, 7, 2, 1998, pp. 161–80.

52 In the financial sector, Hamburg and Frankfurt employed respectively 13,000 and 8,200 people in 1950, and 46,500 and 40,200 in 1970. As far as banking activities alone were concerned, 8,200 people worked in Hamburg in 1950, 25,000 in 1970 and 26,000 in 1987, whereas the equivalent figures for Frankfurt were 6,900, 28,000 and 41,000 people. Holtfrerich, *Frankfurt as a Financial Centre*, p. 255.

53 For further details, see C.-L. Holtfrerich, 'The Deutsche Bank 1945–1957: war, military rule and reconstruction', in L. Gall *et al.*, *The Deutsche Bank 1870–1995*, London, 1995, pp. 357–521.

54 H. Bauer, *Société de Banque Suisse 1872–1972*, Basle, 1972, p. 300.

55 M. Iklé, *Die Schweiz als internationaler Bank- und Finanzplatz*, Zurich, 1970, p. 132.

56 Widely practised by the Bank of England in the interwar period, the technique of *gentlemen's agreements* enabled the BNS to intervene, although it did not have the purely legal competence to do so (see above, chapter 4). During the entire period 1950–80, the Swiss central bank in fact tried almost continually to prevent an excessive influx of funds into Switzerland that, under a fixed exchange rate regime, swelled the money supply, pushed down interest rates and caused inflation. It also feared that the Swiss franc might become a small international common currency over which it would no longer be able to exert any control if borrowers of Swiss francs were no longer to convert them into foreign currencies.

57 In the 1950s the seven main banking houses, members of the Groupement des Banquiers Privés formed in 1931, were Bordier & Cie, Darier & Cie, Ferrier, Lullin & Cie, Hentsch & Cie, Lombard, Odier & Cie, Mirabaud & Cie and Pictet & Cie.

58 Among these were notably the Banque pour le Commerce Suisse-Israélien, founded in 1950 by the Foreign Trade Bank of Tel Aviv, the Discount Bank (Overseas), established in 1952 and in which Israeli interests predominated, and the Banque Intra, founded in 1958 by the Intra Bank of Beirut.

59 The cantonal banks' assets represented 45% of those of the Swiss banks as a whole in 1945 and 40% in 1955, compared with 28% and 31% for the big banks.

60 K. Speck, *Strukturwandlungen und Entwicklungtendenzen im Auslandgeschäft der Schweizerbanken*, Zurich, 1974, p. 35.

61 C. Schenk, 'The origins of the Eurodollar market in London, 1955–1963', *Explorations in Economic History*, 35, 1998.

62 The bank repurchased dollars forward at a premium of $2\frac{10}{8}$%. This operation enabled it to borrow pounds sterling at a rate of 4%, even though the Bank of England's discount rate was $4\frac{1}{2}$% at that time. Arbitrage did not lead to rates on both sides of the Atlantic levelling out, owing to the numerous regulations preventing the free movement of funds, Regulation Q, etc.

63 R. Fry (ed.), *A Banker's World. The Revival of the City 1957–1970. The Speeches and Writings of Sir George Bolton*, London, 1970.

64 In early 1962 Siegmund Warburg, the City's great outsider and innovator during this period, considered issuing a loan on behalf of the ECSC, then abandoned the idea to avoid encroaching upon the territory of Kuhn Loeb, his allies in New York, and turned his attention towards IRI, the Italian state holding company. J. Attali, *Un homme d'influence. Sir Siegmund Warburg (1902–1982)*, Paris 1985, pp. 378–9; Kynaston, *City of London*, vol. IV, pp. 275–80.

65 I. M. Kerr, *A History of the Eurobond Market: The First 21 Years*, London, 1984.

66 'Witness seminar on the origins and early development of the Eurobond market', introduced and edited by Kathleen Burk, *Contemporary European History*, 1, 1, 1992, pp. 65–87.

67 The reference rate of these loans is the famous LIBOR – for London Interbank Overnight Rate.

68 A secondary market was set up at the same time by the American firm White Weld & Co.

69 R. Roberts, *Take Your Partners. Orion, the Consortium Banks and the Transformation of the Euromarkets*, Basingstoke, 2001, p. 13.

70 H. McRae and F. Cairncross, *Capital City. London as a Financial Centre*, London, 1973, p. xiii.

71 Letter to Charles Hambro, head of the famous merchant bank and a director of the Bank of England. Cited by Schenk, 'International financial centres 1958–1971', p. 85.

72 Paris was the only centre to more or less hold its own with London in this sector.

73 Sampson, *Money Lenders*, p. 126.

74 M. Baker and M. Collins, 'London as an international banking centre, 1950–1980', in Cassis and Bussière (eds.), *London and Paris as International Financial Centres*.

75 The American banks were the most numerous in the City: whereas there had been only seven in 1950, there were fourteen in 1966 and thirty-seven in 1970. In that year, they were joined by fifty European banks, thirteen Japanese ones, twenty-six from Commonwealth countries – traditionally well represented in London – and thirty-three banks of various nationalities.

76 See Roberts, *Take Your Partners*, pp. 17–41.

77 Its shareholders were the Chase Manhattan Bank, the National Westminster Bank, the Royal Bank of Canada, the Westdeutsche Landesbank Gironzentrale, the Credito Italiano and the Mitsubishi Bank from 1972.

78 At that time, there were twenty-one in London, compared with seven in Paris, six in Brussels, five in Zurich and two in Luxembourg, Amsterdam and Vienna.

79 S. Battilossi, 'Banking with multinationals: British clearing banks and the Euromarkets' challenge, 1958–1976', in Battilossi and Cassis (eds.), *European Banks and the American Challenge*, pp. 106–7.

80 Kerr, *History of the Eurobond Market*.

81 Baker and Collins, 'London as an international banking centre'.

82 T. Huertas, 'U.S. multinational banking: history and prospects', in G. Jones, *Banks as Multinationals*, London, 1990, p. 253.

83 R. Sylla, 'United States banks and Europe: strategy and attitudes', in Battilossi and Cassis (eds.), *European Banks and the American Challenge*, pp. 66–7.

84 The two measures were taken to limit outflows of funds from American residents, with the aim of reducing the United States' balance-of-payments deficit.

85 The number of mergers and acquisitions rose to 1,951 between 1963 and 1967 and to 3,736 between 1968 and 1972.

86 The product range of the 148 companies, out of the 200 largest in 1950 that survived until 1975, increased from an average of 5.22 per company in 1950 to 9.74 in 1975.

87 M. O'Sullivan, *Contests for Corporate Control*, Oxford, 2000, p. 110.
88 See J. B. Baskin and P. Miranti, *A History of Corporate Finance*, Cambridge, 1997, pp. 273–85.
89 The latter played the leading roles during these years, under the leadership of André Meyer, partner of the Paris banking house, who emigrated to the United States in 1940. He was considered in many respects one of the fathers of corporate finance which would mark the following decades.
90 See *Luxembourg, an International Financial Centre*, Luxembourg, 1972.
91 See R. Roberts (ed.), *Offshore Financial Centres*, Aldershot, 1994.
92 'Witness seminar on the origins and early development of the Eurobond market', p. 80.
93 Holtfrerich, *Frankfurt*, pp. 269–70.
94 G. Franke, 'The Bundesbank and financial markets', in Deutsche Bundesbank (ed.), *Fifty Years of the Deutsche Mark. Central Bank and the Currency in Germany since 1948*, Oxford, 1999, pp. 246–7.
95 P. Gallant, *The Eurobond Market*, Cambridge, 1988, pp. 85–9, 119–21.
96 See E. Bussière, 'French banks and the Eurobonds issue market in the 1960s', in Cassis and Bussière (eds.), *London and Paris as International Financial Centres*.
97 R. Larre, 'Le développement du rôle de Paris dans le marché international des capitaux: Paris, place financière internationale', 13 July 1966, Larre private archives, Comité pour l'histoire économique et financière de la France, typescript. My thanks to Laure Quennouëlle-Corre for passing this document on to me.
98 At that time it comprised six countries: the Federal Republic of Germany, Belgium, France, Italy, Luxembourg and the Netherlands.
99 C. P. Kindleberger, 'European economic integration and the development of a single financial center for long-term capital', *Weltwirtschaftliches Archiv*, 90, 2, 1963, pp. 189–208.
100 Named after Pierre Werner, prime minister of Luxembourg and chairman of the group of experts appointed at the Hague Summit of Heads of State and Government, in December 1969.
101 See D. Ross, 'European banking clubs in the 1960s: a flawed strategy', *Business and Economic History*, 27, 1998, pp. 353–66, and 'Clubs and consortia: European banking groups as strategic alliances', in Battilossi and Cassis (eds.), *European Banks and the American Challenge*, pp. 135–60.
102 Associated Banks of Europe Corporation. The club comprised the nine following banks: the Banque Nationale de Paris, Barclays Bank, the Banca Nazionale del Lavoro, the Dresdner Bank, the Algemene Bank Nederland, the Bayerische Hypotheken und Wechsel Bank, the Banque de Bruxelles, the Banque Internationale du Luxembourg and the Osterreichische Landerbank.
103 European Banks International Company. The club's composition is given below in the text.
104 It comprised the Crédit Lyonnais, the Commerzbank, the Banco di Roma and the Banco Hispano Americano.

105 It comprised the Kredietbank, the Crédit Commercial de France, the Berliner Handels-Gesellschaft und Frankfurter Bank, the Nederlandsche Middenstandbank, Williams and Glyn's, the Banco Ambrosiano and the Privatbanken.

106 A. R. Holmes and E. Green, *Midland. 150 Years of Banking Business*, London, 1986, pp. 253–60; H. E. Büschgen, 'Deutsche Bank from 1957 to the present: the emergence of an international financial conglomerate', in Gall *et al.*, *Deutsche Bank*, pp. 751–9.

107 Among other things, it provided medium-term credit to major industrial projects and became involved in syndicated Eurocredits.

108 It specialised in financing international trade and provided commercial banking services in the United States; it also provided its clients with loans in Eurocurrencies, especially the American subsidiaries of European enterprises through its offshore branch in Nassau, opened in 1969. In 1972 it opened branches in San Francisco and Los Angeles to enter the Californian market, then spread to Australia, founding the Euro-Pacific Finance Corporation in Melbourne, in association with the Fuji Bank, the Commercial Bank of Australia and the United California Bank.

109 Among these were EBICREDIT to speed up and simplify borrowing procedures from one country to another for clients, EBILEASE to offer exporters better financing opportunities, and EBICEM to train employees and increase their prospects for international mobility.

110 H. J. Mast, 'La Suisse place financière – bénédiction ou malédiction?', *Cahiers du Crédit Suisse*, 42, March 1977.

111 The Swiss monetary authorities introduced a whole battery of measures to prevent the excessive influx of funds into the country, including a ban on interest on the bank deposits of non-residents, or even temporarily making the former negative, which separated the eurofranc market from that of the domestic franc, with very different interest rates on forward investments for example.

112 P. Braillard, *La place financière Suisse. Politique gouvernementale et compétitivité internationale*, Geneva, 1987, p. 154.

113 In 1965 American banks held 23.7 % of banks' foreign assets and British banks 17.1%, whereas in 1975 it was the British banks, with 22.2%, which were ahead of the American ones, with 9.7%, the latter being on a par with the banks of the Bahamas at that time. IMF, *International Monetary Statistics*, 1981.

114 'La Suisse, place financière', *Cahier SBS*, 6, 1975.

115 These were investments carried out by a bank, for a commission, on behalf of clients and at their own risk. In fact, they were mainly investments in Swiss eurofrancs in the subsidiaries of Swiss banks in London, which enabled their holder to avoid paying the 35% withholding tax on the interest of such deposits in Switzerland. Bank fiduciary investments thus reflected both the liquid assets in Swiss francs of foreign clients whose wealth was managed in Switzerland, as well as those of Swiss residents who were rich enough to enter the Eurocurrency market and avoid paying this withholding tax.

116 Braillard, *La place financière suisse*, pp. 149–51.
117 Banque Nationale Suisse, *Les banques suisses*, annual publication, 1962 and 1972.
118 Iklé, *Die Schweiz*, p. 180.
119 For a long-term application of this concept, see M. Obstfeld and A. Taylor, 'Globalization and capital markets', in M. Bordo, A. Taylor and J. Williamson (eds.), *Globalization in Historical Perspective*, Chicago, 2003, pp. 121–83.
120 BIS, *Annual Report*, 1980.
121 OCDE, *International Capital Markets Statistics*, 1950–1995.
122 Convertible bonds gave their holders the possibility of converting them into shares in the issuing company or the parent company. Stock warrants allowed their holders to acquire shares in the issuing company or the parent company.
123 Jones, *British Multinational Banking*, p. 550.
124 G. Bird, *Commercial Bank Lending and Third World Debt*, London, 1989, pp. 2–3.
125 Usually calculated in basis points above the LIBOR.
126 A. Sampson, *The Money Lenders*, London, 1981, p. 128.
127 Barclays, National Westminster, Midland and Lloyds. The National Provincial Bank and the Westminster Bank merged in 1968.
128 Fiduciary operations, for example, went from Fr.38 to Fr.121 billion between 1970 and 1980; that is to say, from 16% to 25% of Swiss banks' total assets.
129 Braillard, *La place financière suisse*, pp. 149–59.
130 OECD, *International Capital Markets Statistics*, 1950–95.
131 Donaldson, Lufkin & Jenrette was the first to do so in 1969, quickly followed by Merrill Lynch.
132 E. White, 'Banking and finance in the twentieth century', in S. L. Engerman and R. E. Gallman (eds.), *The Cambridge Economic History of the United States*, vol. III, *The Twentieth Century*, Cambridge, 2000, pp. 799–800.
133 H. C. Reed, 'The ascent of Tokyo as an international financial center', *Journal of International Business Studies*, 11, 3, 1990, pp. 290–1.
134 The main commercial banks were Dai-Ichi Kangyo, Fuji, Sumitomo, Mitsubishi and Sanwa, whereas the biggest investment banks were Nomura, Nikko, Yamaichi and Daiwa.
135 See L. S. Presnell (ed.), *Money and Banking in Japan*, London, 1973.
136 T. Hoshi and A. K. Kashyap, *Corporate Financing and Governance in Japan. The Road to the Future*, Cambridge, Mass., 2001, pp. 124–5.
137 S. Eken, 'Integration of domestic and international financial markets: the Japanese experience', in *International Monetary Fund Staff Papers*, 33, 3, 1984, pp. 501–3.
138 K. M. Dominguez, 'The role of the yen', in M. Feldstein (ed.), *International Capital Flows*, Chicago, 1999, p. 145.
139 Eken, 'Integration of domestic and international financial markets', pp. 505–10.

140 W. Lazonick and M. O'Sullivan, 'Finance and industrial development: evolution to market control. Part II: Japan and Germany', *Financial History Review*, 4, 2, 1997, pp. 124–6.
141 Eken, 'Integration of domestic and international financial markets', pp. 513–17.

6. GLOBALISATION AND INNOVATION, 1980–2005

1 While the first commercial computer admittedly goes back to 1951, the first Intel microprocessor dates from 1971 and the modem, developed in the Bell Laboratories, from 1965. The modem enabled links to be established between computer technologies and telecommunication networks, which took off in the seventies as new technologies, such as fibre optics and data digitisation techniques, progressed. F. Caron, *Les deux révolutions industrielles du XXe siècle*, Paris, 1997, pp. 396–434.
2 M. Obstfeld and A. Taylor, *Global Capital Markets: Integration, Crisis and Growth*, Cambridge, 2004, p. 53.
3 The United States is certainly the largest debtor in these two cases; but it was a new country in 1914, whereas it is now the most developed country in the world, its world status having totally changed in nature within a century.
4 D. Kynaston, *The City of London vol. IV: A Club No More 1945–2000*, London, 2001, p. 585.
5 The name itself is sufficiently evocative and has been used to describe the deregulation measures applied to other markets, including Paris and Tokyo.
6 For example, the foreign assets of British institutional investors went from £10.4 billion in 1978 to £77.3 billion in 1985; R. Roberts and D. Kynaston, *City State. How the Markets Came to Rule our World*, London, 2001, p. 93.
7 This abolition of the monopoly was gradual; external financial institutions, French or foreign, could hold 30% of a charge's capital from 1988 and 100% from 1990, the monopoly disappearing completely two years later. As in London, stockbroker houses lost their independence in turn, the main exceptions to this being Oddo & Cie and the financière Meeschaert.
8 G. Franke, 'The Bundesbank and financial markets', in Deutsche Bundesbank (ed.), *Fifty Years of the Deutsche Mark*, Oxford, 1999, pp. 246–53.
9 Capital exports subject to authorisation went from Fr. 23 billion in 1980 to Fr. 45 billion in 1993, before dropping to an annual average of approximately Fr. 35 billion over the next ten years.
10 See Swiss National Bank, 'Exportations de capitaux soumises à autorisation', in *Rapport annuel de gestion, years 1980–1995*, Zurich.
11 See H. Davies, 'Regulation and politics: the need for a new dialogue' or 'A letter to John Redwood', *Hume Occasional Papers*, 66, 2005.
12 See below p. 269.
13 See P. L. Bernstein, *Capital Ideas. The Improbable Origins of Modern Wall Street*, New York, 1992.

14 Present in the big banks, mainly on Wall Street but also in universities and in consulting firms combining advanced research and product development for financial companies, these scientists contributed above all to statistical risk analysis, which played a central role in all investments, especially those involving forward transactions directly or indirectly.

15 Between 1980 and 2001, the number of salaried employees in New York commercial banks dropped from 170,000 to 105,000, while it more than doubled from 85,000 to 190,000 in the securities industry. R. Roberts, *Wall Street*, London, 2002, pp. 8–10.

16 Technically speaking, one could add swaps (exchanges between maturity dates), which are used mainly by financial intermediaries themselves and thus have no direct influence on the bidders and primary seekers of funds.

17 Potential losses or gains at maturity are thus always known. Too great a potential loss then automatically leads to a margin call or a forced sale, which limits the risk on these instruments for the brokers.

18 Price indices or temperature indices were also traded, with little success.

19 British and foreign banks, merchant banks, discount houses, stockbrokers and commodity brokers, all coordinated by John Barkshire. See D. Kynaston, *LIFFE: A Market and its Makers*, Cambridge 1997, pp. 12–42.

20 A second market, MONEP (Marché des Options Négociables de Paris) was set up in 1987.

21 In the absence of a derivatives market in Germany, in September 1988 LIFFE launched, with Bundesbank approval, its contract on German government bonds (the *Bund Future*), a product that would only return to Frankfurt ten years later, after the founding of Eurex.

22 Euronext was created in 2000 from the merger of the Paris, Amsterdam and Brussels stock exchanges, and was next joined by the Lisbon Stock Exchange.

23 These generally reached 20% of profits above a certain threshold plus $1\frac{1}{2}$% to 2% management fees.

24 They included Julian Robertson from Tiger Management Corporation, Bruce Kovner from Caxton Corporation, Paul Tudor Jones from Tudor Investment or his friend Louis Bacon from Moore Capital Management.

25 See R. Raymond, *L'euro et l'unité monétaire de l'Europe*, Paris, 2001; E. Appel, *European Monetary Integration 1958–2002*, London, 1998.

26 The eleven countries were Austria, Belgium, Finland, France, Germany, Ireland, Italy, Luxemburg, the Netherlands, Portugal and Spain, with Greece joining this group in only 2002. Some small countries having concluded a monetary union with one of their big neighbours – Andorra, Monaco and the Vatican – also adopted the new currency and were allowed to mint their own coin in euros.

27 The Single European Act, signed in Luxembourg and ratified by national parliaments in 1986, came into force on 1 July 1987. The goal that it set itself was to complete the internal market by 1 January 1993, by making a space without internal borders within which the free circulation of goods, people, services and capital was assured.

28 After Jacques Delors, president of the European Commission and of the Committee for the Study of Economic and Monetary Union, the group of experts appointed at the Hanover Conference of Heads of States and Governments in June 1988 and including among others the governors of the twelve central banks of the EEC member countries.

29 These criteria cover the inflation rate, the budget deficit, the public debt, fluctuations in the exchange rate and long-term interest rates.

30 These figures record the amounts of underlying stocks upon which derivatives are based. They are much higher than the amounts actually exchanged by the traders.

31 R. Roberts, *Inside International Finance*, London, 1998, pp. 31–52. Figures published by the Bank for International Settlements and, for derivatives, by the International Swaps and Derivatives Association.

32 Amongst these raiders were notably Carl Icahn, Thomas Boone Pickens and the firm Kohlberg, Kravis, Roberts, which would acquire RJR Nabisco.

33 J. B. Baskin and P. J. Miranti, *A History of Corporate Finance*, Cambridge, 1997, pp. 289–96; M. O'Sullivan, *Contests for Corporate Control*, Oxford, 2000, pp. 161–9.

34 This could have been the case for companies whose ratings had been lowered owing to persistent or temporary difficulties, or for companies that were too young to receive a high rating – generally small and medium-sized enterprises.

35 A. Brummer and R. Cowe, *Hanson. A Biography*, London, 1994.

36 It was the same for Morgan Grenfell and Deutsche Bank, Kleinworts and the Dresdner Bank, Schroders and Salomon Smith Barney/Citigroup, Barings and ING, Flemings and Chase Manhattan, and Hambros and the Société Générale.

37 More precisely, between the end of December 1979 and their absolute peak in March or August 2000, the Dow Jones Industrials index went from 840 to 11,497, the S&P500 from 108 to 1,527, the FTSE 100 from 509 to 6,930, the CAC40 from 421 to 6,922, the Dax30 from 498 to 8,004, and the SMI from 5,617 to 8,317.

38 The NASDAQ actually went from 151 at the end of 1979 to 752 at the beginning of 1995, to reach 5,048 on 10 March 2000.

39 The thrashing was severe. In comparison with their peaks, the NASDAQ fell back by three-quarters, the DAX30 by two-thirds, the FTSE, the CAC40 and the S&P500 by half, whereas the Dow Jones, which included more defensive securities, dropped by only one third.

40 Enron was the seventh American company in terms of market capitalisation, and WorldCom one of the main long-distance telecoms operators.

41 See Y. Cassis, 'Financial elites revisited', in R. Michie and P. Williamson (eds.), *The British Government and the City of London in the Twentieth Century*, Cambridge, 2004, pp. 76–95.

42 The bank was structured into five large divisions – Wealth Management and Business Banking, Investment Bank, Global Asset Management, Wealth Management USA, and Corporate Center – each being managed by its own chief executive officer, who was a member of the executive board, and by

the directors responsible for the division's main duties, who also belonged to the group managing board.

43 D. Hobson, *The National Wealth. Who Gets What in Britain*, London, 1999, p. 536.

44 Sixty per cent of merger and acquisition business was of American origin for the New York investment banks in 2001, 73% for Crédit Suisse First Boston and 53% for Deutsche Bank.

45 White Weld and First Boston from 1978 for Crédit Suisse, and Bankers' Trust in 1999 for Deutsche Bank.

46 See Roberts, *Inside International Finance.*

47 In 2001 the NYSE's capitalisation reached $11,000 billion to which should be added the NASDAQ's $2,900 billion compared with $2,300 billion in Tokyo and $2,150 in London. In spite of stock-market and exchange-rate fluctuations, the proportions remained more or less similar in 2004.

48 In 2000 there were 921 foreign listings in New York, 488 of which were on the NASDAQ, whereas the London Stock Exchange had only 448. Roberts, *Wall Street*, p. 216.

49 The development of the Docklands and Canary Wharf has led to a significant degree of relocation.

50 R. Roberts, *The City*, London, 2004, pp. 246–7.

51 Roberts and Kynaston, *City State*, pp. 67–79; Roberts, *City.*

52 The London shares and futures market – the LIFFE – had, for example, lost its second place to Eurex in 2003.

53 See H. McRae and F. Cairncross, *Capital City. London as a Financial Centre*, 1st edn., London, 1973, 2nd edn., London, 1984.

54 Roberts and Kynaston, *City State*, pp. 95–102; P. Augar, *The Death of Gentlemanly Capitalism*, London, 2000.

55 It was in 1989 that the first, Deutsche Bank, bought up Morgan Grenfell, weakened by losses sustained during the stock-market crash of 1987.

56 In the same year, SG Warburg, weakened by losses and an abortive merger plan with Morgan Stanley, was bought out by the Swiss Bank Corporation (in 2005, the UBS), whereas Kleinwort, considering itself too small to remain both competitive and independent, preferred to become allied with Dresdner Bank. Schroders and Robert Fleming would do likewise by joining up with Citigroup and Chase Manhattan (in 2005, JP Morgan Chase) respectively in 2000.

57 The initially promising attempts by Barclays with BZW, and National Westminster with Natwest Markets ended in failure and in the sale of these subsidiaries in 1997, the first to Crédit Suisse First Boston and the second to the Bankers' Trust of New York, itself bought out the following year by Deutsche Bank.

58 Augar, *Death of Gentlemanly Capitalism.*

59 A. Alletzhauser, *The House of Nomura*, London, 1990, p. 7.

60 See K. Burk, 'Money and power: the shift from Great Britain to the United States', in Y. Cassis (ed.), *Finance and Financiers in European History, 1880–1960*, Cambridge, 1992, pp. 359–69.

61 Partner of the Frankfurt private bank B. Metzler seel. Sohn & Co.

62 C.-L. Holtfrerich, *Frankfurt as a Financial Centre*, Munich, 1999, pp. 293, 304.

63 M. Marshall, *The Bank*, London, 1999, pp. 172–3.

64 See D. Franke, 'Internationale Finanzplätze: Rivalen oder Partner?', *Die Bank*, April 2002, pp. 176–9.

65 A. Straus, 'The future of Paris as an international centre from the perspective of European integration', in Y. Cassis and E. Bussière (eds.), *London and Paris as International Financial Centres in the Twentieth Century*, Oxford, 2005.

66 Roberts, *Inside International Finance*.

67 Straus, 'The future of Paris'.

68 The United Kingdom came top with 20.8% of banks' non-residents' deposits, followed by the United States with 12.6% and Germany with 8.7%.

69 The United Kingdom came top with 19.1% of bank loans to non-residents, followed by the United States with 11.5% and Japan with 9.3%. J.-C. Lambelet and A. Mihailov, 'Le poids des places financières suisse, genevoise et lémanique', Institut 'Créa' de Macroéconomie Appliquée, Université de Lausanne, 2001, pp. 18–20.

70 *FT Global 500*, 27 May 2004.

71 South Korea, Taiwan, Hong Kong and Singapore, quickly nicknamed the four 'dragons', opened up the way from the end of the sixties. They were followed in the following decades by Thailand, Malaysia, Indonesia, the Philippines and, above all, China and are often referred to as the 'tigers'.

72 See, in particular, G. Jones, 'International financial centres in Asia, the Middle East and Australia: a historical perspective', in Cassis (ed.), *Finance and Financiers in European History*, pp. 405–28; C. Schenk, *Hong Kong as an International Financial Centre: Emergence and Development, 1945–1965*, London, 2001; R. C. Bryant, 'The evolution of Singapore as a financial centre', in K. S. Sandhu and P. Wheatley (eds.), *Management of Success. The Moulding of Modern Singapore*, Singapore, 1989, pp. 337–72.

73 These measures included abolishing the 40% withholding tax on income from investments by non-residents in 1968, the 20% liquidity ratio imposed on Asian currency units in 1972, which brought them into line with current practice on the European Eurocurrency markets, and, more generally, the controlled opening up of borders to foreign banks and financial institutions.

74 D. R. Lessard, 'Singapore as an international financial centre' in, R. Roberts (ed.), *Offshore Financial Centres*, Aldershot, 1994, pp. 200–35; Roberts, *Inside International Finance*.

75 Y. S. Park, 'A comparison of Hong Kong and Singapore as Asian financial centres', in P. D. Grub *et al.* (eds.), *East Asia Dimension of International Business*, Sydney, 1982, pp. 21–8.

76 They came to $608 billion for Hong Kong and $439 billion for Singapore.

77 Y. C. Jao, 'Hong Kong as an international financial centre: evolution and prospects', in *The Asian NIEs: Success and Challenge*, Hong Kong, 1983, pp. 39–82; Roberts, *Inside International Finance*.

Bibliography

Ackrill, M., and L. Hannah, *Barclays: The Business of Banking 1690–1996*, Cambridge, 2001.

Adler, D. R., *British Investment in American Railways, 1834–1898*, Charlottesville, 1970.

Albert, M., *Capitalisme contre capitalisme*, Paris, 1990.

Albion, R. G., *The Rise of New York Port (1815–1860)*, New York, 1939.

Alletzhauser, A., *The House of Nomura*, London, 1990.

Ambigapathi, B., 'La stratégie de cartellisation bancaire en France du Crédit Lyonnais entre 1919 et 1925', in B. Desjardins *et al.*, *Le Crédit Lyonnais 1863–1986*, Geneva, 2003.

Andrieu, C., *Les banques sous l'occupation. Paradoxes de l'histoire d'une profession*, Paris, 1990.

Appel, E., *European Monetary Integration 1958–2002*, London, 1998.

Artaud, D., 'Les dettes de guerre de la France, 1919–1929', in M. Lévy-Leboyer (ed.), *La position internationale de la France. Aspects économiques et financiers, XIXe–XXe siècles*, Paris, 1977.

Attali, J., *Un homme d'influence. Sir Siegmund Warburg (1902–1982)*, Paris, 1985.

Aubert, M., J.-P. Kernen and H. Schönle, *Le secret bancaire suisse*, Bern, 1982.

Augar, P., *The Death of Gentlemanly Capitalism*, London, 2000.

Augustine, D., *Patricians and Parvenus. Wealth and High Society in Wilhelmine Germany*, Oxford, 1994.

Autheman, A., *La banque impériale ottomane*, Paris, 1996.

Autin, J., *Les frères Pereire. Le bonheur d'entreprendre*, Paris 1984.

Bagehot, W., *Lombard Street. A Description of the Money Market*, London, 1873.

Bairoch, P., *Commerce extérieur et développement économique de l'Europe au XIXe siècle*, Paris, 1976.

'La place de la France sur les marchés internationaux', in M. Lévy-Leboyer (ed.), *La position internationale de la France. Aspects économiques et sociaux XIXe–XXe siècles*, Paris, 1977.

Victoires et déboires. Histoire économique et sociale du monde du XVIe siècle à nos jours, 3 vols., Paris, 1997.

Baker, M., and M. Collins, 'London as an international banking centre, 1950–1980', in Y. Cassis and E. Bussière (eds.), *London and Paris as International Financial Centres in the Twentieth Century*, Oxford, 2005.

Balderston, T., 'The banks and the gold standard in the German financial crisis of 1931', *Financial History Review*, 1, 1, 1994.

'A comparison of British and German monetary policy 1919–1932', in C. H. Feinstein (ed.), *Banking, Currency and Finance in Europe between the Wars*, Oxford, 1995.

Balderston, T., *The Origins and Course of the German Economic Crisis: November 1923 to May 1932*, Berlin, 1993.

Balogh, T., *Studies in Financial Organization*, Cambridge, 1947.

Bankers' Magazine, 1844–89; 1890–1954.

Banque Nationale Suisse 1907–1957, Bern, 1957.

Banque Nationale Suisse, *Les banques suisses*, various years.

Banque Nationale Suisse, 'Exportations de capitaux soumises à autorisation', in *Rapport annuel de gestion, années 1980–1995*, Zurich.

Barbier, F., *Finance et politique. La dynastie des Fould, XVIIIe–XXe siècles*, Paris, 1991.

Barth, B., *Die Deutsche Hochfinanz und die Imperialismen: Banken und Aussenpolitik vor 1914*, Stuttgart, 1995.

'The financial history of the Anatolian and Baghdad railways, 1889–1914', *Financial History Review*, 5, 1998.

Baskin, J. B., and P. Miranti, *A History of Corporate Finance*, Cambridge, 1997.

Battilossi, S., 'Financial innovation and the golden age of international banking: 1890–1931 and 1958–81', *Financial History Review*, 7, 2, 2000.

'Banking with multinationals: British Clearing Banks and the Euromarkets' challenge, 1958–1976', in S. Battilossi and Y. Cassis (eds.), *European Banks and the American Challenge. Competition and Cooperation in International Banking Under Bretton Woods*, Oxford, 2002.

Battilossi, S., and Y. Cassis (eds.), *European Banks and the American Challenge. Competition and Cooperation in International Banking Under Bretton Woods*, Oxford, 2002.

Bauer, H., *Société de Banque Suisse, 1872–1972*, Basle, 1972.

Beckert, S., *The Monied Metropolis. New York City and the Consolidation of the American Bourgeoisie, 1850–1896*, Cambridge, 2001.

Beckhart, B. H., *The New York Money Market*, 4 vols., New York, 1931–32.

Bergeron, L., *Banquiers, négociants et manufacturiers parisiens du Directoire à l'Empire*, Paris, 1978.

Les Rothschild et les autres ... La gloire des banquiers, Paris, 1991.

Bernstein, P. L., *Capital Ideas. The Improbable Origins of Modern Wall Street*, New York, 1992.

Bird, G., *Commercial Bank Lending and Third World Debt*, London, 1989.

BIS, *Annual Reports*, various years.

Bitsch, M.-T., *La Belgique entre la France et l'Allemagne 1905–1914*, Paris, 1994.

Blakey, G., *The Post-War History of the London Stock Market*, 2nd edn, London, 1994.

Bodmer, D., *L'intervention de la Confédération dans l'économie bancaire suisse*, Basle, 1948.

Bonin, H., 'L'outre-mer, marché pour la banque commerciale de 1875 à 1985?', in J. Marseilles (ed.), *La France et l'outre-mer. Un siècle de relations monétaires et financières*, Paris, 1998.

L'apogée de l'économie libérale bancaire française (1919–1935), Paris, 2000.

La Banque de l'union parisienne (1874/1904–1974). Histoire de la deuxième grande banque d'affaires françaises, Paris, 2001.

La Banque nationale de crédit. Histoire de la quatrième banque de dépôts française en 1913–1932, Paris, 2002.

'Le Crédit Lyonnais, la Société générale et les autres: essai d'appréciation des rapports de force (1864–1966)', in B. Desjardins *et al.* (eds.), *Le Crédit Lyonnais (1863–1986)*, Geneva, 2003.

Bordo, M., and A. J. Schwartz (eds.), *A Retrospective on the Classical Gold Standard, 1821–1931*, Chicago, 1984.

Bordo, M., and B. Eichengreen (eds.), *A Retrospective on the Bretton Woods System. Lessons for International Monetary Reform*, Chicago, 1993.

Bordo, M., and H. Rockoff, 'The Gold Standard as a "Good Housekeeping Seal of Approval"', *Journal of Economic History*, 56, 2, 1996.

Bordo, M., and R. Sylla (eds.), *Anglo-American Financial Systems: Institutions and Markets in the Twentieth Century*, Burr Ridge, Ill., 1996.

Bordo, M., A. Taylor and J. Williamson (eds.), *Globalization in Historical Perspective*, Chicago, 2003.

Born, K. E., *Die Deutsche Bankenkrise 1931*, Munich, 1967.

International Banking in the 19th and 20th Centuries, Leamington Spa, 1977.

Bouvier, J., *Le Crédit Lyonnais de 1863 à 1882. Les années de formation d'une banque de dépôts*, 2 vols., Paris, 1961.

Les Rothschild, 2nd edn, Brussels, 1983.

Braga de Macedo, J., B. Eichengreen and J. Reis (eds.), *Currency Convertibility. The Gold Standard and Beyond*, London, 1996.

Braillard, P., *La place financière suisse. Politique gouvernementale et compétitivité internationale*, Geneva, 1987.

Bramsen, B., and K. Wain, *The Hambros 1779–1979*, London, 1979.

Brummer, A., and R. Cowe, *Hanson. A Biography*, London, 1994.

Bryant, R. C., 'The evolution of Singapore as a financial centre', in K. S Sandhu and P. Wheatley (eds.), *Management of Success. The Moulding of Modern Singapore*, Singapore, 1989.

Buist, M. G., *At spes non fracta: Hope and Co. 1770–1815, Merchant Bankers and Diplomats at work*, La Haye, 1974.

Bullock, H., *The Story of Investment Companies*, New York, 1959.

Burk, K., *Morgan Grenfell 1838–1988. The Biography of a Merchant bank*, Oxford, 1989.

'Money and power: the shift from Great Britain to the United States', in Y. Cassis (ed.), *Finance and Financiers in European History*, Cambridge, 1992.

Burn, G., 'The state, the City and the Euromarkets', *Review of International Political Economy*, 6, 2, 1999.

Burrin, P., *La France à l'heure allemande 1940–1944*, Paris, 1995.

Büschgen, H. E., 'Deutsche Bank from 1957 to the present: the emergence of an international financial conglomerate', in L. Gall *et al.*, *The Deutsche Bank 1870–1975*, London, 1995.

Bussière, E., *Paribas. L'Europe et le monde, 1872–1992*, Anvers, 1992.

'The French 'Banques d'affaires' in the interwar period: the case of the Banque de Paris et des Pays-Bas (Paribas)', in M. Kasuya (ed.), *Coping with Crisis. International Financial Institutions in the Interwar Period*, Oxford, 2003.

'French banks and the Eurobonds issue market in the 1960s', in Y. Cassis and E. Bussière (eds.), *London and Paris as International Financial Centres in the Twentieth Century*, Oxford, 2005.

Cain, P. J., and A. G. Hopkins, *British Imperialism*, 2 vols., London, 1993.

Cairncross, A., and B. Eichengreen, *Sterling in Decline. The Devaluations of 1931, 1949 and 1967*, Oxford, 1983.

Cameron, R., *France and the Economic Development of Europe 1800–1914*, Princeton, 1961

Cameron, R., and V. I. Bovykin, *International Banking 1870–1914*, Oxford, 1991.

Capie, F., 'Structure and performance in British banking, 1870–1939', in P. L. Cottrell and D. E. Moggridge (eds.), *Money and Power. Essays in Honour of L. S. Presnell*, London, 1988.

Capie, F., and G. Rodrik-Bali, 'Concentration in British banking, 1870–1920', *Business History*, 29, 3, 1982.

Caron, F., *Les deux révolutions industrielles du XXe siècle*, Paris, 1997.

Carosso, V., *Investment Banking in America. A History*, Cambridge, Mass., 1970.

The Morgans. Private International Bankers 1854–1913, Cambridge, Mass., 1987.

Cassis, Y., *Les banquiers de la City à l'époque édouardienne, 1890–1914*, Geneva, 1984.

La City de Londres, 1870–1914, Paris, 1987.

'Swiss international banking, 1900–1950', in G. Jones (ed.), *Banks as Multinationals*, London, 1990.

'The emergence of a new financial institution: investment trusts in Britain 1870–1939', in J. J. van Helten and Y. Cassis (eds.), *Capitalism in a Mature Economy. Financial Institutions, Capital Exports and British Industry*, Aldershot, 1990.

'La place financière Suisse et la City de Londres, 1890–1990', in P. Bairoch and M. Körner (eds.), *La Suisse dans l'économie mondiale (15ème–20ème siècle)*, Zurich, 1990.

City Bankers, 1890–1914, Cambridge, 1994.

Big Business. The European Experience in the Twentieth Century, Oxford, 1997.

'Le Crédit Lyonnais à Genève, 1876–2001', in B. Desjardins *et al.*, *Le Crédit Lyonnais 1863–1986*, Geneva, 2003.

'Commercial Banks in 20th Century Switzerland', in Y. Cassis, G. D. Feldman and Olsson U. (eds.), *The Evolution of Financial Institutions and Markets in Twentieth-Century Europe*, Aldershot, 1995.

'Financial elites revisited', in R. Michie and P. Williamson (eds.), *The British Government and the City of London in the Twentieth Century*, Cambridge, 2004.

Cassis, Y. and E. Bussière, *London and Paris as International Financial Centres in the Twentieth Century*, Oxford, 2005.

Cassis, Y., and J. Tanner, *Banques et crédit en Suisse (1850–1930)*, Zurich, 1993.

Cassis, Y., G. D. Feldman and U. Olsson (eds.), *The Evolution of Financial Institutions and Markets in Twentieth-Century Europe*, Aldershot, 1995.

Cassis, Y. (ed.), *Finance and Financiers in European History 1880–1960*, Cambridge, 1992.

Chadeau, E., *L'économie du risque. Les entrepreneurs 1850–1980*, Paris, 1988.

Chancellor, E., *Devil Take the Hindmost. A History of Financial Speculation*, London, 1999.

Chandler, L. V., *Benjamin Strong, Central Banker*, Washington, DC, 1958.

Chapman, S. D., *The Rise of Merchant Banking*, London, 1984.

  'British-based investment groups before 1914', *Economic History Review*, 38, 2, 1985.

  Merchant Enterprise in Britain, Cambridge, 1992.

Chernow, R., *The House of Morgan. An American Banking Dynasty and the Rise of Modern Finance*, London, 1990.

  The Warburgs. A Family Saga, London, 1993.

Chlepner, B. S., *Le marché financier belge depuis cent ans*, Brussels, 1930.

Clarke, S. V. O., *Central Bank Cooperation 1924–31*, New York, 1967.

Clarke, W. M., *The City's Invisible Earnings*, London, 1958.

Clay, C., *Gold for the Sultan: Western Bankers and Ottoman Finance, 1856–1881. A Contribution to Ottoman and to International Financial History*, London, 2000.

Clay, H., *Lord Norman*, London, 1957.

Cleveland, H. Van B. and T. Huertas, *Citibank 1812–1970*, Cambridge, Mass., 1985.

Collins, M., *Money and Banking in the UK. A History*, London, 1988.

Commission Indépendante d'Experts Suisse-Seconde Guerre Mondiale, *La Suisse, le national-socialisme et la Seconde Guerre Mondiale. Rapport final*, Zurich, 2002.

Cope, S. R., *Walter Boyd. A Merchant Banker in the Age of Napoleon*, London, 1983.

Coste, P., *La lutte pour la suprématie financière. Les grands marchés financiers, Paris, London, New York*, Paris, 1932.

Cottrell, P. L., *British Overseas Investment in the Nineteenth Century*, London, 1975.

  'Great Britain', in R. Cameron and V. I. Bovykin (eds.), *International Banking 1870–1914*, Oxford, 1991.

  'A cluster of corporate international banks, 1855–75', *Business History*, 33, 3, 1991.

  'Silver, gold and the international monetary order 1851–1896', in S. N. Broadberry and N. F. R. Crafts (eds.), *Britain in the International Economy, 1870–1939*, Cambridge, 1992.

  'Aspects of commercial banking in Northern and Central Europe, 1880–1931', in S. Kinsey and L. Newton (eds.), *International Banking in an Age of Transition*, Aldershot, 1998.

  'Established connections and new opportunities. London as an international financial centre, 1914–1958', in Y. Cassis and E. Bussière (eds.), *London and Paris as International Financial Centres in the Twentieth Century*, Oxford, 2005.

Crafts, N., *British Economic Growth during the Industrial Revolution*, Oxford, 1985.

Crafts, N., and G. Toniolo, 'Postwar growth: an overview', in N. Crafts and G. Toniolo (eds.), *Economic Growth in Europe since 1945*, Oxford, 1996.

Crick, W. F., and J. E. Wadsworth, *A Hundred Years of Joint Stock Banking*, London, 1936.

Crouzet, F., 'Commerce extérieur et empire. L'expérience britannique du libre-échange à la Première Guerre Mondiale', *Annales E.S.C.*, 19, 2, 1964.

L'économie de la Grande-Bretagne victorienne, Paris, 1978.

'Politics and banking in revolutionary and Napoleonic France', in R. Sylla, R. Tilly and G. Tortella (eds.), *The State, the Financial System and Economic Modernization*, Cambridge, 1999.

Daumard, A., *Les fortunes françaises au XIXe siècle*, Paris, 1973.

Davies, H., 'Regulation and politics: the need for a new dialogue' Or 'A letter to John Redwood', *Hume Occasional Papers*, 66, 2005.

Davis, L. E., and R. J. Cull, *International Capital Markets and American Economic Growth 1820–1914*, Cambridge, 1994.

Davis, L. E., and R. A. Huttenback, *Mammon and the Pursuit of Empire. The Political Economy of British Imperialism, 1860–1912*, Cambridge, 1986.

Davis, L. E., and L. Neal, 'Micro rules and macro outcomes: the impact of micro structures on the efficiency of security exchanges, London, New York and Paris, 1800–1914', *American Economic Review*, 88, 2, 1998.

de Cecco, M., *Money and Empire. The International Gold Standard, 1890–1914*, Oxford, 1974.

de Cecco, M., and A. Giovannini (eds.), *A European Central Bank? Perspectives on Monetary Unification after Ten Years of the EMS*, Cambridge, 1989.

de Clercq, G. (ed.), *A la Bourse. Histoire du marché des valeurs en Belgique de 1300 à 1990*, Louvain-la-Neuve, 1992.

De Long, J. B., 'Did J. P. Morgan's men add value? An economist's perspective on financial capitalism', in P. Temin (ed.), *Inside the Business Enterprise. Historical Perspectives on the Use of Information*, Chicago and London, 1991.

de Vries, J., and A. van der Woude, *The First Modern Economy. Success, Failure, and Perseverance of the Dutch Economy, 1500–1815*, Cambridge, 1997.

Desjardins, B., M. Lescure, R. Nougaret, A. Plessis and A. Straus (eds.), *Le Crédit Lyonnais (1863–1986)*, Geneva, 2003.

Deutsche Bundesbank (ed.), *Fifty Years of the Deutsche Mark. Central Bank and the Currency in Germany since 1948*, Oxford, 1999.

Dickhaus, M., *Die Bundesbank im westeuropäischen Wiederaufbau. Die internationale Währungspolitik der Bundesrepublik Deutschland 1948 bis 1958*, Munich, 1996.

'Fostering "the bank that rules Europe": the Bank of England, the Allied Banking Commission and the Bank deutscher Länder, 1948–51', *Contemporary European History*, 7, 2, 1998.

Dickson, P. G. M., *The Financial Revolution in England. A Study in the Development of Public Credit, 1688–1756*, London, 1967.

Diederiks, H. A., and D. Reeder (eds.), *Cities of Finance*, Amsterdam, 1996.

Diouritch, G., *L'expansion des banques allemandes à l'étranger*, Paris, 1909.

Dominguez, K. M., 'The role of the yen', in M. Feldstein (ed.), *International Capital Flows*, Chicago, 1999.

Dreyfus, J.-M., 'La spoliation des banques juives: Trois études de cas', in M. Margairaz (ed.), *Banques, Banque de France et Seconde Guerre mondiale*, Paris, 2002.

Duffey, G., and I. H. Giddy, *The International Money Market*, New York, 1978.

Dufourcq-Lagelouse, L., *Les banques étrangères en France*, Paris, 1922.

Dulles, E. L., *The Bank for International Settlements at Work*, New York, 1932.

Dupont-Ferrier, A., *Le marché financier de Paris sous le Second Empire*, Paris, 1925.

Edwards, J., and K. Fischer, *Banks, Finance and Investment in Germany*, Cambridge, 1994.

Edwards, J., and S. Ogilvie, 'Universal banks and German industrialization: a reappraisal', *Economic History Review*, 49, 3, 1996.

Ehrsam, P., 'Die Bankenkrise der 30er Jahre in der Schweiz', in Eidgenössische Bankenkommission (ed.), *50 Jahre eidgenössische Bankenaufsicht*, Zurich, 1985.

Eichengreen, B., *Golden Fetters. The Gold Standard and the Great Depression 1919–1939*, Oxford, 1995.

Eichengreen, B., *Globalizing Capital. A History of the International Monetary System*, Princeton, 1996.

Eichengreen, B. (ed.), *Europe's Post-war Recovery*, Cambridge, 1995.

Eichengreen, B., and M. Flandreau, 'The geography of the gold standard', in J. Braga de Macedo, B. Eichengreen and J. Reis (eds.), *Currency Convertibility. The Gold Standard and Beyond*, London, 1996.

The Gold Standard in Theory and History, New York, 1997.

Einaudi, L., *Money and Politics. European Monetary Unification and the International Gold Standard (1865–1873)*, Cambridge, 2001.

Einzig, P., *The Fight for Financial Supremacy*, London, 1931.

Eken, S., 'Integration of domestic and international financial markets: the Japanese experience', *International Monetary Fund Staff Papers*, 33, 3, 1984.

Eldem, E., *A History of the Ottoman Bank*, Istanbul, 1999.

Emden, P., *Money Powers of Europe in the Nineteenth and Twentieth Centuries*, London, 1938.

Feiertag, O., 'La Banque de France et les problèmes monétaires européens de la Conférence de Gênes à la création de la B.R.I. (1922–1930)', in E. Bussière and M. Dumoulin (eds.), *Milieux économiques et intégration européenne en Europe occidentale au XXe siècle*, Arras, 1998.

'Le Crédit Lyonnais et le Trésor public dans l'entre-deux-guerres: les ressorts de l'économie d'endettement du XXe siècle', in B. Desjardins *et al.* (ed.), *Le Crédit Lyonnais 1863–1986*, Geneva, 2003.

'The international opening-up of the Paris Bourse: overdraft-economy curbs and market dynamics', in Y. Cassis and E. Bussière (eds.), *London and Paris as International Financial Centres in the Twentieth Century*, Oxford, 2005.

Feiertag, O., and M. Margairaz (eds.), *Politiques et pratiques des banques d'émission en Europe (XVII–XXe siècle)*, Paris, 2003.

Feiertag, O., and P. Martin-Aceña, 'The delayed modernization of the Central Banks of France and Spain in the twentieth century', in C.-L. Holtfrerich, J. Reis and G. Toniolo (eds.), *The Emergence of Modern Central Banking from 1918 to the Present*, Aldershot, 1999.

Feinstein, C. H. and K. Watson, 'Private international capital flows in Europe in the inter-war period', in C. H. Feinstein (ed.), *Banking, Currency and Finance in Europe Between the Wars*, Oxford, 1995.

Feinstein, H., P. Temin and G. Toniolo, *The European Economy Between the Wars*, Oxford, 1997.

Feinstein, H. (ed.), *Banking, Currency and Finance in Europe Between the Wars*, Oxford, 1995.

Feis, H., *Europe the World's Banker, 1870–1914*, New York, 1961.

Feldman, G. D., 'Banks and banking in Germany after the First World War. Strategies of defence', in Y. Cassis (ed.), *Finance and Financiers in European History, 1880–1960*, Cambridge, 1992.

'The Deutsche Bank from world war to world economic depression 1914–1933', in L. Gall et al., *The Deutsche Bank 1870–1995*, London, 1995.

The Great Disorder. Politics, Economics, and Society in the German Inflation, 1914–1924, Oxford, 1997.

Ferguson N., *The World's Banker. The History of the House of Rothschild*, London, 1998.

The Cash Nexus. Money and Power in the Modern World 1700–2000, London, 2001.

'The City of London and British imperialism: new light on a old question', in Y. Cassis and E. Bussière (eds.), *London and Paris as International Financial Centres in the Twentieth Century*, Oxford, 2005

FT Global 500, 27 May 2004.

Fior, M., *Les banques suisses, le franc et l'Allemagne. Contribution à l'histoire de la place financière suisse (1924–1945)*, Geneva, 2002.

Flandreau, M., 'Central bank cooperation in historical perspective: a sceptical view', *Economic History Review*, 50, 4, 1997.

'The economics and politics of monetary unions: a reassessment of the Latin Monetary Union, 1865–1871', *Financial History Review*, 7, 1, 2000.

'Le service des Etudes financières sous Henri Germanin (1871 1905): une macro-économie d'acteurs', in B. Desjardins et al. (eds.), *Le Crédit Lyonnais 1863–1986*, Geneva, 2003.

Flandreau, M., and Gallice, F., 'Paris, London and the international money market: lessons from Paribas, 1885–1913', in Y. Cassis and E. Bussière (eds.), *London and Paris as International Financial Centres in the Twentieth Century*, Oxford, 2005.

Flandreau, M., and D. Zumer, *The Making of Global Finance 1880–1913*, OECD, 2004.

Franke, D., 'Internationale Finanzplätze. Rivalen oder Partner?', *Die Bank*, April 2002.

Franke, G., 'The Bundesbank and financial markets', in Deutsche Bundesbank (ed.), *Fifty Years of the Deutsche Mark. Central Bank and the Currency in Germany since 1948*, Oxford, 1999.

Fremdling, R., 'Railroads and German economic growth: a leading sector analysis with a comparison to the United States and Great Britain', *Journal of Economic History*, 37, 3, 1977.

Friedman, M., and A. J. Schwartz, *A Monetary History of the United States 1867–1960*, Princeton, 1963.

Fry, R. (ed.), *A Banker's World. The Revival of the City 1957–1970. The Speeches and Writings of Sir George Bolton*, London, 1970.

Fulford, R., *Glyn's 1753–1953. Six Generations in Lombard Street*, London, 1953.

Galbraith, J. K., *The Great Crash, 1929*, Boston, 1954.

Gall, L., G. D. Feldman, H. James, C.-L. Holtfrerich, and H. E. Büschgen, *The Deutsche Bank 1870–1975*, London, 1995.

Gallant, P., *The Eurobond Market*, Cambridge, 1988.

Gallice, F., 'Le Crédit Lyonnais à Londres 1870–1939', in B. Desjardins *et al.* (eds.), *Le Crédit Lyonnais, 1863–1986*, Geneva, 2003.

Geisst, C. R., *Wall Street. A History*, Oxford, 1997.

Gibb, D. E. W., *Lloyd's of London. A Study in Individualism*, London, 1957.

Gille, B., *La banque et le crédit en France de 1815 à 1848*, Paris, 1959.
    Histoire de la maison Rothschild, vol. 1, Des origines à 1848, Geneva, 1965.
    Histoire de la Maison Rothschild, vol. II: 1848–1870, Geneva, 1967.

Girard, L., *La politique des travaux publics sous le Second Empire*, Paris, 1952.

Girault, R., and M. Lévy-Leboyer (eds.), *Le Plan Marshall et le relèvement économique de l'Europe*, Paris, 1993.

Gömmel, R., 'Entstehung und Entwicklung der Effektenbörse im 19. Jahrhundert bis 1914', in H. Pohl (ed.), *Deutsche Börsengeschichte*, Frankfurt am Main, 1992.

Goodhart, C. A. E., *The Business of Banking, 1891–1914*, London, 1972.

Gourvish, T., *Railways and the British Economy 1830–1914*, London and Basingstoke, 1980.

Guex, S., *La politique monétaire et financière de la Confédération Suisse 1900–1920*, Lausanne, 1993.
    'The origins of the Swiss Banking secrecy law and its repercussions for Swiss federal policy', in *Business History Review*, 74, 2000.

Halévy, E., *Histoire du people anglais au XIXe siècle, Epilogue II, Vers la démocratie sociale et vers la guerre (1905–1914)*, Paris, 1932.

Hall, A. R., *The London Capital Market and Australia, 1870–1914*, Canberra, 1963.

Hall, P. A., and D. Soskice (eds.), *Varieties of Capitalism*, Oxford, 2001.

Hardach, G., *The First World War 1914–1918*, London, 1977.

Henning F.-W., 'Börsenkrisen und Börsengesetzgebung von 1914 bis 1945 in Deutschland', in *Deutsche Börsengeschichte*, Frankfurt am Main, 1992.

Hertner P., 'Les sociétés financières suisses et le développement de l'industrie électrique jusqu'à la Première Guerre mondiale', in F. Cardot (ed.), *1880–1980. Un siècle d'électricité dans le monde*, Paris, 1987.
    'German banks abroad before 1914', in G. Jones (ed.), *Banks as Multinationals*, London, 1990.

Hilferding, R., *Finance Capital: A Study of the Latest Phase of Capitalist Development*, London, 1981; 1st edn, Vienna, 1910.

Hirsch, A., 'Les objectifs de la loi sur les banques', in Eidgenossische Bankenkommission, *50 Jahre eidgenossische Bankenaufsicht*, Zurich, 1987.

Hobsbawm, E. J., *The Age of Revolution 1789–1848*, London, 1962.

Age of Extremes. The Short Twentieth Century 1914–1991, London, 1994.

Hobson, D., *The National Wealth. Who Gets What in Britain?*, London, 1999.

Hobson, J. A., *Imperialism: A Study*, London, 1902.

Hoffman, P., G. Postel-Vinay and J.-L. Rosenthal, *Des marchés sans prix. Une économie politique du crédit à Paris, 1660–1870*, Paris, 2001.

Hogan, M. J., *The Marshall Plan. America, Britain, and the Reconstruction of Western Europe, 1947–1952*, Cambridge, 1987.

Holmes, A. R., and E. Green, *Midland 150 Years of Banking Business*, London, 1986.

Holtfrerich, C.-L., 'The monetary unification process in 19th century Germany: relevance and lessons for Europe today', in M. de Cecco and A. Giovannini (eds.), *A European Central Bank? Perspectives on Monetary Unification after Ten Years of the EMS*, Cambridge, 1989.

'The Deutsche Bank 1945–1957: war, military rule and reconstruction', in L. Gall et al., *The Deutsche Bank 1870–1995*, London, 1995.

Frankfurt as a Financial Centre. From Medieval Trade Fair to European Banking Centre, Munich, 1999.

Holtfrerich, C.-L., J. Reis and G. Toniolo (eds.), *The Emergence of Modern Central Banking from 1918 to the Present*, Aldershot, 1999.

Homer, S., and R. Sylla, *A History of Interest Rates*, 3rd ed., Revised with a Foreword by H. Kaufman, New Brunswick, 1996.

Hoshi, T., and A. K. Kashyap, *Corporate Financing and Governance in Japan. The Road to the Future*, Cambridge, Mass., 2001.

Houtman-De-Smedt, H., 'Société Générale from 1822 to 1848: from "Bank of the Crown Lands" to "mixed-type bank"', in H. van der Wee (ed.), *The Generale Bank 1822–1897*, Tielt, 1997.

Houwink ten Cate, J., 'Amsterdam als Finanzplatz Deutschlands (1919–1923)', in G. D. Feldman et al. (eds.), *Konsequenzen der Inflation*, Berlin, 1989.

Howson, S., *Domestic Monetary Management in Britain, 1919–1939*, Cambridge, 1975.

Huertas, T., 'U.S. multinational banking: history and prospects', in G. Jones (ed.), *Banks as Multinationals*, London, 1990.

Iklé, M., *Die Schweiz als internationaler Bank- und Finanzplatz*, Zurich, 1970.

IMF, *International Monetary Statistics*, Washington, DC, 1981.

Imlah A., 'British balance of payments and the export of capital, 1816–1913', *Economic History Review*, 2nd ser., 2, 1952.

James H., 'The causes of the German banking crisis of 1931', *Economic History Review*, 38, 1984.

The Reichsbank and Public Finance in Germany 1924–1933, Frankfurt, 1985.

The German Slump. Politics and Economics 1924–1936, Oxford, 1986.

'Banks and bankers in the German interwar depression', in Y. Cassis (ed.), *Finance and Financiers in European History, 1880–1960*, Cambridge, 1992.

'The Deutsche Bank and the dictatorship 1933–1945', in L. Gall et al., *The Deutsche Bank 1870–1995*, London, 1995.

International Monetary Cooperation since Bretton Woods, New York and Oxford, 1996.

'The Reichsbank 1876–1945', in Deutsche Bundesbank (ed.), *Fifty Years of the Deutsche Mark. Central Bank and the Currency in Germany since 1948*, Oxford, 1999.

'Strukturwandel im Kriegs- und Kriszeiten 1914–1945', in H. Pohl (ed.), *Geschichte des Finanzplatzes Berlin*, Frankfurt, 2002.

James, J., *Money and Capital Markets in Postbellum America*, Princeton, 1978.

Jao, Y. C., 'Hong Kong as an international financial centre: evolution and prospects', in *The Asian NIEs: Success and Challenge*, Hong Kong, 1983.

Jeanneney, J.-N., *Leçon d'histoire pour une gauche au pouvoir. La faillite du Cartel 1926–1926*, Paris, 1977.

   L'argent caché. Milieux d'affaires et pouvoir politique dans la France du XXe siècle, Paris, 1981.

Jenks, L. H., *The Migration of British Capital to 1875*, New York, 1927.

Jöhr, W. A., *Schweizerische Kreditanstalt 1856–1956*, Zurich, 1956.

Jollife, M. F., *The United States as a Financial Centre 1919–1933*, Cardiff, 1935.

Jones, C. A., *International Business in the Nineteenth Century. The Rise and Fall of a Cosmopolitan Bourgeoisie*, New York, 1987.

Jones, G., 'Lombard Street on the Riviera: The British clearing banks and Europe, 1900–1960', *Business History*, 24, 1982.

   'International financial centres in Asia, the Middle East and Australia: a historical perspective', in Y. Cassis (ed.), *Finance and Financiers in European History 1880–1960*, Cambridge, 1992.

   British Multinational Banking 1830–1990, Oxford, 1993.

   The Evolution of International Business, London, 1996.

   Merchants to Multinationals. British Trading Companies in the Nineteenth and Twentieth Centuries, Oxford, 2000.

   Multinationals and Global Capitalism from the Nineteenth to the Twenty-first Century, Oxford, 2005.

   (ed.), *Banks as Multinationals*, London, 1990.

Jonker, J., 'Spoilt for choice? Banking concentration and the structure of the Dutch capital market, 1900–40', in Y. Cassis, G. D. Feldman, and U. Olsson (eds.), *The Evolution of Financial Institutions and Markets in Twentieth Century Europe*, Aldershot, 1995.

   Merchants, Bankers, Middlemen. The Amsterdam Money Market during the First Half of the 19th Century, Amsterdam, 1996.

Jonker, J. and Sluyterman, K., *At Home on the World Markets. Dutch International Trading Companies from the 16th Century until the Present*, La Haye, 2000.

Joslin, D. M., 'London private bankers, 1720–1785', *Economic History Review*, 7, 1954.

   A Century of Banking in Latin America, London, 1963.

Journal of the Institute of Bankers, 1904.

Jung, J., *Von der Schweizerischen Kreditanstalt zur Credit Suisse Group. Eine Bankengeschichte*, Zurich, 2000.

Kasuya, M. (ed.), *Coping with Crisis. International Financial Institutions in the Interwar Period*, Oxford, 2003.

Kaufmann, E., *La banque en France*, Paris, 1914.

Kelly, J., *Bankers and Borders. The Case of American Banks in Britain*, Cambridge, Mass., 1977.

Kennedy, P., *The Rise and Fall of the Great Powers*, London, 1988.

Kerr, I., *A History of the Eurobond Market. The First 21 Years*, London, 1984.

Keynes, J. M., *The Economic Consequences of the Peace*, London, 1919.

The Economic Consequences of Mr. Churchill, London, 1925.

Kindleberger, C. P., 'European economic integration and the development of a single financial center for long-term capital', *Weltwirtschaftliches Archiv*, 90, 2, 1963.

The World in Depression 1929–1939, London, 1973.

'The formation of financial centers', *Princeton Studies in International Finance*, 36, 1974.

Manias, Panics and Crashes. A History of Financial Crises, London, 1978.

A Financial History of Western Europe, 2nd edn, New York, 1993.

King, W. T. C., *A History of the London Discount Market*, London, 1936.

Kinsey, S. and L. Newton, *International Banking in an Age of Transition*, Aldershot, 1998.

Kirby, M. W., *Men of Business and Politics. The Rise and Fall of the Quaker Pease Dynasty of North-East England, 1700–1943*, London, 1984.

König, M., *Interhandel. Die Schweizerische Holding der IG Farben und ihre Metamorphosen (1910–1999)*, Zurich, 2001.

Kopper, C., *Zwischen Marktwirtschaft und Dirigismus. Bankenpolitik im 'Dritten Reich' 1933–1939*, Bonn, 1995.

Kunz, D. B., *The Battle for Britain's Gold Standard in 1931*, London, 1987.

Kurgan-van Hentenryk, G., 'Finance and financiers in Belgium, 1880–1914', in Y. Cassis (ed.), *Finance and Financiers in European History 1880–1960*, Cambridge, 1992.

Gouverner la Générale de Belgique. Essai de biographie collective, Bruxelles, 1996.

'The Société Générale, 1850–1934', in H. Van der Wee (ed.), *The Generale Bank 1822–1997*, Tielt, 1997.

Kurgan-van Hentenryk, G., S. Jaumain, and V. Montens (eds.), *Dictionnaire des patrons en Belgique. Les hommes, les entreprises, les réseaux*, Bruxelles, 1996.

Kynaston, D., 'The London Stock Exchange, 1870–1914: an institutional history', Ph.D. diss., University of London, 1983.

The City of London. Vol. I: A World of its Own, 1815–1890, London, 1994.

The City of London, Vol. II: Golden Age, 1890–1914, London, 1995.

LIFFE: A Market and its Makers, Cambridge 1997.

The City of London, vol. III: Illusions of Gold 1914–1945, London, 1999.

The City of London, vol. IV: A Club No More 1945–2000, London, 2001.

'La Suisse, place financière', *Cahier SBS*, 6, 1975.

Lambelet, J.-C., and A. Mihailov, 'Le poids des places financières suisse, genevoise et lémanique', Institut 'Créa' de macroéconomie appliquée, Université de Lausanne, 2001.

Landes, D., 'Vieille banque et banque nouvelle: la révolution bancaire du XIXe siècle', *Revue d'histoire moderne et contemporaine*, 3, 1956.

Bankers and Pashas. International Finance and Economic Imperialism in Egypt, Cambridge, Mass., 1958.

Larre, R., 'Le développement du rôle de Paris dans le marché international des capitaux: Paris, place financière internationale', 13 juillet 1966, Archives privées Larre, Comité pour l'histoire économique et financière, 46 p. dactylogr.

Laufenburger, H., *Les banques françaises*, Paris, 1940.

Lazonick, W., and M. O'Sullivan, 'Finance and industrial development: evolution to market control. Part I: The United States and the United Kingdom', *Financial History Review*, 4, 1, 1997.

'Finance and industrial development: evolution to market control. Part II: Japan and Germany', *Financial History Review*, 4, 2, 1997.

Lessard, D. R., 'Singapore as an international financial centre', in R. Roberts (ed.), *Offshore Financial Centres*, Aldershot, 1994.

Lévy-Leboyer, M., *Les banques européennes et l'industrialisation internationale dans la première moitié du XIXe siècle*, Paris, 1964.

'La balance des paiements et l'exportation des capitaux français', in Lévy-Leboyer (ed.), *La position internationale de la France. Aspects économiques et sociaux*, Paris, 1977.

Lévy-Leboyer, M. (ed.), *La position internationale de la France. Aspects économique et financiers, XIXe–XXe siècles*, Paris, 1977.

Lindert, P. H., *Key Currencies and Gold 1900–1913*, Princeton, 1969.

Lüthy, H., *La banque protestante en France de la Révocation de l'Edit de Nantes à la Révolution française*, 2 vols., Paris, 1959–61.

Luxembourg, an International Financial Centre, Luxembourg, 1972.

Lysis, *Contre l'oligarchie financière en France*, Paris, 1907.

Maddison, A., *Dynamic Forces in Capitalist Development. A Long-Run Comparative View*, Oxford, 1991.

Margairaz, M., 'La Banque de France et l'occupation', in M. Margairaz (eds.), *Banques, Banque de France et Seconde Guerre mondiale*, Paris, 2002.

(ed.), *Banques, Banque de France et Seconde Guerre mondiale*, Paris, 2002.

Marguerat P., *La Suisse face au IIIe Reich. Réduit national et dissuasion économique*, Lausanne, 1991.

'Banques mixtes et grandes entreprises industrielles en Allemagne, 1880–1913: du mythe à l'antimythe', in P. Marguerat, L. Tissot and Y. Froidevaux (eds.), *Banques et entreprises industrielles en Europe de l'Ouest, XIXe–XXe siècles. Aspects nationaux et régionaux*, Geneva, 2000.

Marguerat, P., L. Tissot, and Y. Froidevaux (eds.), *Banques et entreprises industrielles en Europe de l'Ouest, XIXe–XXe siècles. Aspects nationaux et régionaux*, Geneva, 2000.

Marnata, F., *La Bourse et le financement des investissements*, Paris, 1973.

Marseille, J., *Empire colonial et capitalisme français. Histoire d'un divorce*, Paris, 1984.

Marshall, M., *The Bank*, London, 1999.

Martin, R., *Das Jahrbuch der Millionäre Deutschlands*, Berlin, 1913.

Mast, H. J., 'La Suisse place financière: bénédiction ou malédiction?', *Cahiers du Crédit Suisse*, 42, March 1977.

Mayer, A. J., *The Persistence of the Old Regime. Europe to the Great War*, London, 1981.

Mazbouri, M., *L'émergence de la place financière suisse (1890–1913)*, Lausanne, 2005.

McKay, J. P., 'The House of Rothschild (Paris) as a multinational industrial enterprise: 1875–1914', in A. Teichova, M. Lévy-Leboyer and H. Nussbaum (eds.), *Multinational Enterprise in Historical Perspective*, Cambridge, 1986.

McRae, H. and, F. Cairncross, *Capital City. London as a Financial Centre*, 1st edn, London, 1973; 2nd edn, London, 1984.

Mensbrugghe, J., 'Foreign issues in Europe', *International Monetary Fund Staff Papers*, 11, 1964.

Meuleau, M., *Des Pionniers en Extrême-Orient. Histoire de la Banque de l'Indochine (1875–1975)*, Paris, 1989.

Michie, R., *The London and New York Stock Exchanges 1870–1914*, London, 1987.

The City of London. Continuity and Change, 1850–1990, Basingstoke and London, 1992.

'The invisible stabilizer: asset arbitrage and the international monetary system since 1700', *Financial History Review*, 5, 1, 1998.

The London Stock Exchange. A History, Oxford, 1999.

Michie, R. and Williamson, P. (eds.), *The British Government and the City of London in the Twentieth Century*, Cambridge, 2004.

Milward, A. S., *War, Economy and Society 1939–1945*, London, 1977.

Moggridge, D. E., *British Monetary Policy, 1924–1931*, Cambridge, 1972.

Moreau, E., *Souvenirs d'un gouverneur de la Banque de France. Histoire de la stabilisation du franc (1926–1928)*, Paris, 1954.

Mosse, W. E., *Jews in the German Economy. The German–Jewish Economic Elite 1820–1935*, Oxford, 1987.

Mottet, L., *Regards sur l'histoire des banques et banquiers genevois*, Geneva, 1982.

Mouré, K., *La politique du franc Poincaré (1926–1936)*, Paris, 1998.

Myers, M., *The New York Money Market, Vol. I, Origins and Development*, New York, 1931.

Paris as a Financial Centre, London, 1936.

Nadler, M., S. Heller and S. Shipman, 'New York as an international financial center', in *The Money Market and its Institutions*, New York, 1955.

Neal, L., 'Trust companies and financial innovation, 1897–1914', *Business History Review*, 45, 1, 1971.

'Integration of international capital markets: quantitative evidence from the eighteenth to the twentieth centuries', *Journal of Economic History*, 45, 2, 1985.

The Rise of Financial Capitalism. International Capital Markets in the Age of Reason, Cambridge, 1990.

'How it all began: the monetary and financial architecture of Europe during the first global capital markets, 1648–1815', *Financial History Review*, 7, 2, 2000.

Neue Deutsche Biographie, Berlin, 1952.

O'Sullivan, M., *Contests for Corporate Control*, Oxford, 2000.

Obstfeld, M. and Taylor, A., 'Globalization and capital markets', in M. Bordo, A. Taylor and J. Williamson (eds.), *Globalization in Historical Perspective*, Chicago, 2003.

Global Capital Markets. Integration, Crisis and Growth, Cambridge, 2004.

OCDE, *International Capital Markets Statistics, 1950–1995*, Paris, 1996.

Orbell, J., *Baring Brothers & Co., Limited. A History to 1939*, London, 1985.

Orsingher, R., *Les banques dans le monde*, Paris, 1964.

Paquier, S., 'Banques, sociétés financières, industrie électrique de 1895 à 1914', in Y. Cassis and J. Tanner (eds.), *Banques et crédit en Suisse (1850–1930)*, Zurich, 1993.

Histoire de l'électricité en Suisse. La dynamique d'un petit pays européen 1875–1939, Geneva, 1998.

'Swiss holding companies from mid-nineteenth century to the early 1930s: the forerunners and subsequent waves of creation', *Financial History Review*, 8, 2, 2001.

Park, Y. S., 'A comparison of Hong Kong and Singapore as Asian financial Centres', in P. D. Grub *et al.* (eds.), *East Asia Dimension of International Business*, Sydney, 1982.

Perkins, E., *Wall Street to Main Street. Charles Merrill and Middle-Class Investors*, Cambridge, 1999.

Perrenoud, M. and R. Lopez, *Aspects des relations financières franco-suisses (1936–1946)*, Zurich, 2002.

Perrenoud, M. *et al.*, *La place financière et les banques suisses à l'époque du national-socialisme*, Zurich, 2002.

Pictet & Cie 1805–1855, Geneva, 1955.

Plessis A., *Régents et gouverneurs de la Banque de France sous le Second Empire*, Geneva, 1985.

La politique de la Banque de France de 1851 à 1870, Geneva, 1985.

'Le développement des activités financières à Paris au XIXe siècle', in H. A. Diederiks and D. Reeder (eds.), *Cities of Finance*, Amsterdam, 1996.

'Les grandes banques de dépôts et l'occupation', in M. Margairaz (ed.), *Banques, Banque de France et Seconde Guerre mondiale*, Paris, 2002.

'La création de la Banque de France et la genèse des banques nationales d'émission en Europe au XIXe siècle', in O. Feiertag and M. Margairaz (eds.), *Politiques et pratiques des banques d'émission en Europe (XVIIe–XXe siècle)*, Paris, 2003.

'When Paris dreamt of competing with the City … ', in Y. Cassis and E. Bussière (eds.), *London and Paris as International Financial Centres in the Twentieth Century*, Oxford, 2005.

Pohl, H. (ed.), *Deutsche Börsengeschichte*, Frankfurt am Main, 1992.

Geschichte des Finanzplatzes Berlin, Frankfurt, 2002.

Pollard, S., *The Development of the British Economy, 1914–1980*, 3rd edn., London, 1983.

'Capital exports, 1870–1914: harmful or beneficial?' *Economic History Review*, 38, 4, 1985.

Pollard, S., *Britain's Prime and Britain's Decline. The British Economy 1870–1914*, London, 1989.

Pollard, S. (ed.), *The Gold Standard and Employment Policies between the Wars*, London, 1970.

Porter, M., *The Competitive Advantage of Nations*, London, 1990.

Powell, E. T., *The Evolution of the Money Market*, London, 1915.

Presnell, L. S., 'Gold reserves, banking reserves and the Baring Crisis of 1890', in C. R. Whittlessey and J. S. G. Wilson (eds.), *Essays in Money and Banking in Honour of R. S. Sayers*, London, 1968.

Presnell, L. S. (ed.), *Money and Banking in Japan*, London, 1973.

Price, J. M., 'What did merchants do? Reflections on British overseas trade, 1660–1790', *Journal of Economic History*, 49, 2, 1989, 267–84.

Quelles places financières pour demain?, *Revue d'économie financière*, special edn, 57, 1999.

Quennouëlle-Corre, L., *La direction du Trésor, 1947–1967. L'État-banquier et la croissance*, Paris, 2000.

Rappoport, P. and White, E., 'Was the crash of 1929 expected?' *American Economic Review*, 84, 1, 1994.

Raymond, R., *L'euro et l'unité monétaire de l'Europe*, Paris, 2001.

Reed, H. C., *The Preeminence of International Financial Centers*, New York, 1981.

'The ascent of Tokyo as an international financial center', *Journal of International Business Studies*, 11, 3, 1990.

Reis, J. (ed.), *International Monetary Systems in Historical Perspective*, Basingstoke, 1995.

Reitmayer, M., *Bankiers im Kaiserreich. Sozialprofil und Habitus der deutschen Hochfinanz*, Göttingen, 1999.

Ribeill, G., *La révolution ferroviaire. La formation des compagnies de chemins de fer en France (1823–1870)*, Paris, 1993.

Riesser, J., *Zur Entwicklung der deutschen Grossbanken mit besonderer Rücksicht auf die Konzentrationbestrebungen*, Jena, 1906.

Riley, J. C., *International Government Finance and the Amsterdam Capital Market, 1740–1815*, Cambridge, 1980.

Ritschl, A., *Deutschlands Krise und Konjunktur. Binnenkonjunktur, Auslandsverschuldung und Reparationsproblem zwischen Dawes-Plan und Transfersperre 1924–1934*, Berlin, 2002.

Ritzmann, F., *Die Schweizer Banken. Geschichte, Theorie, Statistik*, Bern and Stuttgart, 1973.

Rivoire, J., *Le Crédit Lyonnais. Histoire d'une banque*, Paris, 1989.

Roberts, P., 'Benjamin Strong, the Federal Reserve and the limits to interwar American nationalism', *Federal Reserve Bank of Richmond, Economic Quarterly*, 86, 2, 2000.

Roberts, R., *Schroders. Merchants & Bankers*, Basingstoke and London, 1992.

'What's in a name? Merchants, merchant bankers, accepting houses, issuing houses, industrial bankers and investment bankers', *Business History*, 35, 3, 1993.

Inside International Finance, London, 1998.

Take Your Partners. Orion, the Consortium Banks and the Transformation of the Euromarkets, Basingstoke, 2001.

Wall Street, London, 2002.

The City, London, 2004.

Roberts, R. and Kynaston, D., *City State. How the Markets Came to Rule our World*, London, 2001.

Roberts, R. (ed.), *International Financial Centres*, 4 vols., Aldershot, 1994.

Rosenbaum, R., and A. J. Sherman, *M.M. Warburg & Co. 1798–1938. Merchant Bankers of Hamburg*, London, 1979.

Ross, D., 'European banking clubs in the 1960s: a flawed strategy', *Business and Economic History*, 27, 1998.

'Clubs and consortia: European banking groups as strategic alliances', in S. Battilossi and Y. Cassis (eds.), *European Banks and the American Challenge. Competition and Cooperation in International Banking under Bretton Woods*, Oxford, 2002.

Rubinstein, W. D., 'Introduction', in W. D. Rubinstein (ed.), *Wealth and the Wealthy in the Modern World*, London, 1980.

Men of Property, London, 1981.

Sabouret, A., *MM Lazard Frères et Cie. Une Saga de la fortune*, Paris, 1987.

Sampson, A., *The Money Lenders*, London, 1981.

Sancey, Y., 'Place financière suisse et émergence d'une régulation para-étatique durant l'Entre-deux-guerres', in S. Guex *et al.* (eds.), Krisen und Stabilisierung. *Die Schweiz in der Zwischenkriegszeit*, Zurich, 1998.

Sassen, S., *The Global City. New York, London, Tokyo*, Princeton, 2001.

Saul, S. B., *Studies in British Overseas Trade, 1870–1914*, Liverpool, 1960.

Saul, S., 'Banking alliances and international issues on the Paris capital market, 1890–1914', in Y. Cassis and E. Bussière (eds.), *London and Paris as International Financial Centres in the Twentieth Century*, Oxford, 2005.

Sauvy, A., *Histoire économique de la France entre les deux guerres*, 3 vols., Paris, 1984.

Sayers, R. S., *Bank of England Operations 1890–1914*, London, 1936.

Lloyds Bank in the History of English Banking, Oxford, 1957.

The Bank of England 1891–1944, 3 vols., Cambridge, 1976.

Scammel, W. M., *The London Discount Market*, London, 1968.

Schenk, C., *Britain and the Sterling Area. From Devaluation to Convertibility in the 1950s*, London, 1994.

'The origins of the Eurodollar market in London, 1955–1963', *Explorations in Economic History*, 35, 1998.

Hong Kong as an International Financial Centre. Emergence and Development, 1945–1965, London, 2001.

'International financial centres, 1958–1971: competitiveness and complementarity', in S. Battilossi and Y. Cassis (eds.), *European Banks and the American Challenge. Competition and Cooperation in International Banking under Bretton Woods*, Oxford, 2002.

Scholey, D., 'Essential features of international financial centres', in Swiss Bankers' Association, *International Financial Centres: Structure, Achievements and Prospects, Proceedings of the 40th International Summer School*, Interlaken/Basle, 1987.

Schuker, S. A., *The End of French Predominance in Europe. The Financial Crisis of 1924 and the Adoption of the Dawes Plan*, Chapel Hill, 1976.

Seitz, J., *Histoire de la Banque à Genève*, Geneva, 1931.

Simon, M., 'The pattern of new British portfolio foreign investment, 1865–1914', in A. R. Hall (ed.), *The Export of Capital from Britain, 1870–1914*, London, 1968.

Smith, G. D., and R. Sylla, 'Wall Street and the U.S. capital markets in the twentieth century', in *Financial Markets, Institutions and Instruments*, 1993.
'Capital markets,' in S. Kutler *et al.* (eds.), *Encyclopedia of the United States in the Twentieth Century*, vol. III, New York, 1996.

Speck, K., *Strukturwandlungen und Entwicklungtendenzen im Auslandgeschäft der Schweizerbanken*, Zurich, 1974.

Stern, F., *Gold and Iron. Bismarck, Bleichröder and the Building of the German Empire*, New York, 1977.

Stoskopf, N., *Banquiers et financiers parisiens*, vol. VII, Les patrons du Second Empire, Paris, 2002.

Strange, S., *Sterling and British Policy*, London, 1971.

Straus A., 'Structures financières et performances des entreprises industrielles en France dans la seconde moitié du XXe siècle', *Entreprises et Histoire*, 2, 1992.
'The future of Paris as an international centre from the perspective of European integration', in Y. Cassis and E. Bussière (eds.), *London and Paris as International Financial Centres in the Twentieth Century*, Oxford, 2005.

Stürmer, M., G. Teichmann and W. Treue, *Wägen und Wagen. Sal. Oppenhein jr. & Cie. Geschichte einer Bank und einer Familie*, Munich and Zurich, 1989.

Supple, B., 'A business elite: German–Jewish financiers in nineteenth century New York', *Business History Review*, 31, 2, 1957.
The Royal Exchange Assurance. A History of British Insurance 1720–1970, Cambridge, 1970.
'Corporate growth and structural change in a service industry: insurance 1870–1914', in B. Supple (ed.), *Essays in British Business History*, Oxford, 1977.

Suzuki, T., *Japanese Government Loan Issues on the London Capital Market 1870–1913*, London, 1994.

Sylla, R., 'Shaping the U.S. financial system, 1690–1913': the dominant role of public finance', in R. Sylla, R. Tilly and G. Tortella (eds.), *The State, the Financial System and Economic Modernization*, Cambridge, 1999.
'United States banks and Europe: strategy and attitudes', in S. Battilossi and Y. Cassis (eds.), *European Banks and the American Challenge. Competition and Cooperation in International Banking under Bretton Woods*, Oxford, 2002.

Sylla, R., R. Tilly and G. Tortella (eds.), *The State, the Financial System and Economic Modernization*, Cambridge, 1999.

Testis, *Le rôle des établissements de crédit en France*, Paris, 1907.

The Economist, 1843– .

Thornton, H., *An Inquiry into Paper Credit*, London, 1802.

Tilly, R., 'Berlin als preussiches und deutsches Finanzzentrum und seine Beziehungen zu den anderen Zentren in Ost und West', in W. Ribbe and J. Schmädeke (eds.), *Berlin in Europa der Neuzeit*, Berlin, New York, 1990.

'International aspects of the development of German banking', in R. Cameron and V. I. Bovykin (eds.), *International Banking 1870–1914*, Oxford, 1991.

Tilman, S., 'Portrait collectif de grands banquiers belges Bruxelles-Liège-Anvers (1830–1935): contribution à une histoire des élites', Thèse de doctorat, Université Libre de Bruxelles, 2003–4.

Toniolo, G., 'Europe's golden age, 1950–1973: speculations from a long-run perspective', *Economic History Review*, 51, 2, 1998.

Torres, F., *Banquiers d'avenir. Des comptoirs d'escompte à la naissance de BNP Paribas*, Paris, 2000.

Treue, W., 'Das Bankhaus Mendelssohn als Beispiel einer Privatbank im 19. und 20. Jahrhundert', in C. Lowenthal-Hensel, *Mendelssohn Studien. Beiträge zur neueren deutschen Kultur und Wirtschaftsgeschichte*, vol. I, Berlin, 1972.

United Nations, *International Capital Movements during the Interwar Period*, New York, 1949.

Van der Wee, H., and M. Goossens, 'Belgium', in R. Cameron and V. I. Bovykin, *International Banking 1870–1914*, Oxford, 1991.

Van der Wee, H., and M. van der Wee-Verbreyt, 'Belgian banking in the nineteenth and twentieth centuries: the Société Générale and the Générale de Banque (1822–1997)', in R. Sylla, R. Tilly and G. Tortella (eds.), *The State, the Financial System and Economic Modernization*, Cambridge, 1999.

Van der Wee, H. (ed.), *The Generale Bank 1822–1897*, Tielt, 1997.

Van Helten, J. J., and Y. Cassis (eds.), *Capitalism in a Mature Economy. Financial Institutions, Capital exports and British Industry*, Aldershot, 1990.

Veraghtert, K., 'Bruxelles éclipse Anvers. Le centre boursier belge se déplace, 1800–1840', in G. de Clercq (ed.), *A la Bourse. Histoire du marché des valeurs en Belgique de 1300 à 1990*, Louvain-la-Neuve, 1992.

Vilar, P., *Or et monnaie dans l'histoire*, Paris, 1974.

Vogler, R., 'The genesis of Swiss banking secrecy: political and economic environment', *Financial History Review*, 8, 1, 2001.

Wake, J., *Kleinwort Benson. The History of Two Families in Banking*, Oxford, 1997.

Wellhöner, V., *Grossbanken und Grossindustrie im Kaiserreich*, Göttingen, 1989.

White, E., *The Regulation and Reform of the American Banking System, 1920–1929*, Princeton, 1983.

'The stock market boom and crash of 1929 revisited', *Journal of Economic Perspective*, 4, 2, 1990.

'Banking and finance in the twentieth century', in S. L. Engerman and R. E. Gallman (eds.), *The Cambridge Economic History of the United States*, vol. III, *The Twentieth Century*, Cambridge, 2000.

Wilkins, M., 'The free-standing company, 1870–1914: an important type of British foreign direct investment', *Economic History Review*, 41, 2, 1988.

'Banks over borders: some evidence from their pre-1914 history', in G. Jones (ed.), *Banks as Multinationals*, London, 1990.

'Cosmopolitan finance in the 1920s: New York's emergence as an international financial centre', in R. Sylla, R. Tilly and G. Tortella (eds.),

The State, the Financial System and Economic Modernization, Cambridge, 1999.

The History of Foreign Investment in the United States to 1914, Cambridge, Mass., 1st edn, 1989, 2nd edn 2004.

The History of Foreign Investment in the United States, 1914–1945, Cambridge, Mass., 2004.

Williamson, P., *National Crisis and National Government: British Politics, the Economy and Empire, 1926–1932*, Cambridge, 1992.

Wilson, C., *Anglo-Dutch Commerce and Finance in the Eighteenth Century*, Cambridge, 1941.

Withers, H., *The Meaning of Money*, London, 1910.

'Witness seminar on the origins and early development of the Eurobond market', introduced and edited by Kathleen Burk, *Contemporary European History*, 1, 1, 1992, 65–87.

Wixforth, H., 'German banks and their business strategies in the Weimar Republic: new findings and preliminary results', in M. Kasuya (ed.), *Coping with Crisis. International Financial Institutions in the Interwar Period*, Oxford, 2003.

Wixforth, H., and D. Ziegler, 'Deutsche Privatbanken und Privatbankiers im 20. Jahrhundert', *Geschichte und Gesellschaft*, 23, 2, 1997.

Worner, M., *La Suisse, centre financier européen*, Argenton, 1931.

Wright, C., and C. E. Fayle, *A History of Lloyds*, London, 1928.

Ziegler, P., *The Sixth Great Power. Barings, 1762–1929*, London, 1988.

Zimmermann, R., *Volksbank oder Aktienbank? Parlamentsdebatten, Referendum und zunehmende Verbandsmacht beim Streit um die Nationalbankgründung 1891–1905*, Zurich, 1987.

Index